M000312979

Handwritten note:

daniel.edmondson
@DminAccess2015

Contact server team
if you want to
schedule a time when
it's safe to do windows
updates + reboot
automatically:

hs-serverteam@
ucsd.edu

SAP® BusinessObjects BI™ System Administration

 **PRESS**

SAP PRESS is a joint initiative of SAP and Galileo Press. The know-how offered by SAP specialists combined with the expertise of the Galileo Press publishing house offers the reader expert books in the field. SAP PRESS features first-hand information and expert advice, and provides useful skills for professional decision-making.

SAP PRESS offers a variety of books on technical and business-related topics for the SAP user. For further information, please visit our website: *www.sap-press.com*.

Greg Myers and Eric Vallo

SAP® BusinessObjects BI™ System Administration

Galileo Press

Bonn • Boston

Galileo Press is named after the Italian physicist, mathematician, and philosopher Galileo Galilei (1564—1642). He is known as one of the founders of modern science and an advocate of our contemporary, heliocentric worldview. His words *Eppur si muove* (And yet it moves) have become legendary. The Galileo Press logo depicts Jupiter orbited by the four Galilean moons, which were discovered by Galileo in 1610.

Editor Sarah Frazier
Acquisitions Editor Kelly Grace Weaver
Copyeditor Julie McNamee
Cover Design Graham Geary
Photo Credit Shutterstock.com/144681674/© bikeriderlondon
Layout Design Vera Brauner
Production Kelly O'Callaghan
Typesetting SatzPro, Krefeld (Germany)
Printed and bound in the United States of America, on paper from sustainable sources

ISBN 978-1-4932-1000-8

© 2015 by Galileo Press Inc., Boston (MA)
2nd edition 2015

Library of Congress Cataloging-in-Publication Data
Myers, Greg.
SAP BusinessObjects BI system administration / Greg Myers and Eric Vallo. -- 1st edition.
pages cm
Includes index.
ISBN 978-1-4932-1000-8 (print : alk. paper) -- ISBN 1-4932-1000-9 (print : alk. paper) --
ISBN 978-1-4932-1001-5 (ebook) - ISBN 978-1-4932-1002-2 (print and ebook)
1. BusinessObjects. 2. Business intelligence--Data processing. 3. Management information systems. I. Vallo, Eric. II. Title.
HD38.7.M94 2014
658.4'038028553--dc23
2014032358

Contents at a Glance

Dear Reader,

Being a system administrator is a lot like being a therapist. Both involve emotionally-charged people coming to you with problems that are often complicated and hard to fix. Perhaps, that was what Greg Myers and Eric Vallo were trying to remedy when they decided to simplify the technical challenges of SAP BusinessObjects BI system administration with this comprehensive guide.

Injecting both wit and practicality between the lines, these authors will not only prepare you for the troubles ahead, but enable you to think preemptively about your system. From installation to configuration, this book has you covered from top to bottom. Revised with additional information on the newest features and improvements since the release of SAP BusinessObjects BI 4.1, you'll emerge from these pages with a renewed confidence, armed with the humor and tools you'll need to maintain your sanity and stay one step ahead.

We at SAP PRESS want to hear from you! What did you think about the second edition of *SAP BusinessObjects BI System Administration*? How could it be improved? As your comments and suggestions are the most useful tools to help us make our books the best they can be, we encourage you to visit our website at *www.sap-press.com* and share your feedback.

Thank you for purchasing a book from SAP PRESS!

Sarah Frazier
Editor, SAP PRESS

Galileo Press
Boston, MA

sarah.frazier@galileo-press.com
www.sap-press.com

Contents

Preface

In the beginning, man created the computer and the database. And the data was without form and void. And Bernard Liautaud said, "Let there be Business Objects." And it was good. SAP BusinessObjects BI 4.0, and later, SAP BusinessObjects BI 4.1, as it is known today, provides the underpinnings of SAP's business intelligence architecture.

It's important to remember that planning and administering an SAP BusinessObjects BI environment is one-third art, one-third science, and one-third trial and error. In the constantly changing landscape of users, system utilization, and increasing adoption, the way you manage your environment will be in a constant state of flux. Don't believe for a second that you take in requirements, design a system with all the right people, and walk away from it for three years until your servers go end-of-life and you can get new ones. This book explores the complexities of the technology, sizing, and scaling as your environment and usage matures. It *is* complex, but fear not! We're here to work through it together.

Our goal for you, the reader, is to lure you in with our wit and charm and, in the process of entertaining you a bit, teach you a thing or two about SAP BusinessObjects system administration. If you are someone who is responsible for the day-to-day operations of an SAP BusinessObjects BI environment, whether a veteran or a newbie, this book is for you. We've taken our collective experience and put it down for you here in writing. We've done our finest job to document the best and the worst of what you need to know to get the job done and do it well.

In **Chapter 1,** we'll give you a tour of the entire SAP BusinessObjects BI system. You'll get a heaping helping of the various reporting tools and an overview of the SAP BusinessObjects BI architecture. We'll get heavy in **Chapter 2** and give you all the tools you'll need to properly size your SAP BusinessObjects BI environment.

Chapter 3 covers the actual installation of the product, no matter what platform you find yourself on, and **Chapter 4** goes over all of the important ways you'll need to configure your system for optimal performance.

We lay down the law in **Chapter 5** and get gritty with security, covering the heady topics of user and content security along with SSL, cryptographic keys, firewalls, and reverse-proxies.

Chapter 6 is dedicated to our pal Promotion Management, and the chapter goes into the murky depths of moving content around from system to system.

Chapter 7 will bring you a tour of the SAP BusinessObjects BI 4.1 monitoring engine. This got a serious upgrade in SAP BusinessObjects BI 4.0 Service Pack 4 (SP4), and we have the scoop.

Chapter 8 is the heart and soul of any SAP BusinessObjects BI administrator's job: troubleshooting and maintenance. Face it, stuff breaks. We'll help you figure out what broke and how to fix it, and show you some things you can do on the preventative side as well.

We take the show on the road in **Chapter 9** and go over SAP BusinessObjects Mobile, which also seriously changed in SP4.

Then, to round out our powerhouse lineup, **Chapter 10** goes over all the ways you can customize and enhance your SAP BusinessObjects BI system. You'll be surprised to learn how this has changed from previous versions as well.

So fasten your seatbelts, sit back, and enjoy the flight. We're pleased you'll be traveling with us today.

Acknowledgments

To my wife, my Lioness, Gia, who fiercely supports me in all of my endeavors. *Il mio cuore e l'anima per sempre.*

To my old friend, Mike Sawyer, who had faith in me and gave me my first job in business intelligence.

To my pal, Chris Randall, who first gave me the idea for this book.

Last but certainly not least, to my brave and dear friend, Eric Vallo, who unleashed me and allowed me to fulfill my potential.

Greg Myers

To my wife, Stephanie, it is still unconditional.

To my first boss, Bob Buser, who took a chance on this rookie and gave me the greatest start I could have had with this technology.

To my team, my friends, you inspire me every day to be better, and I'm insanely proud of every one of you for being on this journey with me.

Lastly, to my pal Greg Myers, who, even though separated by miles, is a constant ally, podcaster, colleague, and friend. No way this was possible without you.

Eric Vallo

"The SAP BusinessObjects BI platform" is a mouthful, but for good reason—it encompasses a lot. This chapter introduces some of the basic concepts behind the platform.

1   Introduction to the SAP BusinessObjects BI Platform: What Am I Getting Into?

The SAP BusinessObjects Business Intelligence (SAP BusinessObjects BI) platform is a robust solution that has a lot to offer for anyone who works with it: developer, administrator, end user, or some combination of all three. As an SAP BusinessObjects administrator, you should have an idea about its fundamental principles, including its semantic layer (*universes*), different tools, and basic architecture. In this chapter, we'll introduce you to all of these, and—once you have the basics down—we'll get you started with what you need to know to plan for a new solution.

1.1   The Hitchhiker's Guide to the Universe

The SAP BusinessObjects BI platform consists of a number of disparate, yet connected, sets of data visualization technologies. These technologies vary in capability from Microsoft Office integration to desktop reporting tools to mobile platforms for viewing content on the go.

As this book progresses, you'll learn that each of these tools, in some way, relies on a semantic layer known as a *universe*. We're going to dive into this in more detail in Chapter 4, but know that ensuring that your platform can scale to support the diverse needs of one or many universes, using these reporting tools will make for happier end users. For now, grab your towel and don't panic.

This universe is part of the magic that makes SAP BusinessObjects BI stand out among its competitors in the industry. As SAP BusinessObjects BI matured and the support for more data sources became available, organizations were able to roll all that complex data into an easily digestible universe for user consumption.

Understanding the benefits and architecture of the universe is an important component of supporting your developers and users. Let's start by extolling the virtues of having a good universe in the first place:

- Masks complex business rules in the data in a simple user interface (UI)
- Brings data dictionary definitions forward to the universe, defined by developers, to empower users with more knowledge of what they are reporting on
- Allows developers to implement application controls on queries to prevent the runaway queries common to direct-to-data access methods
- Allows developers to guide the user through a more carefully sculpted experience, organizing and exposing data based on the user profile or competency
- Creates a single version of the truth for data marts, data warehouses, or other data within your organization
- Powers the multitude of technologies in the SAP BusinessObjects BI product stack with a common user experience

In the versions prior to SAP BusinessObjects BI 4.1, universes (.unv extension) were created using the Universe Design Tool (see Figure 1.1). In SAP Business-Objects BI 4.0 and beyond, SAP BusinessObjects BI has built upon the legacy of the universe's long-standing history as a UNV with the new common semantic layer (CSL), which has a .unx extension. This new universe format expands on the capabilities of the universe with many new features, including the following:

- A new developer interface based on the Eclipse development interface framework (leveraged to create a common experience with other new SAP developer tools)
- Support for multisource universes versus the traditional single-source universe
- Interactive visualization capabilities to preview and profile data from the data source as you develop
- An enhanced Query Panel that now actually permits the preview of data without the need for export for testing in one of the reporting tools
- Support for more data sources including, importantly, SAP HANA

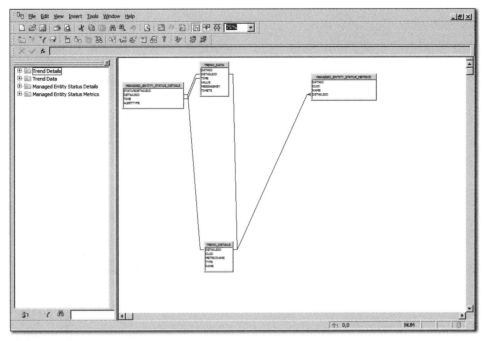

Figure 1.1 The Universe Design Tool

The list goes on as you look at the new and redesigned interface of the newly named Information Design Tool (see Figure 1.2). As administrators, we have to focus on continuing to control access to universes, connections created by the designer, and the definition of access restrictions on each universe as they move through the systems development lifecycle. It's through continued, rigorous enforcement of policy on how developers should control access to data that we're able to ensure that any single application won't run away with the system or create undue bottlenecks in processing time. We'll talk a lot more about tuning for the new CSL as we move into Chapter 4, but just know that many more server-side configuration considerations must be made when you look to support the CSL.

As you wrap your brain around the universe, it's also important to understand, at least at a high level, what end-user consumption of these technologies entails, because ultimately, as an administrator, you're asked to support end users as a part of the SAP BusinessObjects BI platform.

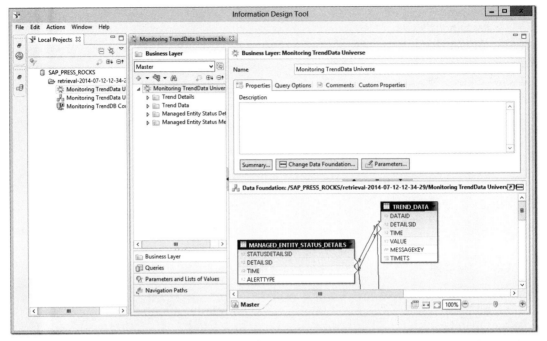

Figure 1.2 The Information Design Tool

Pop Quiz

1. Contrast the Universe Design Tool universe (UNV) to the Information Design Tool universe (UNX).

2. What is the purpose of a universe, regardless of how it's created?

1.2 Introduction to the SAP BusinessObjects BI Reporting Tools

You have a not-so-insignificant bunch of tools in your BI toolbox for solving the reporting needs that plague your day. And, just like a mechanic's toolbox, you have to use the right tool for the right job. No one tool is best for every need. Let's take a tour of the different tools and discuss what each one does and how it works. We'll introduce you, or refamiliarize you, with SAP BusinessObjects Web

Intelligence (Web Intelligence, for short), SAP Crystal Reports, SAP Business-Objects Dashboards (Dashboards, for short), SAP BusinessObjects Analysis, SAP BusinessObjects Explorer (Explorer, for short), SAP Predictive Analysis, and SAP BusinessObjects Mobile. We'll also introduce two new SAP BusinessObjects BI tools: SAP BusinessObjects Design Studio and SAP Lumira.

1.2.1   SAP BusinessObjects Web Intelligence

SAP BusinessObjects Web Intelligence is arguably the flagship reporting technology in the product suite. With a rich history as the ad hoc analysis technology within the suite, SAP BusinessObjects Web Intelligence today provides a mechanism that empowers end users to ponder their own answers to their business questions and seek them out using universes within the platform.

Each SAP BusinessObjects Web Intelligence report consists of one or more data providers or queries that retrieve data from a relational database or online analytical processing (OLAP) data source. Further, in a more decentralized model on user desktops, SAP BusinessObjects Web Intelligence reports can consume text or comma-separated value (CSV) data using the SAP BusinessObjects Web Intelligence Rich Client.

Most popularly, SAP BusinessObjects Web Intelligence is deployed via a Java applet in a user's browser, creating a dependency on a supported Java runtime environment by Oracle Sun. Similarly, a "light" version of SAP BusinessObjects Web Intelligence also exists in a browser-based deployment as a DHTML-based application. This version mimics capabilities contained within the applet-based version of SAP BusinessObjects Web Intelligence and doesn't provide the same feel for interactivity that the applet-based version supports.

The SAP BusinessObjects Web Intelligence Rich Client takes that same power and flexibility of the applet-based version and creates a desktop experience for users. While great strides have been made to eliminate a thick client on users' desktops, this version does indeed replicate the experience from the web browser with the added capability of a few non-universe-based data sources. Administrators must use caution in considering the push of a desktop version of SAP BusinessObjects Web Intelligence. Maintenance costs should be considered in pushing desktop software in an environment in which we've sought to deprecate SAP Business-Objects Desktop Intelligence.

After the data is retrieved and held within the report, additional slice and dice, filters, ranks, sorts, and more can be applied to derive added intelligence about the data, further uncovering trends, patterns, and actionable information.

Query Development

The development interface for SAP BusinessObjects Web Intelligence has followed a common pattern since the 1990s, when SAP BusinessObjects BI first gained traction. This common interface, consisting of a list of usable objects—those to be used in the results objects (the SELECT statement) and those to be used in the filter panel (the WHERE clause)—establishes a common query-building standard for SAP BusinessObjects. The name of this main SAP BusinessObjects BI interface is the Query Panel (see Figure 1.3).

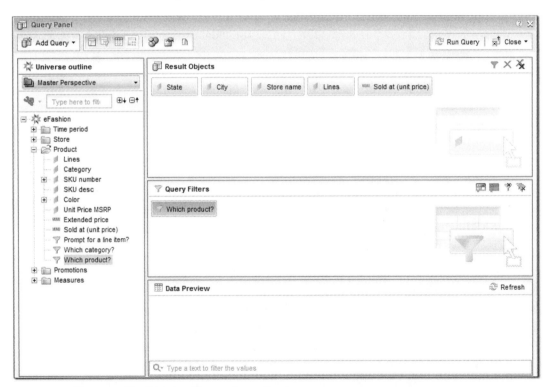

Figure 1.3 The Web Intelligence Query Panel

Developers and power users alike are presented with the capability to define one or more complex queries and manage the general connections to the universes from here. Beyond the ability to use the abstraction layer within this Query Panel, much of the power and flexibility of SAP BusinessObjects Web Intelligence exists within the report development components.

Report Development

With data in tow, the user experience is set to mimic a Microsoft Office-like experience with a tabbed, ribbon interface. Even as we present data to the users, we have the ability to create parameter-driven queries based on either universe-defined filters, or those we create report-side, to build parameter-driven reports (see Figure 1.4).

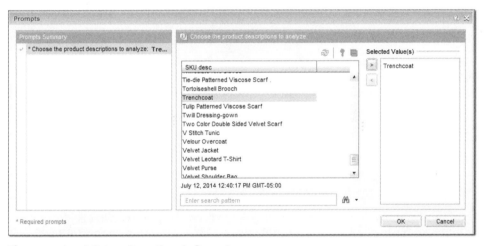

Figure 1.4 Input-Driven Reporting via Prompts

This report development interface (the Report Viewer, shown in Figure 1.5) gives users all the power to pivot, slice and dice, summarize, and visually represent data in the most effective way possible to themselves and other report consumers. Data, possibly from many different data sources, can be organized in a common report or group of reports in a single SAP BusinessObjects Web Intelligence document—even in what is referred to as "blocks" within the body of a single document. This gives the designer a great deal of flexibility in creating robust tabular or graphical reports to guide the user to conclusions or allow for deeper drilldowns on data, both contained in the report and linked to external reports.

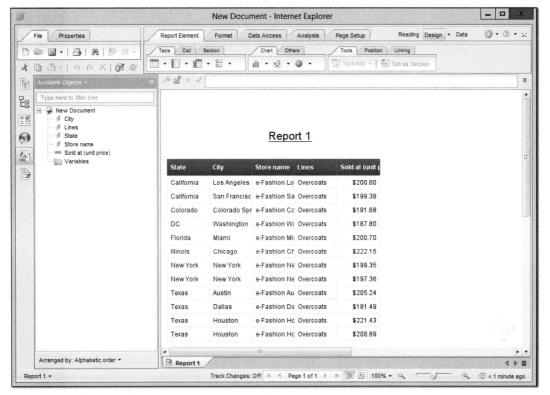

Figure 1.5 The Report Viewer

Using technologies that empower power users to browse seemingly limitless data presents challenges that administrators must constantly monitor and predict. While SAP BusinessObjects BI permits developers to enforce application controls on universes to limit row counts, query times, and so on, many organizations may choose to remove these restrictions to permit users to consume more and more data. Understanding these behaviors is key to making appropriate decisions on scaling an environment to meet the growing needs for data in the SAP BusinessObjects environment, and especially inside SAP BusinessObjects Web Intelligence.

Further, user utilization patterns can change on a whim. Consider an organization with a power user who develops a groundbreaking report. Executives love it, and suddenly you're asked to ensure that 4,000 sales representatives get their own personal copy of this report each day. This is where a practical understanding of the SAP BusinessObjects BI servers is needed; database performance, service level agreements (SLAs), and more, all become variables that require you to be able to thoughtfully scale your environment to support ever-changing requirements for your system.

As SAP has continued to decrease the gap between Web Intelligence and the now less-deprecated Desktop Intelligence, the feature gap between the two reporting tools has decreased. Web Intelligence, now supporting the vast majority of the capabilities of Desktop Intelligence, has won over much of the day-to-day reporting from its predecessor. Customers still holding out for capabilities such as freehand SQL or migration of content based on Visual Basic for Applications (VBA) must still wait for a solution or take matters into their own hands to migrate this content into a modern application.

In SAP BusinessObjects 4.1, SAP announced the reintroduction of Desktop Intelligence to the platform, in a more limited capacity, through an add-on known as the Desktop Intelligence Compatibility Pack (DCP for short). The DCP enabled report developers to patch an SAP BusinessObjects XI 3.1 desktop running the client tools to log on to an SAP BusinessObjects BI 4.1 landscape, allowing reports to be published once again. Further, the Upgrade Management Tool (UMT; see Chapter 6) allows administrators on versions of SAP BusinessObjects prior to BI 4.1 to now migrate that content forward.

Strategically, this solution allows customers that were delaying their upgrade to SAP BusinessObjects BI 4.1, due to the feature gaps of Web Intelligence, to rethink their approach and determine if the barriers to entry are removed. However, the DCP provides a less-than-production-like solution to this problem. The enterprise components of SAP BusinessObjects BI aren't used by the DCP. It only provides repository functions and viewing functions as HTML or PDF. Any automation must still take place on the desktop computers running the DCP itself. Now that's a sticky situation. Migrate your Desktop Intelligence content with caution.

1.2.2 SAP Crystal Reports

SAP Crystal Reports has a long history as an enterprise reporting solution. With its roots in the days of Seagate Systems, SAP Crystal Reports has become a technology that satisfies mass-reporting requirements or integration with other application-development technologies such as Microsoft Visual Studio. SAP Crystal Reports is well known for its ability to consume data from many disparate data sources, generate outputs in many different content types, and distribute to user bases on small to large enterprise scales. It's also popular with application developers thanks to its Software Development Kit (SDK), making it easy to integrate with non-BI-based applications.

The deployment of this reporting solution differs significantly from that of SAP BusinessObjects Web Intelligence. SAP Crystal Reports has long been thought of as the "batch" reporting tool, creating reports during the offline day and distributing them, as opposed to SAP BusinessObjects Web Intelligence, which is known more as the ad hoc technology in the product suite. Therefore, scaling considerations must be made more toward supporting the demands of scheduling SAP Crystal Reports in batches and how users consume that content during the online day.

With the introduction of SAP Business Objects 4.0, SAP Crystal Reports has branched into two unique products: SAP Crystal Reports 2011 (and in SAP BusinessObjects BI 4.1, SAP Crystal Reports 2013) and SAP Crystal Reports Enterprise. We discuss each of these in more detail next.

SAP Crystal Reports 2013

SAP Crystal Reports 2013 most closely resembles prior releases of SAP Crystal Reports. The classic interface will be a familiar technology to classic SAP Crystal Reports developers, providing many of the same layouts and controls found in older versions of SAP Crystal Reports.

While SAP Crystal Reports 2013 is integrated into the SAP BusinessObjects BI 4.1 platform, it's really only integrated from the perspectives of viewing, scheduling, and distributing reports. SAP Crystal Reports 2013 remains today as a standalone, desktop development tool that provides developers with a powerful technology for delivering reports.

Query Development

The developer experience for acquiring data for a report in SAP Crystal Reports 2013 is one that has always provided developers with a common interface. One of the core, key strengths of SAP Crystal Reports 2013 is the multitude of data sources upon which a report can be generated (see Figure 1.6). This makes a Crystal report an ideal delivery mechanism when the SAP BusinessObjects BI universe isn't an option. These types of data sources include native data sources such as Oracle or SQL Server, Open Database Connectivity connections (ODBC), Lightweight Directory Access Protocol (LDAP), delimited files, and much more.

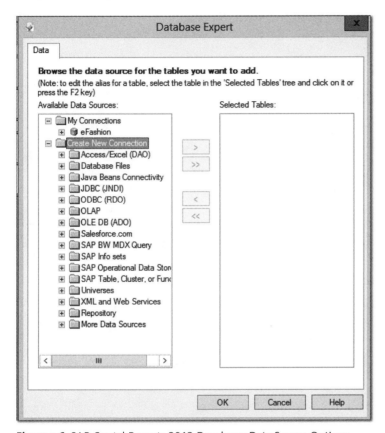

Figure 1.6 SAP Crystal Reports 2013 Developer Data Source Options

These data sources, once mapped to a Crystal report, provide the developer with the ability to create linkages that can combine disparate data sources into usable data across data sources. But even as you delve into creating a Crystal report, our favorite semantic layer, Query Panel, shows itself in Figure 1.7.

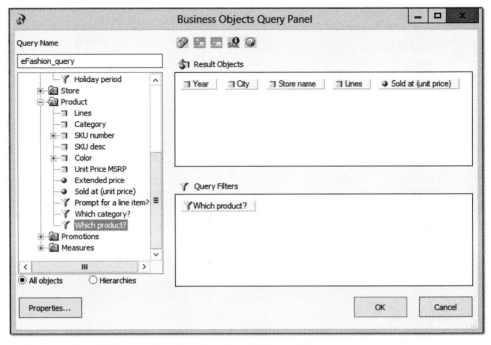

Figure 1.7 The All-Too-Familiar Query Panel in SAP Crystal Reports

Report Development

The report development interface of SAP Crystal Reports 2013 (see Figure 1.8) differs greatly from that of the SAP BusinessObjects Web Intelligence report development interface. Being a desktop-only tool, the typical user profile for an SAP Crystal Reports 2013 developer will be an individual in IT or a *very* technically savvy power user.

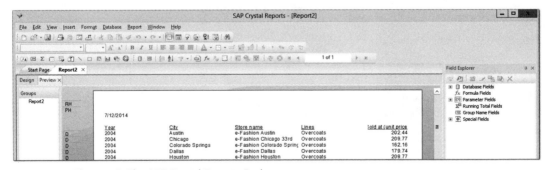

Figure 1.8 The SAP Crystal Reports Body

This interface is very linear in nature. Compared to SAP BusinessObjects Web Intelligence and the power of its report block capability, SAP Crystal Reports 2013 developers must consider carefully the flow of reports in one long report body, capable of carefully crafted pagination, groups, and subreports.

In addition, SAP Crystal Reports 2013 is a popular choice for very finely tuned report formatting and mass distribution of reports, whether by soft media choices such as email or file system distribution or by printer for large-volume distribution of reports.

Considerations for major changes in utilization in SAP Crystal Reports 2013 also push administrators to carefully consider deployment needs. Usage increases in distribution or on-demand viewing put new requirements on the number of deployed SAP BusinessObjects BI servers to ensure maximum availability and fulfillment of Service Level Agreements (SLAs).

SAP Crystal Reports Enterprise

SAP Crystal Reports Enterprise rethinks the approach to creating Crystal reports. Based solely on universe-based data sources, SAP Crystal Reports Enterprise provides a new report design interface for constructing a Crystal report.

Query Development

Compared to its predecessor in SAP BusinessObjects BI 4.0, SAP Crystal Reports Enterprise improves its data source connectivity options significantly, offering native, ODBC, and Java Database Connectivity (JDBC) to many popular database vendors. In addition, access to SAP-specific connectivity, such as UNX or BI Consumer Services (BICS), is much improved.

The design for SAP Crystal Reports Enterprise has been reimagined so that integration with the existing semantic layers by SAP are front and center, leaving behind the complex nature of all the data sources that SAP Crystal Reports 2013 supports today, as shown in Figure 1.9.

Figure 1.9 SAP Crystal Reports Enterprise Query Panel

Report Development

Much like the new approach to getting data into the report in SAP Crystal Reports Enterprise, the report development takes a brand-new, distinctive approach to report layout. Differing from both SAP BusinessObjects Web Intelligence and SAP Crystal Reports 2013, this new report development interface (see Figure 1.10) implements the technique of smart guidelines for easier report formatting and isn't dissimilar to its counterpart in SAP BusinessObjects Web Intelligence—a report-formatting ribbon with a well-thought-out organization of options.

While longtime SAP Crystal Reports developers may look in disdain on developers wanting to use the new SAP Crystal Reports Enterprise as a development platform, this release has the potential to significantly improve the time to delivery for complex Crystal reports in the SAP BusinessObjects BI platform.

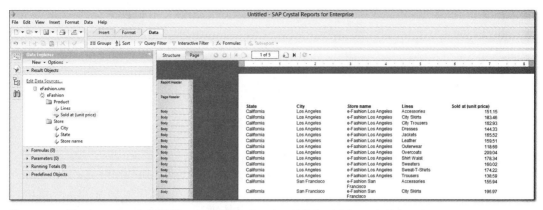

Figure 1.10 The New Smart-Guideline-Based Interface for SAP Crystal Reports Enterprise

The lack of significant change to SAP Crystal Reports 2013 has been felt throughout the lifecycle of SAP BusinessObjects BI 4.1, leaving an impact. Administrators and developers must ask, "why SAP Crystal Reports 2013?" Change and innovation are clearly coming to SAP Crystal Reports Enterprise, as well as support for the modern SAP product stack. Customers making their migration to the new UNX, wishing to use SAP Crystal Reports, have no choice but to transition to SAP Crystal Reports Enterprise, while customers still maintaining UNVs must stay on with SAP Crystal Reports 2013, if using the universe as a source for reporting.

1.2.3 SAP BusinessObjects Dashboards

SAP BusinessObjects Dashboards provides a visually compelling, Adobe Flash-based interface for analyzing data. SAP BusinessObjects Dashboards provides power users and developers with a technology that can deliver visualizations resembling Rich Internet Applications (RIAs). These types of visualizations include controls, alternate views, and, with the help of some third-party integrated technologies, even write-back capabilities. While compiled dashboards can live anywhere an Adobe Flash-enabled browser or device can consume it, dashboards may also live within the SAP BusinessObjects BI 4.1 platform and consume data provided by a universe.

SAP BusinessObjects Dashboards has become a flagship product over recent years. With dashboards becoming more pervasive as lead-in visualizations to more details, they are no longer just for executives or decision makers. Dashboards are becoming more frequent in the area of operational visualizations as well, delivering content to the masses. This further blurs the lines between using standard query and analysis reporting tools such as SAP BusinessObjects Web Intelligence or SAP Crystal Reports to deliver content versus pushing out more interactive content via Dashboards.

Query Development

Like SAP Crystal Reports 2013, SAP BusinessObjects Dashboards has considerable strength in being able to consume a significant number of resources, as you can see in Figure 1.11, and even as defined as dashboard connections in Figure 1.12. While originally more centric to Microsoft Excel, additional capability to integrate into SAP BusinessObjects BI and other platform-agnostic web services makes SAP BusinessObjects Dashboards quite robust in its consumption of data. With the introduction of the SAP BusinessObjects BI 4.0 platform, SAP introduced direct-to-universe connectivity as well, leveraging the Query Panel to the mix for SAP BusinessObjects Dashboards. Rather than require additional layers of abstraction, developers can go straight to the universe.

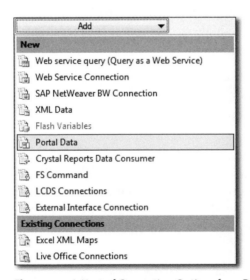

Figure 1.11 A Host of Connection Options for a Dashboard

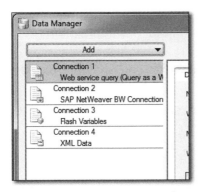

Figure 1.12 Incorporating One or More Data Sources

These connections, and the robust nature of conditional query triggers, give SAP BusinessObjects Dashboards the unique ability to make dashboards mimic web applications (or RIAs, as mentioned earlier). Considering this dynamic and user-driven nature of query triggers, the demands on an environment must be carefully considered. Using Query as a Web Service, for example, puts an increased load not just on the SAP BusinessObjects BI environment, but also on the web tier components that render content and fulfill the HTTP requests. It's this type of activity that makes administrators need to pause and fully understand the net impact of these calls back to SAP BusinessObjects BI as dashboard use becomes more pervasive within the environment.

Dashboard Development

Developing dashboards in SAP BusinessObjects Dashboards is nothing like any other experience for developers in the product family. Developers are exposed to an interface (see Figure 1.13) that appears flat and supports a degree of layered development that enables developers to bind data from the queries developed into dashboard components. These varying types of components enable charting, tabular data displays, and interactive controls to change the view the dashboard.

Administrators must be aware of the development patterns that dashboard developers are following. It's not impossible for them to avoid common data aggregation or row-limit constraints, pulling too much data through a data connection into a dashboard. In addition, new capabilities are available to bind universes built in the Information Design Tool directly into Dashboards. Bypassing more traditional data sources and accessing data in real time may have performance implications that your landscape should be sized to support.

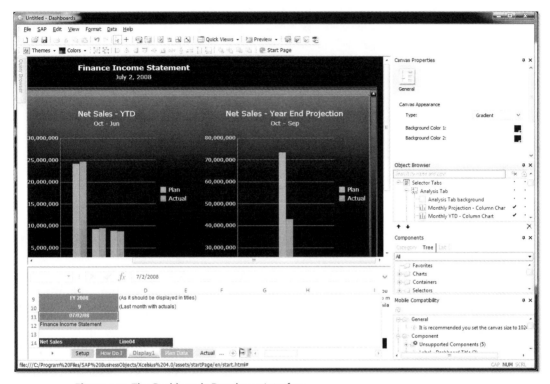

Figure 1.13 The Dashboards Developer Interface

There are also more complex information security concerns, as it's easy for developers to "detach" and let a dashboard run outside of the SAP BusinessObjects BI platform. A developer can simply embed authentication tokens within the dashboard, compile the dashboard, and distribute it to users outside of the platform to enable immediate access to this data. If authentication isn't enforced, consumers have unrestricted, on-demand access to the SAP BusinessObjects BI 4.1 platform that isn't available if a user exports that same data to an Adobe PDF or a Microsoft Excel spreadsheet.

1.2.4   SAP BusinessObjects Analysis

SAP BusinessObjects Analysis comes in two flavors: edition for Microsoft Office and edition for OLAP, as discussed in the following subsections.

Edition for Microsoft Office

SAP BusinessObjects Analysis edition for Microsoft Office is the latest iteration of Microsoft Office-integrated technologies to enable a robust OLAP analytical experience for end users. Much like the classic SAP BusinessObjects BI counterpart, Live Office, SAP BusinessObjects Analysis edition for Microsoft Office extends Microsoft Office's reach into ad hoc OLAP analysis. SAP BusinessObjects Analysis extends this reach beyond the classic SAP data sources into SAP HANA as well.

Intended to satisfy a broad base of needs, SAP BusinessObjects Analysis edition for Microsoft Office provides improved capabilities over legacy products such as SAP BEx Analyzer and an easier-to-use experience for the casual or power user. Users already familiar with pivot tables and other advanced Microsoft Excel capabilities will find integration with this type of analysis friendly and easy to step into.

Edition for OLAP

Your deployment may also be licensed to leverage SAP BusinessObjects Analysis edition for OLAP. The edition for OLAP is integrated into the SAP BusinessObjects BI platform Java BI Launch Pad (BI Launch Pad, for short) as an application, giving your users a web-based UI and the ability to share and disseminate Analysis Views within the SAP BusinessObjects BI 4.1 platform. The beauty here is integrated security within the SAP BusinessObjects BI platform, a distribution mechanism (in SAP BusinessObjects BI) that is mature and capable, and finally, a user experience that isn't tied to the user's desktop tools.

1.2.5   SAP BusinessObjects Explorer

SAP BusinessObjects Explorer was introduced to the suite relatively recently. It differs most fundamentally in the way that data is accumulated. Data, most commonly consumed via a universe or spreadsheet, is indexed and stored on the local file system of the server versus within any type of report file. These indexes, known as InfoSpaces, are very fast file-based indexes, which allow SAP Business-Objects Explorer to digest many more rows of data per dataset than other reporting tools in the set. Much like the other tools in the suite, SAP BusinessObjects BI security, scheduling, and integration into BI Workspaces are available for SAP BusinessObjects Explorer.

SAP BusinessObjects Explorer made a significant appearance on the Apple iTunes App Store ahead of other apps for SAP BusinessObjects BI. This app exposed the same InfoSpaces that the browser-based application delivered to end consumers, creating an interface not dissimilar to the full browser-based version.

SAP BusinessObjects Explorer is also released in an optimized version that takes advantage of SAP's in-memory technologies such as SAP BW Accelerator (BWA) and, more recently, SAP HANA. These technologies give SAP BusinessObjects Explorer additional capability not only to process data faster but also to consume more data than basic InfoSpaces produced against a universe.

Query Development

While query development in SAP BusinessObjects Explorer may vary somewhat based on the version purchased, administrators should know that primarily Microsoft Excel, universes, SAP BW Accelerator, and SAP HANA are leveraged.

While constructing InfoSpaces around a universe, developers are faced with the all-too-familiar Query Panel object browser. However, objects are defined in new buckets known as measures, facets (i.e., dimensions), and filters. While limitations do exist, utilizing the universe to build InfoSpaces leverages the terms universe structure users are accustomed to and improves user experience.

Exploration

Differing once again from counterparts in the reporting and dashboard capability within the platform, SAP BusinessObjects Explorer creates a powerful exploration interface that permits users to rapidly segment and drill down through many more rows of data than the other technologies in the suite, especially in the in-memory-enabled InfoSpaces.

Users walk from left to right in navigating the flow of the simply arranged data. SAP BusinessObjects Explorer automatically orders the facets based on the number of distinct values in the facet, making it easy to see at the highest level the impact each has on a measure. The interface also makes it easy to visualize this data in graphical form with predefined charts, also identified by ideal representation for the data. Lastly, the selected segment for the chart is represented in a table immediately to the right of the chart so users can see the detailed data associated with the selected measure and facets.

1.2.6 SAP Lumira

The release of SAP Lumira and its server counterpart SAP Lumira Server (general availability came in the first half of 2014) marks a significant turning point in the evolution of SAP BusinessObjects BI tools. Regarded initially as a stand-alone BI tool and as an answer to other desktop data discovery tools, SAP Lumira has set a new tone in a more agile release cycle for BI products, recently receiving new releases every six weeks. This has enabled SAP Lumira data visualization capability to mature quickly and to enable additional connectivity into the SAP BusinessObjects BI landscape. Compared to other tools in the SAP BusinessObjects BI portfolio, it fulfills the role of the user that requires data discovery capabilities in a BI tool.

Coupled with the capabilities of SAP Lumira Cloud, SAP seeks to create a more collaborative approach to information sharing among the chief audience of these types of power users, the business analysts. Recently announced as of the writing of this book, SAP Lumira Server will begin to take shape as the on-premise, browser-based user experience for SAP Lumira users. Based on SAP HANA and its robust capabilities as both an in-memory database and an in-memory application server (SAP HANA XS Engine), SAP Lumira Server stands to be the precursor of the future of SAP BI technologies, and the first that doesn't rely on the SAP BusinessObjects BI platform architecture to deliver BI.

What We Know about SAP Lumira Server

SAP Lumira Server is on the horizon and will allow integration with SAP BusinessObjects BI solutions so that visualizations can be secured and viewed through the BI Launch Pad. But for now, this functionality is limited to the desktop or SAP Lumira Cloud, which isn't covered in this text.

SAP has indicated that SAP Lumira Server will function on a runtime version of SAP HANA. The integration into the SAP BusinessObjects BI landscape is performed via a plugin that integrates security and content into the BI Launch Pad, simplifying the administration experience. That integration facilitates the consumption of … you guessed it … universes!

So at the end of the day, we all may be running SAP Lumira Server in some shape or form as a sidecar to our SAP BusinessObjects BI landscapes. Stay tuned.

Query Development

While SAP Lumira is positioned to suit the needs of the business analyst first, so must the needs of data acquisition for this profile of user be satisfied first. In its initial phases, SAP Lumira provided both offline and online access to SAP HANA data; JDBC access to other relational sources; access to comma separated values (CSVs), text, and Microsoft Excel-based flat files; and finally SAP BusinessObjects BI universes. As the user experience of SAP Lumira has evolved, the ability to quickly acquire, transform, and visualize data has become one of the strengths of SAP Lumira (see Figure 1.14).

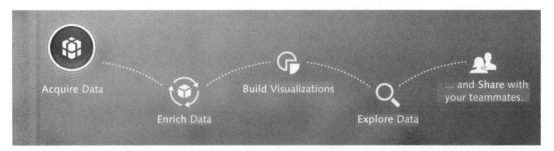

Figure 1.14 Flow for Acquiring, Enriching, Building, and Exploring Data

Like its sibling, SAP BusinessObjects Explorer, SAP Lumira has the ability to connect natively to SAP HANA. This presents the user with the ability to consume tens of millions, or even hundreds of millions of rows of data, inside of an SAP Lumira dataset, without ever bringing a single row of data back to the desktop physically. After the user has selected the appropriate source (see Figure 1.15), he is ready to begin enrichment and more.

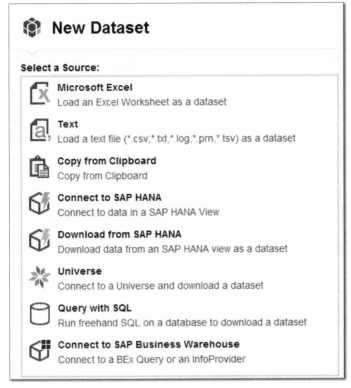

Figure 1.15 Current SAP Lumira Connectivity Options

Data Visualization

Working with SAP Lumira isn't really report development. Working with SAP Lumira isn't really dashboard development. It's known more as data exploration or data discovery. Users enrich and organize content into charts within SAP Lumira on their desktop and have the ability to share with other SAP Lumira users via the storyboard feature or by publishing directly to SAP Lumira Cloud. All this happens while maintaining the idea that this is a self-service BI with a little predictive sprinkled on top.

1.2.7 SAP Predictive Analysis

SAP Predictive Analysis is another new entry into the marketplace. This tool is meant to bring statistical and predictive analysis capabilities to businesses with no data scientists on staff. Nearly everything you need to create accurate, understandable analyses of datasets is included in this easy-to-use tool—without having to have a degree in math.

SAP Predictive Analysis is everything that SAP Lumira is, plus a little more. It's the exact same software for the most part, but it includes an extra set of tools that make the predictive magic happen. In SAP Lumira, you'll notice the familiar menus on the top: PREPARE, VISUALIZE, COMPOSE, and SHARE (see Figure 1.16). SAP Predictive Analysis has the exact same menus, plus one—PREDICT (see Figure 1.17).

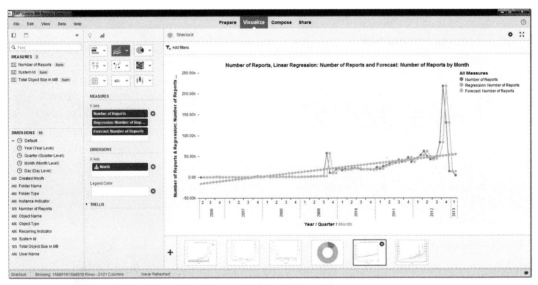

Figure 1.16 Enriching and Exploring Data in SAP Lumira

That PREDICT section packs some serious punch. It adds in the ability for this tool to go toe-to-toe with the other industry-standard predictive analysis tools. Under the PREDICT section, you're given access to what almost looks like an SAP Data Services transformation window (see Figure 1.18).

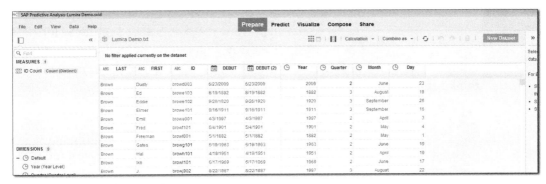

Figure 1.17 SAP Predictive Analysis Menus

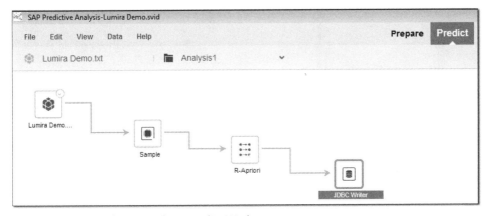

Figure 1.18 SAP Predictive Analysis: Predict Workspace

On the left-hand menu of this workspace, you have access to a whole library of predefined transformations, also not unlike SAP Data Services (see Figure 1.19).

The magic of what makes SAP Predictive Analysis so special is under the ALGO-RITHMS heading. These are nearly all of the types of things you'd need to explore your different datasets in a statistical sense. Some algorithms are written specifically for SAP Predictive Analysis, but most of them are written from the open-source statistical programming language R.

Because SAP Predictive Analysis is based on SAP Lumira, you get access to all of the same data sources, flat files such as a .csv or .xls, and can connect directly to SAP HANA and work from there. SAP Predictive Analysis is smart enough to know when you're directly connected to SAP HANA, and your ALGORITHMS section is replaced with a list of the algorithms that are included in the SAP HANA Predictive Analysis Library (PAL). That way, you can push the prediction "heavy lifting" up onto the SAP HANA server, where it will fly like the wind. Yeah, we think that's pretty cool, too.

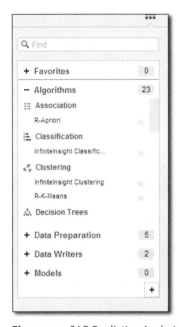

Figure 1.19 SAP Predictive Analysis Transformation Menu

Because this is the same tool as SAP Lumira for all intents and purposes, you can open any SAP Lumira document in SAP Predictive Analysis. This is great if you have someone to prepare a dataset for you first in SAP Lumira, then you, the great Predictor, can just work on the statistical part and not have to worry about all of that data preparation noise.

If you're looking for a way to get your business into the advanced analysis scene (and if you're not, you should be), then look no further than SAP Predictive Analysis. For more information than you could imagine, check out *Predictive Analysis with SAP: The Comprehensive Guide* (SAP PRESS, 2013), by John MacGregor, at *www.sap-press.com*.

1.2.8   SAP BusinessObjects Mobile

SAP BusinessObjects Mobile has been a long-standing part of the SAP Business-Objects architecture, but in recent years gained traction as the mobility market matured with the introduction of the smartphone (in large part thanks to the introduction of the iTunes App Store).

The mobile components made their first appearance with mobile for RIM devices predating the SAP BusinessObjects XI rollout. While crude in implementation, Wireless Application Protocol (WAP)-enabled browsers made it possible to log in to SAP BusinessObjects BI, browse reports, pass limited parameters, and refresh reports on demand.

As smartphones have matured, the capabilities of the mobile applications for SAP BusinessObjects BI have made significant advances as well. As mentioned before, SAP BusinessObjects Explorer delivered the first app for iOS, creating a very robust analytic experience. SAP BusinessObjects Mobile has matured as well, delivering more robust SAP BusinessObjects Web Intelligence content in a sleek, interactive environment that deploys with SAP BusinessObjects BI. Figure 1.20 and Figure 1.21 show examples of this environment.

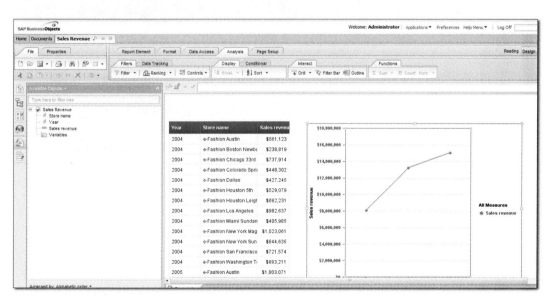

Figure 1.20 Web Intelligence Report on Sales Figures

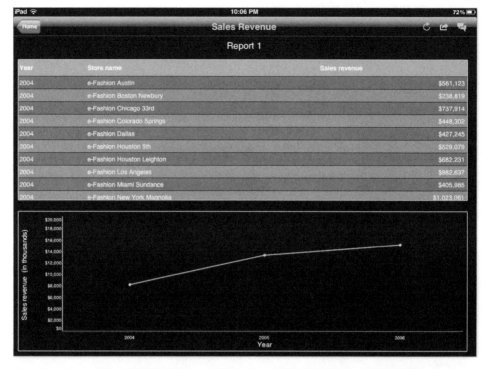

Figure 1.21 Unmodified Web Intelligence Report Opened in SAP BusinessObjects BI

As the demand for mobile devices increases and companies either adopt policies empowering more distribution of mobile devices or use of personal devices on corporate networks, the demand for mobile BI will grow as a consequence. Thus, the way we design solutions for SAP BusinessObjects BI must evolve alongside this demand to ensure that the types of requests made by mobile devices can be sustained.

Query and Report Development

The well-thought-out approach to reports used for SAP BusinessObjects Mobile is simple: reuse the reports you've already constructed. While not necessarily consistent in all mobile platforms, Apple iOS-based devices can benefit from the write once/use once device approach. While extended visualization capabilities exist for iOS-based devices, many out-of-the-box reporting capabilities will transition smoothly to SAP BusinessObjects Mobile. Other devices such as RIM and

Android-based devices require additional report formatting to optimize the report for mobile display.

Another significant difference is in the deployment strategy for these mobile platforms. SAP BusinessObjects Mobile includes layers for integration and security with the mobile platforms that give administrators flexibility in how each is managed and deployed within the enterprise. It also draws on the inherent capabilities within the SAP BusinessObjects BI 4.1 platform for authentication and authorization to simplify deployment of content to users.

1.2.9   SAP BusinessObjects Design Studio

As much as we still want to see this called "Zen," SAP decided that name was too short or something. The now, two-ish-year-old SAP BusinessObjects Design Studio dashboard tool is establishing itself as a helpful feature from which application developers can create interactive dashboards based on SAP HANA, SAP BW, or an SAP BusinessObjects BI universe in UNX form. SAP BusinessObjects Design Studio fills many roles in the suite, serving as a platform for building new dashboards and fulfilling the need for mobility out of the box.

For customers running Dashboards, that leaves a big question: What about my dashboards? This is where we're going to suggest you do a quick search for the SAP Xcelsius Statement of Direction. This was a well-publicized event held where the distinction between these two products was made, and a one-hour webinar was recorded to make these directions clear. The abbreviated version of that story, though, gives customers simple direction:

▶ **Customers using BEx Web Application Designer (WAD)**
BEx WAD customers should adopt SAP BusinessObjects Design Studio as their primary tool for creating dashboards and applications, both on the web and on devices.

▶ **Customers using SAP BusinessObjects Dashboards**
SAP BusinessObjects Dashboards customers should continue with dashboards and leverage the upcoming HTML5 functionality for on-device dashboards. SAP BusinessObjects Dashboards customers using dashboards on top of SAP BW should consider building their new dashboards in SAP BusinessObjects Design Studio.

Yes, customers today must make educated decisions on whether to develop new content on Dashboards or Design Studio. Today, those decisions come down to requirements for form and function and should be based less on the future direction of either of the two tools.

Pop Quiz

1. Which development interface enables developers to create a single, unified interface supporting one or more data sources?
2. What Microsoft Office add-in enables OLAP analysis natively in SAP BW?
3. Which technology creates a file-based index on the server file system for high-speed data analysis?

1.3   Architecture Overview

There should be no misconception that the SAP BusinessObjects BI platform architecture is easy. But on the flip side, it's very robust and scalable. In 2003, when Business Objects announced the purchase of Crystal Decisions, and later BusinessObjects XI, it became clear that this was a decision to leverage the historically strong platform architecture that Crystal Enterprise brought to the table. This technology had already overcome the need to develop a secure service-oriented architecture (SOA) that had built-in fault tolerance capabilities.

As Business Objects integrated the two technologies, classic Business Objects reporting tools were layered onto the Crystal Decisions Crystal Enterprise architecture so that in the end, customers received a best-in-class technology for enterprise reporting.

The core architecture for BusinessObjects, prior to SAP, has evolved but still draws heavily on the same platform. It's important to understand this architecture from a few key points of view. Consider the topmost-level picture you can possibly visualize for SAP BusinessObjects BI, as shown in Figure 1.22.

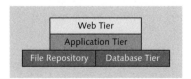

Figure 1.22 Layers of SAP BusinessObjects BI Architecture

As you can see, the SAP BusinessObjects BI architecture has four tiers:

▶ **File repository**
All reports, dashboards, InfoSpaces, and other published content are stored in this layer. This represents the physical output that is retrieved and rendered for the user.

▶ **Database tier**
Metadata pertaining to the reports, dashboards, InfoSpaces, and other published content is stored here in a relational database. Other pertinent information such as access rights, users, groups, and other ancillary information is stored, as well as the pointer on the file repository for the physical report content.

▶ **Application tier**
SAP BusinessObjects BI itself resides here, along with all servers central to granting access to reports, retrieving reports, displaying reports, and scheduling content live in the application tier. Later, in Chapter 3, we'll explore this layer in much more detail, as well as the comprising layers, the application server tier, the intelligence tier, and the processing tier.

▶ **Web tier**
The primary delivery mechanism for SAP BusinessObjects BI content is a web browser, although as mentioned earlier in this chapter, via a mobile device. The web tier provides access via a web browser or other application programming interface (API). These APIs grant access to programmatically access the platform to perform many of the same functions that the included web applications provide via SAP BusinessObjects BI.

> **Note**
>
> See the Product Availability Matrix (PAM) for supported database and web application technologies capable of supporting these tiers, as they will change across major releases and service packs.
>
> The PAM is available at *http://service.sap.com/bosap-support* and is located in the FIND DOCUMENTATION section of the main screen as SUPPORTED PLATFORMS/PARs.

Chapters 3 and Chapter 4 will explore these layers many times over into the distribution of services across multiple nodes, their purposes, and optimizing for use in your environment. Get excited, because our goal here isn't to just walk through the simple deployment of the default install, but to ensure that you get a feel for how to optimize SAP BusinessObjects BI 4.1 within your own environment.

> **Pop Quiz**
>
> 1. Which acquired technology became the underpinnings of the SAP BusinessObjects BI architecture?
> 2. Which tier is responsible for rendering the HTTP content to a user's web browser?
> 3. What document provides insights into the supported technologies for each layer of the SAP BusinessObjects BI architecture?
> 4. Describe the application tier.

1.4 Planning for a New Solution

As you may recall from our preface to the book, administering an SAP BusinessObjects BI system is one-third art, one-third science, and one-third trial and error—and it all begins here, in planning your new solution. Every implementation is different, so the key is knowing the right questions to ask. In this section, we'll introduce you to your options for the three most important areas of solution planning: scope, job rules, and the layout of your deployment.

1.4.1 Scoping Questions

The beginning of the planning process for deploying an SAP BusinessObjects BI environment is to gather facts—as many facts as you possibly can to make the most educated decisions on sizing and scaling the environment. Here we outline some of the major questions you need to be able to answers to plan for a new SAP BusinessObjects BI environment:

- Questions revolving around availability requirements:
    - What days of the week does this system need to be available?
    - What hours of each day does this system need to be available to users?
    - What hours of each day can be allocated to batch reporting?
    - Does the system need to continue to be available if there is a hardware or software failure?

- What percentage of the users need to be available if there is a failure in a single hardware or software component?

- Questions revolving around reporting capacity:

  - What products are licensed: SAP BusinessObjects Web Intelligence, SAP Crystal Reports, SAP BusinessObjects Dashboards, SAP BusinessObjects Explorer, SAP BusinessObjects Mobile, SAP BusinessObjects Analysis?

  - How many total users will use each of the products licensed?

  - What percentage of the user population will only view a report created by someone else?

  - What percentage of the user population will occasionally create a report and browse through existing reports?

  - What percentage of the user population will very frequently create a report and distribute reports to others?

  - Do users require any desktop technologies such as SAP BusinessObjects Web Intelligence or SAP Crystal Reports?

- Questions revolving around the selection process:

  - Do enterprise standards dictate a Windows-based solution versus a UNIX- or Linux-based solution?

  - Is virtualization an option for any component of this environment?

  - Do storage area network (SAN) technologies exist within the enterprise?

  - What database standard exists to host Central Management Server (CMS) and Auditor databases?

  - Are there existing standards for web application containers to host SAP BusinessObjects BI?

Although not an exhaustive list, these are the types of questions that get the ball rolling to determine what assets you have within your organization's technology standards, what SAP BusinessObjects BI technologies you're responsible for managing, and what availability requirements you must fulfill for the user community. We'll also explore these in more detail as we dive into Chapter 2 to learn to effectively size your SAP BusinessObjects BI platform. After all, in this case, it's better to over-deliver than under-deliver on a brand new environment.

1.4.2   Job Roles

This is the point where growing partnerships within your organization becomes important. The following resources in IT and in the business play a critical role in the success of your SAP BusinessObjects BI implementation:

▸ **Business sponsor**
Presumably, this product champion on the user side isn't only responsible for helping you define the target audience and its requirements, but serves as an evangelist to that user community to champion the final solution you seek to deliver.

▸ **Windows/UNIX administrator (also known as a system administrator)**
Soon, this person may become your best friend. The system administrator should be your partner in ensuring that you have a lean, running machine that can handle the load SAP BusinessObjects BI is going to put on that environment. In some distributed models, it's not uncommon for the system administrator to also manage the SAP BusinessObjects BI deployment. In any case, take your system administrator to lunch once in a while.

▸ **Network administrator**
Network designs that involve the lowest latency, or time from one network hop to the other, are really important. Your network administrator should have the intimate knowledge of network subnets, proximity of your servers to the database and storage, and a host of other variables that will ensure inter-server communications in your SAP BusinessObjects BI cluster are optimized and running in top form.

▸ **Web administrator**
With the understanding that most of the SAP BusinessObjects BI platform is accessed via a web browser, it's crucial to make the right technology selection for the web tier. Your enterprise's web administrators are the experts in existing corporate standards and how to deploy them. They will likely be able to assist in deploying and optimizing your environment for your SAP BusinessObjects BI deployment, as well as in serving as an interface to the system administrators and network administrators to ensure that your web tier performs as intended.

▸ **Storage administrator**
You actually owe the storage administrator double. Not only will the storage administrator be able to offer gigabytes of space to support the growth of your file repository, but the storage administrator will likely also pony up space to

support your needs for your CMS and Auditor databases for each of your environments (but in that, directly supports your database administrators). Having a properly configured storage solution for an SAP BusinessObjects BI cluster ensures the availability of the reports users are trying to retrieve.

▸ **Database administration**
No, the database administrator isn't just for supporting your data warehouse or operational reporting needs. Working with the database administrator to ensure that the right enterprise technology standard in your organization is chosen for your CMS and Auditor databases, and placed in a system not over-taxed by other co-located database applications, is critical. If the CMS database isn't available, SAP BusinessObjects BI won't be available.

▸ **Business intelligence architect**
If you're not the business intelligence architect, as an SAP BusinessObjects BI administrator, you need to be not just colleagues, but partners with your architect. This individual is largely responsible for system design, is in tune with incoming platform requirements, is a face to the business users, and will assist in being a voice for change in your constantly evolving SAP BusinessObjects BI environment.

▸ **Extra credit testers**
Many organizations have the luxury of dedicated testers. Those testers may have many different roles:

 ▸ Application/report testing or validation

 ▸ Load or capacity testing

Regardless of the functional need, testers will help to cement the capability of the environment you construct as it pertains to the requirements laid out before you. This also gets you off the hook for being the person solely responsible for figuring out if the environment is actually going to support x users hitting a y-server cluster within a z-minute period. Did you get that formula? It's okay. We'll talk about it more in Chapter 2.

1.4.3 Deployment Layout

With our requirements laid out and the cast of players engaged, we're ready to tackle the SAP BusinessObjects BI deployment layout. The several environment types commonly considered in any enterprise software deployment also apply here. Let's explore the types and functions of each of these environments and how each might be used in your SAP BusinessObjects BI deployment.

▶ **Sandbox**
The sandbox is frequently overlooked as an important part of an SAP BusinessObjects deployment. Consider the need to perform regression test patches, evaluate new versions of the product, and in general, shield your development lifecycle environments from being impacted by change. The sandbox is your answer. It's not needed in the day-to-day environment, demonstrating a great use case for virtualization because it remains dormant until needed.

▶ **Report development**
The report development environment is as important to application developers as production should be to the end-user community. Being able to adhere to project time lines with a reliable development environment is vital and improves the quality of the BI work products delivered by your deployment.

▶ **System/integration test**
After the development of a work product is completed—and before it's put in the hands of developers—reports, universes, dashboards, and other SAP BusinessObjects BI content should be tested against nondevelopment data. Using the system/integration environment to validate this content against base or detail data prior to providing it to end users for review creates an opportunity to avoid unnecessary defects in content delivered to the users.

▶ **User acceptance test**
User sign-off on content avoids big defects. User advocacy and sign-off in a user acceptance test environment creates an opportunity for users to do the following:

   ▶ Validate new data in a near-production environment.

   ▶ Ensure that new universes interpreting data are user friendly and fulfill the ad hoc reporting requirements of the business.

Sign off on reports being delivered as a part of your release to ensure that they meet layout, format, and data integrity requirements for the deliverables.

▶ **Performance test**
So, you've constructed a report in development and used a development database that has 10% of the data of the production environment. What do you do

when you deploy to production with 100% of the data available, and performance slows to a crawl? Whether it stands as a separate environment or is integrated into another test environment, creating a connection to full data to validate performance avoids go-live bumps demonstrated by unseen performance bottlenecks in incomplete data.

▶ **Production**
Production is the real deal. Universes, reports, dashboards, and more are delivered for real scheduling and on-demand consumption.

▶ **Break-fix**
There are organizations that have strict guidelines on not permitting break-fix activities in production. Creating a simple environment that has access to that same representative data and that can be changed as required outside of the systems development lifecycle ensures that you can be flexible in identifying solutions to problems. This may also include hotfixes or other patches provided by SAP for the environment.

Pop Quiz
1. What are the equal parts of creating an SAP BusinessObjects BI environment?
2. Why is the development environment in a systems development lifecycle important?

1.5   Summary

Now that you have a high-level feel for what the tools are doing and how, as well as the types of players that play a role in an SAP BusinessObjects BI deployment, we can start to look ahead to planning deployments. Always be mindful of the uses and behaviors of the users within your environment. They will continue to evolve as their experiences with the technologies and the maturity of your BI capabilities change as well. These fluctuations will keep you on your feet and create the need for you to be in a constant reactive stance to keep your environments running in tip-top shape.

Before you buy a lick of hardware or any kind of licenses, it's crucial for you to understand how big or small a system will need to be to meet your business needs.

2 Sizing and Scalability: Better Make It Big Enough

Now that you've had an overview of the SAP BusinessObjects BI architecture, and you understand the basics of what is involved in the enterprise suite, you have to determine the size of the servers you'll need, either how much or how little. Sizing can be tricky and is likely one of the most important decisions you'll make about your SAP BusinessObjects BI system. The ultimate success or failure of your SAP BusinessObjects BI implementation project hinges not only on your organization's effectiveness in delivering a quality business intelligence solution but also on your sizing decision. Many folks will steer you toward hiring a professional services team to do your sizing estimate for you, which isn't a bad idea—a tad chicken maybe, but not a bad idea. For those a bit more stalwart of heart, you can—with a little time, effort, and diligence—complete a sizing estimate on your own.

Sizing and capacity planning can be a scary task. Many fail to size their solutions properly from the outset, only to get bashed by their customers on opening day. How many times have you tried to visit an overloaded website? Maybe you're old enough to remember getting the following message on Thanksgiving or Christmas when you tried to call Mom: "We're sorry, all circuits are busy. Please try your call later." Not to increase the level of hysteria around this topic, but so much rides on getting your sizing estimates right. Customers have little tolerance for bad capacity planning. They want access to their service whenever they want it, and they want it to be fast. *Slowness* is a prevalent term these days when talking about infrastructure.

The golden rule for sizing is to make your system big enough to perform as well during peak usage hours as it does during nonpeak hours. And that is because users are a fickle species, dear administrator. Users panic when they see error messages. Error messages are scary, and users often don't know what they mean. Scared or angry users mean your phone is going to start ringing. They will call you names, insult your work, and disrupt your Facebook time. So, to preserve your sanity, you should strive to make sure that your users don't ever see a "server is busy" or "out of memory" error, or they will begin to lose confidence in the system and the stones will begin to fly. Users need to be able to trust their SAP BusinessObjects system. After all, they are using the system to get critical information to make decisions about their day or supply information to customers. These are all important things for conducting successful (and profitable) business operations.

While sizing should be taken seriously, it doesn't need to be scary. To break down this ugly beast into something a little more familiar, imagine, if you will, that you're planning a Super Bowl party: Your guests are your business users, and the food is your SAP BusinessObjects BI system. Before you go to the supermarket to purchase the food, plates, plastic utensils, and so on, there are some key pieces of information you need first. How many guests are you going to invite? How long are they going to stay? How much room do you have for seating and game viewing? How much room do you have in your refrigerator? What is your budget for this shindig?

These are all important questions, right? Right!

This Super Bowl party planning is a sizing estimate. We can't be totally sure how many people are going to show up until they actually show up. But we can make some educated guesses at how many people might show up and make sure we have enough of everything so that they have a good time. So, let's get educated so we can start guessing!

Take a deep breath, and get ready for some intense material. Sizing is something you have to get right because when you say it's done, somebody is going to go out and spend money (usually a lot) based on your recommendation. After the money is spent, things get serious very quickly. Up until that point, it's all a theoretical discussion, and your project stakeholders will be friendly and flexible. After the money is spent, the conversation turns very quickly to getting the project done in a timely manner and realizing that return on investment.

First, we'll cover some sizing basics to be sure we're all speaking the same lingo. Next, we'll cover some of the essential tools you have in your sizing toolbox.

Then, we'll discuss some ways you can size an existing environment using Auditor data. If you aren't upgrading, and instead are starting a brand new project, we'll give you some tips on how to handle that sizing job as well. Then we'll scare you with some math you might find handy for more complex sizing projects. We'll round it all out by going over some general things you need to understand about sizing.

2.1 Sizing Basics

If you are new to SAP BusinessObjects BI 4.1, sizing is a totally different ball game than what you may be used to. This is because SAP BusinessObjects BI 4.1 is (finally) a true 64-bit application. That means those antique memory restrictions of old are gone. Gone are the days where processes could only use 2GB of memory each. SAP BusinessObjects BI 4.1 has some serious muscle, and you'll need to be sure you have the proper amount of hardware in place to sustain your business operations, or you might leave stretch marks on your shiny new hardware.

If you strip away all of the scary formulas, math, and statistics and look at sizing for SAP BusinessObjects BI in a purely theoretical way, it all boils down to a few key pieces of information that you need to gather. By starting here, it doesn't seem so scary. What are those basic data points, you ask? Great question! All you really need to know are the following bits of information:

▶ How many users are going to log in to this system?

▶ Of those users, what percentage are information consumers, business users, and expert users? (Don't worry; explanations of these terms are coming soon.)

▶ Which tools in the suite are you going to be using (Web Intelligence, SAP Crystal Reports, SAP BusinessObjects Analysis, etc.)?

▶ How many reports of each type are going to be loaded on the system?

▶ What percentages of those reports are small, medium, and large?

▶ How many days in a typical workweek will this system be operating?

▶ What is the company's tolerance for outages? Can the system be down for a few hours and not impact business, or must it always be up?

That's not so bad, is it? To make a simple sizing estimation, these data points are all you really need. In many cases, this is enough to make a decent sizing decision.

It all boils down to a few key items that are easy to state but a bit more complex to calculate. The main thing we need to estimate is load. *Load* refers to the amount of activities and the types of activities that are going to happen on the system. To estimate load, we need to first figure out how many *total users* will be on the system. Next, we need to estimate how many *active-concurrent* users there will be. And last, what are those active-concurrent users going to be doing concurrently (in other words, what are the *simultaneous requests* going to be)? Active-concurrent users and simultaneous requests are the two main drivers of load.

Before we get into the particulars of how to size, let's discuss briefly what the sizing exercise is going to produce. Yes, you're going to estimate the size of the computer hardware you'll need to run SAP BusinessObjects BI 4.1 in your environment and sustain your level of business activity during peak usage times, smarty-pants. But much simpler than that, the sizing exercise is going to produce two numbers for you. First, is the SAP Application Performance Standard (SAPS) rating, and second is the amount of memory you'll need to support all of your users. Armed with those two key numbers, you'll very quickly be able to determine how much hardware you'll need to buy and, more importantly, how much this is going to cost you.

But wait! Before you go jump in the pool, kids, we'll start by explaining what the SAPS rating is and what you need to know about estimating your different types of users.

2.1.1 Shopping for SAPS

SAP Application Performance Standard, more commonly known as SAPS, is now the standard benchmark for servers running not only classic SAP technology, but also SAP BusinessObjects BI. It's a new concept to folks who came over from the Business Objects-only world, but if you've been around the traditional SAP block, then this is likely a repeat for you. SAPS is a measurement, pure and simple. This measuring stick is used to express a unit of performance you can expect from a certain piece of hardware. It's a way to measure computing power. A little more specifically, SAPS is a hardware-independent unit of measurement that describes the performance of a system configuration in the SAP BusinessObjects BI environment. It is derived from the sales and distribution (SD) benchmark, where 100 SAPS are defined as 2,000 fully business-processed order line items per hour. Wow! That's a mouthful! If you want to get even more scarily technical, this is the throughput required to process 6,000 dialog steps (screen changes), 2,000 postings per hour in the SD benchmark, or 2,400 SAP transactions. If you were thinking this is derived from the legacy SAP products, you'd win a shiny badge. Don't worry, the SAPS ratings you get from your sizing exercise work just fine and dandy for SAP BusinessObjects BI, too.

Now, before you panic, you don't need to calculate the SAPS of a server yourself. SAP has used this measurement for over a decade, and all of your favorite hardware vendors should be able to give you the SAPS rating on any server they are going to sell you. When SAP laid down the law about SAPS as the standard measure for SAP systems, every vendor that wanted a piece of the sales pie stepped up to the plate. Vendors from Dell to VMware (and everyone in between) can tell you what the SAPS rating is on any system they sell (or you configure). Once you figure out your SAPS rating from your sizing exercise, contact the vendor of your choice, and they'll be more than happy to work with you to get the server hardware you need for your shiny new SAP BusinessObjects BI server systems.

All in all, SAPS is just a friendly number. Friendly numbers are nothing to be afraid of. They are warm and fuzzy.

2.1.2 Active, Concurrent, and Active-Concurrent Users

Another important basic concept to wrap your brain around is the "active-concurrent" user. If you already have an SAP BusinessObjects BI environment, you are likely familiar with this term, but if you're new to the game, then read on. An active-concurrent user is pretty much what it says. It's a user that is logged into the system and actually doing something (besides playing Angry Birds). You could have a thousand user accounts in your system, but odds are that less than 10% of them are logged in at any given time. Let's stick with this example, and say you have 1,000 users, and 100 of them are logged in right now. That means you have 100 concurrent users. But are they active? Another smaller percentage of those 100 are likely active at the same time. For the sake of example only, let's say 20% are active. That means you have 20 active-concurrent users. To break this down just a little bit further, you then need to know which tools those 20 troublemakers are using. Are all 20 using Web Intelligence? If only it was that simple. It's more likely a mixture of different tools. The particulars on how to estimate this will come in a bit, but for now, just remember this little bit about active-concurrent users. They're active concurrently. Consider visualizing the breakout of all these users in a pyramid (see Figure 2.1). This picture has been used for what seems like eons in SAP BusinessObjects BI years. It's easy to see where the bulk of your user population will likely shake out as opposed to your heavy users by visualizing them in this manner.

Figure 2.1 The User Breakout Pyramid

All of these concepts and data points you need to collect go back to those first five questions we asked about your system and ran off in search of answers for. These few key factors have the most influence on your SAP BusinessObjects BI system performance. Boiled down, the first is the number of active-concurrent users in the system and the number of documents they have open at any given time. Second is the volume of data being returned by those open reports and the report or query complexity. Third is the type of things users are doing while logged in. And fourth, but not least, is the type of data provider the report is pulling data from.

Before you throw your hands up and scream about your brain hurting, take a deep breath and exhale slowly. Remember that a little headache now will save you a lot of headaches in the coming months and years you have to operate and maintain this SAP BusinessObjects BI system. Keep your eyes on the goal, which is to make sure you provide enough CPU and memory power to meet your business users' needs during peak capacity times. If your system can perform during peak hours, you'll be golden. If it can't, you'll know about it right quick.

Pop Quiz

1. What is SAPS?
2. What is an active-concurrent user?

2.2 Tools in Your Sizing Toolbox

For those who are long-time SAP BusinessObjects BI administrators, you know that sizing information was always extremely hard to come by. Nothing about sizing was made public. You either had to take a class about SAP BusinessObjects BI administration or hire professional services to come in and do it for you. Those days, thankfully, are over. With the release of SAP BusinessObjects BI 4.1, you now have a couple of handy tools in your toolkit, courtesy of our friends at SAP. Those handy tools are the T-Shirt Sizing Guide and the SAP BusinessObjects BI 4 Sizing Estimator. Both of these tools can be found on the spiffy new SAP SIZING page in the SAP Service Marketplace.

2.2.1 T-Shirt Sizing Guide

The simplest of these tools is the T-Shirt Sizing Guide. This is meant to be an extremely simple way to make an estimate of how big your SAP BusinessObjects BI system needs to be. The name is supposed to make you think about sizing just the way you would choose your T-shirt size when you're off buying new ones (which you should do from time to time, especially when they get those indelible yellow stains). Small, medium, large, and extra-large are all terms everyone is familiar with and make people a bit more comfortable when tackling this chore. If you download the entire zip file of T-shirt sizing documents from the aforementioned SAP Service Marketplace, you'll find a guide for each of the different reporting tools you might use in your landscape. You'll find action-packed guides for SAP BusinessObjects Explorer, SAP BusinessObjects Web Intelligence, SAP BusinessObjects Analysis, SAP BusinessObjects BI Workspaces, and SAP Crystal Reports Enterprise. After you scroll past the usual couple of pages of SAP legal disclaimers and a few pages of introduction on what sizing is, you'll find some really interesting charts. These charts break down your sizing for you, in SAPS and in memory, based on how many active-concurrent users you anticipate.

As you can see from Figure 2.2, the sizes are given down the left-hand column, and the different metrics are given across the top. SAP assumes that you'll be using a distributed architecture, and, as written, this might be a tad confusing at first. As far as the T-Shirt Sizing Guide is concerned, the frontend is your SAP BusinessObjects BI web and application tiers, along with the set of SAP BusinessObjects BI services that make up the intelligence tier. And what the T-Shirt Sizing

Guide calls the backend is the SAP BusinessObjects BI services that make up the processing tier. Details on which services belong in which tier can be found in the Sizing Companion for SAP BusinessObjects BI 4.1, which is included in the T-shirt sizing documentation bundle. If you have anything bigger than a medium deployment, you'll likely want to break this down even further, but sit tight until we talk about more advanced sizing in just a few pages. For now, you can see that you get an SAPS rating for both your frontend and backend servers and an amount of memory for both of those as well. See how easy that is? In essence, you should run through this exercise for each of the products you're planning to use, then just add up all the memory and SAPS, and go shopping, right?

Sorry, wrong answer.

Size	Users	SAPS - Front End	SAPS – Back End	Front End Memory in GB	Back End Memory in GB
S	25	3620	1690	8	8
M	50	7230	3380	16	8
L	100	14460	5070	24	16
XL	150	21690	8440	36	16
XXL	>150	*Please contact SAP*			

Figure 2.2 The T-Shirt Sizing Guide

If you find yourself in this boat—that is, a system with multiple SAP products— you probably want to use a different sizing method. T-shirt sizing is quick and simple but is best for planning simple environment landscapes or where "close" is good enough (not involving horseshoes, hand grenades, or nuclear weapons). Although easiest to calculate, T-shirt sizing is the least accurate sizing method because it assumes a doomsday scenario (also not involving nuclear weapons) that all users are always logged in. It really just gives you a wag, a swipe, a guesstimate. Remember all that talk about active-concurrent users? The T-Shirt Sizing Guide assumes that the number of users you're using are all active-concurrent users.

2.2.2   The SAP BusinessObjects BI 4 Sizing Estimator

Those of you not familiar with working on the more traditional SAP products (SAP ERP, SAP ERP HCM, SAP CRM, etc.) probably never heard of the SAP Quick

Sizer. In that case, the folks at SAP who actually built SAP BusinessObjects BI 4.1 sort of feel the same way. To give the SAP BusinessObjects-only crowd a more targeted experience, they put together a tool they call the SAP BusinessObjects BI 4 Sizing Estimator (Sizing Estimator, for short). It's built as a Dashboards Flash file and is free for download from the SAP Community Network (SCN). You can search for it on SCN.

After you download the Sizing Estimator and open it in your favorite web browser, you'll see the typical disclaimer statement that SAP is notorious for. Click off that guy, and you'll land straight in a pretty awesome tool (see Figure 2.3).

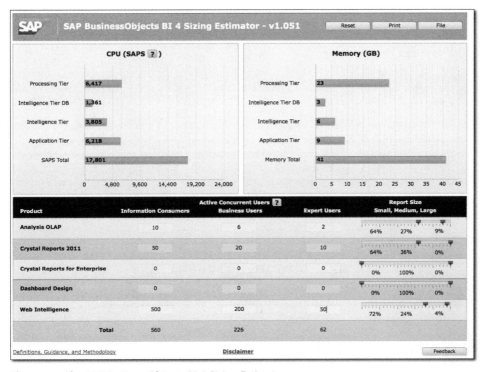

Figure 2.3 The SAP BusinessObjects BI 4 Sizing Estimator

There are a couple of things that are super nice about this tool compared to the others. First, this is the only tool that breaks out your SAPS and memory requirements by tier. Second, this tool is developed and maintained by the SAP BusinessObjects BI 4.1 platform team and is on its own update cycle.

Just like the other tools, you enter in your stratified active-concurrent users by user classification and by reporting tool, and enter in your estimates for report sizes (small, medium, and large in percentages), and you get a nice output.

And, come on, it's pretty cool to estimate an SAP BusinessObjects BI server size using an SAP BusinessObjects BI reporting tool, right?

There are some things to keep in mind when using the SAP BI 4 Sizing Estimator. First, it doesn't calculate sizing for the DSL Bridge Service. This is a big gap that you'll have to factor back in manually afterward. Second, it also doesn't size for SAP BusinessObjects Explorer. You'll have to add that in manually as well. And last, but not least, it won't take a user number greater than 999. So, if you're sizing a monster system, you'll have to step through a few cycles and add up each run to get your final numbers.

Pop Quiz

1. What role does the SAP BI 4 Sizing Estimator fulfill?
2. What technologies does the SAP BI 4 Sizing Estimator take into account when estimating SAPS?
3. How are users classified for use in the SAP BI 4 Sizing Estimator?
4. Which type of users command the highest utilization of the environment?
5. Where can you find the SAP BusinessObjects BI 4 Sizing Estimator?

2.3 Hardware and Software Requirements

It may seem a little odd to shift gears suddenly and have a discussion about hardware and software requirements in the middle of a discussion about sizing. But, rest assured, there is method to this madness. Remember, that the end-goal of a sizing exercise is to go and purchase your servers. It's one thing to know how big a server you require, but you'd also better spend some time in this section and make double- and triple-sure you're buying stuff that is supported.

Can you imagine going out and buying some spiffy server hardware, going through the effort to get it prepared for the big SAP BusinessObjects BI install, and when that day comes, and you push off that install program or script, the installer fails, telling you your system isn't supported? Ouch!

It's worth noting that since the initial release of SAP BusinessObjects BI 4.1, the minimum system requirements have made significant bumps. Even while the minimum system requirements tend to grow, it's not safe to assume today that a minimal chassis with no expansion is wise. Consider in the planning process that your memory requirements, for example, may far exceed initial scoping. Always plan ahead for growth.

An equally important piece of the sizing puzzle is to make sure that what you buy is the right this, that, and the other. Each version, patch, feature pack, and so on has different requirements for hardware and software. The single best place to find that information is, you may have guessed, the SAP Support Portal. Log in with your trusty S-ID, and head over to the RELEASE,UPGRADE & MAINTENANCE INFO tab (see Figure 2.4). There, you'll see the Product Availability Matrix (PAM).

Figure 2.4 SAP Support Portal Navigation Bar

Click on the PAM link, and find the SBOP BI PLATFORM 4.1 link. This is where you're going to find out all you need to know about what is supported on SAP BusinessObjects BI 4.1, and because it's hosted at SAP, it will always be up to date for each release and patch you're looking to install. In addition, this will be your reference to go back to as the rest of the world updates web browsers, databases, and more, to ensure that you're clear on supported technologies for *your* version of SAP BusinessObjects BI. So imagine, when Mozilla releases Firefox 24.5, you'll know that your users still need to keep Firefox 3 installed.

The first page you land on will show you the date the product was released and when support will end (see Figure 2.5).

In the ESSENTIALS section, you'll want to click the OPEN IN NEW WINDOW link to launch the PAM document fully (see Figure 2.6).

Figure 2.5 SBOP BI Platform 4.1 PAM General Information

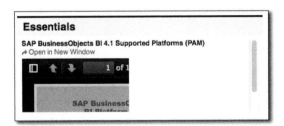

Figure 2.6 Essentials Tab to Launch the PAM

Click the link and download or save the file to the location of your choice. The document has more details for you on what is supported for this version and service pack of SAP BusinessObjects BI 4.1.

The document version of the PAM has several more pages of detailed crosstab information on all of the various flavors of supported pieces (see Figure 2.7 and Figure 2.8). The point being made here isn't to use these images when planning your system but to demystify the PAM for you by showing you what to expect when you get there. This is by no means a substitute for going out to the SAP Service Marketplace and checking the PAM for yourself. Reading through the PAM document in detail is time well spent.

SAP BusinessObjects BI Platform 4.1
Server Components by Operating System

	Windows (*1)				Linux			AIX		Solaris	
	Server 2008 x64	Server 2008 R2 x64	Server 2012	Server 2012 R2	Suse SLES 11 x86_64	Red Hat EL 5 x86_64	Red Hat EL 6 x86_64	AIX 6.1 Power	AIX 7.1 Power	Solaris 10 SPARC	Solaris 11 SPARC
64-bit BusinessObjects BI Server Products	SP2	SP1			(*2)	Update 3 (*2)	Update 2 (*2)	TL5	TL1 SP1		
SAP BusinessObjects BI platform	✓	✓	✓	SP02+ (*6)	✓	✓	✓	✓	✓	✓	✓
SAP BusinessObjects Analysis, edition for OLAP	✓	✓	✓	SP02+ (*6)	✓	✓	✓	✓	✓	✓	✓
SAP BusinessObjects Explorer	✓	✓	✓	SP02+ (*6)	✓	✓	✓	✓	✓	✓	✓
SAP BusinessObjects Web Intelligence	✓	✓	✓	SP02+ (*6)	✓	✓	✓	✓	✓	✓	✓
SAP Crystal Reports for Enterprise	✓	✓	✓	SP02+ (*6)	✓	✓	✓	✓	✓	✓	✓
SAP Crystal Reports 2013	✓	✓	✓	SP02+ (*6)	✓	✓	SP01+	✓	✓	✓	✓
SAP BusinessObjects Dashboards	✓	✓	✓	SP02+ (*6)	✓	✓	✓	✓	✓	✓	✓
Mobile Server (*4)	✓	✓	✓	SP02+ (*6)	✓	✓	✓	✓	✓	✓	(*5)

Figure 2.7 Detailed PAM Crosstab 1

SAP BusinessObjects BI Platform 4.1
Desktop Clients and Operating System

	Windows Server				Windows Desktop			Mac
	Server 2008	Server 2008 R2	Server 2012	Server 2012 R2	Windows 7 SP1	Windows 8	Windows 8.1	Mac OS X 10.9
32-bit BusinessObjects BI Desktop Clients	SP2	SP1			SP1			
SAP BusinessObjects BI Client Tools	✓	✓	✓	SP02+ (*1)	✓	✓	SP02+ (*1)	-
SAP BusinessObjects Live Office	✓	✓	✓	SP02+ (*1)	✓	✓	SP02+ (*1)	-
SAP BusinessObjects Web Intelligence Rich Client	✓	✓	✓	SP02+ (*1)	✓	✓	SP02+ (*1)	-
SAP Crystal Reports for Enterprise	✓	✓	✓	SP02+ (*1)	✓	✓	SP02+ (*1)	-
SAP Crystal Reports 2013	✓	✓	✓	SP02+ (*1)	✓	✓	SP02+ (*1)	-
SAP Crystal Reports Viewer 2013	✓	✓	✓	SP02+ (*1)	✓	✓	SP02+ (*1)	✓
SAP Crystal Presentation Design 2013	✓	✓	✓	SP02+ (*1)	✓	✓	SP02+ (*1)	-
SAP BusinessObjects Dashboards(*2)	✓	✓	✓	SP02+ (*1)	✓	✓	SP02+ (*1)	-

Figure 2.8 Detailed PAM Crosstab 2

Don't forget to check the end of the PAM document, too. Buried down about 20 pages deep, you'll find the minimum hardware requirements by platform (see Figure 2.9 and Figure 2.10).

SAP BusinessObjects BI Platform 4.1
Minimum HW Requirements - Windows

Minimum Screen Resolution
Screen resolution of [1024] x [768] is recommended

Minimum Server Hardware Requirements
For Evaluation Purposes:
CPU performance of at least 8000 SAPS
16 GB RAM minimum
For Deployment:
Please refer to the BI4 Sizing Companion Guide, located at www.sap.com/bisizing and also your SAP representative.
- For more information on SAPS, see the SAP Sizing portal: http://service.sap.com/sizing and also the SAP benchmarked vendor hardware list: http://www1.sap.com/solutions/benchmark/sd2tier.epx
- If deploying to virtualized hardware, it is strongly recommended that the memory and CPU(s) be reserved for each virtual machine that is running the BI services.

Minimum Client Hardware Requirements
Dual Core CPU
2 GB RAM

Recommended Disk Space Requirements
SAP BusinessObjects BI (client installer):
- 3.5 GB for default installation with English language only installed
- 7.5 GB for default installation with all languages installed
SAP BusinessObjects BI (server installer):
- 11 GB for default installation with English language only installed
- 14 GB for default installation with all languages installed

Figure 2.9 PAM Hardware Requirements by Platform 1

SAP BusinessObjects BI Platform 4.1
Minimum HW Requirements - Linux

Minimum Server Hardware Requirements
For Evaluation Purposes:
CPU performance of at least 8000 SAPS
16 GB RAM minimum
For Deployment:
Please refer to the BI4 Sizing Companion Guide, located at www.sap.com/bisizing and also your SAP representative.
- For more information on SAPS, see the SAP Sizing portal: http://service.sap.com/sizing and also the SAP benchmarked vendor hardware list: http://www1.sap.com/solutions/benchmark/sd2tier.epx
- If deploying to virtualized hardware, it is strongly recommended that the memory and CPU(s) be reserved for each virtual machine that is running the BI services.

Note: Compiled binaries of SAP BusinessObjects BI software is supported on versions of the Linux operating system running on CPUs made by AMD or Intel.

Recommended Disk Space Requirements
SAP BusinessObjects BI (server installer):
- 14 GB for default installation with English language only installed
- 16 GB for default installation with all languages installed

Figure 2.10 PAM Hardware Requirements by Platform 2

Administrators plotting their upgrade should really take notice of the minimum system requirements. They are significantly higher than what you may have been used to supporting in SAP BusinessObjects XI 3.x deployments. We've already covered the fact that SAP BusinessObjects BI 4.1 takes us to a mandatory requirement for 64-bit hardware and operating system. On top of that, we have many new services for which to scale that further increase the minimum requirements for an SAP BusinessObjects BI 4.1 system.

Again, these aren't all-inclusive and aren't meant for actual planning. Check the PAM online to find the detailed information about the product and version you're going to install; it's certainly a necessary step in your sizing and planning project. Checking the PAM before you buy any hardware or software will help make sure you have exactly what you need to get going on the day you start installing the product.

Pop Quiz
1. How does the PAM apply in a sizing exercise?

2.4   Using Auditor to Size an Existing System for Migration

One of the best ways to gauge how much infrastructure you're going to need is by taking a look at what you have today. For some, that may be nothing. For others, there may be a long history of business intelligence utilization that must be accounted for to correctly forecast the size and scale of your SAP BusinessObjects BI 4.1 deployment. In this section, we'll focus on how to size an existing system for migration using the Auditor tool.

2.4.1   XI R2 and XI 3.1 as the Way to 4.1

If you're looking at a migration, you certainly have some work cut out for you as the administrator. But luckily, you have a really great resource for estimating how big your SAP BusinessObjects BI 4.1 system needs to be, and that resource is your existing SAP BusinessObjects BI environment. As you may or may not be aware, SAP BusinessObjects BI comes with a pretty comprehensive auditing capability. Nearly every action that takes place inside your SAP BusinessObjects BI system gets recorded in a log file: who logged in, who ran what report, how big that report was, who passed what parameters in which prompt window, and so on.

These log files get written to the Auditor database about every 15 minutes, and SAP BusinessObjects BI comes along with a universe called Activity and about 30 pre-made reports that use it. If you have Auditor enabled on your system (and you really should), you're even more fortunate because you have nearly all the information you need to make a more educated sizing estimate right in your Auditor database. You can break down the number of reports by flavor, by size, and by owner. You can figure out who your power users are, who your information consumers are, and who those zany experts that challenge your existence so much are.

As you begin to grasp the value of the Auditor data in keeping your environment healthy and forecasting for growth, you'll see that the historical Auditor data is a valuable set of key performance indicators (KPIs) for deriving accurate values for correctly setting the scale for the SAP BusinessObjects BI 4 Sizing Estimator for your new SAP BusinessObjects BI 4.1 environment. Remember those key questions you want to have sound estimates for answering:

▶ How many users are logged in at any given time over the day?

▶ When are my peak usage hours?

▶ During peak hours, how many users are logged in?

▶ During peak hours, how many reports are being run?

▶ Which reports are refreshed the most? How big are they?

Next, we'll address how you can use Auditor to answer some of these questions.

Third-Party Tools

Third-party tools are available for improving your experience with Auditor. On the book's website at *www.sap-press.com*, we've included a copy of an enhanced version of the Activity universe we call "Activity – Reloaded" for both SAP BusinessObjects XI 3.1 and 4.0 in the downloadable content. The current Activity universe does an adequate job of putting the detailed Auditor data in front of an administrator. However, many of the business rules applied in this semantic layer don't immediately make it obvious how to derive other KPIs out of this data, which is why third-party tools can sometimes be helpful.

Getting Cozy with the Auditor Database

Let's take a tangent and spend some time getting familiar with Auditor data. Now, we'll have to make a few hefty assumptions here, and we'll leave it up to you whether you'll read on or skip ahead. Read on if you're comfortable with databases and database structures. Read on if you're comfortable operating in your favorite query tool. Read on if you're familiar with a little Structured Query Language (SQL). Skip ahead to Section 2.4.2 if none of those apply to you.

Let's be perfectly clear: *Don't fear the Auditor.* The Activity universe tends to make this look daunting, but we're going to break this into tiny bits so that it might make a little more sense.

Dissecting the Auditor Database

Begin with the core table for this hunk of data, Table AUDIT_EVENT (see Figure 2.11). Think of it as the center of all things audited. Very simply, this table tracks the "who, what, when, where, and, when applicable, how long did it take?" information. It also sets up the unique identifiers for us to uniquely identify each of these events. The primary key is also established for the event with a combination of two fields, the EVENT_ID and the SERVER_CUID. We'll learn more about that in just a moment.

Figure 2.11 The Audit Event Table

The event itself is a look at the rearview mirror of your environment:

- A user logged on
- A report was viewed
- A report was refreshed
- A schedule failed

The list goes on and on. The point is that the Auditor database is storing the accounting of all things that took place within your environment at the highest level of granularity. It's very simple to get a full picture of all the audited event types. Run a query against Table EVENT_TYPE, which is the event type lookup table.

```
SELECT * FROM EVENT_TYPE;
```

Yes, you're an administrator, but don't fear the SQL. This gives you, at a high level, an idea of the types of data that *can* be audited within your environment. So, perhaps you're a little curious about how many events have been audited by an event type. Let's figure that out next, considering the relationship between the event and the event type (see Figure 2.12) and then run our query (see Listing 2.1).

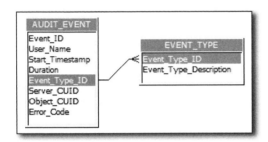

Figure 2.12 Audit Event as It Relates to Event Type

```
SELECT
    COUNT(*) as NUMBER_OF_EVENTS,
    EVENT_TYPE.EVENT_TYPE_DESCRIPTION
FROM
    AUDIT_EVENT,
    EVENT_TYPE
WHERE
    AUDIT_EVENT.EVENT_TYPE_ID = EVENT_TYPE.EVENT_TYPE_ID
GROUP BY
    EVENT_TYPE.EVENT_TYPE_DESCRIPTION
```

Listing 2.1 Query to Return Count of Events by Event Type Description

That was easy. This constitutes a simple distribution of values to illustrate the higher-volume events taking place within your environment. We haven't gotten to the guts of where it ran or what happened when it ran, but we'll get there.

To make sense of all the ancillary bits included in Auditor, we have to move on to the next table in the Auditor schema, Table AUDIT_DETAIL (see Figure 2.13). The detail table is really the one that gives administrators heartache. While this looks like a table with little content, the reality is that it's normalized to return all of the ancillary data for an event, as well as more descriptive information about that event's detail in a sometimes cumbersome character large object (CLOB). A CLOB contains large amounts of character data and can be up to 4GB in size.

Figure 2.13 Audit Detail Table

The detail table goes deep and wide, encompassing everything that Auditor can cram into that CLOB, such as the following:

▶ Full SQL at the time of query execution

▶ Instance destination details

▶ Delimited (albeit ugly) list of groups a report owner was in when he viewed a report

Again, the list goes on and on. Much like Table AUDIT_EVENT, Table AUDIT_DE-TAIL also has a lookup table called DETAIL_TYPE. It's used to identify the list of details available for a given Table AUDIT_DETAIL record.

If it's not already obvious, Table AUDIT_DETAIL can't stand on its own. You need Table AUDIT_EVENT to derive when the event occurred, who owned it, what report it related to, and so on. Figure 2.14 gives a brief look at that relationship and SQL to pull it together.

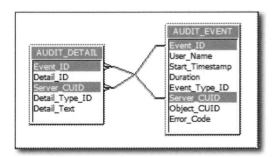

Figure 2.14 Audit Event and Its Relationship to Audit Detail

Caution

Don't really run the query; just observe the syntax (see Listing 2.2). We'll explain in a minute.

```
SELECT
    *
FROM
    AUDIT_EVENT,
    AUDIT_DETAIL
WHERE
    AUDIT_EVENT.EVENT_ID = AUDIT_DETAIL.EVENT_ID
    AND AUDIT_EVENT.SERVER_CUID = AUDIT_DETAIL.SERVER_CUID
```

Listing 2.2 An Example Monster Auditor Query You Should Not Run

Table AUDIT_EVENT alone can have millions of rows on an aging system. Table AUDIT_DETAIL will then contain possibly dozens of rows for each and every event along the way. The net result? We need KPIs to better drive how we use this data. Let's first get our heads around the rest of this data.

The other relevant Auditor data in prior versions of SAP BusinessObjects BI are merely lookup tables, resolving codes for the event type, the detail type, and the server full description. Now that we have the structure laid out nice and neat, let's see the full picture of what a structured Auditor universe with appropriate relationships should look like (see Figure 2.15).

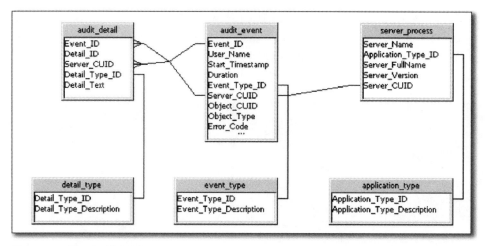

Figure 2.15 The Auditor Schema

With the core tables having taken shape, we can actually learn a lot from the out-of-the-box Activity universe and the way it has decoded fields such as the Universe Name, Document Name, and so on. But further, we can derive other KPIs to begin to more effectively aggregate data. Let's consider looking at three KPIs in one query, to calculate the total number of jobs, the total number of successful jobs, and the total number of failed jobs (see Listing 2.3). Don't run away. This will be worth it.

```
SELECT
    SUM(CASE
    WHEN AUDIT_EVENT.EVENT_TYPE_ID IN (327681,327682,327683) THEN 1
    ELSE 0
    END) AS NUMBER_OF_JOBS,
    SUM(CASE
    WHEN AUDIT_EVENT.EVENT_TYPE_ID IN (327681) THEN 1
    ELSE 0
    END) AS NUMBER_OF_SUCCESSFUL_JOBS,
    SUM(CASE
    WHEN AUDIT_EVENT.EVENT_TYPE_ID IN (327682,327683) THEN 1
    ELSE 0
    END) AS NUMBER_OF_FAILED_JOBS
FROM
    AUDIT_EVENT
```

Listing 2.3 Query for Total Number of Jobs by Status

Now we're getting somewhere! We can slice those KPIs in several ways. Consider using USER_NAME, a format of START_TIMESTAMP to pivot the data to the day, week, month, quarter, or year, and more. In this one example, we can now also look at daily failures on the schedules to identify who generated the job, the frequency and number of times the job failed, and more. That is a pretty powerful rearview mirror.

There are other views of this data we can leverage to make more effective considerations in sizing the environment as well:

- Number of report views
- Number of reports refreshed
- Number of logons

It's through that combination of the AUDIT_EVENT.EVENT_TYPE_ID and the AUDIT_DETAIL.DETAIL_TYPE_ID that our KPIs really take shape and we can identify at an aggregate level—supplemented by the existing detailed-level universe—what is happening in the environment.

Lastly, Table SERVER_PROCESS is the historical accounting of the server in the cluster that handled the event when it took place (see Figure 2.16). We're fans of this table in particular because to top it all off, we now know the "where" of it all.

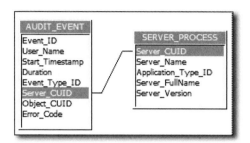

Figure 2.16 Audit Event as It Relates to Server Process

Knowing our events and all the great historical data and KPIs we can derive, and now combining that with our server list, let's look at the distribution of jobs by the Job Server in the environment (see Listing 2.4).

```
SELECT
  SERVER_PROCESS.SERVER_FULLNAME,
  SUM(CASE
    WHEN AUDIT_EVENT.EVENT_TYPE_ID IN (327681,327682,327683) THEN 1
    ELSE 0
    END) AS NUMBER_OF_JOBS,
  SUM(CASE
    WHEN AUDIT_EVENT.EVENT_TYPE_ID IN (327681) THEN 1
    ELSE 0
    END) AS NUMBER_OF_SUCCESSFUL_JOBS,
  SUM(CASE
    WHEN AUDIT_EVENT.EVENT_TYPE_ID IN (327682,327683) THEN 1
    ELSE 0
    END) AS NUMBER_OF_FAILED_JOBS
FROM
  AUDIT_EVENT,
  SERVER_PROCESS
WHERE
  AUDIT_EVENT.SERVER_CUID = SERVER_PROCESS.SERVER_CUID
  AND SERVER_PROCESS.APPLICATION_TYPE_ID = 37
```

Listing 2.4 Query for Finding Jobs by the Job Server

While we took a little shortcut and didn't talk about the lookup table for SERVER_ PROCESS, Table APPLICATION_TYPE, know that it has all of the types of servers nicely bundled up into a code. In this case, scheduling for Web Intelligence is a code of "37." So now, we've taken our query and simply redistributed it across all Job Servers that handle Web Intelligence documents to see how balanced that load is.

Could they be imbalanced? Are server groups defined but ineffective? Are there servers in the cluster that are overpowered compared to others? Do we simply have Job Servers configured to handle more concurrent jobs than others (correctly or incorrectly)? These are the questions you should be able to ask yourself, and with this type of data, you certainly can. It's also relevant to note that this application type relates more precisely to the individual services that run within a defined SAP BusinessObjects BI server. For example, the Adaptive Job Server (AJS) supports scheduling for both Web Intelligence and the Replication Service. These services are broken out so that audit events can be traced to the service that handled the event.

This type of idea is fairly universal, whether you're looking across Web Intelligence Processing Servers, SAP Crystal Reports Job Servers, or any other server audited within the SAP BusinessObjects BI environment. If you're looking to audit SAP BusinessObjects Desktop Intelligence history, you're in luck—if you're on SAP BusinessObjects XI 3.1 or higher. SAP BusinessObjects XI R2 customers are unfortunately going to have to come up with an alternative means of auditing.

2.4.2 So What Do We Audit?

There are a *ton* of properties you can audit within a legacy SAP BusinessObjects BI environment. If you're one of the fortunate few for whom disk availability on your Auditor database isn't a premium, good for you. However, the masses must consider what corporate compliance, system administrators, and common sense say before they audit. In Table 2.1, we take a look back at an SAP BusinessObjects XI 3.1 system and consider exactly what we should be auditing to make good decisions about our environments. Sure, there are a lot of other audit properties. It even varies if you look far enough back to take into consideration what this looks like on an SAP BusinessObjects XI R2 system. However, we're going to put an emphasis on properties we use for sizing and understanding usage for forecasting growth.

Server	Event	Why You Care
Adaptive Job Server	Scheduling Succeeded	Schedules that run to completion without error are great. Having a metric to which you can compare failures is even better; ultimately giving you the ability to count the total number of jobs run in a given period. The Adaptive Job Server (AJS) is going to take point on auditing your Web Intelligence jobs.
Adaptive Job Server	Scheduling Failed	Not only are the details behind this event type important, but it gives you the total number of failures to compare to your successes, as well as the ability to spot users with recurring failures. Consider that users can't figure this out easily on their own without an InfoView-based Instance Manager. You've got the power with this data to keep users informed of scheduling issues.
Adaptive Job Server	Scheduling Failed But Will Be Reattempted	Not dissimilar to Scheduling Failed. Simply creates a bucket to identify failures that will take another crack at it as defined in the job properties.
Central Management Server	Concurrent Logon	Customers who haven't purchased named user licenses have audit events for authentication stored here. With that, they can trend concurrent logons over time to see the growth in user activity and user adoption of the platform.
Central Management Server	Named User Logon	Customers purchasing named user licenses get the same type of events logged here. This is also used for trending user logon events. You start to see the complete picture of user logon volumes over time.
Central Management Server	User Logon Failed	Corporate compliance or security departments typically want to track failed logon attempts to enterprise systems. Be sure to get them engaged on how you track failed logon attempts to your system.
Central Management Server	User Logoff	This audit event gives value in one simple way: identifying first at a high level the percentage of the total user logons versus the percentage that also correctly log off. This can also then be used as a drill-down to identify users that have logged in with a concurrent or a named user logon that haven't logged off correctly.

Table 2.1 Auditing Events by Server

Server	Event	Why You Care
Crystal Reports Cache Server	Report Viewing Succeeded	When a Crystal report isn't run immediately through the SAP Crystal Reports Job Server, a cache hit can be viewed. SAP Crystal Reports can display reports to large numbers of users. So having a full understanding of report view volumes by server is critical in helping scale the environment for Crystal reports consumption.
Crystal Reports Job Server	Scheduling Succeeded	This is similar to the Adaptive Job Server auditing for Web Intelligence but is applicable specifically to SAP Crystal Reports jobs.
Crystal Reports Job Server	Scheduling Failed	This is similar to the Adaptive Job Server auditing for Web Intelligence but is applicable specifically to SAP Crystal Reports jobs.
Crystal Reports Job Server	Scheduling Failed But Will Be Reattempted	This is similar to the Adaptive Job Server auditing for Web Intelligence but is applicable specifically to SAP Crystal Reports jobs.
Desktop Intelligence Cache Server	Document Retrieved	When a Desktop Intelligence report is accessed via the Cache Server, that view event is flagged. This also provides insights into report view activity.
Desktop Intelligence Cache Server	Document Refreshed	When a Desktop Intelligence report is refreshed via the Cache Server, that refresh event is flagged. This also provides insights into report refresh activity.
Desktop Intelligence Job Server	Scheduling Succeeded	This is similar to the Adaptive Job Server auditing for Web Intelligence but is applicable specifically to Desktop Intelligence jobs.
Desktop Intelligence Job Server	Scheduling Failed	This is similar to the Adaptive Job Server auditing for Web Intelligence but is applicable specifically to Desktop Intelligence jobs.
Desktop Intelligence Job Server	Scheduling Failed But Will Be Reattempted	This is similar to the Adaptive Job Server auditing for Web Intelligence but is applicable specifically to Desktop Intelligence jobs.
Program Job Server	Scheduling Succeeded	This is similar to the Adaptive Job Server auditing for Web Intelligence but is applicable specifically to program objects such as Java or .NET programs.

Table 2.1 Auditing Events by Server (Cont.)

Server	Event	Why You Care
Program Job Server	Scheduling Failed	This is similar to the Adaptive Job Server auditing for Web Intelligence but is applicable specifically to program objects such as Java or .NET programs.
Program Job Server	Scheduling Failed But Will Be Reattempted	This is similar to the Adaptive Job Server auditing for Web Intelligence but is applicable specifically to program objects such as Java or .NET programs.
Publication Job Server	Scheduling Succeeded	This is similar to the Adaptive Job Server auditing for Web Intelligence but is applicable specifically to publications.
Publication Job Server	Scheduling Failed	This is similar to the Adaptive Job Server auditing for Web Intelligence but is applicable specifically to publications.
Publication Job Server	Scheduling Failed But Will Be Reattempted	This is similar to the Adaptive Job Server auditing for Web Intelligence but is applicable specifically to publications.
Web Intelligence Processing Server	Document Retrieved	An event of this type is a signal that a Web Intelligence report was at the very least opened and viewed. This doesn't imply that a refresh took place, but it also doesn't preclude that as a subsequent event.
Web Intelligence Processing Server	Document Refreshed	A Web Intelligence refresh event provides insights into the number of users at least one notch above the view-only users. These users are those that will start to tax the system harder than the viewers and, in the case of using Auditor as the rearview mirror, are important to understand.
Web Intelligence Processing Server	Document Edited	This audit event is useful from the perspective of understanding which users are taking an existing report; whether it's a personal report or a standard, enterprise report; and making changes to the queries within.
Web Intelligence Processing Server	Universe Selected	This event type is a signal that a user selected the option to create a new Web Intelligence report by selecting a universe from the list of available universes.

Table 2.1 Auditing Events by Server (Cont.)

You may have noticed that things such as the Multi-Dimensional Analysis Server (MDAS), the Report Application Server (RAS), the List of Values Server (LOV), and others were omitted. Your reporting environment requirements will dictate the auditing requirements. Those mentioned above cover the big three—SAP Crystal Reports, Desktop Intelligence, and Web Intelligence—and for the majority of customers will encompass the "big hit" reporting technologies in legacy SAP BusinessObjects BI systems.

The only real big and scary audit event that comes to mind that should cause concern is that, for Web Intelligence, when the document is refreshed and the SQL-generated events fire, the detail type stores the full SQL statement behind the query or queries. This is a CLOB. CLOBs are gigantic, and they consume a great deal of space. Use caution in storing/retaining this data, as this type of event will lead to significant database bloat as your audit history grows.

With that, you have the building blocks of auditing with historical event data inside SAP BusinessObjects BI. Take advantage of the summarized view of this data, and rest well knowing you'll actually have an easier time estimating the size requirements for your future SAP BusinessObjects BI 4.1 environment than the guy building his first.

The Golden Rule

Remember your golden rule: the system should be able to perform as well during peak usage hours as it does during nonpeak hours. If you can do that, the rest of the business day will be a cakewalk. The key point here is finding out when that peak usage time is and how big it is in terms of users, reports, and data volume.

Pop Quiz

1. Characterize the role of Table AUDIT_DETAIL when auditing events.
2. Should all auditing be turned on with every server?
3. How can Auditor data be used to size a new environment?

2.5 Sizing a System from Scratch

For a fresh start, you'll still need the same information, but you'll need to use sneaker-ware instead of cold, hard data. This means you're going to have to walk around and talk to people. Find out from your different business units how many people will require access to your SAP BusinessObjects BI server. Talk to a few of those users and see if they know what types of reports they are going to want. If you have business analysts to talk to that's even better because they are likely already working on gathering business requirements for the shiny new reporting suite. Find out how many report designs are already in their pipeline and how many they plan to request in the coming year. Which tools do they envision using?

After you have that information, then you can start doing some analysis of your own as the administrator. Talk to the database administrators for the data warehouse or data marts that will be used as data sources for SAP BusinessObjects BI. Get an idea about how big or small those are, and, if you really want to get fancy, see if you can mock up some of the reporting queries and get a feel for how many records will be returned. Keep in mind, "Garbage in, garbage out." The goal is to produce the best guess you possibly can and satisfy the dictates of the golden rule: make this puppy fly well during peak usage hours, so your users can trust the system and do their jobs.

When starting from scratch, use your sizing toolbox to help you get a start. Begin plugging numbers into the SAP BusinessObjects BI 4 Sizing Estimator and see how changing the numbers changes the SAPS and memory ratings. As you continue your project meetings and discussions with the stakeholders, you can refine your model and construct a better picture.

It can't be overstated at this point how clear you must be to all of those stakeholders about how your sizing estimates are just that—estimates. It's extremely difficult to size accurately when you have nothing to build from, and having those conversations earlier in the process will help smooth the inevitable bumps you'll hit in the road later on. Set the expectations early so that you're making the best estimate you can, and leave yourself some elbow room. Estimate 10–20% above where you think you'll need to be to give yourself space and capacity to scale after the system goes live.

Sizing from scratch is just as much about your technical chops as it is about your interpersonal chops. You have to bridge the technical with the business so they understand you're not Superman or Carnac the Magnificent, but instead an extremely bright and helpful SAP BusinessObjects BI administrator who can get the job done.

2.6   Complex Sizing Projects: Where Science Meets Art

No matter if you have an existing system you're upgrading or if you're starting from scratch, there comes a time when the simpler sizing models simply won't be sufficient. When you come to the realization that a single server just isn't going to be enough to support your BI needs and start talking about multiple servers, tiered architecture, and clustering, you might start breaking out in a cold sweat. We're going to spend much more time on this in Chapter 3. But for now, consider how on Earth you're going to make a sizing decision for something that complicated. The solution is quite similar to the age-old question, "How do you eat an elephant? One bite at a time." It often helps to think about finding an answer when you start to understand what some of the questions are going to be. Isn't that why politicians have you submit questions for a town hall meeting in writing prior to the event? The following are some of the questions for which we're going to start looking for answers:

▶ Is a single server going to be sufficient for my project?

▶ If a single server isn't enough, how many do I need?

▶ How far do I need to scale (horizontally and vertically) to meet my company's capacity, availability, and security needs?

It starts getting complicated pretty quickly, doesn't it? When things start getting complex, it's best to go back to basics. T-shirt sizing and the SAP BI 4 Sizing Estimator are fine and dandy, but the old-school sizing methods still work pretty darned well and tend to be a bit more flexible for estimating these more involved projects. Let's examine some more traditional ways of sizing an SAP BusinessObjects BI system.

To start eating our complex sizing project elephant, first we'll need to figure out what "concurrency" means and why you need to care about it a lot. Next we'll walk you through how to create a sizing estimate for your intelligence, processing, and application tiers. And finally, we'll round it out with some general sizing considerations. Tie your thinking caps on tight, and get ready to start sizing!

2.6.1   The Currency of Concurrency

When sizing a complex system, the main concepts we discussed earlier for the sizing tools still apply. The first thing we need to estimate is load. As we said earlier, load refers to the amount of activity that is going to happen on the system and what types of activities those are. The estimation for load hasn't changed. First, we need to figure out how many total users will be on the system. Next, we need to estimate how many active-concurrent users will there be. And last, what are those active-concurrent users going to be doing concurrently? Remember, active-concurrent users and simultaneous requests are the two main drivers of load.

To estimate load, start by counting the total number of users that could potentially access the system. Talk to your business analysts, project managers, or other stakeholders in your SAP BusinessObjects BI build project if you aren't sure how many users are involved. If you have an existing system, the total number of user accounts there is a great place to start. If you find that you're going to be giving access to everyone in the company, then counting user accounts in the Active Directory or Lightweight Directory Access Protocol (LDAP) is a great way to estimate. For example, let's say our total potential user base is going to be 2,000 user accounts.

Now that we have our total, we need to guess how much of that is going to be active-concurrent usage. If you have an existing SAP BusinessObjects BI system, you can look at your historical concurrency in Auditor. For a new system, guessing is totally acceptable—and you should guess high. It's always better to oversize from the beginning rather than undersize.

As we stated earlier in the chapter, active concurrency is typically between 10% and 20% of your total user base. Continuing with our example of 2,000 potential users and sticking with our suggestion to guess high, we'll estimate that this will be a busy system, and we'll see 20% active-concurrent users, which would be 200. Now we're starting to close in nicely on our load estimation. We have 2,000 total users and 200 active-concurrent users. But what types of users are these? They most certainly aren't all using the system the same way. Remember (or turn back to) our discussion on the SAP Sizing Estimator (Section 2.2.2), where active-concurrent users were segmented into a few different types: information Consumers, Business Users, and Experts. The older approach to sizing actually divides active-concurrent users into four different strata: heavy users, active users, moderate users, and light users. Table 2.2 shows the general rule of thumb for how these break out.

User Type	Percentage of Total
Heavy Users	15%
Active Users	45%
Moderate Users	25%
Light Users	15%

Table 2.2 User Type Percentages

If we plug in our example numbers to this formula, we get the results shown in Table 2.3.

User Type	Percentage of Total	Result
Heavy Users	15%	30
Active Users	45%	90
Moderate Users	25%	50
Light Users	15%	30
Total Active-Concurrent	100%	200

Table 2.3 User Type Percentage Calculations

Now, we're getting somewhere. We're really close to our estimation for simultaneous requests. Before you get scared by the formula for simultaneous requests, a bit of explanation is in order. Let's take a leap of faith together and make the following assumptions:

▶ Heavy active-concurrent users will be making simultaneous requests at a 100% rate.

▶ Active active-concurrent users will be making simultaneous requests at a 25% rate.

▶ Moderate active-concurrent users will be making simultaneous requests at a 12% rate.

▶ Light active-concurrent users will be making simultaneous requests at a 6% rate.

The formula for calculating simultaneous requests is described this way:

((((total active-concurrent users * % of heavy users)/100*(1)) +
(((total active-concurrent users * % of active users)/100*(0.25)) +
(((total active-concurrent users * % of moderate users)/100*(0.12)) +
(((total active-concurrent users * % of light users)/100*(0.06))) = calculated simul-
taneous requests (SR)

Now we'll substitute our number estimates into the formula and compute the result:

(((200 * 15)/100*(1)) + (((200*45)/100*(0.25)) + (((200*25)/100*(0.12)) +
(((200*15)/100*(0.06)) = SR

or

(((3000)/100*1) + (((9000)/100*(0.25)) + (((5000)/100*(0.12) + (((3000)/
100*(0.06)) = SR

or

(30) + (22.5) + (60) + (1.8) = SR

or, finally

114.3 = SR

Feel free to round up to 115 just to keep things neat and clean. We're just estimating, after all.

Now, we have our magic number of 115 simultaneous requests estimated for our SAP BusinessObjects BI system. And, we got this magic number using a time-tested methodology that still holds true. Let's fast forward now to the SAP BusinessObjects BI 4 Sizing Companion. The first thing you'll notice is that we're still talking in the exact same language of active-concurrent users and simultaneous requests. Isn't that cool?

So you ask, "Now what?" Going back to the architecture overview, we'll start to break out our sizing estimates by tier. The intelligence tier consists of the following services:

▶ Server Intelligence Agent

▶ Central Management Server (CMS)

- Various cache servers
- Pieces of the Adaptive Processing Server (APS)
- Event Server

The processing tier consists of the following:

- Various processing servers (Dashboards, Web Intelligence, SAP Crystal Reports)
- Various Job Servers
- Multi-Dimensional Analysis Server (MDAS)
- Connection Server

The application tier consists of the following:

- Web application server
- SAP BusinessObjects Live Office

Not every single service is listed in the preceding lists, and that's okay. Not every service in the SAP BusinessObjects BI suite is necessary to consider when sizing because not all services contribute significantly to the capacity plan. Let's spend some time with the ones that do matter the most.

2.6.2 Estimating the Intelligence Tier

Starting at the top of the stack with the Server Intelligence Agent (SIA), you'll want to plan for about 350MB of memory for each SIA you intend to run. How many you run is entirely subject to your architecture plan (think back to Chapter 1). You could have many, or you could have just one. Typically, one SIA per host (node) is sufficient.

For the Central Management Server (CMS), there are a few general sizing rules to abide by. In general, you'll want to have an additional CMS service (e.g., a cluster) for every additional 500 active-concurrent users. So, for our example where we have 200 active-concurrent users, 1 CMS service should be sufficient. Don't think this gets you off the hook for a cluster. This estimate is strictly for capacity of the CMS service. If you had 200 active-concurrent users but no appetite for downtime, you would still want to cluster to add fault tolerance. This is all fine, but what type of hardware should you put that CMS service on? How big or small can you get away with? Those are great questions.

The SAP BusinessObjects XI R2 sizing guide offers the following general guidelines:

▶ 1 CPU (or core) for every 500 active-concurrent users
▶ 1 CMS service for every 600–700 concurrent active users

Or:

▶ 1 CPU (or core) for every 100 simultaneous requests

The Sizing Companion for SAP BusinessObjects BI 4.1 provides the general guidelines of 500 active-concurrent users per CMS instance.

Looks just about the same, doesn't it? And, in the absence of the specific CPU language in the *BusinessObjects Platform Administrator Guide* (because they want you to use SAPS), if the ratings are the same, then our estimate of CPU usage the old-fashioned way is probably pretty darned close. Tie that in with the assumptions the XI R2 guide makes about CPU and memory, and we're well on the way to figuring out our hardware estimates.

If we go back to our example, according to these guidelines, we would be fine with a single CMS service but would want to have it installed on a dual-core (or more) CPU server because our 200 active-concurrent users are well below the 500 user limit per instance, but our 121 simultaneous requests are over the 100 request-per-CPU threshold. But what about memory? If we stick with the version XI R2 estimate, 1 CPU should go with 2GB of memory. Here's where the older model starts to show its age. The older guide was written for a 32-bit application, and now we're dealing with a 64-bit application that isn't bound by a 2GB memory cap. Let's take our 1 CPU/2GB memory estimate with a grain of salt for the moment and talk about the limitations of that after we're through with our initial estimations by tier.

2.6.3   Estimating the Processing Tier

The processing tier is where you'll really start to notice some differences between the older products and SAP BusinessObjects BI 4.1. This is mainly because of the application architecture improvements that make full use of 64-bit technology. Now, the processing tier will vary greatly based on the tools that you're going to use in your environment. Remember that most of these were made by different companies, and through multiple acquisitions over the years, they were put under the same roof and told to go play nicely together. Because each processing tier product works differently, we'll discuss each one and its specific sizing requirements.

Web Intelligence

If you've been doing SAP BusinessObjects BI sizing for a while, you'll probably remember the old golden rule: "Thou shalt have one Web Intelligence Processing Server for each CPU core." And this law was passed down from on high to make the most use of the system's CPU and memory resources and to help users get around the 32-bit 2GB memory cap limit. Well, you can cast that golden rule right off the side of the mountain. It just doesn't apply anymore. Now you only need one Web Intelligence Processing Server per server, because the Web Intelligence Processing Server can spawn its own child processes to multithread and parallel process your Web Intelligence report requests. It will expand as far as you allow it to within the memory heap you allocate for your Web Intelligence Processing Server. Don't get too hung up on the details just yet, because we're going to cover those until your eyes melt in Chapter 4, when we talk about configuration. For now, we need to be concerned with sizing, so understanding a bit about how the services operate is necessary to plan for the proper-sized host. Also, don't get hung up on the considerations for vertical scaling and service redundancy. We'll talk about all of that later as well.

The Sizing Companion for SAP BusinessObjects BI 4.1 says that you'll want 1 Web Intelligence Processing Server for every 25 simultaneous connections. That's about as far as a single process can flex within the confines of a single server, and if you need more, then it's time to seriously think about a clustered architecture solution. If a cluster is on your mind, we'll cover that in detail in Chapter 3.

SAP Crystal Reports

The Crystal Cache Server can take 400 simultaneous requests per instance. The Crystal Reports Processing Server (SAP Crystal Reports 2011) will want 1 service per CPU and will default to 25 simultaneous requests (except on a single-CPU machine, which defaults to 50). Sort of sounds like one of many wonky rules for the English language, doesn't it?

The Crystal Reports Job Server can handle 20 simultaneous jobs per instance or 5 simultaneous report jobs per core, whichever is larger. This is also due to a flex capability of 64 bits.

SAP BusinessObjects Analysis, Edition for OLAP

The AA Analytic Service and AA Dashboard Service both get the best throughput by running one of each of these services per CPU core. Each AA Analytic Service should have 200MB of memory per instance, and each AA Dashboard Service should have 120MB of memory per instance.

Scheduling Things

A lot of what has been discussed in this section so far is about interactive reporting, which is live users actually logged into the system and clicking on things. The other piece of the puzzle is your scheduled report jobs. Users schedule things to run in the background (not interactively) and be generated as an instance to some other place of their choosing. The Adaptive Job Server (AJS) does this scheduling work. The AJS is like most of the other processes in SAP BusinessObjects BI 4.1. It can use up a whole mess of resources. In general, one available CPU core can comfortably support five simultaneous scheduled jobs running at a time. This can vary pretty widely based on the complexity of the report and the size or amount of data being returned in the query. That's not very many, so getting a handle on how many scheduled jobs run at any given time is a must. Clustering and adding dedicated Adaptive Job Server nodes vertically on a node is advisable as well. For example, allocating an Adaptive Job Server for Web Intelligence report jobs and an Adaptive Job Server for Promotion Management jobs splits the resources and permits additional concurrency in processing on a single node.

2.6.4   Estimating the Application Tier

Now that we've got a good feeling for our intelligence and processing tier sizes, it's time to start thinking about our application tier. This is where your Web Application Server will live, and the web application archive files will be deployed so your users can access the BI Launch Pad and Central Management Console (CMC) via their web browser.

There are several flavors of Web Application Server, and the purpose here isn't to endorse one over another or make light of any one over another. They all function in a relatively similar way, and choosing which one to go with for your landscape is really a matter of company preference. Many organizations may already dictate standards that make a particular distribution of a Web Application Server mandatory. However, Apache Tomcat comes bundled with SAP BusinessObjects BI 4.1, as it has for a very long time. It's a *very* safe assumption that the majority of deployments in the wild are running the out-of-the-box deployment of Apache Tomcat. You could also pick IBM WebSphere, Oracle WebLogic, or Microsoft Internet Information Services (IIS). Each of these application servers acts as a container for the web application content and consumes a certain amount of resources. The general rule still mostly applies: 1 Web Application Server can manage approximately 400 simultaneous requests per CPU (or core).

Again, this could be affected by your company's appetite for failover or tolerance for outages. Continuing with our example, a single Web Application Server on a single CPU system would be plenty of horsepower for this deployment. That doesn't mean we wouldn't want to stand up another one and put a load balancer out in front of it to make it more available. Also consider that this doesn't account for or justify how load balancing or failover will be addressed. We'll talk about that later as well. It just means that one would be enough capacity as far as work is involved. Keep in mind that capacity doesn't equal availability.

Now that you understand the key concepts of the three tiers, it's time to add it all up and arrive at a sizing estimate. Now, take an accounting. Go back through all of the notes you scratched in the margins, and put them in this handy tally sheet (Table 2.4).

Service	CPUs	Memory
SIA		
Web Intelligence		
SAP Crystal Reports		
Analysis		
Publications		
Web Application Server		
TOTAL:		

Table 2.4 Handy Dandy Tally Sheet

> **How Far Can the Traditional Model Stretch?**
>
> The traditional formulas for sizing are still helpful, but there are some caveats. For example, while we found that estimating a CPU count was still pretty close, we pretty much have to throw out the assumption about memory. Until now, memory was never really the bottleneck in an SAP BusinessObjects BI system because of the memory constraints of a 32-bit application. Now that SAP BusinessObjects BI 4.1 is 64-bit, those memory constraints are gone. SAP BusinessObjects BI 4.1 can easily consume most of the memory you put on a server system. Do yourself a favor and don't skimp on memory. When configured correctly (see Chapter 4), a default installation of SAP BusinessObjects BI 4.1 on a Windows 2008 R2 server system will consume about 10GB of memory when idle. Before you have a heart attack, keep in mind that that is just the initial allocation, or grab, of memory being taken by the various services and reserved for their private use. Under a light load, you won't see any more memory being consumed. But, if you start pressing the system with work, that number will increase as the services grab more and more memory to flex big enough to get the job done.
>
> The ultimate goal here is to make sure that you're SAP BusinessObjects BI 4.1 system never hits 100% of your system memory and still has work to do. That means jobs are queuing, processing is slowing, and users are fuming. If it won't destroy your budget, consider putting as much memory as possible into your system. Put in the maximum amount that your system board can handle. If you're down here considering a complex architecture, you're going to need that memory.

2.6.5 Overall Considerations for Sizing a Complex System

If you're going to buy multiple servers to act as a part of a cluster, it's important that you buy like-type servers for each tier. For example, if we were buying three servers to cluster an SAP BusinessObjects BI 4.1 system, we would want them all on the same platform (Windows, Linux, etc.), the same number and speed of CPUs, and the same amount of memory. SAP BusinessObjects BI 4.1 is a pretty smart application, but it doesn't include the smarts to be able to determine the difference between a faster server and a slower server. So, you'll want to make sure that if you're planning to use multiple intelligence tier servers, those systems are identical in CPU, memory, and disk speed. Do likewise for any other duplicate systems you plan on deploying. That way, the speed and performance of your system is consistent from node to node across the board. Granted, there are some individual service level parameters you can tune to throttle processes back on smaller boxes or up on larger ones. Just consider that a homogeneous cluster, in terms of both version and capacity, is desirable as you scale your environment to support the ever-increasing needs of your user population.

If at all possible, try to have all of your SAP BusinessObjects BI 4.1 servers on the same network subnet to minimize the number of network hops when communicating between nodes. This includes servers in all tiers, as well as databases that SAP BusinessObjects BI 4.1 must talk to both for CMS and Auditor data, but also for reporting databases. If you anticipate pulling huge amounts of data into SAP BusinessObjects BI 4.1, you might even want to consider having it on its own subnet so you're not facing any contention with other business traffic on your corporate network. This is especially true if you're hooking into some heavyweight data sources, such as SAP Business Warehouse (SAP BW), SAP HANA, or some other data monster like that. Also, keep in mind that the Data Federation Services are now a part of the SAP BusinessObjects BI suite, and if you're going to be making use of the multisource universe feature (who isn't?), that can also be a big consumer of memory and network traffic.

Pop Quiz
1. What role does the processing tier fulfill?
2. Which tiers require sizing estimates when estimating for the growth of your environment?
3. How many Web Intelligence Processing Servers are needed per server?
4. Which server handles scheduling requests for each of the Processing Servers?

2.7 Sizing as an Ongoing Activity

We bet you thought you were done at this point. You made it through your big upgrade project and are now running SAP BusinessObjects BI 4.1, so you don't have to worry about sizing anymore, right? Wrong. Sizing is something that should go on and on and on because your system will continue to grow. You can choose to be like some parents are about their children and live in denial that they will grow up someday, but regardless of your belief, that child will eventually need new sneakers and new jeans because the old ones are too small.

Look at it in a positive light. You did such a good job sizing your SAP BusinessObjects BI 4.1 system the first time that now user adoption is growing at an explosive rate. Your "kid" is about to need new jeans.

2.7.1   How Do I Know When My Server Is All Grown Up?

Where do you start? That's fortunately the easy part. You start with your original sizing estimate. You know how big your servers are, you know how many CPUs you bought, how much memory they have, and how big the disks are. SAP BusinessObjects BI 4.1 also comes with some really spiffy monitoring capabilities, which we'll discuss in detail in Chapter 7. When the system is properly configured, you can have your "sizing metrics" built right into the SAP BusinessObjects BI 4.1 platform. In general, you should watch for the following indicators that you're running out of capacity:

▸ CPU is at 100% usage for 15 minutes or more several times a day.

▸ Memory is at 100% usage for 15 minutes or more several times a day.

▸ Disk is nearing 70% usage.

▸ CPU or memory average usage is 70% or greater during peak hours.

▸ Scheduled jobs aren't completing on time.

▸ Users are reporting "out of memory" errors.

2.7.2   What Do I Do When My Server Is All Grown Up?

So, your indicators are starting to light up. You're using up CPU and memory like they're going out of style. Your disks are full, and your phone is lighting up with angry users. What do you do? Panic? Nah. Just turn on over to Chapter 3 and thumb down to where we tell you how to cluster. Be prepared to get another sizing estimate going. You'll need it in short order if you're going to be adding hardware, and as you remember, if someone is going to be opening their wallet to buy more hardware, you'd better be accurate with your sizing estimate.

2.7.3   Sizing as a Habit

Get used to the fact that you're going to be continually on the hook to watch for signs that you're running out of capacity. Build some dashboards or reports that you can check on occasion to see how your server growth is progressing. These are great to have around for an easy reference on short notice. Park the reports in your Favorites folder (or a public folder if you want to share them) so you can run them whenever you need to. Often requests for such information come swiftly, with little warning and with little time to prepare.

Ever have to attend those monthly or quarterly status updates with your manager or even higher-up leadership? Server growth statistics are a perfect inclusion in these types of meetings. Keep sizing and capacity in your leadership's field of vision by giving periodic updates and showing how the growth has changed since the last time you showed them. If you want to get really fancy, include a simple forecast to project when you think the server will run out of resources, and share that date with your leadership. At least the choice is theirs then.

Here's a tip that will make you look like a champion. For this example, we'll use Microsoft Excel 2010. First, take your statistic that you want to forecast, and lay it up in a spreadsheet, as shown in Figure 2.17. In this example, we've averaged CPU consumption by month.

A	B	C	D	E	F	G	H	I	J	K	L
53.2	53.8	64.6	63.2	68.9	71.6	74.6	78.9	81.2	84.6	86.9	89.8
1-Jan-11	1-Feb-11	1-Mar-11	1-Apr-11	1-May-11	1-Jun-11	1-Jul-11	1-Aug-11	1-Sep-11	1-Oct-11	1-Nov-11	1-Dec-11

Figure 2.17 Average CPU Consumption by Month for Forecast

Next, click an empty cell, then click the FUNCTION (FX) button and choose the FORECAST function, and click OK (see Figure 2.18).

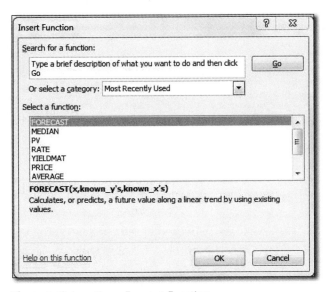

Figure 2.18 Inserting a Forecast Function

The Function Arguments window will pop up (see Figure 2.19). Enter the X value, which is the number for which you want to forecast. For this example, enter the number "100" because we want to predict when CPU consumption will hit 100%. Then, click the array button next to the Known_y's field. Use your cursor to select your row of dates, as these are the Y values. Click the button at the end of the field to go back to the Function Arguments window.

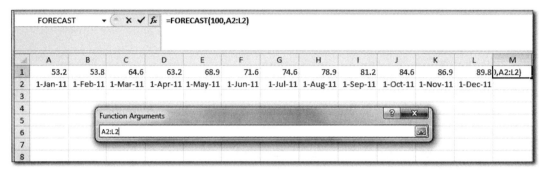

Figure 2.19 Choosing the Array of Known Y Values

Repeat the process for the Known_x's field, and choose your array of percentages this time (see Figure 2.20).

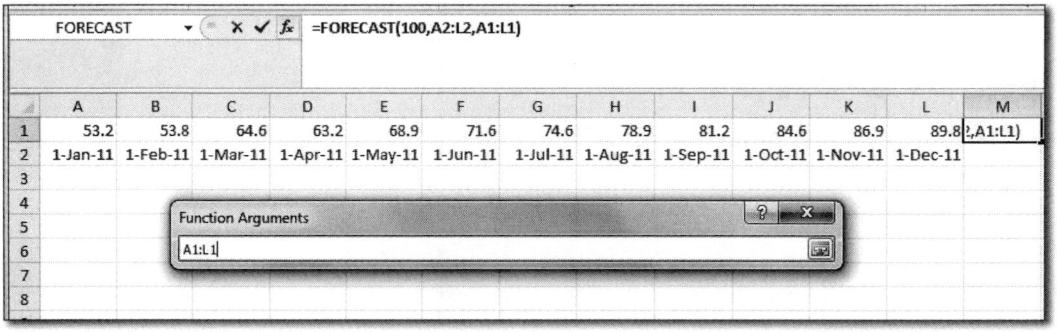

Figure 2.20 Choosing the Array of Known X Values

When you're back in the Function Arguments window, review everything you have in place before you click OK (see Figure 2.21).

You'll return to your spreadsheet with your completed forecast (see Figure 2.22). But wait, what's that funky number in there? That doesn't look right, does it?

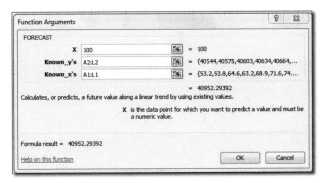

Figure 2.21 The Forecast Function with Completed Arguments

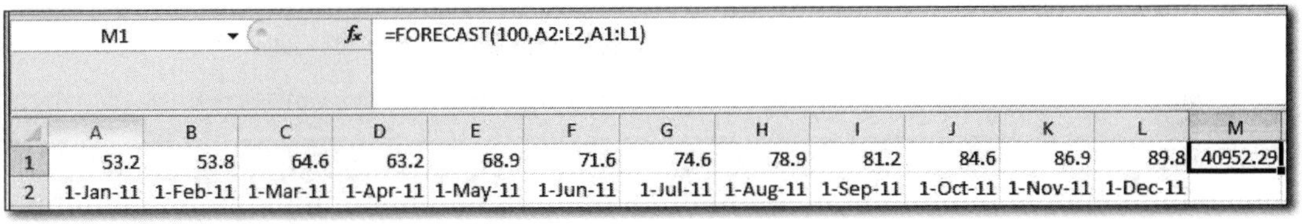

	M1	▼		f_x	=FORECAST(100,A2:L2,A1:L1)								
	A	B	C	D	E	F	G	H	I	J	K	L	M
1	53.2	53.8	64.6	63.2	68.9	71.6	74.6	78.9	81.2	84.6	86.9	89.8	40952.29
2	1-Jan-11	1-Feb-11	1-Mar-11	1-Apr-11	1-May-11	1-Jun-11	1-Jul-11	1-Aug-11	1-Sep-11	1-Oct-11	1-Nov-11	1-Dec-11	

Figure 2.22 The Completed Forecast Function on the Spreadsheet

Aha, but it's correct. It's just not formatted properly. Right-click on that funky number, choose FORMAT CELLS, and then select DATE (see Figure 2.23).

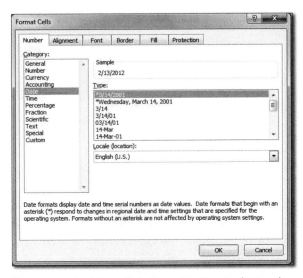

Figure 2.23 Applying a Date Format to Our Funky Number

Click OK, and you'll return to your spreadsheet with something that looks much more familiar (see Figure 2.24).

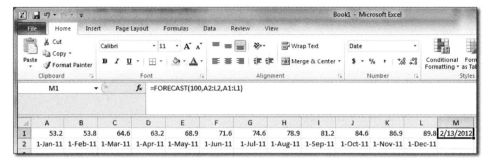

Figure 2.24 The Properly Formatted Forecast Output

And, there you have it. You can now see that based on the consumption trend you put in from your average CPU by month, you'll hit 100% capacity on February 13, 2012.

Pretty cool, eh?

2.8   Summary

SAP BusinessObjects BI architecture sizing is an art not a science.

Say it with us.

SAP BusinessObjects BI architecture sizing is an art not a science.

SAP BusinessObjects BI architecture sizing is an art not a science.

While we tried to present this topic in a light-hearted way to keep it interesting, make no mistake about how serious your sizing estimate is. Sizing is where the rubber meets the road. You started out with a theoretical discussion about an SAP BusinessObjects BI 4.1 project. You sat at dozens of meeting tables and discussed it at length. Then, the gravity really started to pull because somebody went out and spent money on something like hardware, software, and SAP BusinessObjects BI licenses. After the money has been spent, the mood changes. Managers get edgy to deliver the project and demonstrate the return on investment (ROI) to their superiors. Project managers start lathering over milestones and checkpoints.

And developers start salivating to get their hands on the latest and greatest technologies that SAP has to offer. All of these expectations hinge on a successful sizing estimate, or it all falls apart in a spectacular collapse of a failed project, not at all unlike a building implosion in Las Vegas. Always keep in mind, after the money has been spent, it's nearly impossible go to back without some sort of penalty. Nervous parents like to tell their teenagers when learning how to drive a car, "Remember, you have thousands of pounds of machinery and people's lives in your hands. Act accordingly." Sizing isn't all that dissimilar.

For all of the forecasts, historical trends, and SAPS ratings, every sizing exercise comes with the assertion that we make our best guess possible in sizing for future environments. It's true to say, the more historical usage data you have, the more likely your forecasts for hardware and software purchases will be on par. After all, the last thing you want to be is the administrator that brought in too little or way too much hardware to fulfilll reporting requirements.

As your modeling for environment growth matures, never throw it away. This is a model that can be refined and reused over time as you grow beyond your initial deployment of SAP BusinessObjects BI. And rest assured, your environment will grow. Make sizing and capacity a habitual part of your administrator routine. Further, you may be asked to provide said models if you have to justify decisions made in the sizing of your environment. Take your time and check and double-check your estimates. Make full use of the tools that are in your sizing toolbox. Start with the T-Shirt Sizing Guide, and move up through the tools and the Sizing Companion Guide as you build and refine your estimate. If you're really unsure, then it's better to contact someone to come in and help you out.

As a final note on sizing, don't make the mistake of focusing totally on your production environment and ignoring exercises for lower environments such as development and test. The development lifecycle and time lines are often aggressive and depend on having a right-sized and available environment during those infamous development sprints. Developers need the development environment as much as end users need the production environment. Make sure to size and scale lower environments to fit their needs as well.

Now lift your chin up high. You're well-armed to tackle your sizing estimate. Go forth and purchase your hardware. After you have everything in place, patched, and set up, you'll be ready to dive in to Chapter 3 and install SAP BusinessObjects BI 4.1.

Now that you know a little bit more about where SAP BusinessObjects BI has been and how it all works, it's time to get your hands dirty. Get ready to install some stuff!

3   Installation: If You Build it, They Will Come

If you're a rookie SAP BusinessObjects BI administrator, and you're still reading this book, you win two points. Not that those two points are going to do you any good at the end of the book, but we hear that gamification is a big thing now.

You're ready. You've downloaded your media from the SAP Service Marketplace, you have your development/test or production keys in hand, and this book is aaaaallll you need (you've seen Steve Martin in *The Jerk*, right?). You're about to start an install that is going to take a number of hours to complete end-to-end. You're also likely to be installing a patch or patches on top of a base install of the product. There is an important choice to be made here that will determine how much work you do down the road—whether to install *all* components of SAP BusinessObjects BI or just what you intend to use.

Consider the scenario in which your organization hasn't purchased SAP BusinessObjects Dashboards. You could certainly choose to do a custom installation and strip out that part of the installation. But, then also consider the possibility that you may purchase SAP BusinessObjects Dashboards down the road. Uh-oh. No Dashboard Cache Server. No Dashboard Processing Server. No performance optimizing capabilities. Had you done that complete install and simply stopped, disabled, and set to not automatically start, you'd simply need to enable those services now. The same could be true whether the scenario was for SAP Crystal Reports 2013 or SAP BusinessObjects Web Intelligence. So, take an inventory, be aware of your space limitations (or lack thereof), and do the full install if you can.

Upgrading SAP BusinessObjects BI

You're currently at a fork in the road in our choose-your-own-adventure book. Both paths do lead back to this same chapter but result from two entirely different decisions that you have to make before going forward. If you are the reader that is about to step into an upgrade of SAP BusinessObjects BI versus a user that is starting from scratch, step back right now and be sure you know the answer to this question:

Are these the droids you're looking for?

We're totally kidding. That's not it.

Do we have the capital to have a parallel implementation alongside our existing SAP BusinessObjects BI environment, or do we have to upgrade in place?

This is huge. Any administrator will find it difficult to find a clear way to do an in-place upgrade with SAP BusinessObjects BI 4.1. It's big, it's resource-intensive, and it stands to reason, you may have already learned in Chapter 2 that your existing infrastructure doesn't hold up to the demands as forecasted by the SAP Sizing Estimator.

It's relevant to look deeper at the two paths and arrive at the right spot for your deployment. A pro and con list can never hurt, right? See Table 3.1.

As if it can't get more complicated, if your target platform version is SAP BusinessObjects BI 4.1, and this is an upgrade from SAP BusinessObjects BI 4.0, customers must take a holistic look at this approach as well.

Upgrade Path	Pros	Cons
Customers upgrading from versions pre-SAP BusinessObjects BI 4.0 – Flash cut in the same environment	▶ Lowest cost in terms of infrastructure. ▶ Less involvement required by external teams to complete the implementation in your environment.	▶ Difficult rollback scenario. ▶ More blunt for the user community. ▶ May elongate in-flight development lifecycles with out-of-sync lower environments.
Customers upgrading from versions pre-SAP BusinessObjects BI 4.0 – Upgrade in parallel (we like this one)	▶ Leave existing deployments untouched during implementation and regression testing. ▶ Challenges in go-live? Just roll back to the existing environment. ▶ Nondisruptive to the development lifecycle of other projects.	▶ More costly if newer hardware was not required. ▶ A larger project requiring other enterprise resources (storage, database, network).

Table 3.1 Upgrade Path Options

Upgrade Path	Pros	Cons
New for SAP Business-Objects BI 4.0 customers migrating to SAP BusinessObjects BI 4.1 – In-place upgrade	▶ Lowest cost in terms of time. ▶ Lowest risk in complexity. ▶ Generally doesn't require new hardware.	Customers on early versions of SAP BusinessObjects BI 4.0 must reevaluate sizing requirements.
New for SAP Business-Objects BI 4.0 customers migrating to SAP BusinessObjects BI 4.1 – Upgrade in parallel	Provides the opportunity to implement new hardware that meets system requirements.	▶ Higher risk. ▶ Longer duration. ▶ Requires mass migrations, arguably to be done most typically through Promotion Management. ▶ Not recommended by SAP, but let's get real, sometimes you have to rip off the Band-Aid.

Table 3.1 Upgrade Path Options (Cont.)

Before we get started with a concrete installation example, you should understand the overall flow of an implementation:

1. Install the application.

2. Migrate existing content.

3. Configure and tune.

4. Perform regression test.

5. Deploy to users (phased or flash cut).

6. Maintain.

Stick with us as we move into the remainder of this chapter and actually deploy SAP BusinessObjects BI 4.1 in a Linux environment and a Windows environment. (Those of you that are forced down the path of deploying to a UNIX or Linux distribution, don't fret. Even though the flavor is different, in general the deployments are extremely close to being the same.) We'll also talk about how you can perform clustering in an SAP BusinessObjects BI landscape. Finally, we'll introduce you to the concept of virtualization and how this might affect your system.

Let's get the party started without further delay.

Pop Quiz

1. Which upgrade path should be taken if no other servers are available to stage the migration?
2. What is the appropriate tool(s) to size the target SAP BusinessObjects BI 4.1 migration for a new deployment?

3.1 UNIX and Linux Installation

If you're looking for pretty graphical user interfaces (GUIs) and pictures of models in the install screens, then jump on down to the section on Windows because you won't find those here. The UNIX and Linux flavors of operating system are strong and stable but have never been described as pretty. Let's talk through a few prerequisites before we begin the install process:

1. You'll want to make sure you carefully checked the Product Availability Matrix (PAM) and have all of your required operating system patches applied. If you're using a third-party database, make sure the middleware is installed. Another thing to check (constant "gotcha") is your environment variables. These should be a part of your user profile or something that is sourced before you start the installation.

2. After you download your installation software from the SAP Service Marketplace, you'll have your very first nasty surprise waiting for you. SAP packaged the non-Windows binaries as an .exe file. (Insert collective sigh here.) So, first you'll need to download the binaries to a Windows box, run the .exe to unpack the files, and then repack them with a zip tool like 7-Zip. It's best if you first repackage the files to a .tar file, and then a .gz (gzip) after that. After this chore is complete, you'll need to Secure FTP (SFTP) it to your UNIX or Linux server and unpack it. Best-practice alert: If you're going to be installing more than a few SAP BusinessObjects BI environments on a non-Windows platform, stage your install files somewhere centrally located, such as a network attached Storage (NAS), which can be easily accessed from any of your UNIX or Linux hosts. That way, you need only FTP and to unpack the install files once, and they'll provide a lifetime of enjoyment.

3. Ensure that any needed database drivers are installed not just in their 64-bit version but also in the 32-bit counterpart as well.

4. Ensure that you already have appropriate database accounts created with create/modify rights to the schema for both the CMS and Auditor databases for your application.

5. Create a runtime account for the server, such as "boadmin," "bobjadmin," or whatever, for you to run both the installation and the application under. As a nice enhancement to appease the security folks, you actually can no longer run SAP BusinessObjects BI as the root user.

6. Create a location on the file system in which this runtime user will have full control.

When you're ready, and sure you're ready, give the *install.sh* a rip, and you'll start walking through the install screens. Here we go:

1. The first screen (see Figure 3.1) you'll encounter asks you to pick your language. This only sets the language for the installer script to present on the forthcoming screens. Of course, we picked ENGLISH.

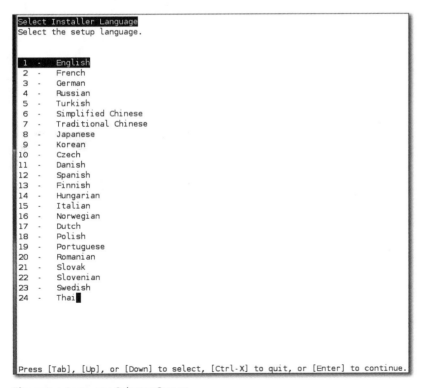

Figure 3.1 Language Selector Screen

2. Next, you'll need to pick the path where you want SAP BusinessObjects BI 4.1 to run from (see Figure 3.2). Think ahead! How large is this file system? Will it accommodate growth from content storage, temporary storage, and general patching in the future? Select a location that lives on its own disk and is easily expanded for future growth.

```
Configure Destination Folder
Enter the full destination path where the product will be installed.

Destination Folder:
[/apps/sapbi4                                                    ]
```

Figure 3.2 Destination Selection Screen

3. The installer script will check your environment and make sure all of the prerequisites it requires are already in place. If they aren't, it will tell you which one failed and then terminate the script if it was a critical prerequisite. We did our homework, so ours went off without a hitch.

```
Check Prerequisites
Summary of any missing critical or optional prerequisites.


Succeeded: Information Steward and Data Services compatibility (Optional)
Succeeded: Information platform services or SAP Crystal Server cannot be installed (Critical)
Succeeded: Operating system patch level (Critical)
Succeeded: BI platform server 4.x cannot already be installed (Critical)
Succeeded: Disk space in /tmp (Critical)
Succeeded: Disk space in /var (Critical)
Succeeded: File Size Limit (ulimit -f) (Optional)
Succeeded: Maximum user processes (ulimit -u) (Optional)
Succeeded: Network settings (Critical)
Succeeded: 64-bit operating system (Critical)
Succeeded: Root user rights (Critical)
```

Figure 3.3 Prerequisite Check Summary

4. It wouldn't be SAP without a legal disclaimer, now would it? You must accept (see Figure 3.4).

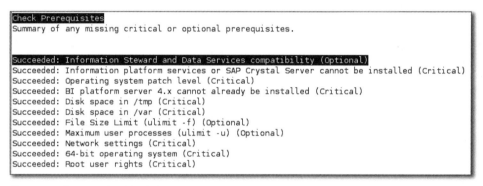

```
SAP BusinessObjects BI platform 4.1 SP3 setup
Welcome to the installation wizard for SAP BusinessObjects BI platform 4.1 SP3.

WARNING: This program is protected by copyright law and international treaties.

Unauthorized reproduction or distribution of this program, or any portion of it, may result in severe civil and
criminal penalties, and will be prosecuted to the maximum extent possible under law.
```

Figure 3.4 Legalese Screen

5. After you get through that license agreement (you did read it, didn't you?), you'll have to put in your product keycode before you go any further. If you didn't get it yet, now would be a perfect time to hop over to the SAP Service Marketplace (*service.sap.com*) and get one, or ping your account manager for a temporary key while you get things sorted on your license agreement.

6. Pick the language packs that can be a part of SAP BusinessObjects BI 4.1 (see Figure 3.5).

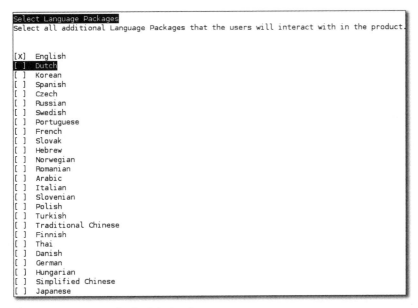

```
Select Language Packages
Select all additional Language Packages that the users will interact with in the product.


[X]  English
[ ]  Dutch
[ ]  Korean
[ ]  Spanish
[ ]  Czech
[ ]  Russian
[ ]  Swedish
[ ]  Portuguese
[ ]  French
[ ]  Slovak
[ ]  Hebrew
[ ]  Norwegian
[ ]  Romanian
[ ]  Arabic
[ ]  Italian
[ ]  Slovenian
[ ]  Polish
[ ]  Turkish
[ ]  Traditional Chinese
[ ]  Finnish
[ ]  Thai
[ ]  Danish
[ ]  German
[ ]  Hungarian
[ ]  Simplified Chinese
[ ]  Japanese
```

Figure 3.5 Language Packs Selector Screen

7. Next, you have to choose your install type (see Figure 3.6). If this is your first time through, the full install is probably best to install the web, application, and database tiers in their entirety. If you're doing something fancier, such as clustering or setting up a separate web tier, then pick those options. We chose FULL.

```
Select Install Type
Select the type of installation.


1  -    Full
2  -    Custom / Expand
3  -    Web Tier
```

Figure 3.6 Install Type Selector Screen

8. Next is the database selection screen (see Figure 3.7). We chose the default. You'll notice that "Uncle Oracle" and his MySQL database have totally gotten the boot here. The new default is Sybase SQL Anywhere.

Figure 3.7 Database Selection Screen

9. Choose your Java Web Application Server (see Figure 3.8). We chose Tomcat.

Figure 3.8 Java Web Application Server Selection Screen

10. You have the choice of installing a new Subversion version control database or using an existing one. You have to tell it which version control system to use at this step. We went with the default Subversion (see Figure 3.9).

Figure 3.9 Version Control Selection Screen

11. Now things are getting interesting. Enter your SIA Port if you have different port standards than the defaults. (See Chapter 5 for specifics on port assignments.) This is also where you'll name your node (see Figure 3.10).

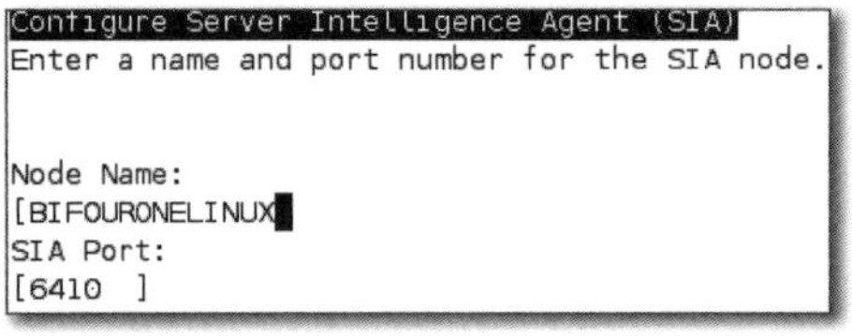

Figure 3.10 Server Intelligence Agent Configuration Screen

12. Now, you'll assign a port for the Central Management Server (CMS), or just use the default. This screen also allows you to set the administrator password and your cluster key (see Figure 3.11). For more on security standards with your cluster keys, see Chapter 5.

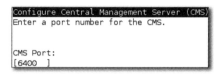

Figure 3.11 Central Management Server Configuration Screen

13. Here you'll want to configure the password for your built-in ADMINISTRATOR ACCOUNT PASSWORD and CMS CLUSTER KEY (see Figure 3.12). You're not one of those administrators that leaves the password blank, are you?

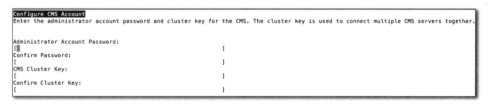

Figure 3.12 CMS Account Configuration Screen

14. If you chose the default Sybase SQL Anywhere database, like we did, then assign it to a port as well (see Figure 3.13).

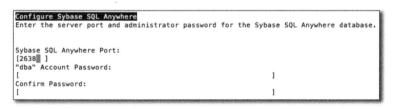

Figure 3.13 Database Configuration Screen

15. Tomcat needs ports as well. For this demonstration, we went with all default values (see Figure 3.14).

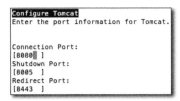

Figure 3.14 Tomcat Configuration Screen

16. Tomcat needs a listening port (see Figure 3.15). Are you still listening?

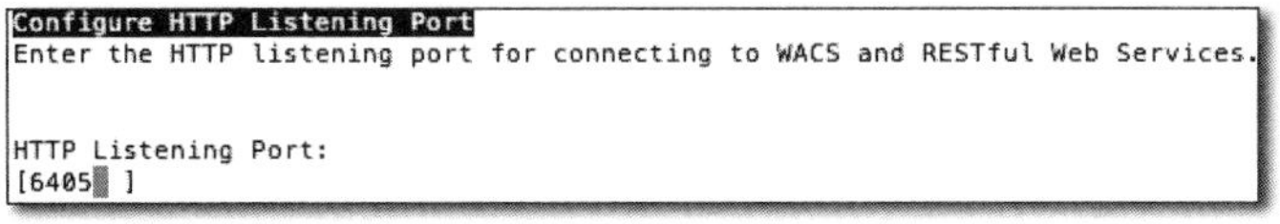

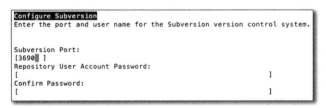

Figure 3.15 HTTP Listening Port Configuration Screen

17. Subversion needs a little time and attention, so we'll give it a port and assign some passwords, as shown in Figure 3.16. (Chapter 5 has some suggestions about passwords to use in these cases.)

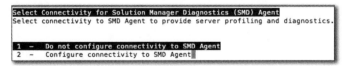

Figure 3.16 Subversion Configuration Screen

18. The Solution Manager Diagnostics (SMD) agent needs some ports to run on. This is necessary if you're going to hook into SAP Solution Manager or Wily Introscope Enterprise Manager (see Figure 3.17).

Figure 3.17 SAP Solution Manager Diagnostic Agent Selection Screen

> **Mark of Excellence**
>
> If you're planning on installing SAP BusinessObjects BI 4 in a production environment, there's a good chance you'll want some enhanced monitoring on it. Do yourself a *huge* favor, and if you don't already have SAP Solution Manager in house, install a copy of Wily Introscope Enterprise Manager (WIEM) and the Solution Manager Diagnostic Agent *first*. By doing that, you'll have the server ready to hook into your SAP BusinessObjects BI 4 system in the following screens. It will configure the collector agents for you as a part of the installation routine. Neat, huh? You can certainly put them in after the fact, but it's a bit tedious and, let's face it, a huge pain. Trust us. Do this first. We'll accept most forms of craft beer as thanks.

19. The Solution Manager Diagnostic (SMD) is on the local host. Enter the details here so it can start collecting all kinds of good info about your system and start shipping it off to WIEM (see Figure 3.18).

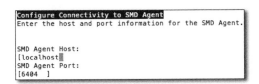

Figure 3.18 SMD Agent Configuration Screen

20. If you're going to configure your connection to WIEM now (if not, you should be), here's where you do so (see Figure 3.19).

Figure 3.19 Select Connectivity to Introscope Enterprise Manager Screen

21. This is the last screen on the Wily stuff. Here's where you put in the digits to your WIEM server (see Figure 3.20).

```
Configure Connectivity to Introscope Enterprise Manager
Enter the host and port information for Introscope Enterprise Manager.


Introscope Host:
[EVTBOBJ41█                                     ]
Introscope Port:
[6001  ]
```

Figure 3.20 WIEM Configuration Screen

22. Now it's time to let her rip (see Figure 3.21 and Figure 3.22)!

Figure 3.21 Are You Ready to Go? Screen

Figure 3.22 Post Installation Steps Screen

Hopefully you had a nice, clean install and you landed with this friendly message in Figure 3.23.

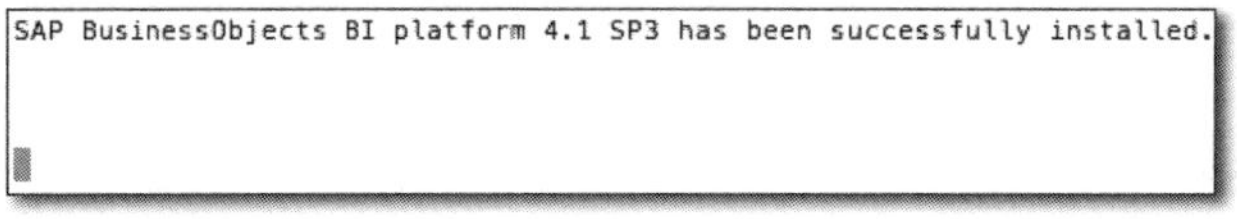

```
SAP BusinessObjects BI platform 4.1 SP3 has been successfully installed.
```

Figure 3.23 Installation Success Screen

If you've gone with that system install, don't forget to have the `init` scripts executed to set SAP BusinessObjects BI 4.1 to run at launch. Otherwise, you're on your own to get it started after reboots.

3.2 Windows Installation

Windows isn't a bad word when it comes to deploying SAP BusinessObjects BI 4.1—as opposed to its estranged cousin, UNIX. If you selected Windows, rest assured that most of the rest of the world did too. That's good enough for us. Let's dive in by thinking through prerequisites for completing a build in a Windows environment.

Don't tell your Windows administrators we told you this, but do yourself a favor before you get started: stop your server-side antivirus application. By now, it's already looked inside your install files. Don't let it bog down your install process. Here are some other helpful tips:

▶ Be sure you're all caught up on your reading for the latest patch. It's wise to understand whether the latest build is appropriate for your efforts.

▶ Get your installers ready and staged on your local file system of your server, including all database drivers and SAP BusinessObjects BI 4.1 installs.

▶ Install the 64-bit database driver for your target CMS and Auditor databases.

▶ Ensure that you have the user name and password for the target CMS and Auditor databases and that a DBA has granted privileges to modify that schema. In addition, if you think the use of the Monitoring application is in your future, request that as well, and assume it's going to be a big one.

▶ While you're at it, go ahead and install the 32-bit versions as well. Connections to other databases through the Connection Server will need these at some point.

▶ Ensure any other dependencies such as network file systems, load balancers, domain, or other entitlement accounts.

▶ Ensure that you have the .NET platform installed and ready to go on your servers.

▶ If you don't already have a permanent key on hand for the SAP BusinessObjects BI 4.1 platform, you either need your permanent key or a temporary key from your SAP account manager.

▶ Read the PAM—again. Make sure your platform, driver, and other configuration components are supported now.

You've made it. The moment of reckoning is here. Your server has all it needs now for you to start your build. With your installs from the SMP residing on your server, let's kick off the installer. And the good news is that once you do, you'll be able to go get coffee, get lunch, take a siesta, or get a nice massage.

3.2.1 Preinstallation Steps

Before you go crazy and start unpacking the giant EXE and RAR files included with SAP BusinessObjects BI 4.1, you should know there are really two ways to go about unpacking all these files:

- ▶ A multipart compressed installer is best unpacked with the leading package file. The uninstaller will uncompress and generally let you select where you want to unpack the files.

- ▶ A single-part compressed installer can be unpacked and reviewed with tools like 7-Zip, which is our choice for a handy compression tool. The great part is that it will also work on the EXE files created by the packagers.

Now, let's get started. Buried deep within the unpacked/extracted install files, the installer has a *setup.exe* executable that you can double-click to run (see Figure 3.24).

Note

You want to run this with a user with elevated/administrative rights to the server.

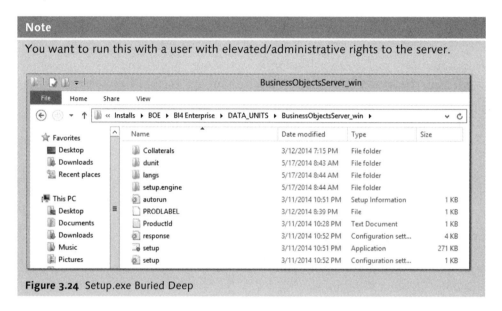

Figure 3.24 Setup.exe Buried Deep

A quick selection of installer language gets you on your way to begin the install process (see Figure 3.25).

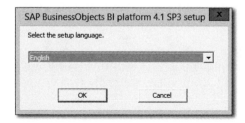

Figure 3.25 Choosing the Setup Language

While we did our best to fulfill the preceding prerequisites, the installer is handy in that it has a much-needed prerequisite checker included in it. The prerequisite check step will ensure you have all you need without a false start (see Figure 3.26). Don't freak out when you see INFORMATION STEWARD AND DATA SERVICES COMPONENTS in this prerequisites check. Even if you're a customer of the two, you'll have the option to add them at a later date, although we're going to strongly advocate right here and now that you not use this platform as your SAP Data Services Information Platform Services server.

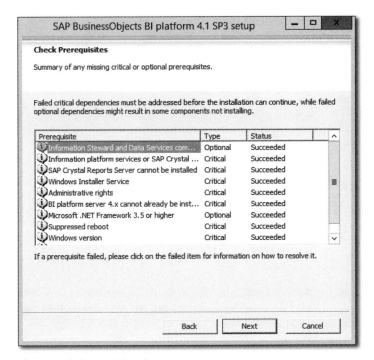

Figure 3.26 Prerequisites Summary

Click through the next informational screen warning of copyright to get to the next step. Additionally, the license compliance screen requires a positive acknowledgment before it will let you proceed to the next install step. While the name and organization are artifacts/novelties of days of Windows installers gone by, the product keycode is still relevant. Get your key ready and enter it in the screen, as shown in Figure 3.27. You may have missed our list of prerequisites earlier. Don't fret. If you haven't gotten your permanent license key, you can request a temp key through the SAP Marketplace to begin your installation. You'll be able to change this key at a later date in the Central Management Console.

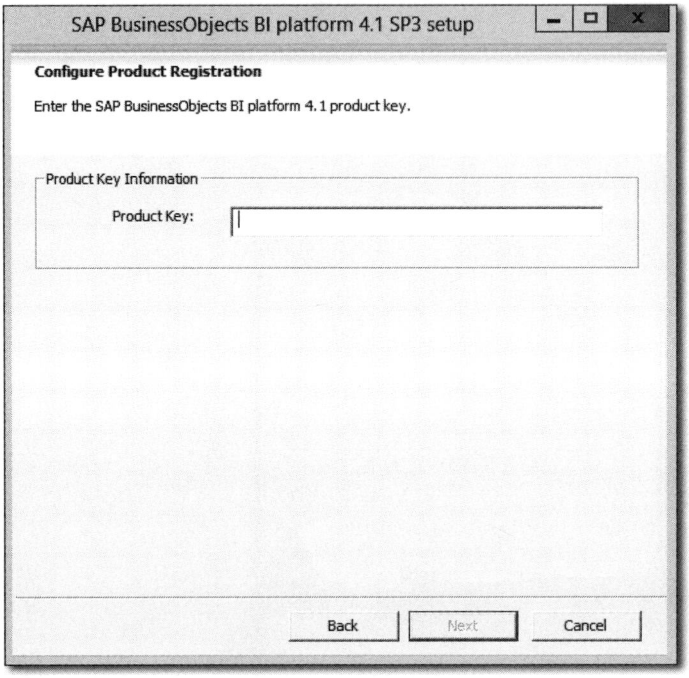

Figure 3.27 Required License Keys, Trial or Permanent

SAP BusinessObjects BI 4.1 has great multilingual support, all ready to go. When you enter the next screen (not shown here), choose the language or languages you want to support within your environment and continue.

3.2.2 Installation Options

Next, we hit our first fork in the road. To be clear, we're going to walk through a single path to start, and we'll talk about variants of the install path a little later. For now, familiarize yourself with the three install types, all of which are shown in Figure 3.28:

▶ FULL
Takes much of the guesswork out of what you're doing, makes broad assumptions, and gives you everything, including the kitchen sink.

► CUSTOM /EXPAND

While fully capable of installing everything, this option allows you to tailor your installation based on the needs of your deployment. We're going to work from this install path.

► WEB TIER

Thinking back to earlier chapters, SAP has done a fine job creating an installer sensitive to building a web tier and an application tier. Choose this option to get the out-of-the-box web tier alone on your server.

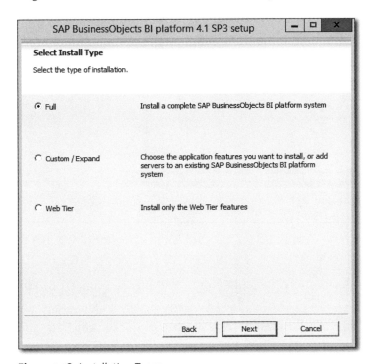

Figure 3.28 Installation Types

For the purposes of this walk-through, a CUSTOM/EXPAND install will be selected to walk through as many of the installer steps in one section as we can. Let's dive in, and click NEXT.

The original/default path supplied by the installer picks a path like *C:\Program Files (x86)\SAP BusinessObjects* (see Figure 3.29). Before you get up in arms over the naming standard here, yes indeed, it's still a 64-bit server. It had to go somewhere.

Figure 3.29 Install Path

As you can see from Figure 3.29, the standard path isn't set in stone. We like to pick a new path for two primary reasons:

▶ Ours is shorter. No, seriously. We do like to put SAP BusinessObjects BI in a short path that makes it easier to reach later.

▶ It's worthwhile to run SAP BusinessObjects BI on a physically separate disk from your operating system and associated swap file if you can. The gain may be tiny, but why not squeeze every ounce of performance out of this box, right?

The next step in the custom install process is to select all of the million components, both large and small, based on your system requirements, and move on (see Figure 3.30). Thinking back to our policy on full installs versus partial installs, this is where you must make that initial decision. Do I install everything? Or do I install the bare minimums? There are a few key pieces of the install that we'll call your attention to here as we move ahead to help with that decision-making process.

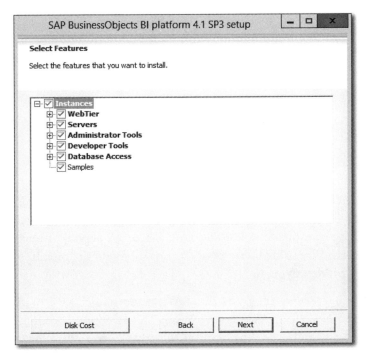

Figure 3.30 Custom Install Overview

The installer selection is simple. Select the checkbox and you get the component installed. Just be sure to note this is a tree-based view of installable components, and caring for each level is relevant (see Figure 3.31). There are a LOT of options here. This platform did not get smaller from a component perspective.

Figure 3.31 Web Tier Components

One of the first custom install pieces to take note of is that Tomcat 7.0 64-bit will get installed alongside SAP BusinessObjects BI. In a distributed architecture, perhaps Tomcat has already been broken out to a dedicated web tier node. Perhaps you've even chosen to deploy another Java application container such as IBM WebSphere to a web tier. With that, this option can be unselected, and you may use the wdeploy application to install your web tier at a later time.

But, also consider that this a great debugging tool. Perhaps users are reporting that the BI Launch Pad works, but they are unable to log in, and you simply can't deduce what the problem is. Just start Tomcat on your application tier and validate that there are no communication failures between your web tier and your application tier.

Setting up Tomcat in the final state to support this is easy. After the installation is completed, just set Tomcat to not automatically start with the system, and you're all set.

New in SAP BusinessObjects BI 4.1 are the options to automatically deploy mobile services. Unlike other application architecture components in SAP BusinessObjects BI 4.1, the mobile servers are simply web applications that get deployed on your web tier. Please consult your SAP account executive or your license agreement for specific terms on using these services, and stop in on Chapter 10 of this book for the scoop on deploying it.

Next, within the individual servers deployed with SAP BusinessObjects BI, an integrated database option is available (see Figure 3.32). This is where additional options will be enabled depending on how you set this install property. New to SAP BusinessObjects BI 4.1, Sybase SQL Anywhere will be installed, and we'll supply the necessary defaults for it later. With this option disabled, the installer will make it mandatory to identify a separate database to support this environment.

Figure 3.32 Platform Services

Consider carefully the implications of this last step. Only you know what you're using this box for, as well as the resources it has available. If this is a sandbox, development, lower test environment, or so on, an integrated database option is a totally viable option. However, in production, seriously consider deploying the database to a separate and distinct server in your environment.

While there are several other platform services here that you may or may not want, the last one that stands out as needing clear definition is Subversion (see

Figure 3.33). Prior to SAP BusinessObjects BI 4.1, it was reasonable to make a case that Lifecycle Manager (now Promotion Management) would exist in its own environment, centrally managing content for all clusters in your systems development lifecycle. Here, enabling SUBVERSION will dictate whether this server will be able to support Promotion Management functions in your cluster. As before, remember that you really only need one Promotion Management Server.

Figure 3.33 Promotion Management Components

From here, there are tons of other options in the customer installer that we'll attempt to highlight, but not micro-manage:

▶ **Connectivity and Data Federator Services**
These provide access to data both via direct connection and via the new common semantic layer (CSL).

▶ **Processing Servers**
Crystal Report Services, Web Intelligence Services, and Analysis Services ensure that users can view and refresh content within your environment.

▶ **Multitenancy Manager**
New with SAP BusinessObjects BI 4.0 SP4, this is a really exciting new capability of the platform. Many organizations are content with a decentralized security model, allowing many different applications to leverage an environment. The Multitenancy Manager allows a primary administrator to create application silos with ease compared to the old days of trying your best to strip away as much as you can from the Central Management Console.

▶ **Data sources**
There are more than a few to mention here. Again, based on your known requirements, or the all-in approach, choose the sources you know you need to make available to developers. If space isn't an issue, don't be stingy with your install options. It's probably also worth noting that the bulk of these are relevant to SAP Crystal Reports only.

▶ **RESTful SDKs**
You never know when you're going to need or want them. The key to integrating applications you develop or those developed by third parties is to install these.

▶ **Upgrade Management Tool (UMT)**

UMT is still not available on the client tools installation. Ensure you install this on at least one server node.

3.2.3   CMS Deployment Options

Moving along, we'll assume that we're starting with a new CMS cluster (see Figure 3.34). This is a branch in the install process if you do want to add this node to an existing CMS cluster, but here we choose the option to start a new one, and click NEXT to continue.

Figure 3.34 Starting a New CMS or Expand Another

As the Server Intelligence Agent (SIA) is named in this next step, be conscious of the fact that at some point, you may add additional SIAs to this physical server, whether it's to scale vertically or to add completely independent clusters to your server. Pick a name indicative of the sequence of the installation of your SIA or maybe, more specifically, the application for which it exists, and click NEXT (see Figure 3.35).

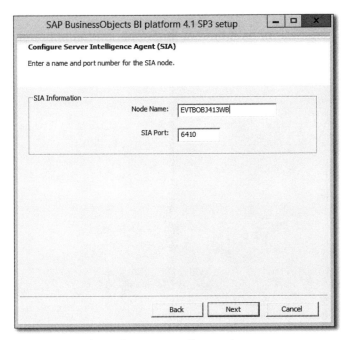

Figure 3.35 Defining the Server Intelligence Agent

The next step is CMS PORT selection (see Figure 3.36). This is critical to get right for a few reasons:

▶ If your organization has standards for port assignment, the CMS port is the first one to ensure you get it right and stay within compliance of your organization's standards.

▶ If this is a secondary or tertiary CMS on this physical box, taking the default will create an automatic conflict when it tries to start this CMS node.

Pick a CMS port that works for your environment and continue to set up the default password and cluster key for this environment.

The next step has to do with CMS security (see Figure 3.37). In a new environment, the administrator account password is as good as root on a UNIX or Linux system. Write this down in your handy password safe and guard it with your life. The cluster key, new with SAP BusinessObjects BI 4.1, is for the protection of adding additional SIAs to your cluster. It's really a simple layer of security to keep people from messing up your cluster. Like the administrator password, you should document and protect this string.

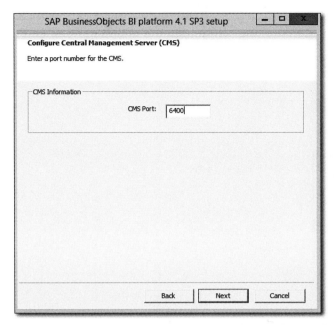

Figure 3.36 CMS Port Specification

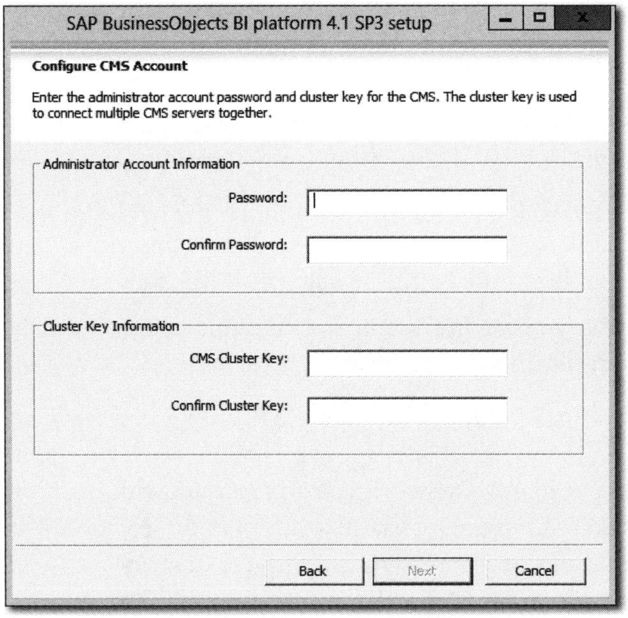

Figure 3.37 CMS Security

Progressing along, we know that in this vanilla installation, we selected the default database included with SAP BusinessObjects BI 4.1. That means we have to give this database some credentials to remember us by (see Figure 3.38).

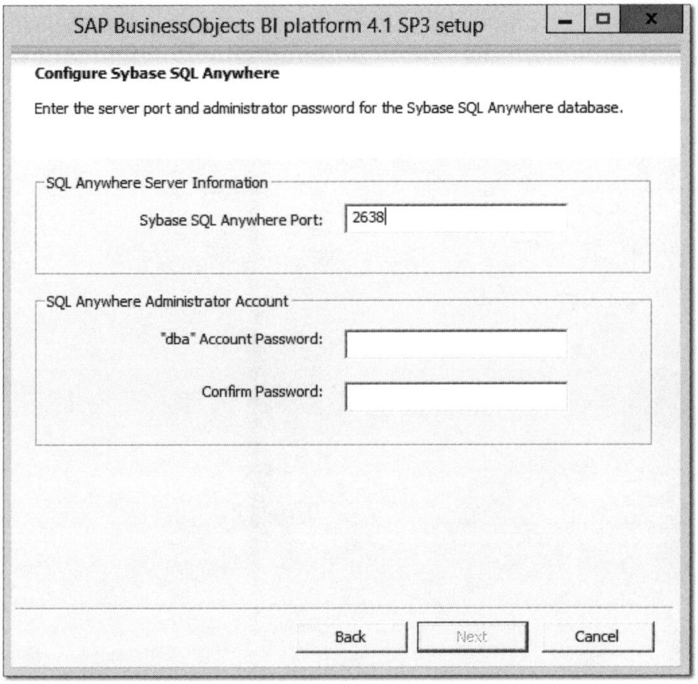

Figure 3.38 Initial Database Setup

Like the SAP BusinessObjects BI administrator, the DBA account is the equivalent of root for Sybase SQL Anywhere. In the same regard, keep it somewhere safe. The user account that gets created in the second set of boxes is actually the runtime user that the CMS will log in with when communicating with the default database. Fill it in, and let's proceed.

Much like the CMS port number, we need to also select ports under which Tomcat can properly function (see Figure 3.39). You'll note that for the purposes of this install, we kept the default port 8080. However, here's a tip. If another server, such as Apache HTTP Server or Microsoft Internet Information Server (IIS), is absent, you can run Tomcat on port 80 instead of 8080. What is the result? Consider this: *http://some_server:8080/BOE/BI* vs. *http://some_server/BOE/BI*

Because modern web browsers will assume port 80 is the standard port, your users don't have to include that on your server. Just remember, if you put Apache or IIS on this server, and they occupy port 80, you'll have to move Tomcat *back* to port 8080 and put the redirect in as appropriate.

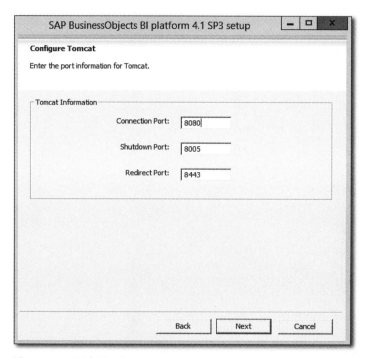

Figure 3.39 Web Tier Ports

Moving to the next screen (new, but not shown), the HTTP Listening Port for connecting to the Web Application Container Server (WACS) or the new RESTful APIs should be validated and confirmed before proceeding.

When Promotion Management is chosen for deployment (back via that SUBVERSION option during the custom installation part of the process), you have to supply some default values for Subversion to deploy on. There really is no flexibility in the REPOSITORY NAME here, but an alternate REPOSITORY PORT can be chosen. Supply a REPOSITORY USER ACCOUNTand REPOSITORY ACCOUNT PASSWORD that you can communicate and refer back to safely, and continue (see Figure 3.40).

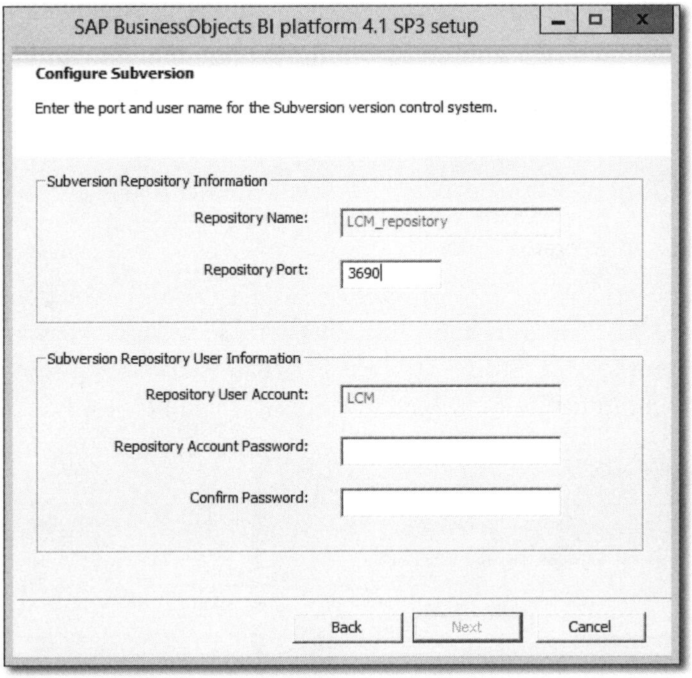

Figure 3.40 Promotion Management/Subversion Setup

The next screen determines whether you want to deploy the Solution Manager Diagnostics agent for integration with Wily Introscope. This deployment isn't covered in this text. Subsequently, it's set to not configure in this step of the installation process. Per our suggestion in Section 3.1 during the installation on Linux, be sure to set this up now for less pain.

In a similar fashion, you may configure SAP BusinessObjects BI 4.1 to integrate with Introscope Enterprise Manager. This text doesn't cover integration with Introscope Enterprise Manager, so this option isn't configured during installation.

While it can be perceived that neither of these options has hit mainstream yet, consider now that SAP does provide runtime versions of Wily Introscope with SAP BusinessObjects BI for advanced monitoring of your SAP BusinessObjects BI landscape.

And with that, you've made it to the end of the installation parameters! Click NEXT to continue. At this point, feel free to use the restroom, go shopping, visit the Diversified Semantic Layer podcast site, and snuggle up to the latest SAP BusinessObjects BI community podcasts (hilarity ensues), or leave for the day and come back later—because it's highly likely that you'll see in excess of a one-hour installation here, especially if you've chosen all components for deployment in your cluster node.

3.2.4   Post-Installation Steps

As the installation comes to a close, a screen with post-installation instructions will pop up (see Figure 3.41). There are some tasty bits here, so be sure to pay attention as the deployment for SAP BusinessObjects BI 4.1, the terminology, and locations of the web applications have changed in a not-so-insignificant way.

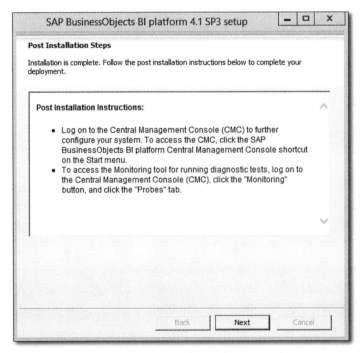

Figure 3.41 Post-Installation Steps

Home run. You made it. Kind of makes you wonder, though, who the guy in this picture is and why he doesn't look happier that the install was successful (see Figure 3.42).

Figure 3.42 The End

Anyway, it's time to hop into your new environment and give it your first review. You'll note that similar to older deployments, the web application shortcuts are in the START menu of Windows servers, but the START menu is missing those client tools that have always accompanied the server install (see Figure 3.43).

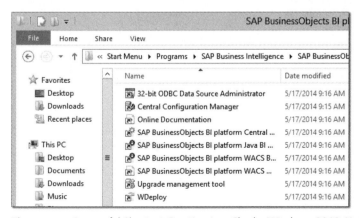

Figure 3.43 Successful Shortcut Creation in a Clunky Windows 2012 Metro

The first step to ensure you're up and running is to always try to access the Central Management Console. Point your browser to *http://your_server_name:8080/BOE/CMC*, and see if the logon page works (see Figure 3.44).

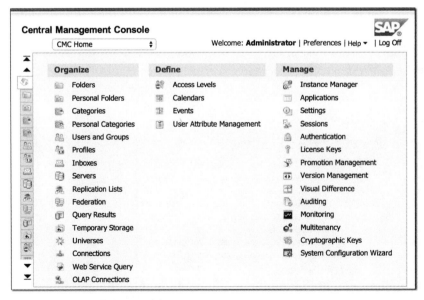

Figure 3.44 Successful Web Tier Deployment

It's an awesome first step to demonstrate that, at least to this point, the web application has deployed successfully and is rendering the content to your web browser. The next step is an actual logon (see Figure 3.45).

Central Management Console

CMC Home

Welcome: **Administrator** | Preferences | Help ▾ | Log Off

Organize	Define	Manage
Folders	Access Levels	Instance Manager
Personal Folders	Calendars	Applications
Categories	Events	Settings
Personal Categories	User Attribute Management	Sessions
Users and Groups		Authentication
Profiles		License Keys
Inboxes		Promotion Management
Servers		Version Management
Replication Lists		Visual Difference
Federation		Auditing
Query Results		Monitoring
Temporary Storage		Multitenancy
Universes		Cryptographic Keys
Connections		System Configuration Wizard
Web Service Query		
OLAP Connections		

Figure 3.45 . . .and a Successful Logon

Ladies and gentlemen, we have lift off. If you're able to successfully log on to the CMC, this means that the web server, database server, and some other moving parts are all clicking, and you have the fundamental building blocks of an SAP BusinessObjects BI 4.1 cluster.

3.2.5 Alternative Installation Paths

Obviously, this install path doesn't fit every need. There are alternative paths for full installs, decentralized database deployments, web tier deployments, and more. Let's take a look at a few alternative deployments and how they shape up based on the varying configuration options. We won't walk all the way through the build process again (nobody wants that), but let's set some context around those scenarios and the impacts on the installer.

Decentralized Database Deployments

We're sure you've already made the wise decision to use a database that won't live on your SAP BusinessObjects BI 4.1 server. This is a good move. Let's give as much horsepower to SAP BusinessObjects BI as we can. During the custom/expanded install process, we already selected the SYBASE SQL ANYWHERE DATABASE-checkbox to ensure that Sybase SQL Anywhere was installed by default.

Here is the easy part. Just *unselect* this checkbox (see Figure 3.46). That's really it. Now we're on our way to supplying new database credentials to the installer.

Figure 3.46 Default Database Selection

In this example, let's assume ORACLE will be the target CMS database for this deployment (see Figure 3.47).

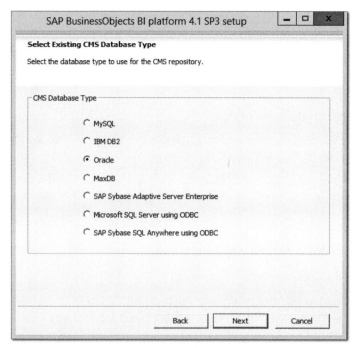

Figure 3.47 Specifying an Alternative CMS Database

Note
A secondary screen will be displayed to indicate your intention to select an Auditor database as well (not shown).

With that done, click NEXT to continue on to supply the database credentials (see Figure 3.48).

The inputs for the credentials will vary based on the database type selected, but for our purposes, know your target database name, the user name with rights to create database objects, and its password, and you'll be good to go here.

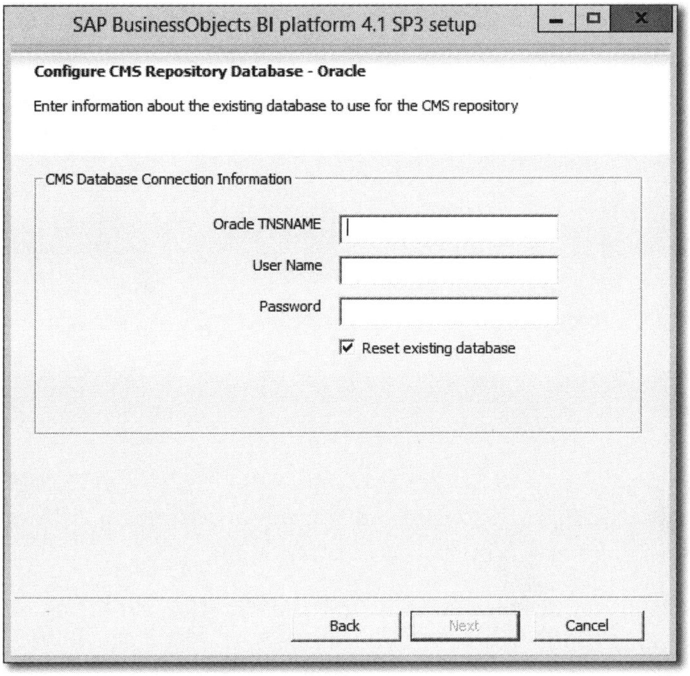

SAP BusinessObjects BI platform 4.1 SP3 setup
Configure CMS Repository Database - Oracle
Enter information about the existing database to use for the CMS repository
CMS Database Connection Information
Oracle TNSNAME
User Name
Password
Reset existing database
Back
Next
Cancel

Figure 3.48 Target Database Definition

Web Tier Installations

Another scenario that you've hopefully caught on to is that distributed web tier. That is easy too! SAP has made the installer for deploying SAP BusinessObjects BI 4.1 really quite simple on a web tier. Backing up to the beginning of the installation process, you're once again presented with the option to do a full, custom/expanded, or web tier installation (see Figure 3.49).

Web Tier
Install only the Web Tier features

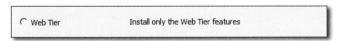

Figure 3.49 The Install Type Option for a Web Tier

The installation process itself is as straightforward as others: selecting the target web server type. At a minimum, the web tier installation provides the necessary components to be able to redeploy the web tier application files to whichever web tier technology your organization has settled on.

1. What is the minimum database driver type required for SAP BusinessObjects BI 4.1 to function: 32-bit or 64-bit?

2. Which type of installation is required of the default CMS database of Sybase SQL Anywhere?

3. If you don't want to install Promotion Management on an environment, which option should be disabled in the custom/expanded install?

4. What is the proper resource to determine supported web servers for any installation?

3.3 Clustering

One thing that SAP BusinessObjects BI has always done well, way back to its roots in the days of Crystal Enterprise, is clustering and scaling for redundancy. Those are some big old terms, so let's try to break it down a little bit.

When we talk about clustering, we need to take into consideration clustering options for both application and web tier perspectives. Clustering in each role varies, but the net result is an environment that is ready for fault.

When adding capacity to a cluster, you have one of two paths: up and out, also more generally known as vertical, and horizontal scaling. *Vertical scaling* is known as the approach to add additional services on a single node to increase capacity. *Horizontal scaling* involves adding additional physical (or virtual) servers to a cluster so that the multiple parts can function as a whole.

If not immediately obvious, there is a logical flow to this type of decision: *scale up, then out*. This is true if you don't already have a secondary node to support immediate failover, which should be your first priority. However, the idea behind growing an environment is to grow it within your existing investment in this technology. After you've reached a practical limit within the confines of your server by adding additional services, then horizontal scaling is appropriate. With that said, let's explore some examples in scaling out servers within the SAP BusinessObjects BI 4.1 cluster, specifically within the application tier.

3.3.1 Adding and Deleting Nodes Using the Central Configuration Manager

The Central Configuration Manager (CCM) provides us with what is perhaps the more crude approach to adding servers to a cluster. Think of it as an all-or-nothing approach to adding services within the cluster.

Adding Nodes

At the highest level, we can indiscriminately add servers by adding additional SIAs to the box. Let's walk through this process using a Windows box as the example, but in all reality, logically, the workflow is the same on a Linux or UNIX environment, just managed via shell scripts.

Within the CCM, no new services have been added. That's for you to fine-tune now. Start out by clicking the ADD NODE icon located on the toolbar (see Figure 3.50). When the wizard begins (not shown), click NEXT to begin the real work.

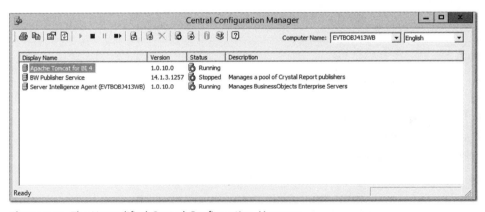

Figure 3.50 The Unmodified Central Configuration Manager

There are several paths you can run down here, but in each, you should specify the node name, or SIA name, and the SIA port. The following options will further dictate how you move from here:

▶ ADD NODE WITH NO SERVERS
A new SIA is created, but no additional servers are added. This assumes the SIA name must be unique, and the SIA port, too, must be unique when deployed.

▶ ADD NODE WITH CMS
Similar to the previous option, the SIA must not conflict, but a new CMS is created, whether you intend to cluster with an existing CMS or create a new one.

▶ ADD NODE WITH DEFAULT SERVERS
Like the first two options, however, all default servers are created when the SIA is built.

▶ RECREATE NODE
As you can surmise, you start from scratch, rebuilding the SIA.

In our example, we're going to go with the assumption that we'll add a node with default servers to demonstrate the ability to scale up (see Figure 3.51).

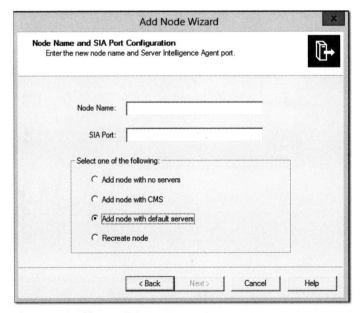

Figure 3.51 Adding an SIA

Because we aren't adding a unique SAP BusinessObjects BI deployment (totally an option here, on the same server, provided you have a beefy enough box), we'll use the existing, running CMS to add the new SIA (see Figure 3.52 and Figure 3.53).

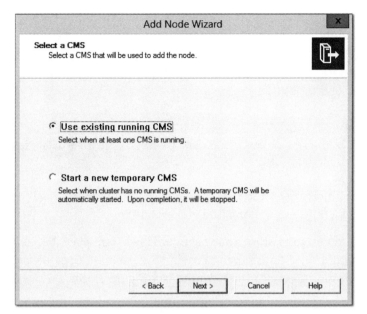

Figure 3.52 Reuse a CMS or Build a New One

Figure 3.53 Data Sources for the CMS

Before selecting a data source, you must specify a new CMS port on this physical server (not shown). This port number can't conflict with the existing CMS port number, which is generally 6400. But still, it must be unique across all running processes on your box. Port 6500 was chosen here as a safe spot.

On this same page, you must select the correct data source connection type for your CMS. Think back a few pages. On this box, we did use the built-in database to build our server, which uses Sybase SQL Anywhere. It also created some Open Database Connectivity (ODBC) connections for us to begin with. Take advantage of those by clicking the SPECIFY button.

> **Note**
>
> Having used Sybase SQL Anywhere as your default data source, use the DBA database account specified during your initial CMS setup.

Select the SAP BusinessObjects CMS 140 data source on your box to leverage the same database, and click OK to move along (see Figure 3.54).

Hopefully, you heeded the note to store your passwords in a safe place because here is the first place you'll need to use them. Provide the database USER ID and PASSWORD for the connection to verify your identity (see Figure 3.55).

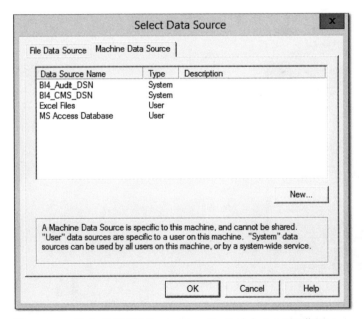

Figure 3.54 Default ODBC Connections Created during Installation

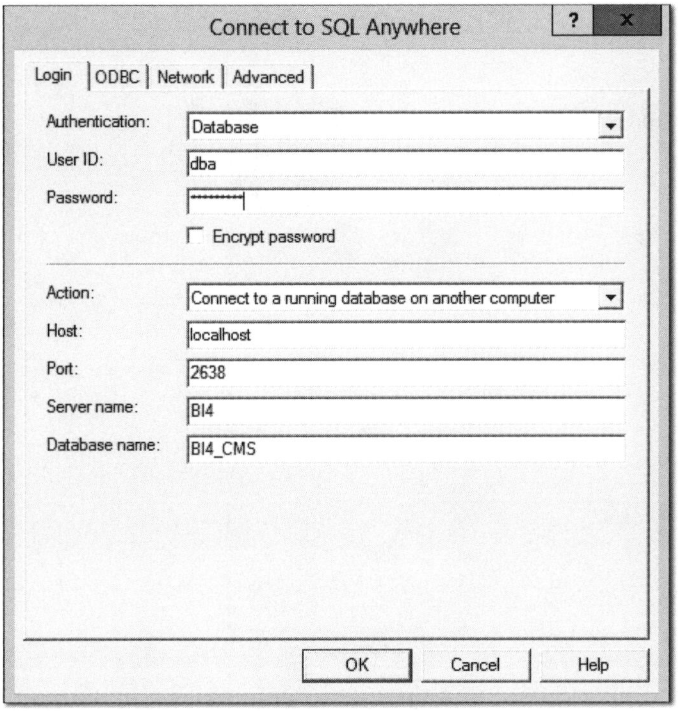

Figure 3.55 Required Data Source Credentials

In addition to authenticating to the database, you still need the cluster key that was defined during installation to complete the connection to the existing cluster (see Figure 3.56).

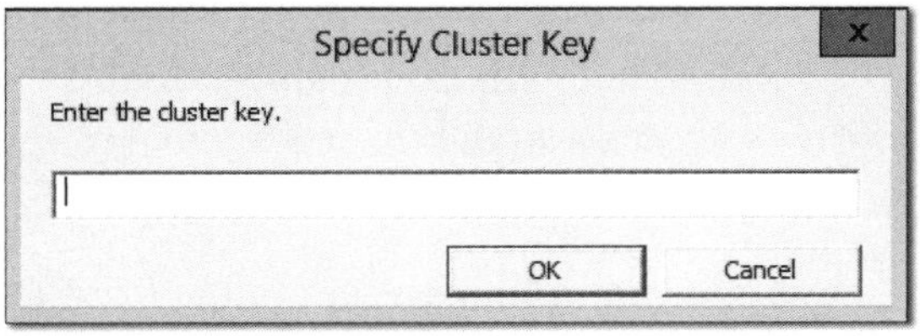

Figure 3.56 The Cluster Key

Not that knowing the database user name and password was enough, nor was knowing the cluster key; the final authentication step is to provide administrator rights to the existing CMS cluster. Another SIA and CMS, at a minimum, must be running on your cluster to permit this authentication step to take place (see Figure 3.57).

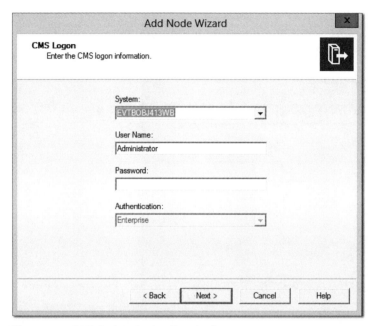

Figure 3.57 CMS Authentication Required

The confirmation step is your last chance to recheck your ports, names, and target CMS before clicking the FINISH button, which will make the CMS database modifications and server modifications to complete this server addition (see Figure 3.58).

That wasn't so bad. When completed, a path to a log file is certainly available for review, but despite being a fairly invasive step, it's a straightforward step (see Figure 3.59).

As long as everything turned out all right, the new SIA is present in the CCM for this specific server but is in a stopped state (see Figure 3.60). This is a good thing. To actually make any servers dependent upon this SIA available, the SIA must be started before logging into the CMC.

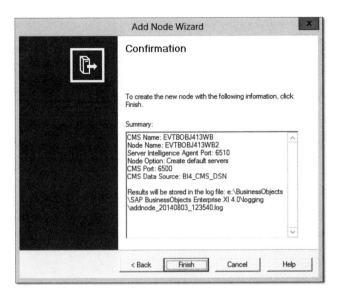

Figure 3.58 Add Node Confirmation

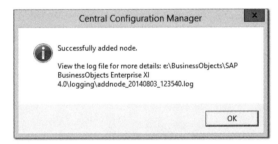

Figure 3.59 Add Node Complete

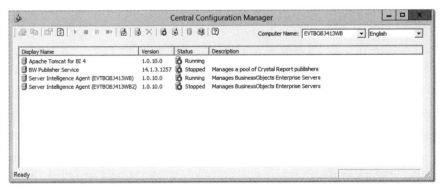

Figure 3.60 New Node in CCM

Log in to your CMC, click on the SERVERS panel, and note that in the NODES portion of the tree, the new SIA is present in the CMC (Figure 3.61), although in this case, it isn't fully aware of the SIA because on this instance it's still not started (see Figure 3.62).

Figure 3.61 The New SIA Present in the CMC

Figure 3.62 New Servers Created under the New SIA

In the preceding options, during creation of the new node, we chose the option to create all of the default servers. While they are created in an enabled state, the servers are all stopped. But, like the other existing SIA's servers, each can be started and controlled individually.

Deleting Nodes

With a new SIA up and running and perhaps running for some time, it stands to reason that the work load on a server node is too great and should be redistributed to new servers. Removing a node from a server is a simple process that walks along the same path.

To delete a node, return to the CMC and first stop the SIA you want to remove from the cluster and server. Next, select it explicitly from the list of available services, and click the DELETE NODE button (see Figure 3.63). You'll note that this process isn't quite as forgiving in letting you walk cautiously through this process. A few button clicks in, and the SIA is gone from your system, and all associated server references are gone from the CMS cluster.

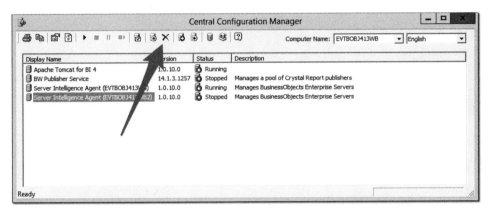

Figure 3.63 Delete Node Button

At the confirmation screen, click YES (see Figure 3.64), and confirm the deletion with the CMS authentication screen that appears next (not shown here). This is a good time to remember that you can't take actions like this to modify the CMS if there isn't a running CMS somewhere in the cluster of which this SIA is a part.

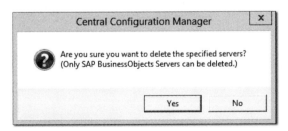

Figure 3.64 Delete Node Confirmation

The SIA is now removed from this node (see Figure 3.65) and can be verified via the CMC by reviewing the node list once again (see Figure 3.66).

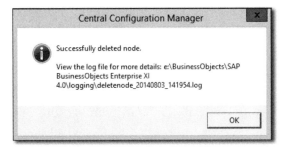

Figure 3.65 Delete Node Log

Figure 3.66 Node List after Removal

Another relevant way this may assist you is in dedicating an existing server to a web tier node. As an environment grows and flexes over time, you may order new hardware or virtual machines to take on the application tier role. Existing unlicensed servers can easily be converted to dedicated web tier nodes as appropriate.

3.3.2 Adding and Deleting Nodes in UNIX/Linux

The CCM on UNIX or Linux does many of the same functions as the prettier Windows version, but it is, of course, completely command-line driven. The following is a helpful listing showing the proper syntax to run the `ccm.sh` on Linux (see Listing 3.1).

```
usage: ccm.sh <command>


To display help:
ccm.sh -help


To start a node:
ccm.sh -start <node identifier>


To stop a node:
ccm.sh -stop <node identifier>
```

To restart a node:
ccm.sh -restart <node identifier>

Node identifiers for start, stop, and restart can be listed by running
serverconfig.sh and selecting 'List all nodes' (for example: node1,
node2). Use 'all' to modify all nodes.

To start a managed server:
ccm.sh -managedstart <fully qualified server name> [
other authentication
information]

To stop a managed server:
ccm.sh -managedstop <fully qualified server name> [other authentication
information]

To restart a managed server:
ccm.sh -managedrestart <fully qualified server name> [other
authentication information]

To force terminate a managed server:
ccm.sh -managedforceterminate <fully qualified server name> [other
authentication information]

To enable a server:
ccm.sh -enable <fully qualified server name> [other authentication
information]

To disable a server:
ccm.sh -disable <fully qualified server name> [other authentication
information]

To disable warnings (only applicable for CMS when -managedstop or
-managedforceterminate is used):
ccm.sh -nowarnings

To display a server's fully qualified name and server status:
ccm.sh -display [other authentication information]

```
OTHER AUTHENTICATION INFORMATION:
To specify which CMS to log on to:
-cms <cmsname:port#>
If a CMS isn't specified, it will default to your local machine name.


To specify a user name when logging onto the CMS:
-username <username>
If a user name is not specified, it will default to Administrator.


To specify a password when logging onto the CMS:
-password <password>
If a password is not specified, it will default to blank.


To specify an authentication type to use when logging onto the CMS:
-authentication <authentication type>
If an authentication type is not specified, it will default to
secEnterprise.


Example:
./ccm.sh -enable vanrdsol03.event.eventserver -cms vanrdsol03:6768
-username jsheldon -password banana -authentication secEnterprise
[boadmin@evtech3 sap_bobj]$
```
Listing 3.1 Linux Options for ccm.sh

3.3.3 Adding a Node Using the Central Management Console

The CMC gives you much more granular capabilities to add individual servers within the cluster and within existing SIAs in the cluster. You can control the individual distribution of servers across each SIA in such a way that you can ensure you configure each with the most efficient configuration possible.

The CMC has a button in the toolbar in the SERVERS panel to create a new server, as shown in Figure 3.67.

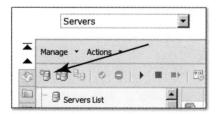

Figure 3.67 New Servers via the CMC

This is a very complicated interface with a somewhat difficult-to-follow list of servers that you can add to your cluster with fine-grained control (see Figure 3.68).

Figure 3.68 Create New Server Dialog

First, servers are organized by SERVICE CATEGORY:

- ▸ ANALYSIS SERVICES
- ▸ CONNECTIVITY SERVICES
- ▸ CORE SERVICES
- ▸ CRYSTAL REPORTS SERVICES
- ▸ DASHBOARDS SERVICES
- ▸ DATA FEDERATION SERVICES
- ▸ EXPLORER SERVICES
- ▸ PROMOTION MANAGEMENT SERVICES
- ▸ WEB INTELLIGENCE SERVICES

Each service category contains one or more related services that while logically organized, can be grouped together in some cases.

Let's explore an example where we need to enhance the Data Federation Server capability on this cluster node. Two servers are required to construct a new Data Federation Server in the Adaptive Processing Server (APS) family. The first is in the SERVICE CATEGORY dropdown list, ANALYSIS SERVICES, and the service is BEX WEB APPLICATIONS SERVICE (see Figure 3.69). Select it and click NEXT to continue.

Figure 3.69 Building a New Data Federation Server

In the composite image shown in Figure 3.70, we must also add the DATA FEDER-ATION SERVICE before we start this new server.

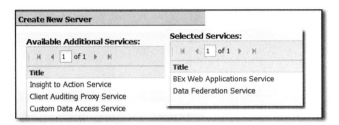

Figure 3.70 Add Additional Services

With the prerequisite services assigned to the new server, name it and select the appropriate node for this new server. Then click the CREATE button to have the new server added (see Figure 3.71).

Figure 3.71 New Server Properties

A new server with the name you chose is added in a stopped and disabled state to the appropriate SIA you selected during the definition steps (see Figure 3.72). That is server scalability with relative ease right there.

Figure 3.72 New Server Added

Alternatively, you can add additional services by cloning servers. Before a server is cloned, it's generally accepted as a first step to set the configuration template on the original server to be cloned first. Select the server to be cloned, right-click it, and choose PROPERTIES (see Figure 3.73).

Figure 3.73 Server Properties

Most major sections of a server's properties include an option to either set or use a configuration template. In this case, let's assume we've tuned this APS, and it's awesome. Select the checkbox to set the configuration template, and click SAVE AND CLOSE (see Figure 3.74).

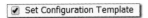

Figure 3.74 Set Configuration Template

With the configuration template set, select the server to be cloned, and right-click to reach the menu with CLONE SERVER near the bottom (see Figure 3.75).

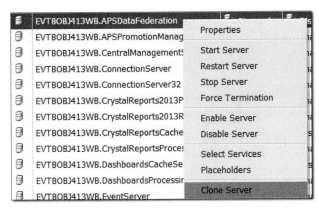

Figure 3.75 Clone Server Option 1

The only two choices of concern in cloning the server initially are to ensure that it has both a unique name on the selected node and to select the SIA/node in which it will run (see Figure 3.76).

Clone Server: EVTBOBJ413WB.APSDataFederation

New Server Name: APSDataFederation2

Clone to Node: EVTBOBJ413WB ▼

Figure 3.76 Clone Server Option 2

The server list is then kind enough to show that now we have two servers (see Figure 3.77). Nice. Now despite the fact that the server is in fact a clone, they aren't linked together in settings. That's why we set the configuration template earlier. Enter the properties for your cloned server.

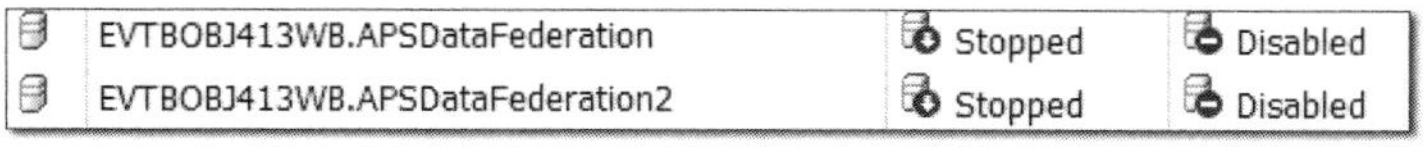

🗐	EVTBOBJ413WB.APSDataFederation	🔴 Stopped	🔴 Disabled
🗐	EVTBOBJ413WB.APSDataFederation2	🔴 Stopped	🔴 Disabled

Figure 3.77 Cloned APS

In each section where you want the clone to inherit the parent's configuration, select the USE CONFIGURATION TEMPLATE checkbox (see Figure 3.78). Any subsequent changes in properties should be made on the parent server. Those changes will then propagate to any clones using the configuration template. It's worth noting that not every server must be a clone to use the configuration template, but it sure helps.

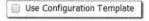
☐ Use Configuration Template

Figure 3.78 Use Configuration Template Checkbox

We've spent considerable time thinking about scaling out the application tier. You as the administrator must also remember, you're in charge of ensuring that you scale the web tier and that the file system and database tiers are at the very least being addressed by your other administrator pals. The web tier, depending on the technology platform you've chosen, will vary in terms of how you scale it out. We highly recommend that, at this point, you research the configuration for your web tier of choice and implement it. Importantly, remember that hardware load balancing is, in our opinion, the best way to achieve the desired result.

3.3.4 Failover and High Availability

Now that we know how to expand an environment, either up or across, we also need to continue to explore configurations that avoid single points of failure. Let's ensure once again that we're on the same page when it comes to the terminology. The term *failover capabilities* implies that a redundancy exists within an environment so that while it may not be able to actively swap to another running server without interruption to the user, an environment can be resumed within a reasonable amount of time to a passive node. This is also known as an *active/passive configuration*.

High availability paints a different picture. Also known as an *active/active configuration*, it means that more than one node in the cluster functions in such a way that they simultaneously handle requests to process user interactions.

Ultimately, your service level agreement with the business will dictate which approach you take in your environment, even going so far as to formulate requirements for disaster recovery. Designing this type of architecture, however, doesn't necessarily have to crush your budget. Budgets and environments come in all shapes and sizes, ranging anywhere from zero budget, to more money than sense. Therefore, you must formulate your redundancy strategy based on those types of variables. Consider a phased approach for those that are budgetarily challenged:

▶ **Failover: active/passive**
A second server, whether physical or virtual, is mirrored to the active node but not started or actively handling requests. In addition, database, file store, and web tier components have similar capability of cold swapping processes.

▶ **High availability : active/active**
That second server just got a promotion and now is actively fulfilling requests. This also implies that other components of the architecture, such as the web tier, database tier, and file store, can function despite either software or hardware failure within the environment.

▶ **Disaster recovery**
Shops with deep pockets will have a backup plan to recover SAP BusinessObjects BI in some other area of the country. This backup strategy will either call for mirrored servers in the backup data center or a strategy to quickly recover from backup to alternate servers in that backup data center. The mean time to recovery is dictated by the mission criticality of BI in your organization compared to the size of your deployment to be recovered.

Pop Quiz

1. What is the difference between the CMC and the CCM?
2. Describe the purpose of a configuration template.
3. True or False: The CMC can be used to add new SIAs.

3.4 Virtualization

We're big, big fans of virtualization. This book is by no means an endorsement of any particular virtualization vendor, but in generally accepted guidelines, we'll refer to VMware throughout this book as a solution to virtualization for SAP BusinessObjects BI.

Sometime shortly after BusinessObjects XI hit the shelves, virtualization topics really started to get lively. "Would Business Objects (now SAP) support my environment if I put it on VMware?" "Is there any performance decrease if I virtualize my environment?" The concept of having many operating systems on a single big-boy server confounded some and became an opportunity to avoid underutilization of hardware platforms for those who saw the chance to improve their investment in technology.

As the years after BusinessObjects XI and XI R2 ticked by, and Business Objects became more and more open to the idea that enterprises could virtualize their environments, administrators were really now left with the only question: "How is performance?"

There are no benchmarks in this book to tell you with any real evidence what the actual performance hit on an SAP BusinessObjects BI environment is, but there are some considerations you have to factor in as you talk with your systems/virtualization architect about the performance of your virtual environment:

▶ How saturated is the virtual host environment? In other words, did everybody have the brilliant idea to virtualize their servers too?

▶ How many virtual hosts make up the virtualization environment, and how easily can it scale to support additional demand?

▶ Are there enough virtual hosts to create a distributed virtual environment for SAP BusinessObjects BI?

▶ How fast is the interconnect to storage for the virtual machines (VMs)?

▶ How many network interconnects are available to the virtual host to create network connections for virtual machines?

▶ Are CPU and memory reservations for the SAP BusinessObjects VMs set appropriately?

As you factor all of these things together, you can expect a VM running SAP BusinessObjects BI to take a hit of anywhere from 2% to 10% of what a physical box of similar stature could. Again, only you and your system/virtualization architect can get real on these numbers. However, as you go through your sizing exercise that we set up in Chapter 2, do take into account that loss in capacity as you get to the upper end of your environment's capacity.

In addition, know that you absolutely should talk to your SAP account manager when deciding to virtualize your SAP BusinessObjects BI environment. Based on your existing master agreement with SAP, the language in your license may dictate the validity of virtualizing components of SAP BusinessObjects BI.

This section won't go into extensive detail about virtualization, but it will give you the basics you need to know to do further research: your main virtualization options, and what they mean for a UNIX/Linux landscape.

3.4.1 Virtualization Options

Only you and your leadership can decide what exactly you *should* virtualize with the SAP BusinessObjects BI environment. Especially, with the significant increase in system requirements for an SAP BusinessObjects BI 4.1 cluster, administrators in the virtual server farms may have a heart attack when you ask them for servers with more than quadruple the minimum requirements of your old SAP BusinessObjects environments. However, let's take this in tiny steps:

▶ **The web tier**
This is an easy call. If you're using Apache Tomcat, distributed with SAP BusinessObjects BI, your only cost to implement is the VM and the operating system license. In addition, you're free to start with the safest/smallest amount of CPU and memory resources you think your web tier will need and can easily scale up as CPU and memory utilization goes up. We like to think this will also give your systems/virtualization administrators the warm and fuzzy feeling that you really do care about conserving resources in their environment. On the

other hand, if your boss is a tyrant and wants all the horsepower you can get, go big or go home. The web tier is also a simple environment to build and rapidly deploy within your cluster. So if you add additional web tier nodes, throw them behind a load balancer, and move along, and then you have a really inexpensive footprint to allow more HTTP traffic. This will be especially relevant not only to all of your users that use the BI Launch Pad, but also to your Dashboards developers and Dashboards consumers that are using web tier resource-hungry dashboards.

► **The application tier**
As we make the transition to SAP BusinessObjects BI 4.1, the reality of virtualization will inevitably come into question for enterprises of all sizes. With minimum memory requirements of 8GB of RAM (but in reality, pushing more toward a need for 16GB of RAM minimum), the strategy behind using virtualization must be carefully considered. Will SAP BusinessObjects BI be the straw that broke the proverbial camel's back? Many will fall in the camp that says "get the best performance out of the investment in SAP BusinessObjects." In other words, throw as much and as big of a piece of hardware as you can out there for your licenses to eat up. The mission of any organization supporting BI should not only be to deliver effective BI but also to be the best stewards of the investment in this technology. We do that by getting the most mileage out of the software and the hardware as we can.

► **Other virtualization opportunities**
Outside of the web tier and application tier, there isn't necessarily a lot of mileage in virtualizing other components of this platform *unless* you have no choice. Database servers, if wisely chosen to outsource to your enterprise database team, should not be an issue. However, if you're stuck in a situation where you have a small enough enterprise with no central environment for databases, consider virtualizing a database to support your CMS and Auditor databases on a machine that isn't the same as your web or application tiers.

There is clearly still the remote possibility that you have a multiserver environment and no SAN or NAS solution to centralize your File Repository Server (FRS). Fear not. A virtual machine is a great place to create a shared file system that your cluster can leverage for its File Repository Servers. Is this ideal? Probably not. Could you just use a share on one of the members of your cluster? Probably. But if you want a clean location to house your files and simplify backup and recovery, a simple virtual machine may be your fix.

Consider Figure 3.79, which shows a part of the standard VMware stencil set. In this diagram, two physical VMware ESX hosts make up a two-node cluster. While technologies such as VMware are smart enough to redistribute the load automatically, the implications for both members of the cluster being on the same node in the event of a failure are significant.

With that, just as we cluster SAP BusinessObjects BI across multiple machines, it also can be a credit to consider forcing individual members of an SAP Business-Objects BI cluster onto distinct virtual hosts to ensure not only redundancy but also resource availability within the virtual host cluster.

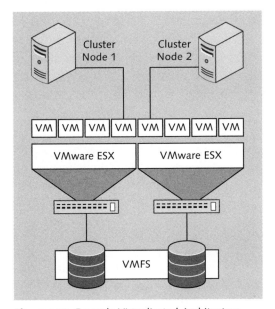

Figure 3.79 Example Virtualized Architecture

3.4.2 UNIX and Linux Landscapes

As you work toward defining a virtualization strategy, realize too that UNIX and Linux landscapes give an even more distinctive opportunity to virtualize applications. When we talk about virtualization in the land of non-Windows, just like the operating system, things look a little different. While Linux is supported by VMware very much like Windows is, the other versions of UNIX are quite different.

Both Solaris and AIX support the concept of a virtual machine. Just to confuse you, they're called different things. On AIX, a virtual machine is called a *workload partition*, or WPAR. On Solaris, they are called either containers or zones. Both of these funny names do the same thing. They segment off a portion of a large physical host into a distinct virtual host. Each zone or WPAR is totally separate from the others and, to the untrained eye, appears and acts exactly like a separate physical host. So, in essence, if you had a huge Solaris host with six different local zones, you could have six different installations of SAP BusinessObjects BI (one on each). Or, you could stratify your tiered architecture across three or four different zones, and while the workloads are separated, they all physically reside on the same host server.

The non-Windows operating systems make it a little easier for you to put multiple installations of SAP BusinessObjects BI on the same host. This is due to how UNIX and Linux handle the concept of roles. You could have one physical host machine and six different installations of SAP BusinessObjects BI running from six different directories running under six different roles. These additional levels of functionality really help you push the utilization of your physical hardware to the max.

One of the major advantages of this approach is the cost of licensing. If you purchased CPU-based licenses, you have the physical host licensed. If you put 10 zones or workload partitions on that hardware, they are covered by the CPU license for that physical box. It's like getting 10 servers for the price of one. Don't get too excited, though. CPU licenses are expensive. Contact your account manager for more details.

> **Pop Quiz**
>
> 1. Is it ever OK to blindly use a virtual machine farm to host SAP BusinessObjects BI servers?

3.5 Summary

SAP BusinessObjects BI 4.1 is a robust architecture with many paths that can be taken to make the technology fulfill business needs. As the technology matures, and additional capabilities are added, it becomes increasingly important for an administrator to comprehend those requirements, the technology components that are used to fulfill them, and potential impacts on business users as implementations are planned and executed.

As you design your environment, make an implementation plan that lays out key players, time lines for each environment build, and even, at a more granular server build level, cite dependencies and roles. Not tracking action items and key deliverables in builds as complex as SAP BusinessObjects BI can be a recipe for disaster at some point, whether it's by your hand or the poor guy that comes along next.

Remember, too, that frequent conversations with organizational architects and business stakeholders about both the needs for your environment and the targets for fulfilling business requirements will keep everyone in the know and avoid leaving people in the dark.

Go forth, build, and configure.

After you have SAP BusinessObjects BI 4.1 installed on your server, the work really begins. This chapter will discuss the many configuration settings available for administrators to optimize their SAP BusinessObjects BI 4.1 system for peak performance.

4 Configuration: Getting the Most for Your Money

If you thought that after planning, sizing, buying, and installing, you could really get started building your ultra-cool reports and dashboards, think again. Now comes another round of vitally important tasks: configuring this monster so it performs properly for what you're about to put it through. SAP has made some great strides since the first days of SAP BusinessObjects BI to help you get this right, and get it right without as much of a headache as it used to be. One of these major strides is the new System Configuration Wizard, which we'll step you through in detail. The challenge has always been that the SAP BusinessObjects BI 4.1 platform is so flexible that it can be configured in any number of ways to suit any number of business workflows. No two BI requirements are exactly alike from company to company, and leaving the platform flexible gives you the ability to maximize it to best suit your needs. For example, not every customer uses SAP Crystal Reports. Not every customer uses Dashboards. Some customers use Web Intelligence, SAP BusinessObjects Analysis, and Explorer. And further still, some use only SAP BusinessObjects Mobile. There's no one "right way" to configure SAP BusinessObjects BI 4.1 out-of-the-box, so it comes out like a big piece of plain vanilla cake. With a little time and attention, you can take that plain vanilla cake and transform it into an award-winning dessert, so to speak.

4.1   How Sizing and Configuration Go Hand-in-Hand

Now you're probably thinking, "Sizing. Didn't I get beat to death with that in Chapter 2? What does sizing have to do with configuration?" You might be surprised to find out that it has a lot to do with configuration—in short, because there are settings you'll need to change to properly set your system up to deal with the business traffic you're about to throw on it.

As you may recall from Chapter 2, SAP BusinessObjects BI offers a document called the Sizing Companion for SAP BusinessObjects BI 4.1, which also contains some sizing considerations that are relevant for configuration. This section is based on the fundamental principles discussed in the sizing guide—but minus the confusing stuff and plus our own additional notes and recommendations.

This isn't a step-by-step configuration guide. Instead, this guide will review both default and recommended setting changes based on the usage of a given server in a very methodical way, one service type after another. So, consider that a Web Intelligence shop will never need those SAP Crystal Reports servers. Skip it. If in the future SAP Crystal Reports becomes a requirement in your deployment, review it and implement based on these guidelines.

4.1.1   Central Management Server

The CMS has just a few settings to tweak to make it perform better. Because it has a relatively light workload compared to some of the other processes, it isn't surprising that there isn't much you can change to make it behave differently. Table 4.1 shows some arguments you can add to the CMS command line via the Central Management Console.

In previous releases, the `-ndbqthreads` argument in the CMS command line in the CMC could be edited to increase the number of threads servicing the CMS repository requests to the repository database. This setting in SAP BusinessObjects BI 4.1 is now available in the CMC under the CMS PROPERTIES tab. The default setting of 14 for SYSTEM DATABASE CONNECTIONS REQUESTED should be sufficient in most cases (see Figure 4.1).

Option	Argument Units	Behavior	Recommended Setting(s)
`-receiverPool`	Number	Specifies the number of threads the CMS creates to receive client requests.	Default value is 5, which is normally enough, unless you create a custom application with many clients.
`-maxobjectsin-cache`	Number	Specifies the maximum number of objects that the CMS stores in its cache.	Default value is 100,000. Increasing this number reduces the number of database calls required and greatly improves CMS performance. However, placing too many objects in memory may result in the CMS having too little memory to process queries. The default value is recommended in most cases.

Table 4.1 Central Management Console Parameters (Source: Sizing Companion for SAP BusinessObjects BI 4.0)

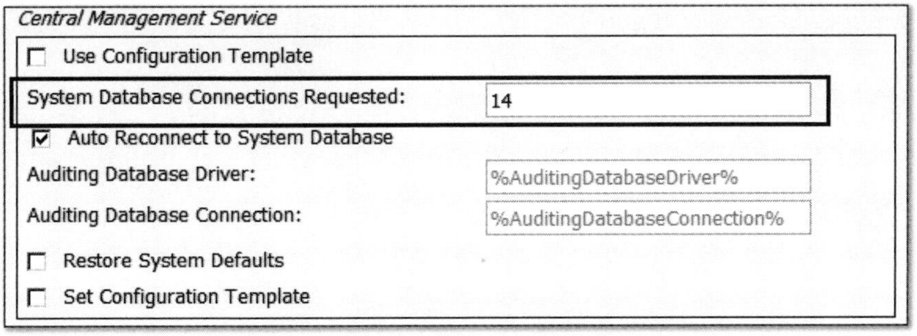

Figure 4.1 CMS Server Properties in Central Management Console

The default for `-MaxObjectsInCache` is set at 100,000 because this was found to be the optimum number during performance testing at SAP and during the ramp-up at customer sites. It's not a hard limit, but it seems to work the best in most deployments. Add too many more or take away too many, and performance can degrade. This number can be changed, but make sure you test any changes carefully before proceeding. This is really just a function of how much memory you have available on the server.

The Central Management Server, being central and all, is quite a chatty little guy. It likes to talk a lot to all of the other processes in the enterprise. More accurately, it needs to talk to everything because it's the boss, applesauce. As far as configuration goes, remember the CMS's chatty nature when you're adding additional services to your cluster for load balancing or failover. You'll want to have no more than four CMS instances in your cluster. Any more than four, and the network traffic they generate becomes problematic. The CORBA chatter will start to degrade your network and system performance. Do your best to minimize network latency between your multiple CMS services and the repository database, and engage your networking and database administration teams if you need additional help. Keeping those communications speedy will really help your system performance overall.

4.1.2   SAP Crystal Reports Cache Server

The purpose of the Cache Server, in case you couldn't guess, is to store (i.e., cache) report pages generated by the Processing Server. This is meant to reduce the number of trips to the database and speed performance, because everyone knows (or should know) that going to the database is costly in terms of processing time and processing resources.

The parameters in Table 4.2 are set in the Central Management Console and should be made on both the SAP Crystal Reports Cache Server and the SAP Crystal Reports Processing Server.

Option	Values	Behavior	Recommended Setting(s)
OLDEST ON-DEMAND DATA GIVEN TO CLIENTS	Seconds	Specifies the amount of time that the server uses cached data to meet requests from on-demand reports.	Default value is 0 seconds, which means ON DEMAND DATA is disabled. Recommended setting is 300,000.
VIEWER REFRESH ALWAYS YIELDS CURRENT DATA	On/off	Controls caching effectiveness.	On.
SHARE REPORT DATA BETWEEN CLIENTS	On/off	Controls caching effectiveness.	On.

Table 4.2 SAP Crystal Reports Cache Server Settings (Source: Sizing Companion for SAP Business-Objects BI 4.1)

4.1.3   File Repository Servers (iFRS and oFRS)

File Repository Servers are like opinions: everybody has one, and they all stink. Joking aside, these are a critical part of your system because they handle the physical storage of your content coming in to the SAP BusinessObjects BI platform and content going out of the platform. When you create a report and save it in the enterprise, this is where it's stored. Because these servers interact with the hard disk quite a bit, it's important to make sure these are placed somewhere with some really good input/output rates where there is plenty of space.

In the properties of the Input File Repository Server (iFRS) and the Output File Repository Server (oFRS), you can select the location where you want these to live. They don't both have to be on the same server. If you're in a clustered environment, you probably want these on network attached storage (NAS) or storage area network (SAN) space somewhere where all nodes in the cluster can communicate with them.

Another setting you can change is shown in Table 4.3.

Option	Argument Units	Behavior	Recommended Setting(s)
MAXIMUM IDLE TIME	Minutes	This setting limits the length of time that the server waits before it closes inactive connections.	Default value is 20. Setting a value too low can cause a user's request to be closed prematurely. Setting a value too high can cause excessive use of system resources.

Table 4.3 File Repository Server Parameters (Source: Sizing Companion for SAP BusinessObjects BI 4.1)

4.1.4 Adaptive Job Server

The Adaptive Job Server (AJS) is a rather large service that houses many of the services that process schedule requests for the various reporting tools. Each tool requires some different settings to make the most out of performance. Remember, that we still live in a world where products that were developed by different companies were acquired and put inside the same platform. Just because they all say SAP on the front doesn't mean they all work the same in the back. Next, we'll spend our time on the surviving reporting tools, Web Intelligence, SAP Crystal Reports, and Dashboards.

Web Intelligence Job Service

The Web Intelligence Job Service does just what the name indicates. It handles schedule requests for Web Intelligence reports. It doesn't do the actual processing of Web Intelligence reports (that job belongs to the Web Intelligence Processing Server, as its name indicates), but instead acts as the scheduling manager and routes schedule requests to an available Processing Server.

The setting shown in Table 4.4 can be changed.

Option	Argument Units	Behavior	Recommended Setting(s)
`-requestTimeout N`	Milliseconds	Specifies the number of milliseconds to wait for a report to return from the Web Intelligence Processing Server.	Default is 600,000. Minimum allowed is 30,000. If it's expected that reports will run longer than 10 minutes, increase this setting.

Table 4.4 Web Intelligence Job Server Parameters (Source: Sizing Companion for SAP Business-Objects BI 4.1)

Here's where a little knowledge of your system behavior can really come in handy. If you know from past experience (or auditor data) that it's normal for your Web Intelligence reports to run 20 to 30 minutes, then you definitely want to increase this timeout setting. Otherwise your scheduled jobs will fail because the Job Server will give up waiting for the Processing Server to finish before the report has a chance to fully complete. Hop over to *www.google.com*, type in "30 minutes in milliseconds", and you'll get the right number to put in your command-line argument. For the record, 30 minutes in milliseconds is 1,800,000.

SAP Crystal Reports Job Service

SAP Crystal Reports is a more mature product than Web Intelligence, so it behaves a bit differently under the covers. Unlike Web Intelligence, the SAP Crystal Reports Job Service doesn't hand off a schedule request to a Processing Server to generate the report. Instead, the SAP Crystal Reports Job Service spawns a child process to create the report, and it will spawn a child service for each report request.

There aren't any command-line settings you can change here, but it's important to keep in mind any information you learned from your sizing estimate. Because the SAP Crystal Reports Job Service is more of a heavyweight, it needs more resources to support your business activity. A single SAP Crystal Reports Job Service can optimally support five maximum jobs (processes) per available CPU core. This default of five simultaneous jobs can be changed, but your available resources and your architecture plan should be taken under careful consideration.

Other Job Servers

There are several other Job Server types rolled into the Adaptive Job Server. There is equal benefit in splitting the Adaptive Job Servers into smaller components to support Job Servers supporting Promotion Management, Platform Search, and so on.

4.1.5 Dashboards Cache Server

The settings shown in Table 4.5 can be configured in the Central Management Console to improve the Dashboard Design Cache Server performance.

Option	Default Value	Recommendation or Comments
MAXIMUM CACHE SIZE	256,000KB	Changing this value will likely have no effect in most scenarios because it's not likely to be reached. Disk space is only consumed if needed, so a lower value will only be beneficial if disk space is limited; this would negatively affect performance.
IDLE CONNECTION TIMEOUT	15 minutes	This can safely be lowered to 2 minutes. Do this if you see unusually high thread counts in your Cache Server.
SHARE DATA BETWEEN CLIENTS	True	Disabling this turns off caching. Disable this only in extremely sensitive security environments. This will slow performance in cases where data could otherwise be shared but will increase performance in cases where the cache hit rate is 0.

Table 4.5 Dashboards Cache Server Parameters (Source: Sizing Companion for SAP BusinessObjects BI 4.1)

Option	Default Value	Recommendation or Comments
OLDEST ON-DEMAND DATA GIVEN TO CLIENTS	0 seconds	Set this to 900 (15 minutes) for more realistic environments.
SECURITY CACHE TIMEOUT	20 minutes	Lower this value only if you need security changes in the CMS to be reflected by the Dashboards servers more frequently. This will negatively impact performance.

Table 4.5 Dashboards Cache Server Parameters (Source: Sizing Companion for SAP BusinessObjects BI 4.1) (Cont.)

4.1.6   Dashboards Processing Server

Just in case you hadn't had enough Central Management Server settings you can adjust, Table 4.6 shows some more things you can tweak on the Dashboards Processing Server.

Option	Default Value	Recommendation or Comments
MAXIMUM CONCURRENT JOBS	Automatic	By default, automatic is 250 jobs per CPU core. This can be adjusted if the Processing Server children are reaching their maximum without consuming too much CPU (e.g., most jobs are idle).
MAXIMUM LIFETIME JOBS PER CHILD	10,000	Keep this value above 1,000, or you'll find that your Java children may restart too often. Otherwise, this has no performance effect.

Table 4.6 Dashboards Processing Server Parameters (Source: Sizing Companion for SAP BusinessObjects BI 4.1)

Option	Default Value	Recommendation or Comments
MAXIMUM NUMBER OF PRE-STARTED CHILDREN	1	Set this higher if you anticipate more than 25 concurrent users for the very first request. Otherwise, this has no performance effect.
IDLE CONNECTION TIMEOUT	15 minutes	This can safely be lowered to 2 minutes. Do this if you see unusually high thread counts in your Processing Server or children.
IDLE JOB TIMEOUTS	15 minutes	This can safely be lowered to 2 minutes. Do this if you see "Maximum concurrent job" errors.

Table 4.6 Dashboards Processing Server Parameters (Source: Sizing Companion for SAP Business-Objects BI 4.1) (Cont.)

4.1.7 Web Intelligence Processing Server

We mentioned a bit earlier that the Web Intelligence Processing Server is the one that does all of the report creation work as far as Web Intelligence is concerned. It's the "big cheese" as far as Web Intelligence reports go. Many of these are deviations from the defaults, and deservedly so. Never forget that we're now working in a 64-bit world. This process in particular can use up a whole bunch of resources. Don't be afraid to experiment with these settings in your own performance testing, but the performance testing conducted at SAP suggests the parameters in Table 4.7 for optimal behavior from Web Intelligence.

Information Engine Service	
LIST OF VALUES BATCH SIZE (entries)	1,000
MAXIMUM CUSTOM SORT SIZE (entries)	100
UNIVERSE CACHE MAXIMUM SIZE (universes)	20
MAXIMUM LIST OF VALUES SIZE (entries)	50,000

Table 4.7 Web Intelligence Processing Server Parameters (Source: Sizing Companion for SAP BusinessObjects BI 4.1)

Interactive Analysis Core Service	
Timeout Before Recycling (seconds)	1,200
Idle document timeout (seconds)	9,000
Server polling interval (seconds)	120
Maximum documents per user	5
Maximum documents before recycling	100
Allow document map maximum size errors	Selected
Idle connection timeout (minutes)	90
Maximum connections	300
Enable memory analysis	Selected
Memory lower threshold (MB)	3,500
Memory upper threshold (MB)	4,500
Memory maximum threshold (MB)	6,000
Enable APS service monitoring	Selected
Retry count on APS service ping failure	3
APS service monitoring thread period	300
Enable current activity log	Not selected
Interactive Analysis Common Service	
Cache timeout (minutes)	4,370
Document cache cleanup interval (minutes)	120
Disable cache sharing	Not selected
Enable document cache	Selected
Enable real-time caching	Selected
Maximum document cache size (KB)	1,000,000
Maximum document cache reduction space (percent)	70
Maximum character stream size (MB)	20
Binary stream maximum size (MB)	50
Single sign-on expiry (seconds)	86,400

Table 4.7 Web Intelligence Processing Server Parameters (Source: Sizing Companion for SAP BusinessObjects BI 4.1) (Cont.)

4.1.8 Crystal Reports Enterprise Processing Server

This is the big guy in charge of making sure all of your Crystal reports are processed properly. And remember from Chapter 1, where we discussed the reporting tools, that this is the brand new version of SAP Crystal Reports that uses the universe. SAP recommends the settings in Table 4.8 for optimal performance of the Crystal Reports Enterprise Processing Server.

Option	Values	Behavior	Recommended Setting(s)
MAXIMUM CONCURRENT JOBS	0 for automatic	Specifies the maximum number of concurrent jobs allowed to run.	0 for automatic.
MAXIMUM LIFETIME JOBS PER CHILD	Number	Specifies the total number of jobs a child process can run. When the process hits the maximum, the parent process will kill the child process.	Default is 1,000.
MAXIMUM NUMBER OF PRESTARTED CHILDREN	Number	Specifies the number of child processes the parent process will start when it starts.	Default value is 1.
IDLE CONNECTION TIMEOUT	Minutes	Specifies the amount of time a connection to a database can remain idle before closing.	Default value is 20.
IDLE JOB TIMEOUT	Minutes	Specifies the amount of time a report job can remain idle before closing.	Default value is 60 seconds.
OLDEST ON-DEMAND DATA GIVEN TO CLIENTS	Seconds	Specifies the amount of time that the server uses cached data to meet requests from on-demand reports.	Default value is 0 (disabled). Recommended setting is 300,000.

Table 4.8 SAP Crystal Reports Enterprise Processing Server (Source: Sizing Companion for SAP BusinessObjects BI 4.1)

Performance testing conducted at SAP showed that the following parameters for the SAP Crystal Reports Enterprise Processing Server Java Virtual Machine (JVM) provided optimal performance. Add these to the command line in the CMC under PROPERTIES:

```
XX:MaxPermSize=128m,Xms1536m,Xmx2048m,XX:+UseParallelOldGC,XX:
ReservedCodeCacheSize=256m,XX:CompileThreshold=5000
```

The items in that string to really take note of are the Xms and Xmx arguments. Those are going to define your minimum starting memory (Xms) and the maximum amount (Xmx) of memory that this process's Java heap is allowed to consume.

4.1.9 Crystal Reports 2013 Processing Server

This guy is the "legacy" SAP Crystal Reports processing product and works a lot like what was in previous releases of SAP Crystal Reports. Although the product hasn't changed much, let's beat the 64-bit horse again and remind you that things can get mighty beefy in our world. The recommended settings in Table 4.9 will help keep you out of trouble.

Option	Value	Behavior	Recommended Setting(s)
DATABASE RECORDS READ WHEN PREVIEWING OR REFRESHING (0 FOR UNLIMITED)	Number of Records	Specifies the maximum number of database records to read when the report is being previewed or refreshed. Allows you to limit the number of records that the server retrieves from the database when a user runs a query report.	Default value is 20,000. Recommendation is to schedule large reports to reduce the load on your database from these large queries.
IDLE JOB TIMEOUT	Minutes	Specifies the length of time the server waits between requests for a given job.	Default value is 60 minutes.

Table 4.9 SAP Crystal Reports 2013 Processing Server Parameters (Source: Sizing Companion for SAP BusinessObjects BI 4.1)

Option	Value	Behavior	Recommended Setting(s)
ALLOW REPORT JOBS TO STAY CONNECTED TO THE DATABASE UNTIL THE REPORT JOB IS CLOSED	On/off	Allows the report jobs to stay connected to the database until the entire report process completes. This will limit the total number of connections made to your data source database.	On
OLDEST ON-DEMAND DATA GIVEN TO CLIENTS	Seconds	Specifies the amount of time that the server uses cached data to meet requests from on-demand reports.	Default value is 0 (disabled). Recommended setting is 300,000.

Table 4.9 SAP Crystal Reports 2013 Processing Server Parameters (Source: Sizing Companion for SAP BusinessObjects BI 4.1) (Cont.)

Here is a good place to stop and think again about the architecture plan you devised while sizing your environment. It's important to keep in mind that these Processing Services are now 64-bit and can grow quite large. In many cases, SAP recommends you house the Processing Server on a completely separate piece of hardware as a dedicated Processing Server. If this is the case, then you should set the MAXIMUM SIMULTANEOUS REPORT JOBS to UNLIMITED, and allow the Processing Server to consume as much of that server's capacity as possible. If this isn't the case, and the Processing Server is housed on a machine hosting other processes, then you should limit the MAXIMUM SIMULTANEOUS REPORT JOBS somewhere between 25 and 75 for each available CPU unit. Values below 25 jobs per CPU core should be considered if other processes such as the CMS, Job Servers, or Web Intelligence are present on the same host machine and sharing resources.

4.1.10 Report Application Server

The Report Application Server (RAS) is similar in many ways to the Crystal Reports Processing Server. It does mainly the same job but is the guy that serves up reports when users view a Crystal report in the BI Launch Pad with the Interactive DHTML viewer. The RAS also gives users the ability to create and modify Crystal reports in a web browser (also through the BI Launch Pad).

The default Maximum Simultaneous Report Jobs is set to 75 for each RAS service. As with the Crystal Reports Processing Server, this setting is highly dependent on how you've configured your system architecture. The general guideline is to run one RAS per available CPU core. Make sure to factor in any other services that might be sharing resources when deciding how many RAS instances to deploy.

Table 4.10 shows the parameters you can set for the RAS.

Option	Argument Units	Behavior	Recommended Setting(s)
Browse data size (records)	Number	Specifies the number of distinct records returned from the database when browsing through a particular field's values.	Default value is 100 records.
Idle connection timeout	Minutes	Specifies the amount of time, in minutes, that the RAS waits for requests from an idle client before timing out.	Default value is 30 minutes.
Batch size	Records	Specifies how many rows from the result set are returned by the database during each data transfer.	Default value is 100 records.
Number of database records to read when previewing or refreshing a report	Records	Specifies the number of database records that will be read when viewing or refreshing a report.	Default value is 20,000 (–1 for unlimited).
Maximum concurrent report jobs	Jobs	Specifies the maximum number of independent jobs allowed to run concurrently on the RAS.	Default is 75 (0 for unlimited).
Oldest on-demand data given to a client	Minutes	Specifies the amount of time, in minutes, an on-demand report will serve cached report data.	Default value is 20.

Table 4.10 Report Application Server Parameters (Source: Sizing Companion for SAP BusinessObjects BI 4.1)

4.1.11   Web Application Server

Last, but not least, we need to take some time to consider the configuration settings needed to get the most out of your favorite flavor of Web Application Server. The recommended settings are shown in Table 4.11.

Web Application Server	Java Heap Recommended Settings
Tomcat 6	Change the JVM heap size in the JAVA OPTIONS box. Add the line `-XX:MaxPermSize=256m`. Fill in the MAXIMUM MEMORY POOL field with the host server's total amount of memory.
WebLogic 10.0	`-Xms1024m -Xmx1024m -XX:MaxPermSize=512m`
Oracle Application Server 10gR3 (10.1.3.0)	`-Xms1024m -Xmx1024m`
SAP Composition Environment 7.20	Use default settings for SAP NetWeaver.
WebSphere Community Edition 2.0	Use default settings for WebSphere CE 2.0.
Tomcat 5.5	Change the JVM heap size in the JAVA OPTIONS box. Add the line: `-XX:MaxPermSize=512m` Fill in the MAXIMUM MEMORY POOL field with the host server's total amount of memory.
WebLogic 9.2.2	Update the following in the file (substitute your drive letter as appropriate): *C:\bea\user_ projects\domains\boe_domain\bin\ setDomainEnv.cmd* before starting up WebLogic. From: `MEM_ARGS="-Xms256m -Xmx512m"` To: `#MEM_ARGS="-Xms256m -Xmx512m"` `MEM_ARGS="-Xms820m -Xmx820m"` Also change the `MaxPermSize` under the JAVA_ VENDOR section inside `setDomainEnv.cmd`. From: `"-XX:MaxPermSize=128m"` To: `"-XX:MaxPermSize=512m"`

Table 4.11 Web Application Server Parameters (Source: Sizing Companion for SAP Business-Objects BI 4.1)

Web Application Server	Java Heap Recommended Settings
WebSphere 7.0	Use default settings for WebSphere 7.0.
WebLogic 10.3	`-Xms512 -Xmx1024m -XX:PermSize=256m` `-XX:MaxPermSize=1024m`
Sun Java System Application Server 9.1	Use default settings.
JBoss 5.0	`-Xms128m -Xmx512m -XX:MaxPermSize=256m`

Table 4.11 Web Application Server Parameters (Source: Sizing Companion for SAP Business-Objects BI 4.1) (Cont.)

As you can see from page after page of settings, there is a lot to tweak inside all of your different server processes. Pay closest attention to the services you need and will use the most, and configure those so they will perform the best for you.

> **Mark of Excellence**
>
> If there are servers or service categories of processes you won't be using in your environment or aren't licensed for, shut down and disable them. Leaving them running doesn't constitute a lot of overhead, but taken in total, it can add up to CPU, memory, and disk that is being wasted. It's best, and helps, to simplify your landscape (as well as your shutdown and startup times) to just shut down and disable servers you aren't using. For example, if you know you'll only be using Web Intelligence and not SAP Crystal Reports, shut down and disable all of the SAP Crystal Reports processes.

4.2 Taming the Adaptive Processing Server Beast

If you got through all of those settings and were left scratching your head thinking, "They missed a whole bunch of stuff," then you're correct. That's because the rest of the stuff is stuff that runs under the Adaptive Processing Server (APS). The APS is a special little monster and, as such, deserves a special section of its own. In fact, it's so special, that it has recently received its very own System Configuration Wizard! If you're new to the SAP BusinessObjects BI 4 game and starting with the most recent version, boy are you a lucky one! The System Configuration Wizard is SAP's response to the pain in the neck that used to be splitting the Adaptive Processing Server by hand. Now, in some cases, like really super-large deployments, or any complex SAP BusinessObjects BI landscape, you're probably better off still splitting the APS up by hand, and we have the steps to do it right here. But for a large majority of you reading this, the System Configuration Wizard is going to get the job done quickly and easily for you, and suit your needs just fine.

But just what is an Adaptive Processing Server? The APS has been around since the SAP BusinessObjects XI 3.1 days and was an early attempt at standardizing all of the various products (Web Intelligence, SAP Crystal Reports, Dashboards) into one standard grouping. The SAP BusinessObjects XI 3.1 version didn't really go very far. But, the APS in SAP BusinessObjects BI 4 isn't your granddaddy's APS. It's a lot different from the SAP BusinessObjects XI 3.1 version. It contains a lot more. It now closely resembles the junk drawer in your kitchen. You know the one drawer where you shove all the little odds and ends lying around that don't really deserve a place of their own? It's like that, only different. If you think about it from a packaging and delivery point of view, it makes sense that SAP would jam all these things together. They really are birds of a feather, in that they all process in some way, shape, or form, but beyond that, the variety of what will be needed at any given deployment site is just too wide and varied to deliver it configured any differently. But, an extremely common mistake is leaving the APS in this default delivery configuration. This is similar to buying some really nice furniture and having it delivered to your living room, but not taking it out of the packaging. It's really nice furniture underneath, but you're left sitting on plastic and cardboard. Ouch! So let's take an inventory of what we have in our junk drawer and work out a plan to organize it so we're planting our backsides firmly on the nice furniture we paid for.

Navigate to the SERVERS area of the CMC, and find the Adaptive Processing Server. Right-click on it, and choose EDIT COMMON SERVICES. You'll see something eerily similar to Figure 4.2.

Wow! Look at all those services! They don't even all fit in one window. If you read some of the not-so-fine print in the Sizing Companion for SAP BusinessObjects BI, you'll see that it pretty clearly states that if you don't care about performance, you should leave the APS like this. And who, pray tell, doesn't care about performance—even in a development or demo system?

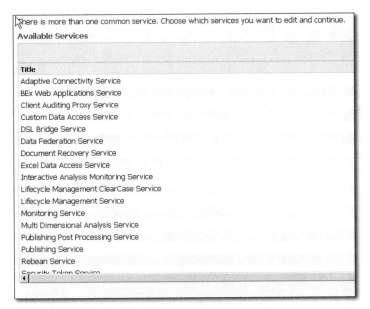

Figure 4.2 The Unsplit Adaptive Processing Server Beast

Your best bet is to split this bad boy up according to your specific performance needs. If Web Intelligence is critical for you, then you need to split out the Web Intelligence processes into their own APS. If you're into publications, split it. If you're into SAP Crystal Reports, multisource universes, split it. There are two ways you can go about splitting this bad boy up to best meet your needs. You can use the handy dandy new System Configuration Wizard, or you can do it the old-fashioned way, by hand. Ready? Great! Let's start with the System Configuration Wizard.

4.2.1 The Wonderful System Configuration Wizard of SAP Business-Objects BI 4.1

You asked for it, you got it. The SAP BusinessObjects BI 4.1 System Configuration Wizard was a direct response from SAP to answer the public outcry on how confusing and difficult the Adaptive Processing Server was to split and configure correctly. Despite the fact that it could cut a huge chunk out of this book, we're big fans of the System Configuration Wizard. It took something really hard and complicated, and made it pretty easy and painless.

For better or for worse, the SYSTEM CONFIGURATION WIZARD screen will be right there to greet you the first time you log in to the Central Management Console of any newly minted SAP BusinessObjects BI 4.1 system (see Figure 4.3).

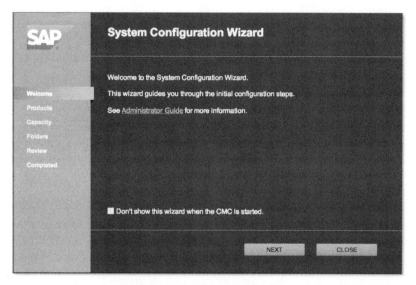

Figure 4.3 System Configuration Wizard Welcome Screen

You'll notice it has a little check box to suppress the Wizard for next time. Go ahead and click NEXT, and let's get this party started:

1. The first screen you land on is the PRODUCTS selection screen (see Figure 4.4). Here you can choose which of the various SAP BusinessObjects BI tools you plan to be using in this environment. Pick only the ones you need (you can always add some back later on). This will only install servers for the products you want to use. This saves space and precious server resources. Uncheck the boxes next to the products you aren't going to use, and then click NEXT.

2. Next up is the CAPACITY screen (see Figure 4.5). This screen assumes you've already done a sizing exercise, and you at least know the T-shirt size of your SAP BusinessObjects BI 4.1 deployment. It also has a couple of disclaimers on this screen about performing your sizing. It just wouldn't be an SAP product without disclaimers, would it? Use the slider bar to select the proper sizing for your server. If you aren't sure, there are several question mark buttons on this screen that link you to helpful information. It also has a few links to the SIZING COMPANION GUIDE. Choose wisely.

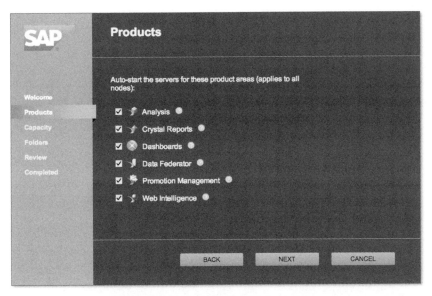

Figure 4.4 System Configuration Wizard: Products Selection Screen

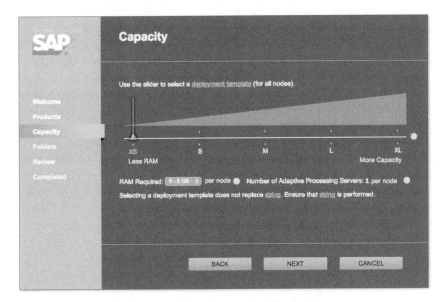

Figure 4.5 System Configuration Wizard: Capacity Selection Screen

3. The FOLDERS screen is a stroke of genius (see Figure 4.6). Here you can set up where you'd like to put the various things in a SAP BusinessObjects BI 4.1 system

that will take up disk space. This is especially handy in a clustered environment where you have to move all of these things anyway. Here's a one-stop shop.

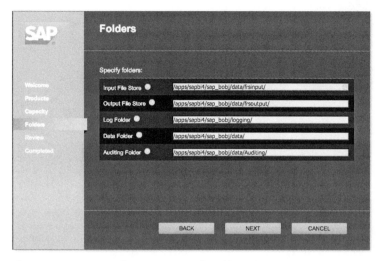

Figure 4.6 System Configuration Wizard: Folder Selection Screen

4. That was easy, wasn't it? So, now that you're about to make changes to your system, do yourself a favor and double-check your work on the REVIEW screen (see Figure 4.7 and Figure 4.8).

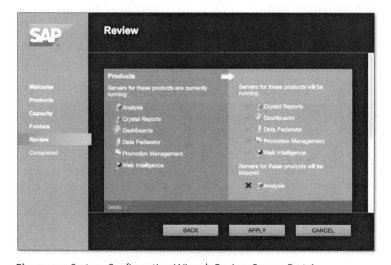

Figure 4.7 System Configuration Wizard: Review Screen Part 1

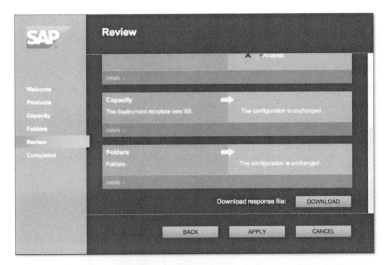

Figure 4.8 System Configuration Wizard: Review Screen Part 2

5. And just for good measure, you'll get asked one more time if you're sure that you want to make these changes (see Figure 4.9).

Figure 4.9 System Configuration Wizard Are You Sure Screen

6. After you click that APPLY button, the Wizard is off and running, doing much of the heavy lifting on splitting up that Adaptive Processing Server for you. When

it's done, it will give you a success or failure message, and provide a few links for you to use if you wish (see Figure 4.10).

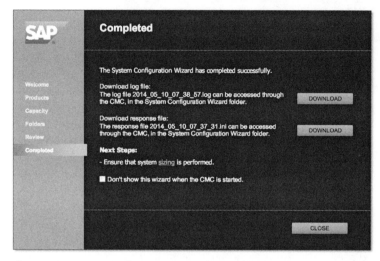

Figure 4.10 System Configuration Wizard Completed Screen

Here, you can download the log file for the Wizard transaction, and/or download the response file for this Wizard transaction. The response file is simply a file that contains all of your responses to the Wizard screens. If you need to configure another system exactly the same way, you can just use the response file the second time and make it even easier! Hey, SAP BusinessObjects BI 4.1 administrators, we'll take easier any day. We have enough complicated things to deal with on a daily basis.

That's it for the new System Configuration Wizard. It's clean, easy to use, and can save you a ton of time, but it's not a silver bullet or magic pill. While the Wizard is perfectly sufficient for smaller, less-complicated SAP BusinessObjects BI 4.1 deployments, it's not recommended for large, complex, distributed landscapes. For those, you'll still want to do it the "old-fashioned" way.

4.2.2 Going Old School—Splitting the Adaptive Processing Server By Hand

Still reading? Good! That means you want to learn how to split an APS like Grandpa did. By hand! There's something to be said for "Artisan APS Splitting." Let's dig into the nitty-gritty. One important thing to know before we get into how to split up the APS is how to remove services from the original big fella. As a best practice, you'll want to shut down the original APS and remove services from it as you create new ones that are split up. This will help you be precise in removing the services you want to run under their own APS instances. Split one out, and then go immediately back and take it out of the old APS — nice, neat, and tidy. After you stop the original APS, you'll see a new right-click option, SELECT SERVICES. Click that option, and you'll go into a big selection window where you can add or remove the services from the APS. It's a little tricky because SELECT SERVICES only appears when the APS is stopped.

Let's break down the major pieces of the APS that you'll want to split out. We'll cover publications, Web Intelligence, the Data Federation Service, Multi-Dimensional Analysis, SAP Crystal Reports, the Dashboards Server, Promotion Management, the Publishing Server, and the Monitoring Server. Then we'll wrap up with some general APS configuration considerations.

4.2.3 Publications

If you're into publication of reports, you'll want to have a separate Adaptive Processing Server with the Publishing Server and publishing post-processing server for every three concurrent publications. You'll want to set each publishing APS to have a 1GB heap size by adding -Xmx1024M into the command line under PROPERTIES. At 1GB of memory a pop, you can see how this could start getting large quickly. This is where you hopefully paid attention in Chapter 2.

4.2.4 Web Intelligence APS Services

Web Intelligence has two services in the default APS that you need to pay attention to. If you use Web Intelligence, you'll want to split one or both of the following services out into one or more new APS instances:

- DSL Bridge Service (BICS connector)
- Visualization Service (CVOM Charting Library Service for Web Intelligence)

DSL Bridge Service

The DSL Bridge Connector is designed to use the maximum memory available for concurrent requests, and there is no way to put a governor on that service. Watch this one very carefully, especially during peak usage times. Keep in mind that this service is used to connect to two different types of services, SAP Business Warehouse (SAP BW; the infamous BICS connector) and any of your new-type .unx universes. If you don't have SAP BW and aren't going to use the .unx, then skip ahead. If you do, then read on.

The minimum recommended heap size for this guy is 4GB; 8GB of memory or more is preferred. And if you're a heavy consumer of SAP Business Explorer (BEx) queries, you might want to consider having the DSL Bridge APS Service on its own server node (as a part of the overall cluster). If you're new to this and want to be conservative, it's best to start small, test it out, and then scale up as needed. Keep in mind that the maximum memory heap for this service is 30GB of memory! Whoa!

Split the DSL Bridge Service out into its own APS, but with this one, you'll also need to add a couple of other services it depends on:

▶ Adaptive Connectivity Service

▶ Custom Data Access Service

▶ Excel Data Access Service

Put all three into their own APS, and don't forget to go right back and remove them from the original APS. In the CMC, under PROPERTIES, add one of the following to the end of the command-line parameters:

▶ -Xmx8192 for an 8GB memory heap

▶ -Xmx4096 for a 4GB memory heap

Visualization Service (CVOM Charting Library Service for Web Intelligence)

The Visualization Service is dedicated to Web Intelligence and has the dubious honor of being responsible for creating all of those beautiful charts that are displayed in a Web Intelligence document, including the notorious exploding pie chart. Split the Visualization Service out into its own APS, and bump the heap size up to 2GB at a minimum. In the CMC, under PROPERTIES, at the end of the line, add -Xmx2048M to the command-line parameters. As stated earlier, start small and scale up if you see your utilization getting too high. The Visualization Service doesn't have any dependent services and should be alone in its own APS instance.

4.2.5 Data Federation Service

Once upon a time, this used to be a separate product called Data Federator. Now it's a part of the enterprise, and this guy is responsible for the magic behind your multisource universes. It allows for joins of disparate data in memory—it's memory. So, you'd better make sure this guy has his own memory and plenty of it. As you can imagine, federating data can be an intensive operation. Split the Data Federation Service out into a separate APS along with the BEx Web Applications Service, which it depends on. Bump the heap up to 4GB to start. Go into the CMC, and at the end of the command-line parameters, add -Xmx4096M. See Section 4.3 for some more information on the Data Federation Service and how to best configure it for great performance.

4.2.6 Multi-Dimensional Analysis Server

The Multi-Dimensional Analysis Server (MDAS) is the engine behind your analysis for OLAP reports. This is another potentially huge resource consumer, so this one gets to go to Splitsville with the original Adaptive Processing Server. You'll want one MDAS running for every 15 active-concurrent users of SAP BusinessObjects Analysis, edition for OLAP. And each MDAS should have a 4GB memory heap. In the CMC, at the end of the command-line parameters, add -Xmx4096M.

4.2.7 SAP Crystal Reports Servers

Depending on which of the SAP Crystal Reports products you're using (or perhaps both), you'll want to split out the SAP Crystal Reports processes as well.

For SAP Crystal Reports 2013, pull out the SAP Crystal Reports 2013 Processing Service into its own process. Also, pull out the SAP Crystal Reports 2013 Viewing and Modification Process so it's running on its own as well.

For SAP Crystal Reports Enterprise, pull out the Crystal Reports Processing Service and the SAP Crystal Reports Cache Service both into separate, individual processes.

4.2.8   Dashboards Design Server

If you're using SAP BusinessObjects Dashboards, then pull out the Dashboards Design Processing Server and Dashboards Design Cache Server into their own processes.

4.2.9   Promotion Management Server

You'll want to pull the Promotion Management processes out of the main APS as well, but you can bundle them together. Make one process that contains the Promotion Management Services, Visual Difference Service, and Promotion Management ClearCase Service.

4.2.10   Monitoring Server

The SAP BusinessObjects BI 4.1 monitoring engine does some pretty amazing things, as you'll see in Chapter 7, but the server just doesn't run well bundled in that junk drawer APS. Pull the Monitoring Server out into its own process.

4.2.11   General Adaptive Processing Server Considerations

When you create a new APS, the default name that comes up is simply ADAPTIVE-PROCESSINGSERVERX, where X is an iterative number of how many APS instances you've created. Do yourself a huge favor. Don't use those default names. Give each APS instance you create a meaningful name so when you look at it in six months, you won't have to wonder, "What is APS6 running?" Name the APS for what it is (i.e., Web Intelligence Visualization, DSL Bridge, etc.). You'll thank yourself down the road. It will likely be helpful as well to prefix the server names with "APS" to keep them grouped within the server list inside the CMC.

> **Don't Split the Adaptive Job Server!**
>
> In previous versions of the sizing recommendations from SAP and in the previous edition of this book, it was recommended that the Adaptive Job Server be split out in the same fashion as the Adaptive Processing Server (for every set of individual Adaptive Processing Servers, split out a matching Adaptive Job Server). This is no longer the case. The best way to configure the Adaptive Job Server is to leave it alone. You want one AJS per processing tier server. Just make sure it has plenty of memory to use to get your scheduling work done. It will spawn child services to expand itself as big as it's allowed to go based on the amount of memory you allocate to the service.

4.3   Multisource Universe Preparation and the Data Federation Administration Tool

Multisource universes were arguably one of the most highly anticipated features of the entire SAP BusinessObjects BI 4.0 release. For many years, the Universe Design Tool has remained largely unchanged and minimally improved. As the BI industry grew and changed around it, this pillar remained a stalwart reminder of what we used to be. One of the most frustrating features of the old universe is the fact that it could only use one database connection at a time. Those days are over.

SAP BusinessObjects BI 4.1 actually comes with two universe-related tools. You get the new one, the Information Design Tool, which does the new fancy multi-source magic. You also get an updated version of the old one, the Universe Design Tool. At first, you might scratch your head and ask, "Why did they do that?" And you'd be asking a valid question. SAP bundled both because, unfortunately, the Information Design Tool is so radically different from the Universe Design Tool that the two types of universes aren't compatible with one another. There is no way to import or migrate your old universe files (which have a .unv extension) into the new universe files (which have a .unx extension).

Thankfully, there is a version of the old Universe Design Tool that comes along with the SAP BusinessObjects BI 4.1 client tools installation so you can maintain your old universes (which you can migrate up, and they work perfectly well) while you get to work on creating some multisource UNX goodness.

Multisource universes are brought to you by the product formerly known as Data Federator. In a time not long gone by, this was a separate tool in the SAP Business-Objects BI stack. It was used for a relatively unique purpose: to eliminate the need for extraction, transformation, and loading (ETL), at least to some degree.

Think of the old way of doing things, where you have various disparate data sources around the company. For example, imagine you have a transactional system in DB2, an HRIS system in Microsoft SQL Server, and an accounting system in Sybase ASE. If your reporting teams wanted to create reports that joined up all of that data together in a couple of different ways, you really had only one choice. You would have to use ETL to create extracts of data from all of those data sources, then transform the data so each data source matched up nicely with similar data being called the same thing, and you would then have to load that data into a central repository somewhere like a data mart or data warehouse. If it sounds long and complicated, that's because it is. This type of project could take months, with a couple of resources being tied up on it full-time. And chances are that the reporting analysts might not even know what all of that data is going to look like after you put it all together. So, the whole process could be for naught.

Now, let's think about the Data Federator way of doing things. Data Federator takes the place of that whole middle tier of complex processes. It allows you to tie all of those disparate data sources into one common layer and do your joins and "transforms" all in its memory. This method is faster to develop and easier than the old one.

As of SAP BusinessObjects BI 4.0, Data Federator is now built into the platform. You no longer have to use a separate product to get this cool functionality. Data Federation Services is the whole basis by which the multisource universe works.

Now you can also imagine that bringing a whole bunch of different data sources into memory and doing ETL-like joins in memory sounds like an infrastructure challenge. Setting up Data Federation Services takes some careful planning and some keen configuration, but for you, dear administrator, the future is now.

Content Federation versus Data Federation

Content federation is a totally different animal. This is the process by which reporting content is moved from one SAP BusinessObjects BI system to another, typically not in a cluster. Why would you want to do that? This type of federation comes in handy when you have multiple SAP BusinessObjects BI 4.1 deployments in a global environment. In this type of Wide Area Network (WAN) architecture landscape, clustering servers that are physically located in different countries around the globe isn't recommended. The WAN traffic those cluster nodes would generate would be just as much as if they were all in the same room together, and they would be exponentially slower. Imagine you're in Spain, and you log in to an SAP BusinessObjects BI server that's hosted in Hong Kong, and you try and run a report. Ugly picture? Yep.

Content federation helps to solve this problem. The Replication Service inside the SAP BusinessObjects BI 4.1 platform drives it. You set up origin and destination sites and

---

schedule your replication jobs to run when it's convenient for you. So, back to our example: You're in your office in Spain, and every morning you need a report from the database that is located in Hong Kong. Your highly thoughtful and intelligent SAP Business-Objects BI administrator has that report you need scheduled to run from the system in Hong Kong and a federation job to push that report instance to your SAP Business-Objects BI server in Spain, all while you sleep. When you come in each morning, your report is ready and waiting for you, and it opens up blazingly fast because all of the heavy lifting was already done for you.

Earlier we discussed splitting out the Data Federation Server from the Adaptive Processing Server monster and giving it its own Java heap so it has some room to work. But now we have to spend a little time talking about how to actually make those multisource queries you wrote move a little faster.

As an obvious homage to "If it ain't broke, don't fix it," SAP left the old, separate Data Federation Administration Tool as a thick client tool. In this section, we'll walk you through the highlights of this tool.

Note

For more information about the Data Federation Administration Tool, we recommend *BusinessObjects Platform Administrator Guide*, SAP's guide for administrators, which can be found on the SAP Help Portal.

4.3.1 Introduction to the Data Federation Administration Tool

If you're already trying to locate the tool, you'll find it among the various other applications that come with the client tools installation (see Figure 4.11).

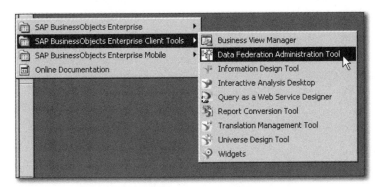

Figure 4.11 The Data Federation Administration Tool Location

This tool will allow you to administer aspects of the Data Federation Service that are specific to the way the service treats data. This includes managing properties of connectors to specific data sources, configuring memory, or setting parameters that affect queries on the Data Federation Query Engine.

With this tool, you can browse and manage connectors, browse data sources and run queries against them, manage statistics, and view the lists of past queries and running queries. This can obviously be useful in a production system to have visibility into what queries are running at any given time. The Data Federation Administration Tool doesn't allow you to manage user accounts or handle logging. That is done from within the Central Management Console.

The Data Federation Administration Tool can also be used for tuning when you want to adapt your connectors or your queries to the data in your data sources. Tuning involves setting capabilities of each connector to make it pass as much work as possible to each data source, setting appropriate statistics for each data source, and configuring parameters to optimize each query that is sent to the server. Optimization typically means making your data sources do as much processing as possible and sending as little data over the network as possible. The Data Federation Service has multiple options for pushing work to sources and reducing data transfer, as well as tools that help you understand how the system is processing your queries.

To grant users access to the Data Federation Administration Tool, you'll first have to assign them the proper rights. Head on over to the Central Management Console and add the needed users into the Data Federation Administrators group. Members of this group have access to the tool. The tool requires a login to the CMS just like all of the other client-based tools. After you're in, you'll land on the WELCOME page (see Figure 4.12).

OVERVIEW is much of what was just described above. WEB RESOURCES takes you to the SAP Business Analytics web page for more information. The real meat and potatoes are inside the GO TO ADMINISTRATION WINDOWS link (see Figure 4.13).

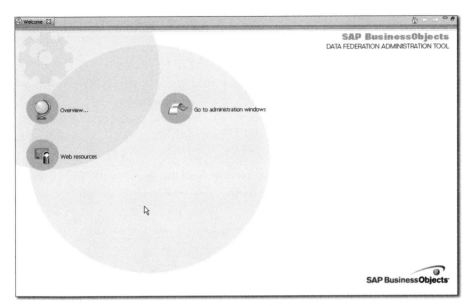

Figure 4.12 Data Federation Administration Tool Welcome Page

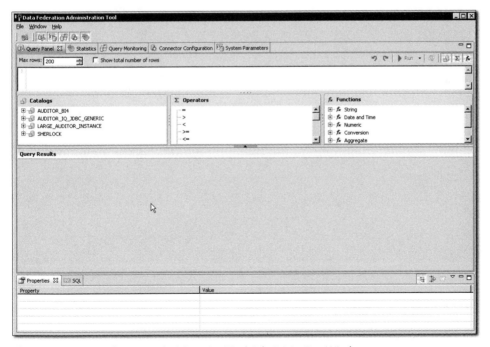

Figure 4.13 Data Federation Administration Tool Administration Windows

The QUERY PANEL tab allows you to test your multisource SQL queries. Enter the query in the white box, and click RUN to execute. When it finishes, the results will be, surprisingly, displayed in the QUERY RESULTS pane.

If you're the cautious type, you can also choose to explain the query without actually executing it. The tool will analyze your SQL queries and decide how to translate them so that you get the correct data from multiple data sources as fast as possible. To perform this analysis, the query engine distributes as much work as possible among the data sources and writes sub-queries to fetch as little data over the network as is needed to produce the final result. Explaining the query first is typically wise if you're working on a brand new query and you're not sure what the result set is going to look like. To run an explain query, enter your query in the pane as before, but click the little dropdown arrow next to the RUN button and choose EXPLAIN QUERY (see Figure 4.14).

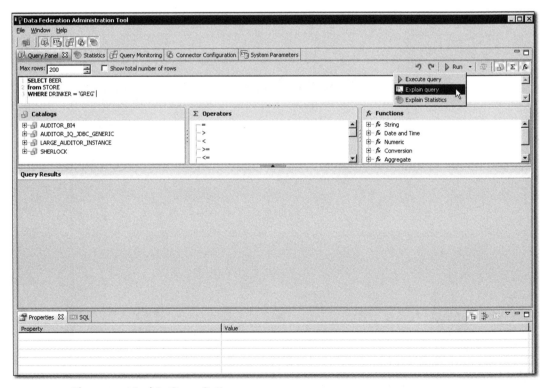

Figure 4.14 Explain Query Option

As far as the Query Panel goes, Table 4.12 gives a more concise list of all of the different things you might need to know about it.

Panel	Description
SQL TEXT	Where you can type your SQL query. You can insert elements into your query by double-clicking or dragging and dropping from the CATALOGS, OPERATORS, and FUNCTIONS panels. The controls include the following: ► MAX ROWS: The maximum number of rows to retrieve. ► SHOW TOTAL NUMBER OF ROWS: Specifies whether or not to show the total number of rows in the result, even if you don't retrieve all of them.
CATALOGS	Shows all existing catalogs on the Data Federation Service.
OPERATORS	Shows list of all possible operators.
FUNCTIONS	Shows list of available functions grouped by categories.
QUERY RESULTS	Container for query results; displayed when you run a query by clicking RUN.
RAW DATA	Shows raw data results of the last query run; displayed when you click RUN or EXECUTE.
AUTO CHARTS	Simple chart (pie) presentation of query results; displayed when you click RUN or EXECUTE.
QUERY PLAN	Shows the query plan without executing the query; displayed when you click EXPLAIN QUERY. Contains two internal panels: ► PLAN: Shows the plan structure as a tree view. ► DETAILS: Shows the details about the selected node in the PLAN panel. You can find more details about the selected nodes in the properties view.

Table 4.12 Query Panel (Source: Data Federation Administration Tool Guide)

For the complete list of detailed descriptions of the Query Panel and all of the various buttons and contextual menus, see the *Data Federation Service Sizing and Tuning Companion Guide* for SAP BusinessObjects BI 4.1.

If you already have users or applications that have sent multisource queries to the Data Federation Server, you can see the list of those queries using the Data Federation Administration Tool. Hop on over to the QUERY MONITORING tab, and under the STATUS field, click the dropdown and choose EXECUTED QUERIES. This will populate a list of historical queries for your review.

The QUERY MONITORING tab also gives you the ability to cancel a query. If, for example, you decided not to take our advice and explain a query before running it, and it turns out you unleashed a monster on your database systems, you do have the ability to back it out. From the QUERY MONITORING tab, choose RUNNING QUERIES from the STATUS field, find your monster query in the list pane, right-click the query, and choose CANCEL (see Figure 4.15, Figure 4.16, and Figure 4.17).

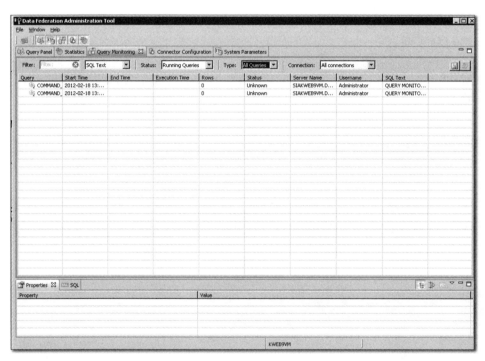

Figure 4.15 Viewing Executed Queries

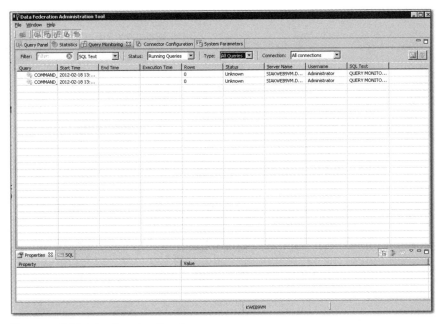

Figure 4.16 Viewing Running Queries

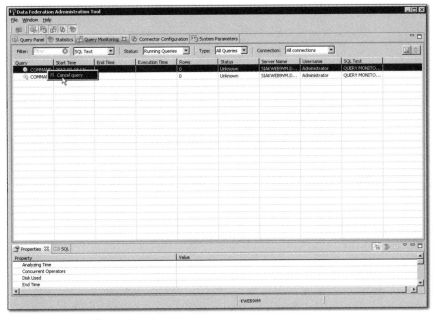

Figure 4.17 Cancelling a Running Query

Table 4.13 gives you the basics you'll need to know about the QUERY MONITOR-ING tab.

Column Name	Description
QUERY	The ID of the query or subquery. The different icons are listed here: ▶ RUNNING: The query is running. ▶ CLOSED SUCCESS: The query is closed and has succeeded. ▶ CLOSED FAILED: The query is closed and has failed. You can use the PROPERTIES view to see the exception.
START TIME	Start time of the query execution.
END TIME	End time of the query execution.
EXECUTION TIME	The elapsed time between the start and end time of execution.
ROWS	The number of rows extracted by the query.
STATUS	The query statuses: ▶ ANALYZING: The query is being analyzed by the Federation Engine. ▶ EXECUTING: The query is being executed by the Federation Engine. ▶ CLOSED: The query closed (either success or failure).
SERVER NAME	The name of the server that handles the query.
USERNAME	The name of the user who launched the query.
SQL TEXT	The SQL text of the query.

Table 4.13 Query Monitoring Tab (Source: Data Federation Administration Tool Guide)

For the complete list of detailed descriptions of the QUERY MONITORING panel and all of the various buttons and contextual menus, see the *Data Federation Service Sizing and Tuning Companion Guide* for SAP BusinessObjects BI 4.1, which can be found on the SAP Help Portal.

There are several techniques you can use to tune the performance of your data federation queries. In order of the degree of efficacy, those strategies are listed here:

▶ Use system parameters to optimize the use of memory.

▶ Use statistics to let the application choose the best algorithms for querying sources.

▸ If the application didn't automatically activate the semi-join operator, verify if you can change the parameters to activate the semi-join.

▸ If the semi-join isn't appropriate, verify if you can change parameters to activate the merge join.

▸ If your data supports capabilities that are disabled by default, activate the capabilities in your connector.

For example, while DB2 doesn't support predictable ordering of null values, if you know that your data has no nulls, you can still use a merge join. In this case, set the capabilities of the source to force it to perform an ORDER BY.

As a side note, if you're going to promote your data foundation to another system and you've changed system parameters to optimize the query against the data foundation, you also need to promote the system parameters. You can use the Promotion Management console for SAP BusinessObjects BI to do this.

4.3.2   System Parameters that Optimize the Use of Memory

System parameters are the most effective way to boost your query performance. You can change those settings from the SYSTEM PARAMETERS tab in the DATA FEDERATION ADMINISTRATION TOOL (see Figure 4.18).

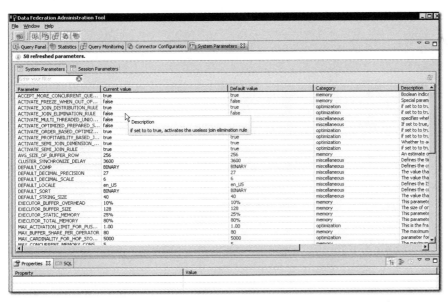

Figure 4.18 System Parameters Tab of the Data Federation Administration Tool

The following strategies will help you get the most out of your system memory:

- Set the amount of memory used by the Java virtual machine (JVM) that is running your Data Federation Server. See Section 4.2.3 for specifics.

- Set the server parameter EXECUTOR_TOTAL_MEMORY. This parameter lets you configure the amount of memory used for query execution. Set it either as a percentage of memory used by the JVM or as a fixed value with a suffix defining the unit of measure (e.g., 512MB, 512MB, 1024KB, or 1024kb). If you use a fixed value, it must be lower than the total number allocated for the JVM.

- Set the server parameter EXECUTOR_STATIC_MEMORY. This parameter lets you set the minimal amount of memory allocated to operators upon initialization. You can also set this as a percentage or a fixed value. And again, if you used the fixed value, it must be lower than the total allocated to the JVM.

- Set the server parameter MAX_CONCURRENT_MEMORY_CONSUMING_QUERIES. This setting defines the number of queries that consume memory that can run concurrently. Other queries aren't affected. Select a small value for this setting if you have many large queries. Select a large value if you have many small queries.

- Set the server parameter MAX_CONCURRENT_MEMORY_CONSUMING_OPERATORS. This parameter limits how many operators that consume memory can run in parallel. Decrease this number if the operators in your queries are consuming too much memory. You can approximate the average size and number of large tables in different data sources accessed. For example, four large tables in different data sources in one mapping rule result in three joins that consume memory.

Walking through all of these settings in an example might help make this a little clearer. Suppose we set the total JVM memory to 1,000MB, which will allocate 1,000MB of memory to the JVM. Following the preceding guides, we'll then set EXECUTOR_TOTAL_MEMORY to 80% to allocate 800MB of memory for the query execution. Next we'll set EXECUTOR_STATIC_MEMORY to 25% to allocate 200MB of memory for each operator. And finally, we'll set MAX_CONCURRENT_MEMORY_CONSUMING_QUERIES to 2, which will limit concurrent operators to two.

With the settings like this, two queries will be able to run concurrently, and each will have 100MB of minimal memory, and each will be able to access a dynamic pool of 600MB of memory.

4.3.3 Operators That Consume Memory

The following operators are the main consumers of memory on your Data Federation Server when you use them in your queries:

- `Join`
- `Cartesian product`
- `Orderby`
- `Groupby`
- `Groupby` (when you have a lot of different values in the group; i.e., a large group set)

The Data Federation Query Engine doesn't use a significant amount of memory when it performs scans of tables, projections, filters, and function evaluations or when it pushes the operations down to the source databases.

4.3.4 Using Statistics to Let the Application Choose the Best Algorithms for Querying Sources

The Data Federation Query Engine internally uses statistics to optimize queries. Statistics aren't refreshed continuously. In your production system, where performance matters the most, run the statistics gather process. Then, any subsequent query plan will take them into consideration.

The statistics subsystem is made up of two parts:

- A tool that computes cardinalities from the measures that are known at the data source level.
- A recorder that counts the number of times a table or attribute is requested when a query is executed.

You can override cardinalities with manual values to influence their usage in optimizing query plans.

Cardinality is the number of rows in a column. You can measure cardinality on other elements, too. It's possible to measure cardinality for a table, for a schema that contains tables, or for an entire catalog. In each case, talking about the cardinality of the object is a shortcut for talking about the cardinalities of all the objects it contains. For example, if we say that the cardinality of a schema is 1,000, then we mean that most of the columns in most tables of the schema have 1,000 rows.

When working with the Data Federation Service, the system can optimize its queries better with more accurate cardinality of the columns in the data sources. For this reason, the Data Federation Query Engine can estimate the cardinalities of the sources of data but also allows you to set the cardinalities if you know them better. Estimating and setting cardinalities is part of the optimization task of gathering statistics.

Another task of gathering statistics is estimating and setting fanout values. The *fanout* measures an association between the data in two columns. If there are two columns, then for each distinct value in the first column, the fanout is the average number of values in the second column. For example, if one column lists countries and the other column lists cities, then the fanout can measure the average number of cities for each country. When you're working with the Data Federation Service, the query engine can optimize its queries better the more precisely it knows the fanout of the columns in the sources of data.

Because gathering statistics can be a resource-intensive process, you have the ability to compute only those statistics that your queries need to speed up your process. The following example of gathering statistics is based on the refresh of a Web Intelligence document, but the process stays the same for any content type.

1. Inside the BI Launch Pad, open the Web Intelligence document in EDIT mode. In the DATA ACCESS tab, click EDIT (see Figure 4.19).

Figure 4.19 Editing Data Providers

2. In the QUERY PANEL, click VIEW SCRIPT, copy the SQL of the query to the clipboard, and close the Web Intelligence document (see Figure 4.20).

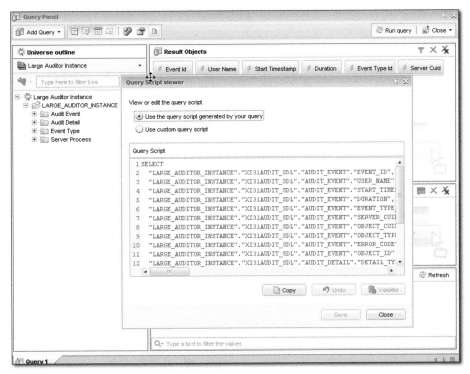

Figure 4.20 The Query Script Viewer in the Web Intelligence Query Panel

3. In the DATA FEDERATION ADMINISTRATION TOOL, paste the SQL in the text area of the QUERY PANEL tab, and then click RUN (see Figure 4.21).

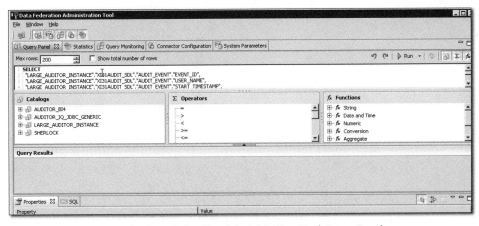

Figure 4.21 SQL Text in the Data Federation Administration Tool Query Panel

4. In the STATISTICS tab, click the REFRESH STATISTICS FROM SERVER button. The tables and columns that are used to optimize your query are recorded in the NUMBER OF REQUESTS column.

5. In the STATISTICS tab, make sure that the value of the filter in the NUMBER OF REQUESTS column is set to RECORDED (see Figure 4.22).

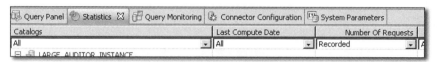

Figure 4.22 Setting the Number of Requests to Recorded

6. Press ⌨Ctrl and click to select all the rows with a value in the NUMBER OF REQUESTS column, and then click the COMPUTE button. The Data Federation Administration Tool computes only those statistics that are useful to your query (see Figure 4.23).

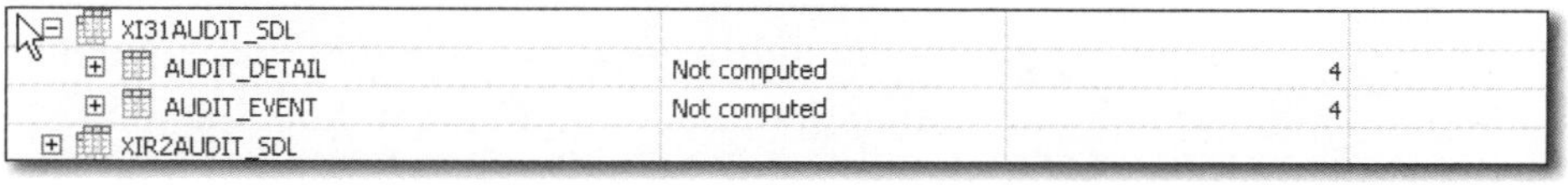

Figure 4.23 Finding the Tables with Recorded Requests

7. Run the actual query by refreshing the Web Intelligence document. The Data Federation Query Engine will now use the gathered statistics and generate an optimal query plan (see Figure 4.24).

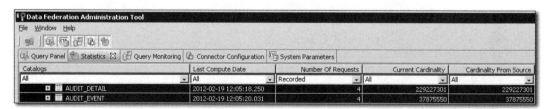

Figure 4.24 Statistics Computed

If you were sitting there thinking this sounds pretty complicated, and a lot like a database administrator job, you'd be right. In many ways, this tool is replacing some database functionality. Just because you're taking that stuff out of the database doesn't mean it doesn't still need to be managed. If you're not the DBA type yourself, you probably want to enlist the help of someone who is. Having properly tuned multisource queries is the "secret sauce" in your recipe for reporting success.

Pop Quiz
1. Which client tool manages federated data sources in SAP BusinessObjects BI 4.1?
2. What technique is used to analyze a query's behavior before it's executed?
3. What characteristic of the query engine is used to make querying more intelligent?
4. What is content federation?
5. What is data federation?

4.4   Configuration Best Practices

Best practices mature with age, like a great single-malt scotch. Industry-accepted best practices are certainly out there. But also, you'll learn that best practices will emerge based on your end users' usage of the tools, the growth trends and tuning needs that arise, and as the technologies mature and comingle with other enterprise technologies. We should spend some time walking through some good practices on configuration, whether we've hit them in earlier chapters or will hit them again later:

▶ Another golden rule to remember when it comes to configuration is to use only what you need. SAP BusinessObjects BI 4.1 is like a massive cruise liner. It can offer you speed and luxury on the high seas. If you only need a pontoon boat, you don't need to pay the fuel costs for the ocean liner. Make sure you enable the services you need to get your job done and shut down and disable the rest. If you do shut something down, make sure to unselect the START THIS SERVICE WHEN THE SERVER INTELLIGENCE AGENT STARTS checkbox so it stays off after a reboot. Oh yeah, you'll be rebooting. For example, if you're a Web Intelligence-only shop, then you don't need to be running any of the SAP Crystal Reports processes, let alone waste the time configuring them. All too often, people leave all of those processes running needlessly, and even though they aren't being used, they will consume some of your server resources. This is especially true in SAP BusinessObjects BI 4.1. After a process starts up, it will reserve a chunk of memory for its own use. That's memory that could be used for something that is actually doing some work. Do yourself a favor and tighten up your deployment by shutting down unnecessary services.

▶ It's easy to forget that SAP BusinessObjects BI 4.1 is a 64-bit process, especially if you've been working with the product for many years. There are a lot of changes in the way things are done because of that. Remember that with your various Processing Servers, you only need to have one per server host because they can spawn child processes until the system dies of a stroke. The days of multiple processing services are a thing of the past. Don't add multiples! In large, heavily used environments, consider having a server node dedicated just to processing. Your other services will thank you. If you do have a dedicated processing machine, set all of your maximum simultaneous report jobs to unlimited, and let that monster flex out. Your users will thank you.

▶ It's always important to keep all of your other component configurations in mind. Make sure you're using supported versions of your operating systems, web browsers, databases, application servers, and especially your local Java runtime environment.

▶ On any client computer that is going to use the SAP BusinessObjects BI 4.1 client tools or access the BI Launch Pad in its browser, it's really important that the computer has the proper version of Java installed. Check the Product Availability Matrix if you're unsure. In many cases, it's best to uninstall Java completely from the client workstation, and then have the user log in to the BI Launch Pad and create a new Web Intelligence report. The user will get prompted then to install Java, and it will push the proper, supported version down from the SAP BusinessObjects BI server. Also make sure to turn auto-updating off on the Java applet options in your Control Panel. Under the UPDATE tab of the JAVA CONTROL PANEL, unselect the CHECK FOR UPDATES AUTOMATICALLY checkbox, and when it warns you about the folly of what you're about to do, tell it to NEVER CHECK (see Figure 4.25). Auto-updating Java will cause you issues because at some point, a version will creep in that isn't compatible with SAP BusinessObjects BI 4.1, and you'll have upset users.

▶ Create a build sheet. By that, we mean that you should have a plan based on the tool requirements for your BI solution that lays out the servers, the services on each, and any nonstandard tuning you need to accommodate for. And keep it documented as to when and why the change was made.

▶ Take custom builds in your environments, and do your best to ensure that your development, test, and production environments follow that build plan. This will ensure consistency in testing and that content will behave as you expect between migrations.

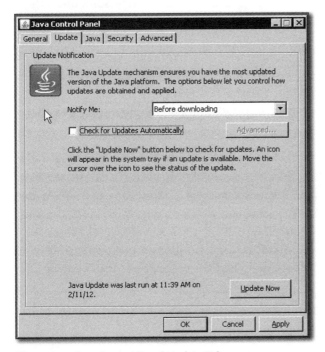

Figure 4.25 Java Control Panel Update Tab

One of the better ideas of the past few years is automatically updating software. This helps users stay up-to-date with the latest and greatest patches, fixes, and security on all of their favorite software components. Unfortunately, SAP Business-Objects BI 4.1 doesn't have this feature, which means that as your operating system, web browsers, Java applet, and so on are all getting updates on a periodic basis, SAP BusinessObjects BI 4.1 isn't (not automatically anyway). You can very easily have these other components update themselves right off the Product Availability Matrix and become unsupported.

Pop Quiz

1. Why should you *not* leave all servers up and running at all costs?

4.5 Summary

Configuration is another one of those fluid topics, and it can make your head spin a bit. Keep in mind that every installation of SAP BusinessObjects BI 4.1 is different. Each customer that lays it down does it in a different way. Sometimes those differences are slight, and other times they are radical. The key to your success is to make sure it's configured properly for your business needs. No one book, white paper, or administration guide can tell you what that is. Whether you're using Windows or Linux, Microsoft SQL Server or IBM DB2, you use what is best for you or what is available for you because of a company standard. There is no substitute for benchmarking your own installation and configuration and adjusting accordingly. Only you can say what is going to work best in your environment.

Take the configuration advice here in that spirit. Nothing is carved in stone. These are merely recommendations on what has worked at the testing labs at SAP and what has worked in some customer installations. Knowing which parts of the enterprise apply to you (Web Intelligence, SAP Crystal Reports, Dashboards, etc.) and configuring those most important parts for optimum performance in your environment under your workloads will yield the greatest results.

Securing your data is critically important, and the complexity of SAP BusinessObjects security can be daunting. In this chapter, we break it down and help you make sense of it so that putting a sound security model in place will be painless.

5 Security: Laying Down the Law

Security is a touchy thing. We all need it, yet we all complain about it, too. How many different user name and password combinations do you have to remember? Are they all on sticky notes deftly tucked under your keyboard? Security is like air. You don't need it anymore after you're dead. But also like air, the best security models are invisible to the end user. Put simply, your goal should be to secure what needs to be secured in a way that is the least disruptive to your user experience. Of course, that's easy to say and much harder to actually do.

Security has always been important when it comes to company information, but over the past decade, that importance has really come to the forefront of company awareness. As we interconnected computers via Local Area Networks (LANs), and then even more via the Internet, it very soon became apparent that some would not rest until they were able to cause digital chaos. Computer viruses, zombie computers (not the brain-hungry kind), and hacking became part of the common global lexicon. As work computers shifted, and the laptop became standard, the challenge of security literally grew legs. Connecting computers is a good thing. It allows us to share information quickly with sources we used to have challenges reaching. It allows us to see what is happening in our business right now, this very minute, or second. It even now allows us to get this information when we're not at our desk, or even without a traditional computer system. Portability and mobility are also good things. Our ability to work is no longer tied to a wooden desk, a clunky desktop computer, and a landline telephone. We can work anywhere, anytime, and always be in touch. With each "next best thing" the need for security becomes even greater. Just watch the evening news any day of the week. Nearly every month, we hear about another company data breach: credit card banks, online retailers, and news and intelligence agencies. It happens far too often. For most companies, the proprietary business data stored in company data stores and data warehouses is the lifeblood of the company. These data stores contain trade secrets, customer data, and all sorts of things that companies and consumers would rather remained private. Data is business.

SAP BusinessObjects BI is now in the forefront of that corporate data access. As businesses become more and more dependent on BI and analytics, more and more of the SAP BusinessObjects system gets used. That means more of your extremely valuable customer and business information is being aggregated, summarized, and analyzed by more and more users. And with each report that is opened, refreshed, and used, you run the risk of a data breach, plain and simple.

Enough with the gloom and doom! Building a good security model isn't "mission impossible." You can protect your data and allow your business users to access what they need to make their critical business decisions securely. SAP BusinessObjects security is mature and robust and allows you to mold your security model in a way that makes sense for you.

Security is more than just rights. Security, more holistically, is about protecting your sensitive business data from unauthorized access. Rights are a part of security, but only one part. Other parts of the security puzzle include firewalls, cryptography, reverse-proxies, and the Secure Sockets Layer (SSL). We'll discuss them each, but let's start with rights.

5.1 User and Content Management

Let's start off with another golden rule. If you're new to SAP BusinessObjects BI security, then put any shame aside, and say this phrase out loud to yourself 10 times: "Principals have rights to objects." Go on, don't be shy!

This is important because it will help reinforce the proper names for the things you're about to be doing. All done? Good! Time to break down the lingo and explain:

▶ **Principals**
These are people, that is, users (typically human, but not a requirement). A principal can also be a group, which is really just a bunch of people.

▸ **Rights**

There are only three rights you can have, which we'll go over in just a bit: GRANTED, DENIED, and NOT SPECIFIED.

▸ **Objects**

This is your content, such as reports, dashboards, universes, and connections. Anything you load into your SAP BusinessObjects BI system that is meant to be used by a user in some way, shape, or form is an object.

We'll start with principals, or your users. If you don't have any users, you don't really have a BI system, right? Skynet isn't self-aware just yet. Every person that needs to access SAP BusinessObjects BI content will need to be authenticated in some way. There are several ways to authenticate a user, the details of which are coming. The main reasons for authenticating a user are to determine if that person is allowed to access the system at all, and if he is, what content he is allowed to see and use. Users log in, see a report they need, launch it, and see the data. *Principals have rights to objects*.

While it may be pointing out the obvious, note that all of the assignment and management of user accounts and rights will be taking place from within the CMC. Now before you go off and start clicking things in the CMC, there are some key concepts you'll need to understand first. We'll cover all of the essentials of rights hierarchy, rights inheritance, and rights overrides.

5.1.1 Hierarchy of Rights

The first thing to get under your belt is a solid understanding of how rights are applied. As with any ordered system in existence, there is a hierarchy in place that is critical to understand. After you get this down, the rest all starts to fall into place. There are three levels of rights that can be assigned to a principal: DENIED, GRANTED, and NOT SPECIFIED. Figure 5.1 shows how this hierarchy works.

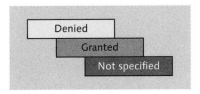

Figure 5.1 Rights Hierarchy

To explain a little further, DENIED is the strongest right you can apply on a principal. No matter what else might be assigned to that principal, DENIED is DENIED. There are a few exceptions, but in general, it will overrule any other settings you might want to apply. The security-frenzied types will try to get you to use this setting frequently, but in many cases, it's not needed. Use the DENIED setting sparingly and strategically. Let's finish discussing the other two, then we'll dive into just how that can be done.

The middle-of-the-road right is GRANTED. This is the one your users really like. They want to be allowed to see things, run reports, crunch data, and do all those other fun things that make business analytics so sexy. As long as there's no DENIED on top of it, GRANTED is what it says. It gives the user access.

Down on the bottom is NOT SPECIFIED. He looks a little lonely there on the bottom, doesn't he? Believe it or not, NOT SPECIFIED is about to get a new best friend—you! The reason you're going to fall heels over head in love with NOT SPECIFIED is because of how elegantly you can use it to achieve your beautiful, invisible security model. Think back to the much harsher and stronger DENIED right. Think of that one as a "hard" deny. There's no way around it. It's off-limits. Now think about NOT SPECIFIED as a "soft" deny. If a right is set to NOT SPECIFIED, it's for all intents and purposes denied. Here's where the elegance comes in. NOT SPECIFIED won't muck with any of your other rights inheritances like a hard DENIED will. That object will simply not be accessible to that principal. NOT SPECIFIED is the kid in the sandbox that will share his toys with all of the other kids. It plays nice with the rest of the system and doesn't make headaches for your hardworking administrators.

Because this is so important to understand, let's review. The three main rights that can be applied to a principal are DENIED, GRANTED, and NOT SPECIFIED. DENIED is the big bully. It will get its way at the cost of all else. GRANTED sits in the middle and is the class favorite, and down on the bottom is your new bestie, NOT SPECIFIED. Use DENIED only when and where you need to because it will do the job you ask of it.

5.1.2 Understanding Inheritance

Inheritance is meant to help you, the administrator, do your job better and make that job easier. Instead of having to explicitly set rights on every single object in

the system, there is inheritance. In a similar fashion to how traits and characteristics pass from parents to children in human biology, rights will pass from top-
level objects to all of their child objects inside SAP BusinessObjects BI. By default,
users or groups who have rights to a folder will inherit the same rights for any
subsequent object placed in that folder. Each area in the system where you're going to set rights also has a top-level folder, or the folder from which all other folders will be children. For example, take a gander at the FOLDERS section, which you
can access via the following menu path: CENTRAL MANAGEMENT CONSOLE • FOLD-
ERS • MANAGE • TOP-LEVEL SECURITY • ALL FOLDERS (see Figure 5.2). The resulting
screen is shown in Figure 5.3.

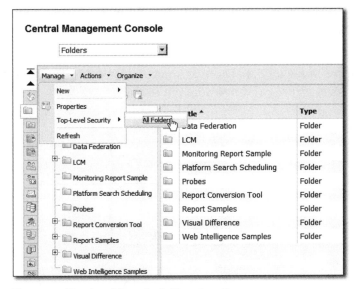

Figure 5.2 Top-Level Security Settings Location

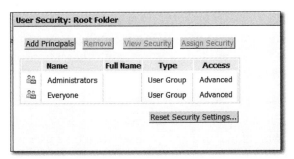

Figure 5.3 Inside the Top-Level Rights Assignment Screen

Before we get into the nitty-gritty of how to set rights and whatnot, let's just pause for a moment and stay up at a higher level. Here, we're at the top. We're the "CEO" of rights assignments. Whatever we set here will be automatically inherited in every other folder we create, so we want to be really careful about what rights we set up here at the top.

An important thing to note about rights inheritance is that it can be broken or overridden. Just like the wayward child that strikes out on his own and doesn't want any of Mommy or Daddy's money, you can set a child folder to tell the top-level folder where to stick its rights. There are a few valid cases where you'll want to consider breaking inheritance, but as a general best practice, sticking with inheritance is best. You can also override rights that have been inherited. We'll get into the specifics of a rights override in just a bit. For now, it's important just to understand that such an exception exists.

Take a look at the example in Figure 5.4. This was a new folder called TEST that was made after the top-level security settings were put in place.

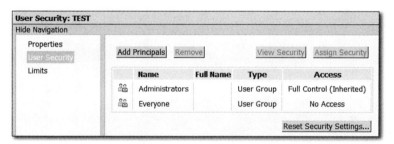

Figure 5.4 Group Rights Inherited

SAP BusinessObjects BI does a good job showing you where rights have been inherited from a tier somewhere above this one. You can pretty plainly see after the ADMINISTRATORS group, under ACCESS, it has FULL CONTROL that was inherited. Don't get bent about what full control means just yet. That's coming up in just a sec. For now, focus on the fact that this set of rights was not explicitly set here on this new folder but that it appeared here on its own through the magic of inheritance.

If you have a really keen eye, you'll have noticed in those previous screenshots that the rights that were assigned were done on a group rather than on a user account. Brace yourself for another best practice. Whenever possible, you should *always* assign rights on groups and not on individual users. If you do it the other way around, you're in for an administrative nightmare. The best way to enforce the proper rules is to create groups that fit your usage models, assign all of the rights needed to those groups, and then add users into those groups based on their access needs. This works really well because inheritance works inside groups as well. Whatever rights you set at the group level, each subsequent user account that becomes a member of that group will inherit the rights assigned to that group, including all of the content and applications that group has permission to. That way, after you get your group security model set, all you're doing as the administrator is moving users in and out of groups, which is much easier than having to assign rights all over the system every time you add a new user.

Let's add a group to have permissions to this folder just to outline this basic step. Drop back to the FOLDERS tab in the CMC, right-click on the TEST folder, and choose USER SECURITY (see Figure 5.5).

Figure 5.5 Choosing User Security

In the next window, click ADD PRINCIPALS (see Figure 5.6). Now we've landed in the ADD PRINCIPALS window, and for this example, we'll want to add the TRANS-LATORS group (see Figure 5.7).

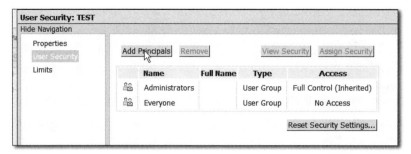

Figure 5.6 Adding Principals

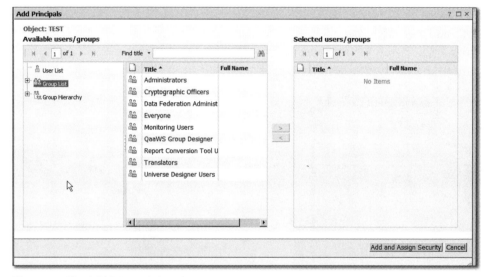

Figure 5.7 The Add Principals Window

Click the TRANSLATORS group, and then click the right-arrow in the middle to push the group over (see Figure 5.8).

Next, we'll choose an access level (see Figure 5.9). Remember, we're outlining the process here. Access levels are discussed in detail starting in Section 5.1.5.

Pick the level you want, use the right arrow and push it over, and then click OK. And there you have it! You just followed the path of "principals have rights to objects."

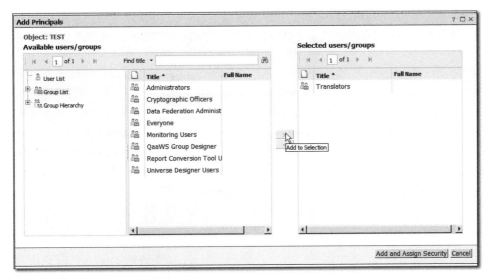

Figure 5.8 Adding the Group

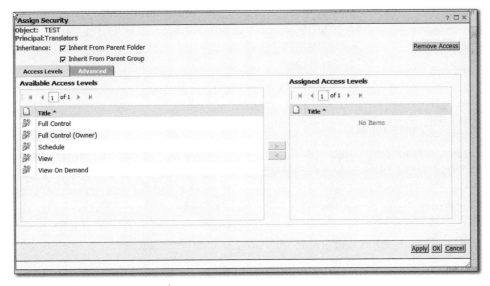

Figure 5.9 Assign Security Window

5.1.3 Determining Effective Rights

It can be pretty easy to get lost in the sea of conflicting rights and inheritance. Keep the following thoughts in mind when setting rights on an object:

- Each access level grants some rights, denies some rights, and leaves the other rights unspecified. When a user is granted several access levels, the system aggregates the effective rights and denies any unspecified rights by default.

- When you assign multiple access levels to a principal on an object, the principal has the combination of each access level's rights.

- Advanced rights can be combined with access levels to customize the rights settings for a principal on an object. For example, if an advanced right and an access level are both assigned explicitly to a principal on an object, and the advanced right contradicts the right in the access level, the advanced right will override the right in the access level. Advanced rights can override their identical counterparts in access levels only when they are set on the same object for the same principal. For example, an advanced ADD right set at the general global level can override the general ADD right setting in an access level; it can't override a type-specific ADD right setting in an access level. However, advanced rights don't always override access levels. For example, a principal is denied an EDIT right on a parent object. On the child object, the principal is assigned an access level that grants him the EDIT right. In the end, the principal has EDIT rights on the child object because the rights set on the child object override rights that are set on the parent object.

- Rights override makes it possible for rights set on a child object to override rights that are inherited from a parent object.

5.1.4 Rights Override

Some cases will come up that will leave the typically sage administrator scratching his head wondering how to solve a rights issue problem. And sometimes, just sometimes, it becomes necessary to override your beautiful and perfect security model to make an exception. This is different from breaking inheritance as we described in Section 5.1.2. In an override scenario, inheritance can stay in place. Rights override will occur in the following two circumstances:

- In general, the rights that are set on child objects override the corresponding rights that are set on the parent objects.

- In general, the rights that are set on subgroups or members of groups override the corresponding rights that are set on groups.

"How does this happen?" you ask. This is an intentional back door SAP functionality left in the security system to help you solve exceptions where there isn't any other good way to solve your security issues. Child objects will inherit the rights of the parent except for rights that are explicitly set on the child object. Confused? Let's walk through a couple of examples.

Figure 5.10 demonstrates how a rights override would work on a parent and child object scenario. In this case, our user, Fred, is denied access to our top-level folder, Beer Sales. Fred likes beer a whole lot, but we don't want him to see what our sales figures are. The subfolder, U.S. Beer Sales, inherits the deny from the parent folder, and poor Fred is still left out in the cold. However, the beer sales manager knows that Fred drinks more beer than anyone and is knowledgeable about many different brands of beer. So, he asks the administrator to allow Fred access to the document, Beer Brands, which is in the U.S. Beer Sales subfolder. This will allow Fred to see and edit this document, which the sales team will use as a reference for new beers to try or hot products to watch. By placing an explicit grant on the Beer Brands document, Fred will be able to see only this document and not any of the other sensitive sales documents in those folders (see Figure 5.10).

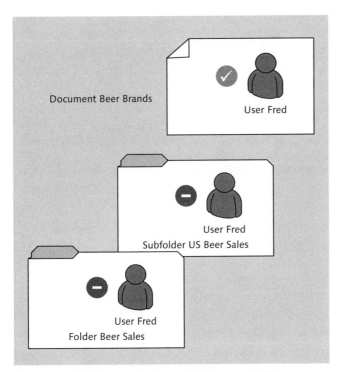

Figure 5.10 Rights Override Example 1: Users and Objects

For our next example (see Figure 5.11), let's stick with our pal Fred. Fred is in the Operations Group and in the Beer Bottlers Subgroup. The Operations Group is denied access to the Beer Sales folder, so the Beer Bottlers Subgroup inherits the deny. But now the sales manager not only wants Fred to access his Beer Brands document, he also wants Fred to do some analysis on all of his sales reports. Instead of moving Fred to a different group against the grain of the security model, he asks you, the administrator, to set an explicit grant on the folder, so it will override the inherited rights and allow Fred (and only Fred) access to the folder.

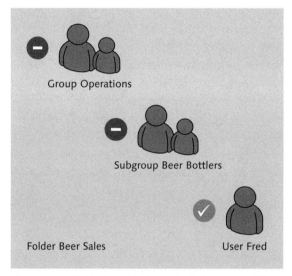

Figure 5.11 Rights Override Example 2: Groups and Users

Let's say for this example that the sales manager doesn't know about SAP BusinessObjects BI 4.1 security and certainly doesn't know anything about overrides. So, to try to get Fred the access he needs to the Beer Brands document, the sales manager asks you, the administrator, to also put Fred in the Beer Sales group because she knows that her Beer Sales group definitely has access to that folder (see Figure 5.12). But Fred logs in and still can't even see that folder. Why? This is happening due to a different type of override. Because Fred is now a member of both the Beer Sales and Beer Bottlers Subgroups, and those two groups aren't related (and neither are their parent groups, Operations and Sales), then the right that will win in case of a conflict is the deny. With only the exceptions of the two override scenarios we demonstrated earlier, SAP BusinessObjects BI is a denial-based rights model. In any case where there is a conflict like this, the deny will win. Clear as mud?

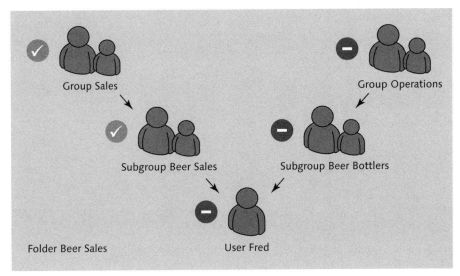

Figure 5.12 Complex Override Scenario

5.1.5 Access Levels

After all of this talk about access levels, now is probably a good time to explain exactly what those are. There are two types of access levels, default access levels and custom access levels. Let's spend some time with each, shall we?

Default Access Levels

Let's take a moment and walk through an example to show how default access levels come into play and to reinforce what we've already learned about how principals have rights to objects.

Let's revisit our TEST folder example from earlier. In this example, the object is our new folder named TEST. From the FOLDERS page in the CMC, follow these steps:

1. Navigate to the TEST folder, right-click, and choose USER SECURITY (see Figure 5.13).

Figure 5.13 Step 1: Setting User Security

2. Click the ADD PRINCIPALS button (see Figure 5.14).

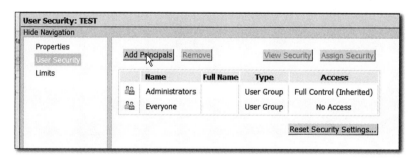

Figure 5.14 Step 2: Adding Principals – Clicking Add Principals

3. Click the GROUP LIST tree, remembering that it's a best practice to assign rights to groups (see Figure 5.15).

4. Click to highlight the TRANSLATORS group, and then click the right arrow button to add the group to your selection (see Figure 5.16). This takes you to the AS-SIGN SECURITY screen.

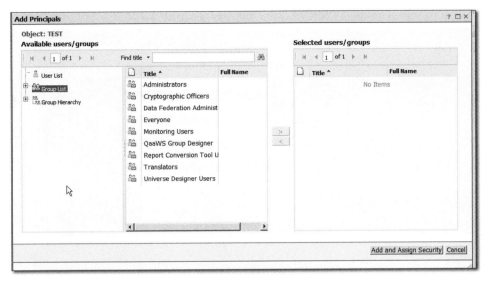

Figure 5.15 Step 3: Adding Principals – Selecting a Group

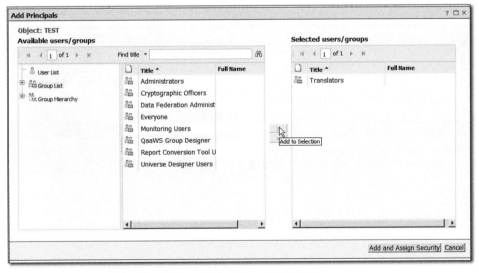

Figure 5.16 Step 4: Adding Principals – Adding Group to Selection

5. In the ASSIGN SECURITY screen (see Figure 5.17), you can see generic sets of pre-defined rights you can use to quickly assign a set of permissions to a user or group.

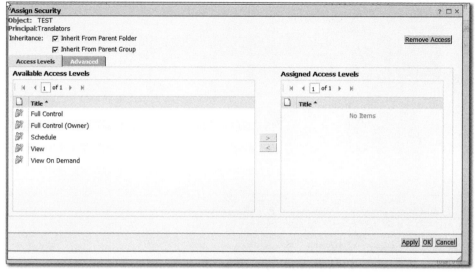

Figure 5.17 Step 5: Adding Principals – Assigning a Default Access Level

Table 5.1 lists the access levels in order of their restrictions. VIEW has the most restrictions; FULL CONTROL (OWNER) has the least.

Access Level	Description	Rights Involved
VIEW	If set on the folder level, a principal can view the folder, objects within the folder, and each object's generated instances. If set at the object level, a principal can view the objects, their history, and their generated instances.	► View objects ► View document instances

Table 5.1 Default Access Levels (Source: BusinessObjects Platform Administrator Guide)

Access Level	Description	Rights Involved
SCHEDULE	A principal can generate instances by scheduling an object to run against a specified data source or on a recurring basis. The principal can view, delete, and pause the scheduling of instances that he owns. He can also schedule to different formats and destinations, set parameters and database logon information, choose servers to process jobs, add content to the folder, and copy the object or folder.	VIEW access level rights plus: ▸ Schedule the document to run. ▸ Define server groups to process jobs. ▸ Copy objects to another folder. ▸ Schedule to destinations. ▸ Print the report's data. ▸ Export the report's data. ▸ Edit objects that the user owns. ▸ Delete instances that the user owns. ▸ Pause and resume document instances that the user owns.
VIEW ON DEMAND	A principal can refresh data on demand against a data source.	SCHEDULE access level rights plus the right to refresh the report's data.
FULL CONTROL	A principal has full administrative control of the object.	All available rights, including the following: ▸ Add objects to the folder. ▸ Edit objects. ▸ Modify rights users have to objects. ▸ Delete objects. ▸ Delete instances.
FULL CONTROL (OWNER)	A principal has full administrative control of the object and becomes the owner of the objects.	FULL CONTROL rights plus object ownership rights.

Table 5.1 Default Access Levels (Source: BusinessObjects Platform Administrator Guide) (Cont.)

A common question for new administrators is "What's the difference between VIEW and VIEW ON DEMAND?" Great question.

The VIEW access level, the most restrictive access level, really only allows users to open up and look at a report. They can't do much else with it, including doing a refresh. This access level is really great for your information consumer-type users. (Remember them from Chapter 2?) These are people that just need to eyeball some information and get on with their day. It's also great for reducing network and database traffic because the report must be prepared for a VIEW user. They're only looking at saved data—an instance.

VIEW ON DEMAND, however, allows users to refresh the report directly. This means they can click the pretty little REFRESH button, and that report is going to go and hit the data source database and run a query, return data, and render the page directly into the web browser or reporting tool. These are more your business users and expert-type users. They need to run things on their own and explore the data a bit.

Custom Access Levels

The default access levels are great for a large majority of your rights-assignment tasks, but they are pretty generic and certainly don't meet every use case. In the olden days, administrators used to have to set "advanced" rights on every folder or object where the default access levels weren't enough. This became another administrative nightmare, as you can well imagine. Enter the custom access level to save the day. The custom access level lets you create your own specific set of grants, denies, and not specified to meet your own business needs and save them in the platform so they are consistent and repeatable throughout. Pretty nifty, huh?

To create a custom access level, you can either copy one of the default access levels or start a new one from scratch. If you just need to tweak the rights in a default level, then copying an existing one is the way to go. Go to the ACCESS LEVELS section of the CMC; in the DETAILS panel, select the level you want to copy, and then click ORGANIZE • COPY. A copy of the access level you selected will now appear in the DETAILS panel, and you can modify it and rename it to suit your needs.

If you want to create a new custom access level from scratch, from the same ACCESS LEVELS area of the CMC, click MANAGE • NEW • CREATE ACCESS LEVEL (see Figure 5.18), and the CREATE ACCESS LEVEL dialog box will appear.

Figure 5.18 Create Access Level Menu Path

Enter a TITLE and DESCRIPTION of your new access level (see Figure 5.19), and then click OK.

Figure 5.19 Create New Access Level Dialog Box

After you click OK, you'll return to the ACCESS LEVELS area, and you'll see your new access level in the DETAILS panel (see Figure 5.20).

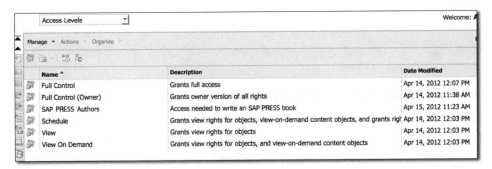

Figure 5.20 New Access Level in the Details Panel

You can then modify the access level to add the rights you want to include. To do that, click to highlight your access level, and then choose ACTIONS • INCLUDED RIGHTS (see Figure 5.21).

227

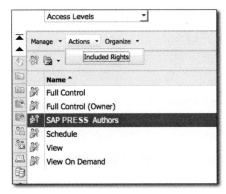

Figure 5.21 Accessing the Included Rights Dialog Box

The INCLUDED RIGHTS dialog box will appear and display a list of effective rights (see Figure 5.22).

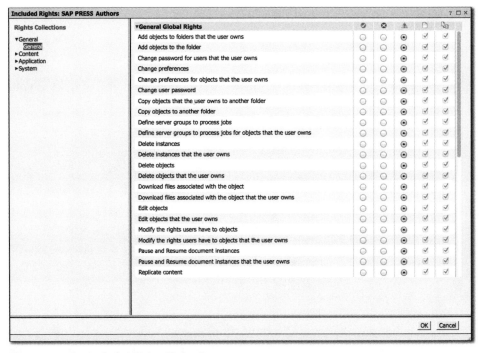

Figure 5.22 The Included Rights Dialog Box

From here, you'll want to choose all of the specific, granular rights you want to be a part of this new custom access level. This part will definitely take some time, and be sure to take what you know about inheritance and rights override into consideration when planning what to put into your custom access levels.

Custom access levels can be an extremely powerful and useful way to extend your security model into one of those ideal invisible ones we discussed in the beginning of the chapter. Custom access levels allow you to get really specific about what types of rights you want your users and groups to have and to tailor those rights to fit your organization perfectly.

5.1.6 Delegated Administration

In previous versions, the only way to administer an SAP BusinessObjects BI environment was by using the built-in Administrator user. This user was a "super-administrator" and had rights beyond what you could grant even to a new user in the Administrators group. This user was really the only recommended account to use when doing content migrations with the now-defunct Import Wizard and even most other administrative tasks one would perform inside the platform. It was common practice that several administrator people would all share the password for this account so they all could use it when they needed to. Obviously, this was a bad practice (nobody ever shares passwords, do they?), and SAP understood this from talking with customers.

SAP added a nifty feature back in SAP BusinessObjects 4.0 Service Pack 4 (SP4) that comes with the ability to divide and conquer when it comes to SAP BusinessObjects administration. This is a great idea for several reasons. First of all, it's great because the job is certainly bigger than a single person these days. Second, many SAP BusinessObjects BI environments need to run 24 hours a day, 7 days a week. A single person can only work so much. So, here comes delegated administration to make our collective lives, and jobs, easier. You can now grant users the proper rights to help out with administrative tasks without giving away the keys to the kingdom.

You can now use rights to divide administrative tasks between functional groups within your organization. You may want to give users from different departments the ability to manage their own users and groups, or you may have one administrator you want to handle the high-level management of the environment, but you want all of the server management to be handled by folks up on the service desk.

Let's assume that your group and folder structure aligns with your delegated administration security structure. You'll want to grant your delegated administrator rights to groups but grant the delegated administrator less than full rights on the users he controls. For example, you might not want the delegated administrator to edit user attributes or reassign them to different groups, or certainly not to be able to delete users in another group.

Table 5.2 summarizes the rights that are required for delegated administrators to perform common actions.

Action for Delegated Administrator	Rights Required by the Delegated Administrator
Create new users.	ADD right on the top-level users folder.
Create new groups.	ADD right on the top-level user groups folder.
Delete any controlled groups, as well as individual users in those groups.	DELETE right on relevant groups.
Delete only users that the delegated administrator creates.	OWNER DELETE right on the top-level users folder.
Delete only users and groups that the delegated administrator creates.	OWNER DELETE right on the top-level user groups folder.
Manipulate only users that the delegated administrator creates.	OWNER EDIT and OWNER SECURELY MODIFY RIGHTS right on the top-level users folder.
Manipulate only groups that the delegated administrator creates (including adding users to those groups).	OWNER EDIT and OWNER SECURELY MODIFY RIGHTS on the top-level user groups folder.
Modify passwords for users in their controlled groups.	EDIT PASSWORD right on relevant groups.
Modify passwords only for principals that the delegated administrator creates.	OWNER EDIT PASSWORD right on top-level users folder or on relevant groups. Note: Setting the OWNER EDIT PASSWORD right on a group takes effect on a user only when you add the user to the relevant group.

Table 5.2 Required Rights for Delegated Administrators (Source: BusinessObjects Platform Administrator Guide)

Action for Delegated Administrator	Rights Required by the Delegated Administrator
Modify user names, descriptions, and other attributes, and then reassign users to different groups.	EDIT right on relevant groups.
Modify user names, descriptions, and other attributes, and then reassign users to different groups, but only for users that the delegated administrator creates.	OWNER EDIT right on the top-level users folder or on relevant groups. Note: Setting the OWNER EDIT right on relevant groups takes effect on a user only when you add the user to the relevant group.

Table 5.2 Required Rights for Delegated Administrators (Source: BusinessObjects Platform Administrator Guide) (Cont.)

It's time for another best practice alert. You may be tempted to take the easy road and just assign all of your delegated administrators FULL CONTROL. It's better to spend a little time up-front and use the advanced rights settings to withhold the MODIFY RIGHTS right and give your delegated administrator the SECURELY MODIFY RIGHTS right instead. You should also consider giving your delegated administrator the SECURELY MODIFY RIGHTS INHERITANCE SETTINGS right instead of the MODIFY RIGHTS INHERITANCE SETTINGS right. Let's talk about the difference between the two to help make it clearer why this is a good idea.

The right MODIFY THE RIGHTS USERS HAVE TO OBJECTS allows a user to modify any right for any user on that object. If our beer bottler Fred has the rights VIEW OBJECTS and MODIFY THE RIGHTS USERS HAVE TO OBJECTS ON A REPORT, Fred could simply change his rights on that report to FULL CONTROL and do some damage.

The right SECURELY MODIFY THE RIGHTS USERS HAVE TO OBJECTS allows a user to grant, deny, or revert to unspecified only the rights he is already granted. If Fred has VIEW and SECURELY MODIFY THE RIGHTS USERS HAVE TO OBJECTS, then Fred can't give himself any more rights and can grant or deny to other users only these two rights. Additionally, Fred can only change the rights for users on objects for which he has the SECURELY MODIFY RIGHTS right.

The following conditions must all be in effect for Fred to modify the rights for another user, Ed, on the object Beer Sales Report:

- Fred has the SECURELY MODIFY RIGHTS right on the Beer Sales Report.

- Each right or access level that Fred is changing for Ed is granted to Fred.

- Fred has the SECURELY MODIFY RIGHTS right on Ed.

- If an access level is being assigned, Fred has the ASSIGN ACCESS LEVEL right on the access level that is changing for Ed.

The scope of rights can further limit the effective rights that a delegated administrator can assign. For example, a delegated administrator may have SECURELY MODIFY RIGHTS and EDIT rights on a folder, but the scope of these rights is limited to the folder only and doesn't apply to its subobjects. Effectively, the delegated administrator can grant the EDIT right on the folder (but not on its subobjects) only, and with an APPLY TO OBJECTS scope only. On the other hand, if the delegated administrator is granted the EDIT right on a folder with a scope of APPLY TO SUBOBJECTS only, he can grant the other principals the EDIT right with both scopes on the folder's subobject; but on the folder itself, he can only grant the EDIT right with an APPLY TO SUBOBJECTS scope.

The delegated administrator would additionally be restricted from modifying rights on those groups for other principals that don't have the SECURELY MODIFY RIGHTS right. This is useful, for example, if you have two delegated administrators responsible for granting rights to different user groups for the same folder, but you don't want one delegated administrator to be able to deny access to the groups controlled by the other delegated administrator. The SECURELY MODIFY RIGHTS right ensures this because delegated administrators generally won't have the SECURELY MODIFY RIGHTS right on each other.

The SECURELY MODIFY RIGHTS INHERITANCE SETTINGS right allows a delegated administrator to modify inheritance settings for other principals on the objects that the delegated administrator has access to. To successfully modify the inheritance settings of other principals, a delegated administrator must have this right on the object and on the user accounts for the principals.

To summarize delegated administration, you now have the ability to grant users limited administrator rights that will ease the burden for just one person to have to perform all of the administration tasks in the SAP BusinessObjects BI system. You can now protect the built-in Administrator account because it still is a "super-administrator," and allow your delegated administrators to use their own accounts with more limited access. This helps protect the system from any accidents related to too much access and not enough knowledge, and it provides greater accountability because people are changing the system in an auditable way. For tired, old administrators, delegated administration is a gift from above.

5.1.7 Owner Rights

Owner rights, quite simply, are rights that apply only to the owner of an object. In SAP BusinessObjects BI 4.1, the owner of an object is the principal who created the object. If that principal is ever deleted from the system, ownership will default to the administrator.

Owner rights are useful in managing owner-based security. For example, you may want to create a folder or hierarchy of folders in which various users can create and view documents but can only modify or delete their own documents. Owner rights are also useful for allowing users to manipulate instances of reports they create, but not other instances. Take, for example, the SCHEDULING access level, which permits users to edit, delete, pause, and reschedule only their own instances.

Owner rights work similarly to their corresponding regular rights. However, owner rights are effective only when the principal has been granted owner rights, but regular rights are denied or not specified.

5.1.8 Rights Administration Summary

To wrap up this huge gob of information on SAP BusinessObjects BI 4.1 rights administration, keep the following recommendations in mind as takeaways:

▶ Use access levels wherever possible. These predefined sets of rights (whether default or custom) simplify administration by grouping together rights associated with common user needs.

▶ Set rights and access levels on top-level folders. Enabling inheritance will allow these rights to be passed down through the system with minimal administrative effort.

▶ Avoid breaking inheritance wherever possible. By doing so, you can reduce the amount of time it takes to secure the content you have added to the system.

▶ Set appropriate rights for users and groups at the folder level, and then publish objects to that folder. By default, users or groups who have rights to a folder will inherit the same rights for any object that you subsequently add to that folder.

▶ Organize users into user groups, assign access levels and rights to the entire group, and assign access levels and rights to specific members when necessary (for rights overrides).

▶ Create individual administrator accounts for each administrator in the system, and add them to the Administrators group to improve accountability for system changes.

▶ Use delegated administration rights to allow users to assist with certain administrative tasks without granting them full administrator rights and putting the system at risk.

▶ By default, the Everyone group is granted very limited rights to the top-level folders. After installation, review the rights of the Everyone group members, and adjust security accordingly.

Pop Quiz

1. What is a principal?
2. The most restrictive right that may be enforced is _____.
3. Describe application rights.
4. What is the minimum access level required to refresh data on demand?
5. What is the purpose of a custom access level?

5.2 Data and Data Source Security

It's possible, to some extent, for you as the administrator to manage the way sensitive data is secured inside the SAP BusinessObjects BI 4.1 platform. In overview, here are some of the measures you can take:

▶ Manage a security setting at the cluster level that determines which applications and clients can access the CMS. This setting is managed through the Central Configuration Manager (CCM).

▶ Use a two-key cryptography system that controls both access to the CMS repository and keys used to encrypt/decrypt objects within the repository. Access to the CMS repository is set in the CCM, while the CMC has a dedicated management area for cryptographic keys.

These features allow administrators to set SAP BusinessObjects BI 4.1 platform deployments to particular data security compliance levels and to manage encryption keys used to encrypt and decrypt data within the CMS repository.

SAP BusinessObjects BI 4.1 can operate in two possible data processing security modes:

▶ **The default data processing security mode**
In certain instances, systems running in this mode use hard-coded encryption keys and don't follow a specific standard. The default mode enables backward compatibility with previous versions of the SAP BusinessObjects BI platform client tools and applications.

▶ **A data security mode designed to meet guidelines stipulated by the Federal Information Processing Standard (FIPS)—specifically FIPS 140-2**
In this mode, FIPS-compliant algorithms and cryptographic modules are used to protect sensitive data. When the SAP BusinessObjects BI 4.1 platform runs in FIPS-compliant mode, all client tools and applications that don't meet FIPS guidelines are automatically disabled. The platform client tools and applications are designed to meet the FIPS 140-2 standard. It's important to note that older clients and applications won't work when SAP BusinessObjects BI 4.1 is running in FIPS-compliant mode.

The data processing mode is transparent to your end users. In both data processing security modes, sensitive data is encrypted and decrypted in the background by an internal encryption engine.

If you're not sure if you need to be FIPS-compliant, here are a few circumstances where you'll probably want to consider it:

▶ Your SAP BusinessObjects BI 4.1 platform won't need to use or interact with any legacy BI platform client tools or applications.

▶ Your organization's data processing standards and guidelines prohibit the use of hard-coded encryption keys.

▶ Your organization is required to secure sensitive data according to FIPS 140-2 regulations.

The data processing security mode is set through the CCM on both Windows and UNIX platforms. Also important to note, every node in your SAP BusinessObjects BI 4.1 cluster must be set to the same data processing security mode.

FIPS-compliant mode is off after SAP BusinessObjects BI 4.1 is installed. To enable FIPS-compliant mode in Windows, follow these steps:

1. Launch the Central Configuration Manager (CCM).

2. Right-click the Server Intelligence Agent (SIA), and choose STOP.

3. Wait for the SIA to be marked STOPPED before proceeding.

4. Right-click the SIA, and choose PROPERTIES.

5. Click the COMMAND field, press the [End] key on your keyboard (or laboriously scroll to the end with the right arrow key), and after the last bit of text, put in a space, then add "fips", and click APPLY (see Figure 5.23).

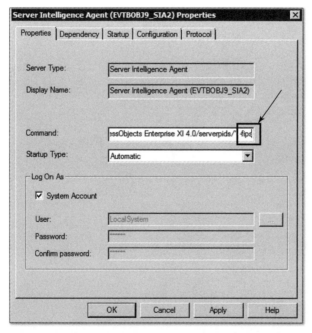

Figure 5.23 Adding the –fips Switch to the Windows Command Launch

6. Click OK, and close the PROPERTIES dialog box.

7. Start the SIA.

Now your SIA is running in FIPS-compliant mode. If you have multiple SIAs running in a cluster, be sure to enable FIPS on all of them, or you'll cause yourself some trouble.

To enable FIPS-compliant mode in UNIX/Linux, follow these steps:

1. Navigate to the directory where SAP BusinessObjects BI 4.1 is installed on your non-Windows server.

2. Change to the *sap_bobj* directory.

3. Use your favorite editor and open the *ccm.config* file in EDIT mode (ours is *vi*).

4. Add the `-fips` switch to the end of the node launch command parameter (see Figure 5.24).

```
SIANODENAME="SAPPRESSRocks"
SIAPORTNUMBER="6410"
FIPSModeValue="undefined"
SapPressRocksLAUNCH=' "/app/bobj/sap_bobj/enterprise_xi40/generic/bobjrestart.sh" -protect "/app/bobj/sap_bobj/enterprise_xi40/generic/javalaunch.sh
" "-Dbobj.product.languages.dir=/app/bobj/sap_bobj/enterprise_xi40/Languages/" -Djava.net.preferIPv4Stack=false -Djava.awt.headless=true "-Xms64m"
"-Xmx256m" "-XX:+ExitVMOnOutOfMemoryError" "-XX:+HeapDumpOnOutOfMemoryError" "-XX:+PrintGCTimeStamps" "-XX:+PrintGCDetails" "-XX:LogGcMaxFileCount=
3" "-XX:LogGcMaxFileSize=5m" "-XX:HeapDumpPath=/app/bobj/sap_bobj/logging/" "-XtraceFile=/app/bobj/sap_bobj/logging/SapPressRocks_jvm_@PID.log" "-X
X:GCHistoryFilename=/app/bobj/sap_bobj/logging/SapPressRocks_gc.prf" "-Xloggc:/app/bobj/sap_bobj/logging/SapPressRocks_gc.log" "-XX:ErrorFile=/app/
bobj/sap_bobj/logging/SapPressRocks_dump_@PID.log" -jar "/app/bobj/sap_bobj/enterprise_xi40/java/lib/SIA.jar" -boot "/app/bobj/sap_bobj/enterprise_
xi40/linux_x64/_boe_SapPressRocks.bootstrap" -port "6410" -pidFile "/app/bobj/sap_bobj/serverpids/SapPressRocks.pid" -loggingPath "/app/bobj/sap_bo
bj/logging/" -traceinipath "/app/bobj/sap_bobj/enterprise_xi40/conf/BO_trace.ini" -name "SapPressRocks" -dbinfo "/app/bobj/sap_bobj/enterprise_xi40
/linux_x64/_boe_SapPressRocks.dbinfo" -piddir "/app/bobj/sap_bobj/serverpids/" -noauditor -fips '
~
```

Figure 5.24 Adding the –fips Switch to the UNIX/Linux Launch Command

5. Save your changes, and exit the editor.

6. Restart the node.

As with the Windows version, if you have more than one SIA in the cluster, you'll want to be sure you turn FIPS on for all of them, or you'll be making headaches for yourself.

If you decide that FIPS compliance just isn't for you, and you want to remove it, just backtrack and remove the `-fips` command from wherever you put it. Make sure to stop the SIA on Windows before you start, and make sure to restart your SIA after you're done on UNIX.

Pop Quiz

1. True or false: SAP BusinessObjects BI 4.1 may be configured to use varying encryption levels for data stored within the CMS.

5.3 Securing Communication Using Cryptography and SSL

One of the scariest parts about implementing a business analytics solution such as SAP BusinessObjects BI 4.1 is that you're now exposing sensitive data. It's like the helicopter parents who just can't bear to let their children out of their sight for even a moment. Technology professionals, especially security-minded ones, like to keep data locked away safely in a database behind several firewalls and secured with a dozen randomly generated passwords. The hitch is that data that is locked away doesn't do the business any good when making critical decisions. So, it's time to take a deep breath and put some measures in place that will help protect your data as it goes out into the wide world to enlighten your business decision makers. The two protection measures we'll discuss now are cryptography and Secure Sockets Layer (SSL).

5.3.1 Cryptography

SAP BusinessObjects BI 4.1 was designed to use cryptography to protect sensitive data that is stored in the CMS repository. By "sensitive data" we mean the following:

▶ User credentials

▶ Data source connectivity data

▶ InfoObjects that store passwords

These data elements are encrypted to keep them private, to keep them free from corruption, and to maintain positive access control. All of the requisite encryption resources (including the encryption engine, RSA libraries) are installed by default on each SAP BusinessObjects BI 4.1 deployment. SAP BusinessObjects BI 4.1 uses a two-key cryptography system.

Encryption and decryption of sensitive data are handled in the background through the SDK interacting with the internal encryption engine. System administrators manage data security through symmetric encryption keys without directly encrypting or decrypting specific data blocks.

In SAP BusinessObjects BI 4.1, symmetric encryption keys (cryptographic keys) are used to encrypt and decrypt sensitive data. The CMC has a dedicated management area for cryptographic keys (see Figure 5.25).

Use the cryptographic keys management area to view, generate, deactivate, revoke, and delete keys. The system makes sure that any key required to decrypt sensitive data can't be deleted.

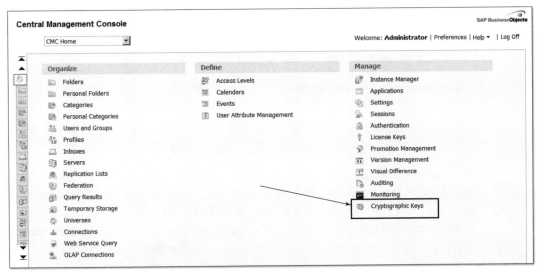

Figure 5.25 Cryptographic Keys Management Area in the CMC

Cluster keys are symmetric key-wrapping keys that protect the cryptographic keys stored in the CMS repository. Using symmetric key algorithms, cluster keys maintain a level of access control to the CMS repository. Each node of the SAP BusinessObjects BI 4.1 environment is assigned a cluster key during installation setup. System administrators can use the CCM to reset the cluster key. Let's get into the specifics on how to work with cluster keys and cryptographic keys.

Working with Cluster Keys

When you run the installation setup for SAP BusinessObjects BI 4.1, a six-character cluster key is specified for the SIA. This key is used to encrypt all of the cryptographic keys in the CMS repository. Without the correct cluster key, you can't access the CMS. The cluster key is stored in encrypted format in the *dbinfo* file. You can find the *dbinfo* file in the following paths depending on your operating system platform as listed in Table 5.3.

Platform	Path
Windows	*<INSTALLDIR>\SAP BusinessObjects Enterprise XI 4.0\win64_x64*
AIX	*<INSTALLDIR>/sap_bobj/enterprise_xi40/aix_rs6000_64/*

Table 5.3 File Paths for dbinfo

Platform	Path
Solaris	*<INSTALLDIR>/sap_bobj/enterprise_xi40/solaris_sparcv9/*
Linux	*<INSTALLDIR>/sap_bobj/enterprise_xi40/linux_x64/*

Table 5.3 File Paths for dbinfo (Cont.)

The file name is based on the following convention: *_boe_<sia_name>.dbinfo*, where *<sia_name>* is the name of the SIA for the cluster.

It's important to note here that you can't retrieve a cluster key from the *dbinfo* file. As a system administrator, you should take very careful measures to protect your cluster keys. Only users with administrative rights can reset cluster keys. If needed, use the Central Configuration Manager to reset the six-character cluster key for every node in your deployment. New cluster keys are automatically used to wrap the cryptographic keys within the CMS repository.

To reset a cluster key on Windows:

1. Launch the CCM, and stop the SIA.

2. Right-click the SIA, and choose PROPERTIES.

3. Click the CONFIGURATION tab.

4. Click CHANGE under CMS CLUSTER KEY CONFIGURATION. A warning message will appear (see Figure 5.26). Confirm that all requirements are met before proceeding.

Figure 5.26 Warning Message for Changing Cluster Keys

5. The CHANGE CLUSTER KEY dialog box will appear (see Figure 5.27). You can either enter your own cluster key or generate a random key.

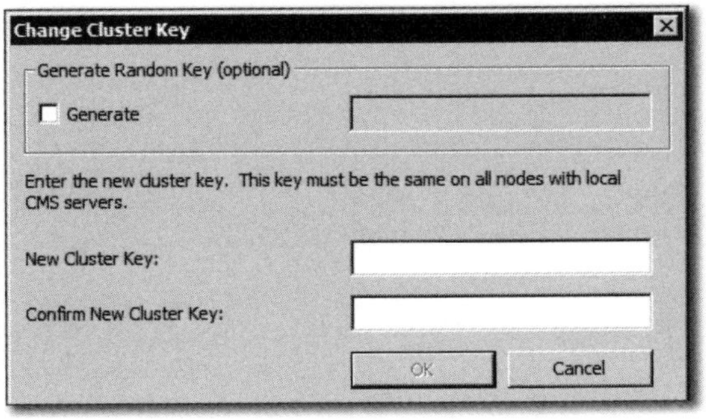

Figure 5.27 The Change Cluster Key Dialog Box

If you enter your own key, the cluster key must contain two of the following character types: lowercase, uppercase, numeral, or punctuation. If your organization must be FIPS-compliant, then you must use a randomly generated key.

6. Click OK to submit the new cluster key to the system, and a message will appear that the cluster key was successfully reset.

7. Start the SIA.

8. In a multinode cluster, you must reset the cluster keys for all of the SIAs in your cluster to the new key.

To reset a cluster key on UNIX/Linux:

1. Navigate to the install directory for SAP BusinessObjects BI 4.1.

2. Change to the *sap_bobj* directory.

3. Execute the `cmsdbsetup.sh` script, and the CMS DATABASE SETUP screen appears.

4. Enter the name of the node, and press Enter (see Figure 5.28).

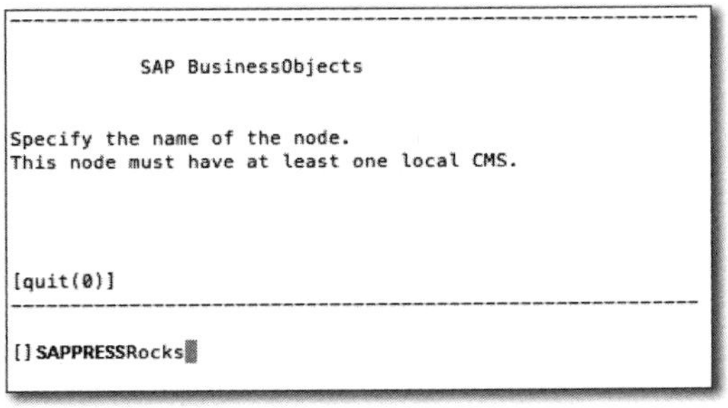

Figure 5.28 The CMS Database Setup Screen

5. Choose YES to allow the script to stop your SIA.

6. Select 2 to change the cluster key (see Figure 5.29).

```
--------------------------------------------------------------
            SAP BusinessObjects

Current CMS Data Source: BOE14

Current cluster name: evtech3.evtintranet.com:6400

Current cluster key: [[OavOvSpp2DVL1qUJ2Fp0Qw]]


update (Update Data Source Settings)
reinitialize (Recreate the current data surce)
copy (Copy data from another Data Source)
change cluster (Change current cluster name)
change cluster key (Change current cluster key)


[update(6)/reinitialize(5)/copy(4)/change cluster(3)/change cluster key(2)/back(1)/quit(0)]
--------------------------------------------------------------
[update]2
```

Figure 5.29 Selecting Option 2 to Change the Cluster Key

7. A warning message will appear. Select YES to continue.

8. The script will ask if you want to randomly generate a cluster key. If you do, choose YES. If you prefer to enter one manually, choose NO.

9. If you chose to enter your own, enter a new eight-character cluster key, and press ⌈Enter⌋. It's important to note a difference here. On UNIX, a valid cluster key contains any combination of eight characters without restrictions.

10. Reenter the new cluster key in the field provided, and press ⌈Enter⌋. A message will appear informing you that the cluster key has been successfully reset.

11. Restart the SIA.

12. As with Windows, you must reset all of the SIA cluster keys in the cluster using the same cluster key.

Just like the information security folks at your company will tell you, when in doubt, go with the randomly generated keys. They're much more secure and much harder to compromise. They really stink to remember, so make sure you keep them cataloged somewhere very safe but that others can access if necessary.

A group password vault program is ideal. At the very least, have a password-protected document or spreadsheet that a few other people have access to in case you go on vacation or get hit by a beer truck.

Cryptographic Officers

Our friends at SAP have given this role a really fancy name. When you boil it down, if you need to manage cryptographic keys in the CMC, then you'll need to be a member of the Cryptographic Officers group. The default Administrator account is also a member of the Cryptographic Officers group, as it should be (and yet another reason to protect that account by limiting who can use it). We highly recommend that membership to the Cryptographic Officers group be extremely limited. Thankfully, just adding someone to the Administrators group doesn't make them a member of the Cryptographic Officers group, and just being a member of the Administrators group doesn't grant you the rights required to perform management tasks on cryptographic keys.

Viewing Cryptographic Keys in the Central Management Console

To view cryptographic keys and the objects that are associated with those keys, head over to the Cryptographic Keys section of the CMC (see Figure 5.30). To view the objects associated with a key, right-click the key entry and choose Properties. The cryptographic keys Properties dialog box will appear.

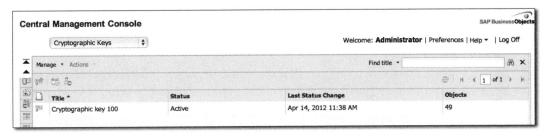

Figure 5.30 The Cryptographic Keys Tab in the CMC

On the left-hand navigation menu, choose Object List, and you'll see the right-hand Object Listdetail panel populated with the list of objects that are encrypted by this key (see Figure 5.31).

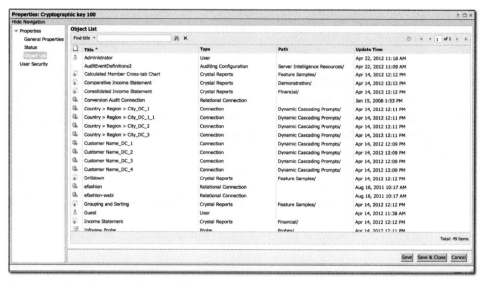

Figure 5.31 The Cryptographic Key Object List

Creating a New Cryptographic Key

If you're still reading this far, then you're likely concerned about this topic and/ or work in an industry where cryptography is required on these types of systems. If that's the case, you'll probably have to change your cryptographic keys periodically to maintain a standard of security.

Before we start with how to create a new key, there's some important functionality to understand first. When you create a new key, the SAP BusinessObjects BI 4.1 system automatically deactivates the current active key. After a key has been deactivated, it can't be restored as the active key. Consider yourself fairly warned, and let's proceed.

1. In the CRYPTOGRAPHIC KEYS tab of the CMC, click MANAGE • NEW • CRYPTOGRAPHIC KEY. The CREATE NEW CRYPTOGRAPHIC KEY dialog box will appear.

2. A warning will appear reiterating that the current key will be deactivated and giving you a chance to chicken out or proceed.

3. Type a NAME and a DESCRIPTION of your new cryptographic key, and click OK to save your information (see Figure 5.32).

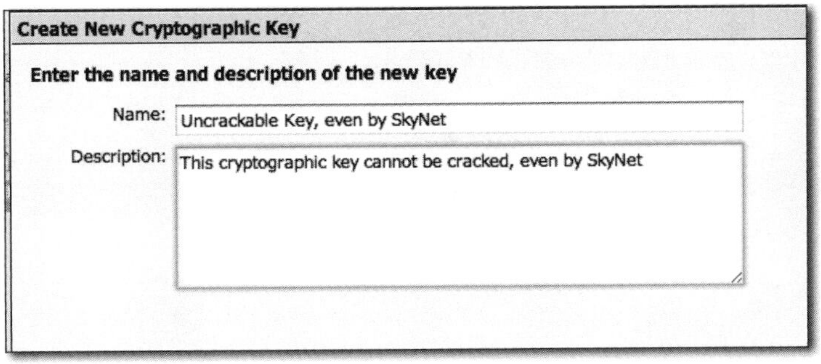

Create New Cryptographic Key

Enter the name and description of the new key

Name: Uncrackable Key, even by SkyNet

Description: This cryptographic key cannot be cracked, even by SkyNet

Figure 5.32 Creating Your New Cryptographic Key

4. Now, you'll see that the new key is marked active and the old key is deactivated.

All new sensitive data that is generated and stored in the CMS database will now be encrypted with the new cryptographic key. You also have the option to revoke the previous key and reencrypt all of its data objects with the new active key.

Marking a Cryptographic Key as Compromised and Revoking Keys

You can mark a cryptographic key as compromised if for some reason the key is considered to no longer be secure. This is useful for auditing and tracking purposes, and you can proceed to identify which data objects are associated with the key. A cryptographic key must be deactivated before it can be marked as compromised. You can also mark a key as compromised after it has been revoked.

1. In the CRYPTOGRAPHIC KEYS tab of the CMC, select the key you want to mark as compromised.

2. Click ACTIONS • MARK AS COMPROMISED, and the MARK AS COMPROMISED dialog box appears (see Figure 5.33).

Mark as Compromised

You have selected the following cryptographic keys to mark as compromised:
Cryptographic key 100

Do you wish to continue?

Figure 5.33 Mark as Compromised Warning

3. Choose CONTINUE to proceed (or choose CANCEL to bail).

4. Next, you'll be asked if you want to reencrypt all of the affected objects with the active key (see Figure 5.34). Choose YES or NO.

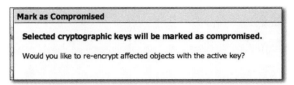

Mark as Compromised

Selected cryptographic keys will be marked as compromised.

Would you like to re-encrypt affected objects with the active key?

Figure 5.34 Option to Reencrypt Affected Objects

If you chose YES, you'll return to the CRYPTOGRAPHIC KEYS tab, and you'll now see your old key with a status of REVOKED – COMPROMISED and with 0 objects. Your new key will now have all of the objects that used to be under the revoked one (see Figure 5.35).

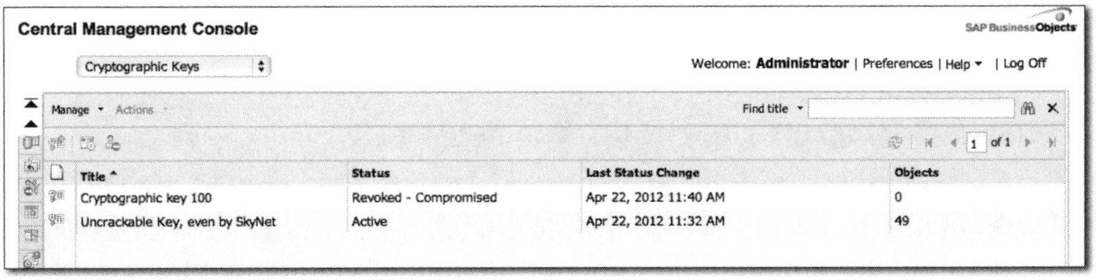

Central Management Console				SAP BusinessObjects
Cryptographic Keys			Welcome: **Administrator** | Preferences | Help ▼ | Log Off	
Manage ▼ Actions ▼			Find title ▼	
Title ▲	Status	Last Status Change	Objects	
Cryptographic key 100	Revoked - Compromised	Apr 22, 2012 11:40 AM	0	
Uncrackable Key, even by SkyNet	Active	Apr 22, 2012 11:32 AM	49	

Figure 5.35 New Key with All Objects and Old Key Revoked

A deactivated cryptographic key can still be used by the data objects associated with it. To break the association between the encrypted objects and the deactivated key, you must revoke the key. When we marked the key in the previous example as compromised, this revoked it as well, as evidenced by its status.

But, if you just want to revoke the key without marking it compromised, you can do that, too.

1. Select the key you want to revoke.

2. Click ACTIONS • REVOKE, and the REVOKE CRYPTOGRAPHIC KEYS dialog box appears with a warning message.

3. Click OK to revoke the cryptographic key. A process is launched to encrypt all of the key's objects with the currently active key. If the key is associated with a bunch of objects, it will be marked as DEACTIVATED: RE-ENCRYPTION IN PROCESS until the reencryption process is complete.

After a cryptographic key is revoked, it can be safely removed from the system because no sensitive data objects require the key for decryption.

Deleting a Cryptographic Key

After your key has been revoked, either by marking it compromised or by revoking it, you'll have the option to delete it. Simply click the key, and then click MANAGE • DELETE, or right-click the key, and choose DELETE.

After you delete a cryptographic key, it's gone for good. You can't get it back.

Cryptographic Keys in Summary

Cryptographic keys are a great new addition to the SAP BusinessObjects BI platform. They address some age-old concerns regarding security of sensitive information inside your SAP BusinessObjects BI system. Users must be members of the Cryptographic Officers group to manage cryptographic keys. Membership of this group should be kept to an absolute minimum. You can have more than one cryptographic key in the system at any given time, but only one key can be active at a time. A deactivated key can still be used by objects that are encrypted by it, but new objects created or added will be encrypted to the active key only. You can revoke a key and have all of its dependent objects reencrypted to the active key. Likewise, you can mark a key as compromised, which will also revoke it. After a key is revoked, you can safely delete it from the SAP BusinessObjects BI 4.1 platform.

Cryptography is great for keeping things locked down on the system, but what about when you're worried about what is being transmitted off of your SAP BusinessObjects BI 4.1 server and out into the ether? That, my friend, is where we'll want to discuss Secure Sockets Layer (SSL).

5.3.2 Configuring Servers for Secure Sockets Layer

In case you've been living under a rock for the past 20 years, SSL is the standard security technology for establishing an encrypted link between two systems that communicate over a network. This could be a web server talking to a web browser, or it could be an application on a user's workstation communicating with a server in a remote location. SSL is an industry standard and is used in millions of websites and applications to protect online transactions and network communications over the Internet.

SAP BusinessObjects BI can use SSL to communicate between the application and the end-user web browsers, as well as any thick client SAP BusinessObjects BI 4.1 tools that need to connect back to the repository. Assuming that your SAP BusinessObjects BI deployment is SSL-enabled, you can perform the following high-level steps to set up SSL for all SAP BusinessObjects BI 4.1 server communication:

1. Create key and certificate files for each machine in your deployment.

2. Configure the SSL protocol; in other words, configure the location of these files in the CCM and in your Web Application Server.

3. Configure any thick client tools such as SAP BusinessObjects Web Intelligence Rich Client or the Information Design Tool.

We discuss these steps in more detail next.

Creating Key and Certificate Files

The first step in setting up SSL is to create a key file and a certificate file for each server in your deployment. To generate these files, you'll have to drop down to the trusty command line and work with the SSLC program.

Following are some important notes for a successful SSL deployment:

▶ You'll need to create certificates for all machines in the deployment, including machines running the thick client components such as Web Intelligence Rich Client. (For client machines, use the `sslconfig` command-line tool to complete the configuration.)

▶ For maximum security, all private keys should be protected and should not be transferred through unsecured communication channels.

▶ Certificates created for previous versions of SAP BusinessObjects BI won't work for SAP BusinessObjects BI 4.1. These certificates will need to be re-created.

To create key and certificate files for a server machine, the steps are the same whether you're on Windows or on UNIX/Linux. Only the beginning path is different:

1. Run the *SSLC.exe* (or `sslc` command on UNIX/Linux) command-line tool. The SSLC tool is installed with your SAP BusinessObjects BI 4.1 software, by

default, in *<INSTALLDIR>\SAP BusinessObjects Enterprise XI 4.0\win64_x64* , or for UNIX/Linux in *<INSTALLDIR>/sap_bobj/enterprise_xi40/<PLATFORM>*.

2. Type the following command: `sslc req -config sslc.cnf -new -out cacert.req`. This command creates two files, a certificate authority (CA) certificate request (`cacert.req`) and a private key (`privkey.pem`).

3. To decrypt the private key, type the following command: `sslc rsa -in privkey.pem -out cakey.pem`. This command creates the decrypted key, *cakey.pem*.

4. To sign the CA certificate, type the following command: `sslc x509 -in cacert.req -out cacert.pem -req -signkey cakey.pem -days 365`. This command creates a self-signed certificate, `cacert.pem`, that expires after 365 days. Choose the number of days that best suits your security requirements.

5. Using a text editor, open the *sslc.cnf* file, which is stored in the same folder as the SSLC command-line tool. Using a text editor is highly recommended because Windows Explorer may not properly recognize and display files with a .cnf extension.

6. Perform the following steps based on the settings in the *sslc.cnf* file:

   ▶ Place the *cakey.pem* and *cacert.pem* files in the directories specified by the *sslc.cnf* file's `certificate` and `private_key` options. By default, the settings in the *sslc.cnf* file are the following:

   ```
   certificate = $dir/cacert.pem
   private_key = $dir/private/cakey.pem
   ```

   ▶ Create a file with the name specified by the *sslc.cnf* file's database setting. By default, this file is *$dir/index.txt*. This file should be empty.

   ▶ Create a file with the name specified by the *sslc.cnf* file's `serial` setting. Ensure that this file provides an octet-string serial number (in hexadecimal format). To ensure that you can create and sign more certificates, choose a large hexadecimal number with an even number of digits, such as 111111111111111111111111111111111.

   ▶ Create a directory specified by the *sslc.cnf* file's `new_certs_dir` setting.

   a) To create a certificate request and a private key, type the following command: `sslc req -config sslc.cnf -new -out -servercert.req`. The certificate and key files generated are placed under the current working folder.

b) Run the following command to decrypt the key in the *privkey.pem* file:
`sslc rsa -in privkey.pem -out server.key`.

c) To sign the certificate with the CA, type the following command: `sslc ca -config sslc.cnf -days 365 -out servercert.pem -in servercert.req`. This command creates the *servercert.pem* file, which contains the signed certificate.

d) Use the following commands to convert the certificates to Distinguished Encoding Rules (DER)-encoded certificates:

- `sslc x509 -in cacert.pem -out cacert.der -outform DER`

- `sslc x509 -in servercert.pem -out servercert.der -outform DER`

▶ The CA certificate (*cacert.der*) and its corresponding private key (*cakey.pem*) need to be generated only once per deployment. All machines in the same deployment must share the same CA certificates. All other certificates need to be signed by the private key of any of the CA certificates.

a) Create a text file (*passphrase.txt*) for storing the plain text passphrase used for decrypting the generated private key.

b) Store the following key and certificate files in a secure location (under the same directory, *d:/ssl*) that can be accessed by machines in your SAP BusinessObjects BI 4.1 platform environment:

- The trusted certificate file, *cacert.der*

- The generated server certificate file, *servercert.der*

- The server key file, *server.key*

- The passphrase file

This location will be used to configure SSL for the CCM and your Web Application Server.

Configuring the SSL Protocol

If you made it this far and thought you were done, think again. You're only part of the way there (nobody ever said security was easy). After you've created keys and certificates for each and every machine in your deployment and have tucked them safely away in your secure location, you'll need to get your CCM and Web Application Server hip to all that great SSL information.

To configure the SSL protocol in the CCM on Windows, follow these steps:

1. In the CCM, stop your Server Intelligence Agent.

2. After it has stopped, right-click the SIA, click PROPERTIES, and then go to the PROTOCOL tab.

3. Select the ENABLE SSL checkbox.

4. Provide the file path for the directory where you stored the key and certificate files.

Figure 5.36 shows the CCM PROTOCOL tab, which contains the following fields:

▶ SSL CERTIFICATES FOLDER
Folder where all the required SSL certificates and files are stored. For this example, it is *d:\ssl*.

▶ SERVER SSL CERTIFICATE FILE
Name of the file used to store the server SSL certificate. By default, it is *server-cert.der*.

▶ SSL TRUSTED CERTIFICATES FILES
Name of the file with the SSL trusted certificate. By default, it is *cacert.der*.

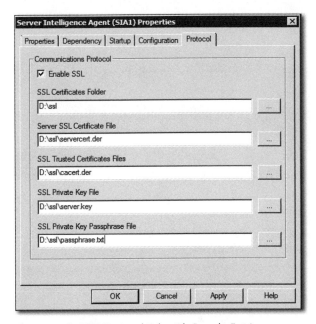

Figure 5.36 CCM Protocol Tab with Sample Entries

▶ SSL PRIVATE KEY FILE
Name of the SSL trusted certificate. By default, it is *server.key*.

▶ SSL PRIVATE KEY PASSPHRASE FILE
Name of the text file containing the passphrase used to access the private key. By default, it is *passphrase.txt*.

To configure the SSL protocol on UNIX, follow these steps:

1. You'll use the `serverconfig.sh` script to configure SSL for the SIA. While not as pretty as its Windows counterpart, the CCM, this script is a text-based program that will enable you to view server information and to add and delete servers from your installation. The `serverconfig.sh` script is installed to the *sap_bobj* directory of your installation.

2. Use the `ccm.sh` or the `stopservers` script to stop your SIA and all SAP BusinessObjects BI servers.

3. Run the `serverconfig.sh` script.

4. Select 3 – MODIFY NODE, and press ⸢Enter⸣.

5. Specify the target SIA, and press ⸢Enter⸣.

6. Select the 1 – MODIFY SERVER INTELLIGENCE AGENT SSL configuration option.

7. Select SSL.

8. When prompted, specify the SSL certificate locations.

9. If your SAP BusinessObjects BI 4.1 platform deployment is an SIA cluster, repeat steps 1–6 for each SIA.

10. Start the SIA with the `ccm.sh` or `startservers` scripts and wait for the servers to start.

To configure the SSL protocol on your Web Application Server if you're running a J2EE Web Application Server, the following example entries will need to go in your Java launch string:

```
-Dbusinessobjects.orb.oci.protocol=ssl -DcertDir=d:\ssl
-DtrustedCert=cacert.der -DsslCert=clientcert.der
-DsslKey=client.key -Dpassphrase=passphrase.txt
```

The example entries can be described as follows:

- `DcertDir=d:\ssl`
  The directory to store all the certificates and keys.

- `DtrustedCert=cacert.der`
  Trusted certificate file. If specifying more than one, separate with semicolons.

- `DsslCert=clientcert.der`
  Certificate used by the SDK.

- `DsslKey=client.key`
  Private key of the SDK certificate.

- `Dpassphrase=passphrase.txt`
  The file that stores the passphrase for the private key.

If by some chance you're instead using a Microsoft Internet Information Services (IIS) Web Application Server, run the `sslconfig` tool from the command line, and follow the configuration steps.

Configuring Thick Client Tools

The last step is to configure any thick client tools, such as Web Intelligence Rich Client or the Information Design Tool. To do this, follow these steps:

1. Make sure you've created and saved all of the required SSL resources in a known directory.

2. Make sure the thick client application isn't in operation.

3. Run the `sslconfig.exe` command line tool.

4. The SSLC tool is installed with your SAP BusinessObjects BI 4.1 client tools software by default in *<INSTALLDIR>SAP BusinessObjects Enterprise XI 4.0\ win64_ x64* (see Figure 5.37).

5. Type the following command:

   ```
   sslconfig.exe -dir d:\SSL -mycert servercert.der
   -rootcert cacert.der -mykey server.key -passphrase passphrase.txt
   -protocol ssl
   ```

6. Restart the thick client application.

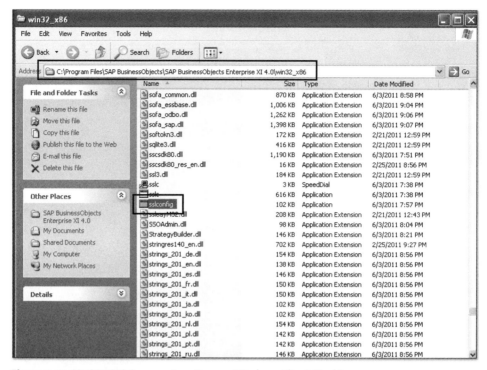

Figure 5.37 SSLCONFIG Program Location on Windows Client Machine

Secure Sockets Layer (SSL) Summary

While the process may seem extremely manual (well, it kind of is), the benefits of implementing SSL are numerous. By going through the somewhat tedious exercise of getting your SSL up and running, you'll be able to rest assured that all of the communication between your SAP BusinessObjects BI 4.1 environment and the various access points (web browsers, thick client tools) are encrypted and protected. This is especially important if you're exposing your reporting portals and content to the greater Internet. This leads really nicely into the next topic, firewalls and reverse-proxies.

Pop Quiz
1. Where are cryptographic keys managed in SAP BusinessObjects BI 4.1?
2. What is the purpose of the cluster key?
3. True or False: Cryptography is fun!

5.4   Working with Firewalls and Reverse-Proxies

If your business needs include allowing access to people outside of the walls of your organization (or even other departments in the same company), then grab a cup of your favorite caffeinated beverage and perk up because this section is especially important for you. All the encryption keys and SSL in the world won't help you much if you're swimming in the big shark tank that is the Internet.

Don't be too frightened—be cautious and vigilant, but not frightened. Allowing your business analytics content to be consumed from a remote location over a Wide Area Network (WAN) can be done, and done with relative safety. Cryptography and SSL are a part of that recipe, but the two main building blocks for a secure deployment are firewalls and reverse-proxies.

In general, a firewall is for computer systems what it's "real" counterpart is: a nearly impenetrable barrier. A brick-and-mortar firewall is meant to stop a blaze from passing through a large building. It can withstand intense heat and, to a large extent, falling, burning debris. A software firewall will block access to your servers and only allow network traffic that knows the secret handshake. This keeps curious hackers out of your system and allows your critical business traffic to get through.

If you aren't familiar with a reverse-proxy, we're betting you're familiar with the Hollywood actor, Kevin Bacon. Think of a reverse-proxy like the popular trivia game "Six Degrees of Kevin Bacon." In the game, players attempt to link any individual to Kevin Bacon as quickly as possible and in as few links as possible. The concept is that the person at the beginning doesn't personally know Kevin Bacon, but someone in the middle of the process does. That's a reverse-proxy! You don't want people in the wide world to know what your internal URLs or IP addresses are, so you put a reverse-proxy in between. You know a public URL, which then gets sent to the reverse-proxy server, and it knows the internal IP or URL of where to route the request. Presto! You have a public way to access your internal systems without compromising their delicate inner workings to the more nefarious elements of our digital society who may be lurking with bad intentions.

So, let's get into the details. First, we'll go over why request ports are important. Then we'll give you the skinny on planning for your firewall and request ports. Next we'll outline how to implement your request port and firewall plan, without forgetting to cover the all-important guide to troubleshooting a firewall deployment. We'll follow up with more than you ever wanted to know about reverse-proxies.

5.4.1 SAP BusinessObjects BI 4.1 Platform Servers and Communication Ports

Every one of your servers and services needs a way to communicate with the others. And, they need a way to communicate that doesn't interfere with the other servers. As you can imagine, behind the scenes, there is a lot of chatter going on between the different server components during normal operations. Having collisions of internal communications would mean lost signals and really shoddy performance. So, just like each of you has your own phone number (so people know how to route a call to you and only you) each SAP BusinessObjects BI platform server binds itself to a request port when it starts.

These request ports are dynamically generated by default. Go to any of your platform servers, right-click, and select PROPERTIES. In the COMMON SETTINGS section, you'll find the request ports (Figure 5.38).

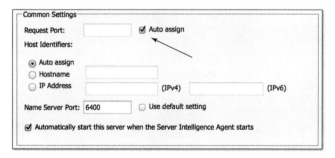

Figure 5.38 Request Port Settings in a Server Properties Window

When each server in SAP BusinessObjects BI 4.1 starts, the first thing it does is register with the Central Management Server. Part of that registration process is telling the CMS what request port this server is going to be communicating on for the duration of this operating period. The CMS itself is the exception to the rule because it's the boss. The CMS has two ports, a name server port and a request port. Each server added to the platform knows what the CMS name server port is, and it will communicate initially on that port to the CMS. The CMS will respond and kindly inform the server of the value of its request port and then also kindly make sure that all subsequent communication takes place over the request port.

So, the CMS gets all the dish on what request ports are being used by whom during a particular running period of the platform. The CMS maintains that information, of course, in the system database for every server that has registered with it. This is great internally within the SAP BusinessObjects BI 4.1 system, but also keep in mind that there are client tools that will want to connect to the platform as well (Web Intelligence Rich Client, SAP Crystal Reports Designer, Information Design Tool, etc.). And, to make matters just a tad more complicated for you, the SIA also uses the CMS request port to communicate with it. And to top things off, many of the processing tier servers will spawn a child process to handle tasks. Each child process will also get its own request port. Ports, ports everywhere, but there's not a packet to send.

Before you get frustrated and chuck this book into the nearest incinerator, let's break it down into some simple, general rules to remember before we configure our firewall:

▶ Every SAP BusinessObjects BI 4.1 server (and service) must be able to initiate communication with every other SAP BusinessObjects BI 4.1 server (and service) via the destination server's request port.

▶ The CMS uses two ports. Every SAP BusinessObjects BI 4.1 server, Rich Client, and the Web Application Server that hosts the SDK must be able to initiate communication with the CMS on both of its ports.

▶ Every Job Server child process must be able to communicate with the CMS.

▶ Thick clients must be able to initiate communication with the request port of the input and output File Repository Servers (iFRS and oFRS).

▶ If auditing is enabled for thick clients and web applications, they must be able to initiate communication with the request port of the Adaptive Processing Servers (APSs) that host the Client Auditing Proxy Service (CAPS).

▶ In general, the Web Application Server that hosts the SDK must be able to communicate with the request port of every SAP BusinessObjects BI 4.1 platform server.

▶ The CMS platform server must be able to communicate with the CMS system and auditing databases.

▶ The Connection Server, and most Job Server child processes, must be able to initiate communication with the reporting databases (your data sources).

Seems a little daunting, doesn't it? Don't let it get you down. Remember that you only need to worry about ports for servers that you're using. If you aren't using SAP Crystal Reports, for example, you don't have to concern yourself with the SAP Crystal Reports ports. Go ahead and try to say "Crystal Reports request ports" five times fast. We dare you.

When you need to get specific, Table 5.4 shows you which servers need to use which ports for the SAP BusinessObjects BI products.

Product	Client Application	Associated Servers	Server Port Requirements
SAP Crystal Reports	SAP Crystal Reports 2011 Designer	▸ CMS ▸ iFRS ▸ oFRS ▸ RAS ▸ SAP Crystal Reports 2011 Processing Server ▸ SAP Crystal Reports Cache Server	▸ CMS name server port (6400 by default) ▸ CMS request port ▸ iFRS request port ▸ oFRS request port ▸ RAS request port ▸ SAP Crystal Reports 2011 Processing Server request port ▸ SAP Crystal Reports Cache Server request port
SAP Crystal Reports	SAP Crystal Reports for Enterprise Designer	▸ CMS ▸ iFRS ▸ oFRS ▸ SAP Crystal Reports Processing Server ▸ SAP Crystal Reports Cache Server	▸ CMS name server port (6400 by default) ▸ CMS request port ▸ iFRS request port ▸ oFRS request port ▸ RAS request port ▸ SAP Crystal Reports Processing Server request port ▸ SAP Crystal Reports Cache Server request port

Table 5.4 Server and Port Requirements for SAP BusinessObjects BI Tools
(Source: BusinessObjects Platform Administrator Guide)

Product	Client Application	Associated Servers	Server Port Requirements
SAP BusinessObjects Dashboards	SAP BusinessObjects Dashboards	▸ CMS ▸ iFRS ▸ oFRS ▸ Web Services provider application (*dswsbobje.war*)	▸ CMS name server port (6400 by default) ▸ CMS request port ▸ iFRS request port ▸ oFRS request port ▸ HTTP port (80 by default)
Live Office	Live Office Client	Web services provider application (*dswsbobje.war*)	HTTP port (80 by default)
SAP BusinessObjects BI platform	Web Intelligence Rich Client	▸ CMS ▸ iFRS	▸ CMS name server port (6400 by default) ▸ CMS request port ▸ iFRS request port
SAP BusinessObjects BI platform	Universe Design Tool	▸ CMS ▸ iFRS ▸ Connection Server	▸ CMS name server port (6400 by default) ▸ CMS request port ▸ iFRS request port ▸ Connection Server request port
SAP BusinessObjects BI platform	Business View Manager	▸ CMS ▸ iFRS	▸ CMS name server port (6400 by default) ▸ CMS request port ▸ iFRS request port
SAP BusinessObjects BI platform	Central Configuration Manager (CCM)	▸ CMS ▸ SIA	▸ CMS name server port (6400 by default) ▸ CMS request port
SAP BusinessObjects BI platform	Server Intelligence Agent	Every SAP BusinessObjects platform server, including the CMS	▸ SIA request port (6410 by default) ▸ CMS name server port (6400 by default) ▸ CMS request port

Table 5.4 Server and Port Requirements for SAP BusinessObjects BI Tools (Source: BusinessObjects Platform Administrator Guide) (Cont.)

Product	Client Application	Associated Servers	Server Port Requirements
SAP BusinessObjects BI platform	Report Conversion Tool	▸ CMS ▸ iFRS	▸ CMS name server port (6400 by default) ▸ CMS request port ▸ iFRS request port
SAP BusinessObjects BI platform	Repository Diagnostic Tool (RDT)	▸ CMS ▸ iFRS ▸ oFRS	▸ CMS name server port (6400 by default) ▸ CMS request port ▸ iFRS request port ▸ oFRS request port
SAP BusinessObjects BI platform	SAP BusinessObjects 4.1 SDK hosted in the Web Application Server	All SAP BusinessObjects BI 4.1 platform servers required by the associated products (SAP Crystal Reports, Web Intelligence, etc.)	▸ CMS name server port (6400 by default) ▸ CMS request port ▸ Request port for each server required by the associated products
SAP BusinessObjects BI platform	Web Services provider (*dswsbobje.war*)	All SAP BusinessObjects BI 4.1 platform servers required by the products accessing the Web Services	▸ CMS name server port (6400 by default) ▸ CMS request port ▸ Request port for each server required by the associated products
SAP BusinessObjects BI platform	SAP BusinessObjects Analysis, edition for OLAP	▸ CMS ▸ APS hosting the MDAS ▸ iFRS ▸ oFRS	▸ CMS name server port (6400 by default) ▸ CMS request port ▸ iFRS request port ▸ oFRS request port ▸ APS (MDAS) request port

Table 5.4 Server and Port Requirements for SAP BusinessObjects BI Tools (Source: BusinessObjects Platform Administrator Guide) (Cont.)

Table 5.5 will give you a clearer picture of the port requirements for the various third-party products that interact with the platform.

Third-Party Application	SAP BusinessObjects BI 4.1 Component That Uses It	Third-Party Application Port Requirement	Description
CMS System Database	CMS	Database server listen port	The CMS is the only server that communicates with the CMS system DB.
CMS Auditing Database	CMS	Database server listen port	The CMS is the only server that communicates with the auditing DB.
Reporting Database	▶ Connection Server ▶ Every Job Server child process ▶ Every Processing Server	Database server listen port	These servers retrieve information from the reporting (data source) database.
Web Application Server	All SAP BusinessObjects web services and web applications, including the BI Launch Pad and the CMC.	HTTP port and HTTPS port	The HTTPS port is only required if secure HTTP communication is used (SSL).
FTP Server	Every Job Server	▶ FTP in (port 21) ▶ FTP out (port 22)	The Job Servers use the FTP ports to allow send to FTP.
Email Server	Every Job Server	SMTP (port 25)	The Job Servers use the SMTP port to allow send to email.
UNIX Servers (to which the Job Servers can send content)	Every Job Server	▶ rexec out (port 512) ▶ (UNIX only) rsh out (port 514)	(UNIX only) The Job Servers use these ports to allow send to disk.
Authentication Server	▶ CMS ▶ Web Application Server that hosts the SDK ▶ Every thick client	Connection port for third-party authentication	User credentials are stored in the third-party Authentication Server. The CMS, SDK, and thick clients need to communicate with this Authentication Server when a user logs in.

Table 5.5 Server and Port Requirements for Third-Party Tools (Source: BusinessObjects Platform Administrator Guide)

Wow! That's a lot of ports! We need to come up with a plan, or when we put a firewall in place, we'll be sunk. Read on, fearless admin, read on.

5.4.2 Planning for Firewalls

So, we're not putting the cart before the horse, the first question you'll need to answer is "How many firewalls am I going to need?" Great question, and like so many other questions posed to us as administrators, it really depends on your organization's security requirements. Let's assume you need at least one firewall, and we'll discuss a few different configuration landscapes. Don't take this to mean that you can't have a firewall on a "black box" installation, but for the sake of firewall discussions, it's easier to indicate each tier of the SAP BusinessObjects BI 4.1 platform separately.

Configuration Option 1: Single Firewall Protecting CMS and Downstream

In this configuration, we'll put a single firewall in between our SAP BusinessObjects BI 4.1 platform servers and the Web Application Server (see Figure 5.39). This will protect the data being housed in our iFRS and oFRS and restrict direct access to the server.

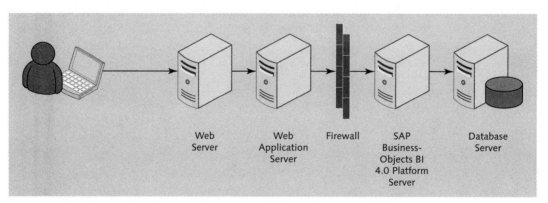

Figure 5.39 Configuration Option 1: Single Firewall in Front of CMS

For this example, we'll assume that the SAP BusinessObjects BI 4.1 platform server and the database server are safely tucked behind the firewall. All communication between SAP BusinessObjects BI 4.1 and the reporting databases is unhindered, yet the CMS can send information back to the web tier through the firewall securely.

Configuration Option 2: Single Firewall Protecting Web Application Server and Downstream

In this configuration, we really just want to restrict communication between the web server and the Web Application Server (see Figure 5.40). Everything downstream of the firewall has unhindered access to each other.

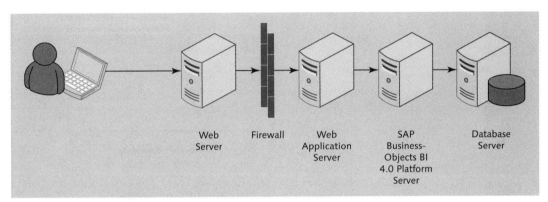

Figure 5.40 Configuration Option 2: Single Firewall in front of Web Application Server

Options 1 and 2 are probably sufficient if you just want to have some extra security in place for an SAP BusinessObjects BI 4.1 deployment that is only accessible from within your corporate network. Your network has its own set of security measures to prevent prying eyes, and you can leverage that layer of security that is already in place and not needlessly complicate your SAP BusinessObjects BI 4.1 landscape.

But, if you work in a highly regulated organization, or if you need to have people outside of your corporate network access SAP BusinessObjects BI 4.1, then you'll need something a bit more robust in place before you'll be able to sleep well at night.

Configuration Option 3: Multiple Firewalls for Maximum Protection

If you do need to let users come in and run reports from somewhere outside of your corporate network, then you'll likely want to put in the maximum amount of protection that your risk appetite (and budget) can support. In this situation, you'd likely want to put a firewall in between each tier of the application stack (see Figure 5.41). This will give your data the most protection from any sort of outside intrusion.

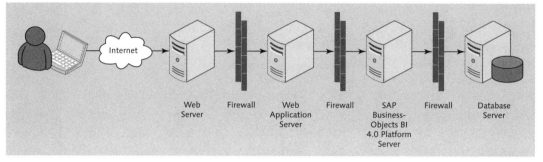

Figure 5.41 Configuration Option 3: Multiple Firewalls

This configuration makes pretty darned sure that nothing gets across to your reporting databases except authorized traffic on an authorized port. This doesn't guarantee that you're hacker-proof, by any stretch of the imagination, but it provides about as much protection as you can get and still allow SAP BusinessObjects BI 4.1 to function.

These aren't the only ways you can deploy a firewall in your system. Be imaginative, and you'll find at least a dozen other ways you could put firewalls in to add security. These are meant to be general examples to spark your interest and get you thinking about how best to deploy a firewall into your environment.

5.4.3   Planning Port Ranges

Now that you've picked your firewall configuration, you have to start thinking about those pesky request ports that your SAP BusinessObjects BI 4.1 servers need to talk with one another. By default, your SAP BusinessObjects BI 4.1 deployment won't work through firewalls, plain and simple. That's because all of those request ports are dynamically assigned when each server starts up. It's pretty hard (and pointless) to try to tell a firewall to just let everything through. Why have a firewall then? This is where some more planning is needed.

As a general outline of the process, you'll need to now go into the Central Management Console and open up the PROPERTIES page of every server you want to talk through the firewall and manually assign it a request port. Next, you'll have to build firewall rules in your firewall to allow those ports you just assigned to be accessible from the appropriate server above and no one else.

It's best to come up with a plan ahead of time. First, take some inventory of your SAP BusinessObjects BI server. See what ports are already in use and which ones are available for you to use. Create a list of all of the servers you know are going to be in play and will need to communicate through the firewall. Take your list of servers and jot them down in a document or spreadsheet. Start with the CMS and the SIA. If you're stuck with the default ports, the CMS will be on port 6400 for its name server, and the SIA will be on port 6410. From there, assuming nothing else is using those ports, it's safe to start incrementing down your port range, for example, as shown in Table 5.6.

Server Name	Request Port Number
CMS	6400 (name server port)
SIA	6410
CMS	6411
oFRS	6412
iFRS	6413
Connection Server	6414

Table 5.6 Cataloging your Request Port Ranges

And on, and on, and on it goes. Build out your entire list in a separate document because when you're done, it will be much easier to hand this off to your firewall administrator or to use as a guide if you have to configure the firewall yourself.

It's important to keep in mind that your Job Servers will spawn child processes that each need their own request ports. If you don't specify the port range for your Job Servers to use, they'll go and assign something dynamically that probably won't be able to get through your firewall.

5.4.4 Implementing a Request Port Plan for Firewalls

To assign request ports for your SAP BusinessObjects BI 4.1 servers, go to the CMC SERVERS tab, right-click the server you want to configure, and choose PROPERTIES (see Figure 5.42).

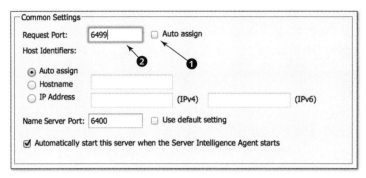

Figure 5.42 Manually Assigning a Request Port

First, unselect the AUTO ASSIGN radio button ❶. Second, enter the REQUEST PORT value ❷ for this server from your spreadsheet list. Click the SAVE & CLOSE button near the bottom of your window, and then restart your server to put the change into effect. Go through your spreadsheet list and repeat this process for each and every server you need to get through the firewall.

For your Job Server, the assignment is a little less elegant. You'll need to enter a switch into the command line of the server launch (see Figure 5.43).

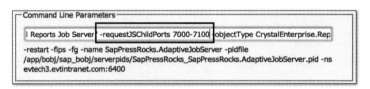

Figure 5.43 Specifying a Port Range for Job Server Child Processes

Click into the command line, scroll to the end, press `Space`, and then enter the following switch: `-requestJSChildPorts <port range>`. Put a dash in between your start and end ports, as shown in Figure 5.43. Click SAVE & CLOSE, and then restart your Job Server. For the preceding example, we gave the Job Server 100 ports to work with. Ideally, you want to make this number as small as possible so you have just enough for your needs because each one of those ports will have to be opened in the firewall. The more holes you poke in your firewall, the more risk of intrusion gets introduced to the system.

Every brand of firewall is different, so it's a tad futile to try to describe how to implement your request port matrix into it. So, keep in mind the general, high-level process. You want to allow traffic from the tier above to access your SAP BusinessObjects BI 4.1 servers on their assigned request ports. Generally speaking, it will be *Allow [From (Web Application Tier IP Address)] [To (BI 4 Enterprise Tier IP Address)] on [Port (Request Port)]*. Enter an allow rule for every one of your request ports from your matrix.

5.4.5 Troubleshooting a Firewall Deployment

Invariably, you're going to hit a snag. It's easy to deploy an SAP BusinessObjects BI 4.1 environment that's wide open, but after you start locking things down, things can get dicey. There are three major areas where you can hit a snag when implementing a firewall/static request port strategy:

▸ You assigned the same request port number to more than one server in the stack.

▸ You assigned a request port number that was already in use by something not in the SAP BusinessObjects BI 4.1 stack.

▸ You didn't open the firewall rule properly.

Let's discuss each of these in a little more detail next.

Problem 1: You assigned the same request port to more than one server.

This is common, because the process is manual. Any manual process can fall prey to human error. This is where building your port matrix on the side in a spreadsheet or document table really helps. For one thing, it keeps you on track where you can easily see your port list. It's even better if you're using a spreadsheet to create a formula to let the spreadsheet calculate the port values (less room for error). It's also best when you're entering the request ports in the CMC to copy and paste them from your port matrix. This helps eliminate the possibility of a typo. If you're already in trouble, then pull out your port matrix, and go back and double-check every single entry. It's time-consuming but necessary.

Problem 2: You assigned a request port that was already in use somewhere else.

This can happen if you're not careful when you're planning. It's super important for you to understand what ports are already in use on your system. If you aren't sure, check with someone who can help, such as a system administrator or network administrator. Check and see if you can find the offending process. The Windows Event Log is a great place to look because port conflicts are written right in there. On UNIX, check /var/adm/messages to see (or your OS's equivalent). After you find the offending process, you either have to change the port that process is using or change your conflicting request port. Fix the conflict, bounce the process, and you should be good to go.

Problem 3: You didn't properly implement the firewall rule.

This one is a tough one to spot. Again, a bunch of caution while implementing can save you hours of troubleshooting. The port matrix is very important in these cases. Go back and double-check your firewall rules. If you don't have access to administer the firewall yourself, then get on the source server (such as the Web Application Server), and try to telnet to your SAP BusinessObjects BI 4.1 server on each request port in your matrix. If the firewall rules are in place properly, the telnet should connect right up. If it can't, you found your problem. Check all of your ports that way, and make sure they're open and running properly.

5.4.6 Firewall Takeaways

Quite simply, a firewall is like your linebackers. It's a line of defense in front of your quarterback. The firewall, when properly implemented, will protect your data sources and your SAP BusinessObjects BI 4.1 server by making sure only authorized traffic can access those servers from a specific host on a specific port. SAP BusinessObjects BI 4.1, by default, randomly assigns request ports for each server when it starts. To create firewall rules around those ports, you have to manually assign a static request port for every SAP BusinessObjects BI 4.1 server that must go through the firewall. Create a plan to assign your ports, and be sure to check ahead of time to see if any of those ports are already in use. Use a separate document or spreadsheet as a port matrix to be your guide to what you assign. Copy and paste the port numbers from your port matrix into the assignment window in the CMC to help eliminate typos and headaches down the road. Get a system administrator or firewall expert to help you out if you get stuck.

5.4.7   Reverse-Proxies

Just like Kevin Bacon doesn't want to be directly associated with you, you don't want your Web Application Server to be directly associated with a dirty, exposed web server. Hackers love to get their hands on internal IP addresses and server names. It makes their disruptive shenanigans all the easier. So, wherever and whenever you need to give access to your SAP BusinessObjects BI 4.1 environment outside of your corporate network, you'll want to use a reverse-proxy to add that extra layer of security (see Figure 5.44).

There are really just a few supported reverse-proxy servers: IBM Tivoli Access Manager WebSEAL 6, Apache 2.2, and Microsoft ISA 2006. Be sure to set up your reverse-proxy server according to the vendor's instructions.

Without getting into the specifics about configuration here (there are too many variables for this discussion), think again about the general process. The reverse-proxy will have a publicly accessible URL (e.g., *http://myreportingsolution.com/ BOE/BI*). This URL will map traffic to the appropriate web application behind it in the Web Application Server, while not exposing that exact location to the end user. This keeps your private IP address schemes private.

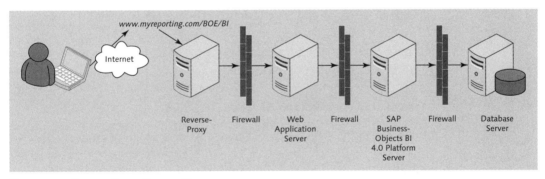

Figure 5.44 Reverse-Proxy Process Flow

> **Note**
>
> For all the specifics around how to set up your particular reverse-proxy server with your particular Web Application Server, we recommend that you consult your reverse-proxy documentation and the *BusinessObjects Platform Administrator Guide*.

Pop Quiz

1. What port is required to be open if a web tier is placed within the demilitarized zone (DMZ) on the web server?
2. What port (default) must be open on the SAP BusinessObjects BI server if restricted by a firewall to be accessed by client tools or DMZ web tier servers?
3. Describe a scenario in which all service ports would need to be explicitly defined.
4. How do I get closer to Kevin Bacon?

5.5 General Recommendations for Securing Your SAP BusinessObjects BI 4.1 Deployment

Get ready for a great big steaming pile of security goodness in summary:

▶ Use firewalls to protect the communication between the CMS and other system components. If possible, always hide your CMS behind a firewall. At a minimum, ensure that the system and Auditor databases are safely behind a firewall.

▶ Add additional encryption to the FRSs. After the system is up and running, sensitive business data will be stored in these servers. Add additional encryption through the operating system or use a third-party tool. It's important to note here that SAP BusinessObjects BI 4.1 doesn't support SFTP. If you require the use of SFTP, there's an SAP Note for that, and it's SAP Note 1556571. Either that or you should consider an SAP partner solution.

▶ Deploy a reverse-proxy server in front of the Web Application Servers to hide them behind a single IP address. This configuration routes all Internet traffic that is addressed to private Web Application Servers through the reverse-proxy server, thus hiding the private IP addresses.

▶ Strictly enforce corporate password policies. Make sure that your pesky users are changing their passwords regularly.

▶ Use randomly generated strong passwords, especially for your service accounts (Administrator account, System Database account, Subversion account, etc.).

▶ If you have opted to install the system database and Web Application Server provided with your SAP BusinessObjects BI 4.1 install, review the relevant documentation to make sure these components are deployed with adequate security.

▶ If you're using the default installation of Apache Tomcat, be sure to check the Apache website often for security updates. You'll likely have to manually update your version of Tomcat to make sure the latest security fixes are in place. Refer to the Apache Tomcat security recommendations for running the Web Application Server, and refer to the SAP Product Availability Matrix before applying any patches to make sure you don't patch yourself out of a supported version.

▶ Use the SSL protocol for all network communication between clients and servers in your deployment.

▶ Install SAP BusinessObjects BI 4.1 on a dedicated server and restrict access to who can log in. The installation directory and subdirectories must be secured. Sensitive temporary data may be stored in these directories during normal system operations.

▶ Access to the CMC should be restricted to local access only.

▶ If you're not a big enough company to have your own data center, make sure that the room where your SAP BusinessObjects BI 4.1 server and your database servers are has controlled access. This could even be a locked closet, albeit a rather warm one unless you have some special cooling installed. It sounds silly, but lock up your servers! Literally.

▶ Make sure the built-in Guest account is disabled. There are other ways to allow "anonymous" access that don't pose as great a risk. Really, just turn it off. Maybe in a future release we'll finally be able to delete this monster.

Security is all about diligence. You have to take a look at all of those possible touch points where data could leak or where someone could see something they aren't supposed to see.

5.6 Multitenancy

What in the great wide world is multitenancy, you ask? Think about the places where people live. A single-family home is analogous to how most people build an SAP BusinessObjects BI platform system. One group from one company has access, creates and uses content, and administers the system. Now, picture a high-rise apartment building in New York City. It's one big building, but has many smaller, individually occupied apartments within its four walls. This is multitenancy. It allows you to divide up one large SAP BusinessObjects BI platform into several smaller "tenants"; each tenant has separate content, security, administrators, rules, and so on. This can be useful in many ways:

- You, as the administrator, have fewer servers to maintain.
- You, as a company, have less infrastructure to purchase and maintain.
- You can apply patches and upgrades to every tenant in the system at the same time because it's really just one big system. So there's less overall downtime and shorter maintenance windows in general.
- You can delegate administrators for each tenant, making your job as the "Super-Administrator" less stressful.

The following are some drawbacks to consider to implementing multitenancy:

- You have one big, honkin' system. If it goes down, all of your tenants go down.
- It definitely requires you to pay careful attention to sizing and capacity.
- Tenants can often be tied to a specific patch level of SAP BusinessObjects BI. Tenants like that can hold up a patch for all of the others.

If this sounds like a great idea to you (it does to us), then learn more on the SAP Community Network and the SAP Help Portal for specifics on how to set up your own system for multitenancy. Happy land lording!

5.7   Summary

Wow, that was quite a chapter! All jokes aside, security is a huge topic and is certainly deserving of your careful attention. Hopefully, we were able to help make a very heavy topic somewhat enjoyable for you to read, learn, and, most of all, remember. Keep those basic principles in line while working with security. If you remember nothing else, you should endeavor to remember that "Principals have rights to objects." You'll seldom go wrong if you keep that phrase in mind. Keeping your SAP BusinessObjects BI 4.1 system safe, secure, and dependable is critical to earning your users' trust and keeping them happily using the system.

Reports aren't going to move themselves. If you're a good administrator, you should ensure your developers have good development and test environments in which to write reports. Now, you have to get used to the new approach to managing content movement in SAP BusinessObjects BI 4.1.

6 Migrating Content: Moving Stuff Around and Keeping It Straight

We've been being groomed over the past few years for one big change: the existence of Lifecycle Manager, currently known as Promotion Management, as the sole mechanism to move content from cluster to cluster after you've completed your migration to SAP BusinessObjects BI 4.1. While the UI changes in the reporting technologies will leave some organizations to reeducate themselves about the new tools, administrators must also consider how to reeducate in a decentralized support model in which we've all come to rely on the Import Wizard. Love it or hate it—rest in peace, dear Import Wizard.

Back in Chapter 3, we completed our buildout and landed with a husk of an environment, ready to serve up your awesome SAP BusinessObjects BI content. At this point, we need to dive deeper into the technologies used in SAP BusinessObjects BI 4.1 to move content around and make the most effective use of these tools as we can. In this chapter, we'll discuss the three options available for migrating content: the Upgrade Management Tool (UMT), Promotion Management, and content federation and replication. We'll spend most of our time on Promotion Management, however, because in the majority of cases, this will be the most commonly used method for migrating content after you've made it to SAP BusinessObjects BI 4.1.

6.1 The Upgrade Management Tool versus Promotion Management

With the release of SAP BusinessObjects BI 4.1, the tool we've all come to know and **love**, the Import Wizard, is at the end of its lifecycle. SAP BusinessObjects XI 3.1 is the last version that will support the use of the Import Wizard. Instead, in SAP BusinessObjects BI 4.1, we're left with two tool choices for two distinctly different roles: the UMT and the more recent Promotion Management. If you're building a brand-new SAP BusinessObjects BI 4.1 cluster, here is the next choose-your-own-adventure fork in the road: Should you use the UMT or Promotion Management?

The UMT is only used for older, rogue SAP BusinessObjects BI deployments that you'll have to assimilate into your SAP BusinessObjects BI 4.1 environment. (Go on, tell them: "Resistance is futile." You know you want to.) If you're migrating from SAP BusinessObjects XI R2 SP2 or SAP BusinessObjects XI 3.1 version of SAP BusinessObjects BI, the UMT is what you need.

> **Migrating Content from Older Releases**
>
> If you're still (embarrassingly) on an older, out-of-support version of SAP BusinessObjects BI, first consider a careful implementation path that gets you to a supported migration path. Then come back to the UMT. In other words, if you're running old-school SAP BusinessObjects 4, 5, or 6, then you really missed out on Y2K and should jump in your DeLorean, generate 1.21 gigawatts of electricity, and head back 14 years or so.
>
> But seriously, systems prior to SAP BusinessObjects XI R2 SP2 can't make the leap to SAP BusinessObjects BI 4.1 as-is. You'll need to identify an interim migration step to a higher SAP BusinessObjects XI version (R2 or higher), regression test to ensure you made the jump successfully, and then stage your migration to SAP BusinessObjects BI 4.1.

On the other hand, if your task is just to move content from one SAP BusinessObjects BI 4.1 system to another, you must now change gears and prepare to use Promotion Management. There is no migration path from older versions. Promotion Management is it. And the truth is, you're utilizing the best practice in deploying Promotion Management.

In this section, we'll discuss the process of deploying both the UMT and Promotion Management.

6.1.1 The Upgrade Management Tool

Now, let's peel back the process of migrating content with the UMT and see how it all works. Personally, we like to hang on to the idea that the UMT is the closest thing to the old Import Wizard we're ever going to get. Now that it's gone, we miss it. Really, we do. However, the UMT does take a much cleaner, wizard-based approach to migrating content from legacy SAP BusinessObjects BI systems into SAP BusinessObjects BI 4.1.

We need to break it down a little bit from here. The UMT gives us the approach of both full and incremental migrations. We'll begin with a full migration strategy.

Full Migration

The very first choice in our migration path is to determine if we'll do a full migration or an incremental migration. We'll explore the full migration first. The first piece of advice in considering a full migration is: *choose your battles wisely.*

A full migration is like a loaded gun, poised and ready to waste your time and energy. Considering that you might have a CMS with 1,000 reports, a full migration isn't all that scary. However, considering that you might have a CMS with 100,000 reports—that is a different story. We'll spend time differentiating the value of the incremental migration over the full migration in a bit. But for now, just let us stress the importance of making an objective assertion about the safety of moving *large* numbers of CMS objects between systems.

With that disclaimer out of the way, let's walk through this option of the full migration (see Figure 6.1).

A complete upgrade implies that we'll indiscriminately pick up and move all CMS objects (including users, groups, security, reports, universes, dashboards—everything) into the target CMS. When you select the COMPLETE UPGRADE option shown in Figure 6.1, the screen shown in Figure 6.2 appears.

Figure 6.1 The Complete Upgrade Path

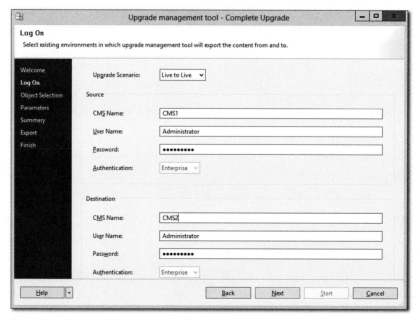

Figure 6.2 A Live-to-Live Complete Upgrade Scenario

The migration in a complete upgrade can't get much simpler. The UPGRADE SCE-NARIO field provides several options for migration:

▶ BIAR
A BI Archive Resource (BIAR) file (created by the UMT, not other BIAR-capable tools such as the Import Wizard or Promotion Management) is a safe way to create a complete export of an environment, giving the administrator more control over when and where to migrate the content. It also facilitates a scenario where the CMS clusters may be on exclusive networks to selectively migrate via a BIAR file where a direct system-to-system copy is possible (to be created by the UMT, not other BIAR-capable tools such as the Import Wizard or Promotion Management).

▶ LIVE TO LIVE
A source environment and a target environment are defined, allowing you to do an active migration without the manual step of importing a previously created BIAR file.

In our example, we'll use the LIVE TO LIVE option. On the screen shown in Figure 6.2, supply the SOURCE CMS NAME and port, administrator USER NAME and PASSWORD, and the DESTINATION CMS NAME and port. When you click NEXT, the screen shown in Figure 6.3 appears.

Delegated Administration

In the past, administrators have often asked "What about delegated administration?" In other words, should migration of content be trusted to the few (administrators) or delegated to the many (content creators)? In this case, you're moving content. You're upgrading. You're making the final leap (or a test leap at least) to move your content between environments. Just use the Administrator user.

When the UMT is kicked off to collect all the metadata about that source CMS, depending on the size, once again, you might want to take a break. After all of the information about the source CMS is aggregated, a simple decision is required before clicking NEXT once again. Selecting AUTOMATICALLY START UPGRADE PROCESS AFTER ALL OBJECTS HAVE BEEN RETRIEVED will ensure that during this migration, the files requiring modification to be hosted in the SAP BusinessObjects BI 4.1 environment will be touched and made compatible. (You went through this process during the migration to SAP BusinessObjects XI 3.1, so there's no reason to not allow that upgrade to happen again here—but it's nice they gave you a choice.) Click NEXT to move along, and you'll see the screen shown in Figure 6.4.

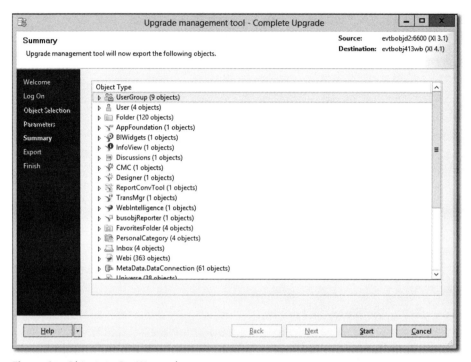

Figure 6.3 Objects to Be Migrated

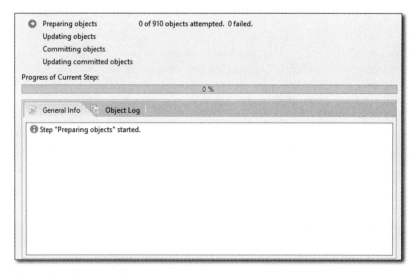

Figure 6.4 Migration Progress

The UMT will give a verbose overview of its progress while it's importing objects, touching them, and placing them in the destination CMS. Once again, depending on the size of your source CMS, the size/performance of your environment, network speeds, and so on, this process may take some time. If you're anything like us, you'll be watching this process in a state of deep hypnosis, hopeful that every tick on the progress bar will be successful and not throw an error.

That never happens.

As this process comes to a close, the overall summary, good or bad, will be displayed (see Figure 6.5). It's beyond the scope of this book to diagnose every possible error that will be displayed during a migration. Simply put, read the logs. A percentage of the reports you're trying to migrate are going to fail.

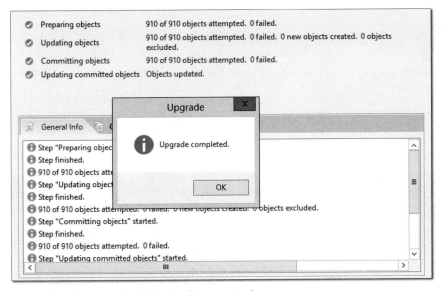

Figure 6.5 Migration Completed and Summarized

This is an important reason to actually review the object log that gets generated with the migration. This will be your key to identifying failed objects and will give you some reasonable guess (hopefully) as to why they failed. There will indeed be easy issues to identify, such as orphans, broken connections to universes, and so on. These things happen every day in an environment. But, the object log will give you more evidence on how to handle the fallout of the full migration. There are a few common things you can watch out for and, likely count on, as you move content that has been stuck in CMS-limbo for the past several years in your environment:

▶ **Orphaned objects**

If you haven't been performing regular maintenance on your system using the Repository Diagnostic Tool (RDT), your source system will most likely contain a number of orphaned objects, whether they are objects in the CMS database that don't exist in the file store or objects in the file store that don't exist in the CMS database. The records that do exist in the CMS database that aren't in the file store will be those that get picked up for migration. The bottom line is, if the UMT can't move them in this case, your users haven't been able to use those reports either.

▶ **Universe not found**

Over time, reports may simply lose their connection to their source universe. It happens. You, as the administrator, must decide the following: If it didn't work before, why should I move it now? Your users may disagree, and ultimately you may have to put someone on the receiving end of a report fix prior to migration.

▶ **Failed instances not migrated**

This should really not be thrown up as a red flag. The reality is that failed instances are failed. There nothing to migrate anyway. Move along.

Nice Try, But . . .

Oh, and one more thing about all of those Desktop Intelligence reports you were *really* hoping to sneak by: No, they won't survive the migration if you're migrating with a version prior to SAP BusinessObjects BI 4.1. If you really did try to sneak those by, go back, convert them to Web Intelligence or SAP Crystal Reports, and take a do-over. If you made the wise choice to implement SAP BusinessObjects BI 4.1, your reports are safe, but for an uncertain time frame. SAP hasn't necessarily shared what the next end-of-life for Desktop Intelligence will be.

For more information about Web Intelligence and SAP Crystal Reports, check out *SAP BusinessObjects Web Intelligence,* third edition (Brogden et al., SAP PRESS, 2014) and *Using Crystal Reports with SAP* (Garrett, SAP PRESS, 2010) at *www.sap-press.com*.

Incremental Migration

Hopefully, you were scared enough by the size of your migration to reconsider performing an incremental migration. Okay, "scared" is probably not the right frame of mind. Caution is really the right one, though. Taking an incremental approach allows you to methodically plan and migrate content, evaluating errors, triaging the easy stuff, and understanding where you can ignore errors.

Going back to the beginning of the UMT options, we choose the INCREMENTAL UPGRADE (see Figure 6.6). There is no correct formula for staging an incremental migration. Similar to the full migration, the approach to break it into bite-sized chunks and then migrate and test it absolutely applies to the incremental migration as well.

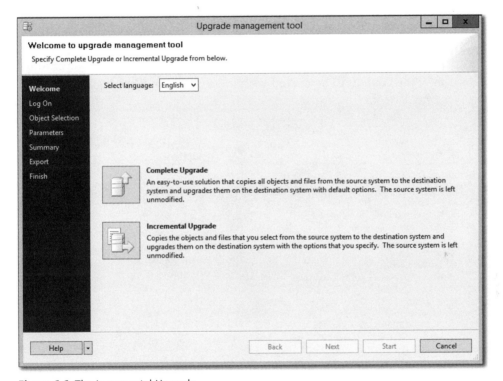

Figure 6.6 The Incremental Upgrade

A sample of a migration broken into phases might entail the following:

▶ Users, groups, and application rights, including favorites and inboxes

▶ Universes and connections

▶ Reports and report folders (including dashboards, etc.)

There are certainly migrations that even broken into those three chunks are way too big and take far too many hours to give you a feel for the right way to migrate all of that content. This is where you might need to get more granular on the number of users migrated in each pull. What is the right number? Only you can gauge that, based on your estimates of the number of users and number of reports in each folder. While we don't specifically endorse any third-party product to inspect CMS metadata, this is exactly the reason to own one: to understand the sizes and volumes across all folders, as well as content, used or not, that should be migrated.

Click NEXT to move on. When the incremental upgrade process has begun and you've supplied the same CMS source and destination details as shown earlier in Figure 6.2, the next step in the process is a variation, which begins the granular selection of the content to be moved within this migration (see Figure 6.7).

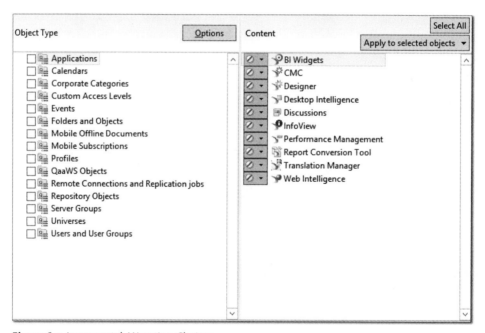

Figure 6.7 Incremental Migration Choices

This view of the repository content is a welcome change from the individual screens on different pages that the Import Wizard once employed. Looking closer, content is categorized by a container that groups it all by content type. Much like you might expect from a view of folders and objects, the list of public folders from the source CMS is displayed for selection in its entirety or in a drilled-down path (see Figure 6.8).

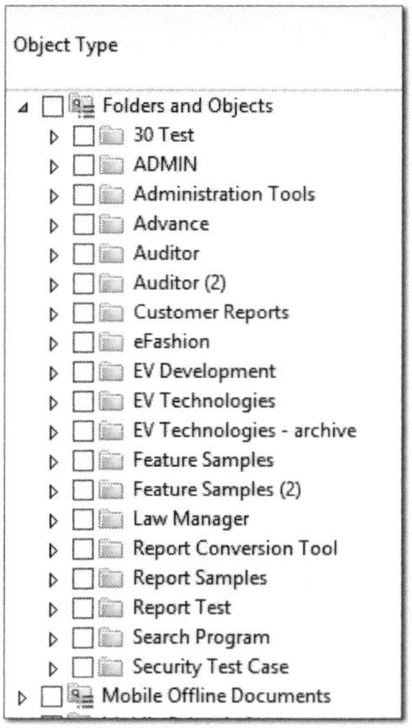

Figure 6.8 Selection of One or More Objects and Children

In addition to the granularity of selecting content, you have the flexibility in an incremental upgrade to migrate dependent objects or objects with dependencies. Consider the case where publications or Dashboards content has been developed. It may be useless to migrate and test if all dependencies aren't fulfilled.

Utilize the dropdown selectors next to each application type to select the desired migration mode (see Figure 6.9) from the following options:

▶ EXPORT THIS OBJECT AND ITS DEPENDENCIES
Not only will this object be exported, but any objects that reference it in the CMS will be included in the migration.

▶ EXPORT THIS OBJECT
This is the cleanest and most straightforward migration option. No dependents or dependencies are migrated with the object.

▶ EXPORT THIS OBJECT ONLY IF IT IS DEPENDED ON
When selecting a larger group of objects, this rule of least selection will ensure that if there is nothing looking for the object in its dependency list, it won't be migrated.

283

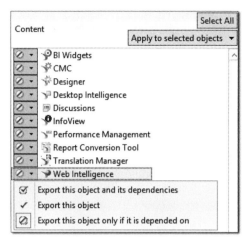

Figure 6.9 Managing Dependencies

After you make your selection, click NEXT to continue.

One final note that lets the incremental stand out from the full upgrade is the ability to fine-tune how content is upgraded if existing content is migrated. The options shown in Figure 6.10 first made their appearance back in the Import Wizard days and are still relevant today.

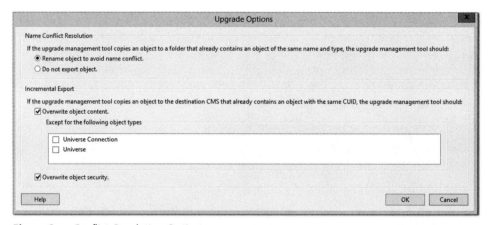

Figure 6.10 Conflict-Resolution Options

You won't hear anything other than the fact that a cluster unique identifier (CUID) match is considered to be the most effective way to migrate content between environments. The CUID identifies objects in a unique way across any SAP

BusinessObjects BI cluster. By maintaining the integrity of this CUID in each environment, the accuracy and capability of both the UMT and, later, Promotion Management, are greatly enhanced. However, there are always different strokes for different folks. So, naming the conflict-resolution option that makes the most sense for your deployment is your call. Renaming the object will result in potentially more than one object in your CMS after each migration, so be warned.

Finalizing the incremental upgrade is the same as finalizing the full upgrade: you'll see a progress screen and then a log of any errors. Always remember to test your migration as many times as your project plan will allow prior to committing to a final production release of SAP BusinessObjects BI 4.1 within your environment. Knowing the challenges to expect before you go live will help you save face later before your users get their hands on your SAP BusinessObjects BI 4.1 environment.

6.1.2 Promotion Management

With the shoe tied firmly to the other foot, you must now change gears and prepare to use Promotion Management for moving content between like SAP BusinessObjects BI 4.1 environments. There is no migration path from older versions. Promotion Management is it.

As much as we'd like Promotion Management to be a full-on replacement for the Import Wizard, the reality is that it requires a change in perspective. Promotion Management isn't the pick-up-everything-and-move-it-in-one-fell-swoop tool that the Import Wizard often served as in prior releases of the product. There are two distinct functions that Promotion Management fulfills: the movement of content between disparate CMS clusters (specifically the promotion management functionality), and version management for development teams. This book will address the movement of content between disparate CMS clusters.

Like many elements of maintaining an SAP BusinessObjects BI environment, Promotion Management is an art and not a science. By now that probably seems cliché, but it's still true. Promotion Management in SAP BusinessObjects BI 4.1 is the process of defining collections of migration processes responsible for testing and copying content from a source CMS cluster to a target CMS cluster while fulfilling any dependencies required by said content. In addition, Promotion Management facilitates the mechanization and automation of these processes so that organizations with more rigid promotion schedules can eliminate the human factor in migrating content between environments. The way you move the content is really the administrator's choice, coupled with the shared vision with your report developers.

That seems pretty technical and wordy, so let's deconstruct some of the most common scenarios that make Promotion Management a great fit for your new home for migrating content between environments:

- ▸ A regularly scheduled migration from a development environment to a test environment is needed every Tuesday and Thursday at 7:00 pm, migrating reports, dependent universes, and associated connections.

- ▸ An initial migration is required to populate content from a development environment to a new test environment, including users, groups, folders and reports, and all associated rights.

- ▸ A report of significant visibility was created in the production environment that requires a reverse migration back to the development environment so that it can be maintained as part of your organization's normal systems development lifecycle.

Promotion Management is designed in such a way that you may control the movement of content between two or more SAP BusinessObjects CMS BI clusters. Thanks to the installer, Promotion Management servers can be deployed in each environment within your cluster. However, you may choose whether to use a single Promotion Management repository, or alternatively, multiple subversion repositories, and even use multiple Adaptive Processing Servers (APSs) managing Promotion Management Services within your cluster.

In other words, there is certainly an option if you want to segregate development to test migrations on one server or test to production migrations on another server. With the scalability of using the SAP BusinessObjects BI framework for storing content in migration jobs within the CMS, it becomes easier to manage and secure these jobs down the road.

Let's consider that deployment in which we have centralized migrations on a single Promotion Management Server in our environment (see Figure 6.11). This leaves our development, test, and production environments free to manage just reporting tasks specific to their environment. The Promotion Management Server in this case acts as the gateway for content between each cluster in the systems development lifecycle (SDLC). It will hold the reports for all environments in your SDLC.

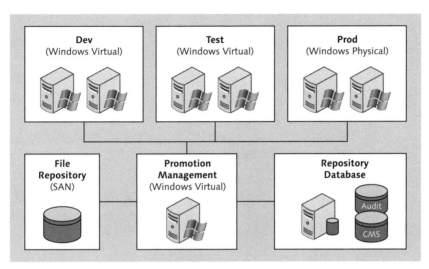

Figure 6.11 A Centralized Deployment Approach

Conversely, while Promotion Management can coexist within the environment, an administrator may choose to isolate the movement of development content by using Promotion Management in the development environment and the movement of test content by using Promotion Management in the test environment (see Figure 6.12). This further prevents unnecessary access to the production system, where it's not needed. In addition, Promotion Management won't require additional CMS or Auditor databases, nor will it need additional physical or virtual hosts on which to run SAP BusinessObjects BI 4.1.

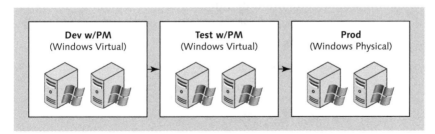

Figure 6.12 A Decentralized Deployment Approach

It will, however, require better and more thoughtful organization of the Promotion Management folder structure you define in the PROMOTION JOBS section of the CMC, as shown in Figure 6.13.

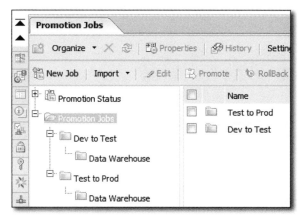

Figure 6.13 Using Folders to Manage Centralized Promotion Jobs

The folder structure that evolves from your design may then be further expanded to delineate jobs by environment, and then further secured by the promotion manager role if the ability to promote to production is isolated to release managers versus developers. In either case, the root-most level (whether in a centralized Promotion Management environment or decentralized Promotion Management environment) of the folder structure is designed with a pattern mindful of the possible moves, and it's further segmented to foster a content move that mimics the structures of the target production environment.

In other words, face the fact that production is the final stop for all of this content. Setting up a folder structure in Promotion Management that stops short of what production will look like is a disservice to you as an administrator because you have to maintain it when it's done.

Pop Quiz
1. What is the purpose of the Upgrade Management Tool?
2. Contrast a full versus an incremental migration in the Upgrade Management Tool.
3. True or False: The Upgrade Management Tool can be used to import BIAR files created by Promotion Management.
4. Name the conflict resolution options available in an incremental migration.

5. What is the purpose of the Promotion Management?

6. Describe a decentralized Promotion Management environment.

7. True or False: Centralized Promotion Management environments require their own CMS, Auditor, and possibly physically separate hardware resources.

6.2 Overview of Promotion Management

In this section, we'll assume that your Promotion Management deployment (discussed in Section 6.1.2) was successful and that you're ready to start migrating content. Before we dive into the steps of doing this, though, we'll offer a brief introduction to Promotion Management: specifically, its changes in SP4 and a brief description of each of its main administrative functions. Let's get this little party started by visiting your CMC: *http://yourserver:8080/BOE/CMC*.

6.2.1 Changes in SAP BusinessObjects BI 4.0 SP4

For the customer still hanging back on SAP BusinessObjects BI 4.0, aside from the perceived stability enhancements over SP2 and some cosmetic changes, the workflows in Promotion Management haven't changed significantly in SAP Business-Objects BI 4.1. We'll dig in by taking a look at the cosmetic changes in this release.

Promotion Management Integration with the CMC

First, note that Promotion Management is no longer a stand-alone web application, but instead, is now integrated directly into the CMC. No way is this a deal breaker. The CMC isn't *that* crowded yet, and the look and feel is more consistent from an administrative function perspective. It simply leaves you with the reality that you do need to care about who has rights to the Promotion Management console and who you want to be able to access the CMC.

Accessing Promotion Management and Creating New Folders

You'll note that on logon, Promotion Management has been tucked within the MANAGE section of the CMC, to the far right (see Figure 6.14).

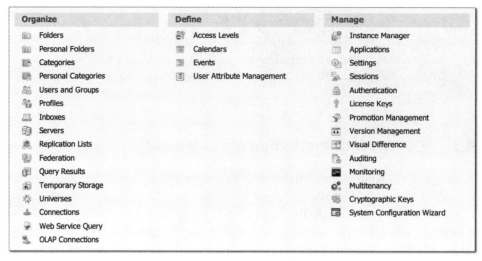

Figure 6.14 Accessing Promotion Management

After you select PROMOTION MANAGEMENT, you're ready to dig into it. The first thing you'll notice is that there's no way to create a new folder within this interface. There's no need to panic. While not necessarily the best user experience change, given that this is a common need, it's still possible to achieve the addition of new folders via the traditional FOLDERS menu in the CMC.

Going with the assumption that your Promotion Management deployment was successful and you're seeing it in your brand-new environment, you have a blank canvas in which to begin implementing your PROMOTION JOBS (see Figure 6.15 and Figure 6.16).

Figure 6.15 Promotion Jobs View within the CMC

Figure 6.16 Creating a New Promotion Job Folders

The net result of adding a subfolder to the Promotion Management folder under PUBLIC FOLDERS is that the PROMOTION MANAGEMENT page in the CMC can now see that subfolder. As you can see in Figure 6.17, we created the DEV TO TEST folder.

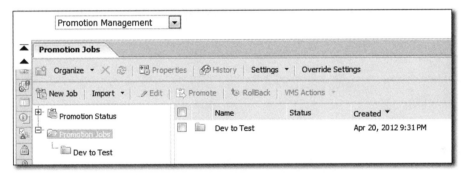

Figure 6.17 Newly Created Folder within Promotion Jobs Screen

Stop Panicking, Seriously

We'll offer more detailed information about adding folders and organizing content in a bit. Our intent here is simply to prevent widespread panic in the first few paragraphs of this section. You can sit back down now.

Menu Changes

Now that Promotion Management is held within the CMC, screen space is at a new premium, and Promotion Management-specific options have been shifted into menus within the application (see Figure 6.18).

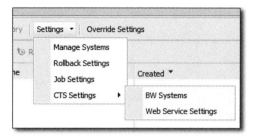

Figure 6.18 Promotion Management Options

These options don't vary wildly from prior releases but do appear much more polished.

6.2.2 Administrative Functions of Promotion Management

To use Promotion Management effectively, you must be familiar with the administrative functions of the tool:

▶ Manage systems

▶ Rollback settings

▶ Job settings

▶ CTS settings

▶ Override settings

Each of these functions is accessed from the PROMOTION MANAGEMENT console within the CMC. Let's look at them in more detail next.

CTS Settings

If you're a classic SAP customer with access to SAP's Change and Transport System, this release supports integration of Promotion Management jobs. This topic isn't covered within this text.

Manage Systems

To centrally manage each system between which Promotion Management has the ability to move content, the systems must be defined by their names, CMS hosts, ports, and users in the Promotion Management Server. These settings are specific to the CMS cluster in which you have Promotion Management running, and are simply a placeholder to store this definition on this CMS cluster for the purpose of moving files around. On initial view, this page of the CMC will display all currently defined systems (see Figure 6.19).

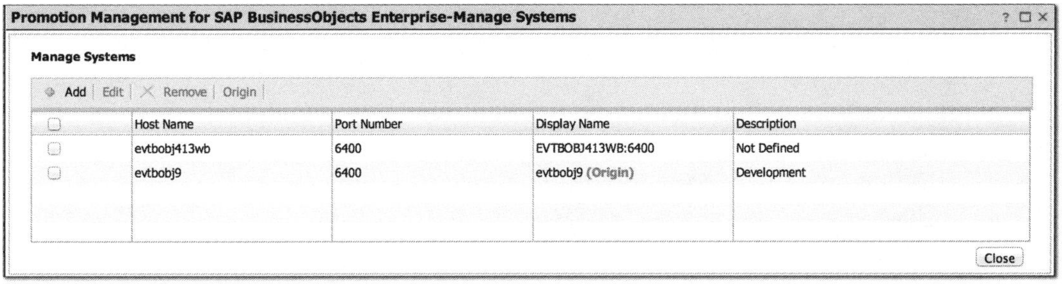

Figure 6.19 Manage Systems

While you take the time to define each system, it's important to give yourself enough useful information to use each system defined via the console. Click the ADD button to drop in a new system as a target for migrating content.

The fields shown in Figure 6.20 are as follows:

▶ HOST NAME
Ensure that a fully qualified host name is supplied to properly locate the other CMS cluster on your network.

▶ PORT NUMBER
Unlike other tools in the platform, the port is supplied on a secondary field.

▶ DISPLAY NAME
Lastly, pick a *logical* display name. This isn't a place we recommend calling the display name, for example, "someserver.somesubdomain.someothersubdomain.companydomain.com". Keep it simple, like "Development" or "QA" or something easy to identify during migrations.

▶ DESCRIPTION
Give the system a verbose and meaningful description.

▶ MARK AS ORIGIN
Also take care to properly mark the correct server in the Promotion Management build as the origin. The origin system will be used to identify all base content to make it eligible for overrides, which we'll cover a bit later.

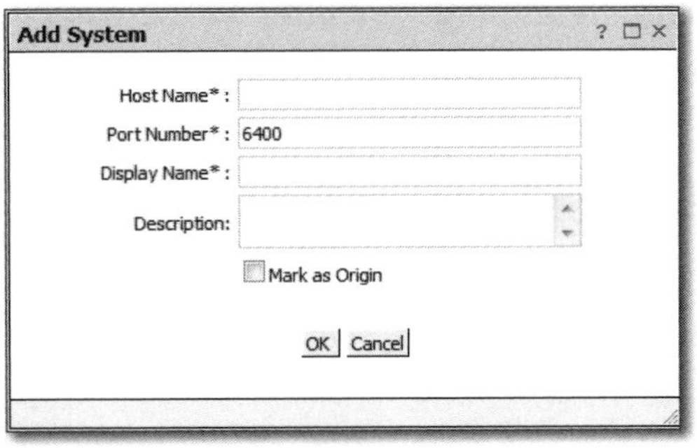

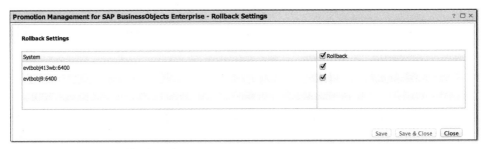

Figure 6.20 Defining a New System

Rollback Settings

Rollback settings are really straightforward. Rollbacks are the opportunity to take a botched upgrade and revert to the prior state. Do you want to keep a running history of content as you migrate between environments? Are you willing to accept any space implications of keeping that history? Select the ROLLBACK SETTINGS menu option to display the status of each system (see Figure 6.21).

Figure 6.21 Defining Rollback Preferences

After you have systems defined in Promotion Management, modify the ROLLBACK property for each as appropriate. This is a simple on/off scenario. Either you want to enable rollbacks or you don't.

Job Settings

Promotion Management's promotion jobs are, well, jobs in the CMC. You probably already know them by now and know how they behave in the CMC when you schedule other report objects. Promotion Management has its own Job Server and behaviors. Promotion Management will give you options to control that job history as well, as shown in Figure 6.22.

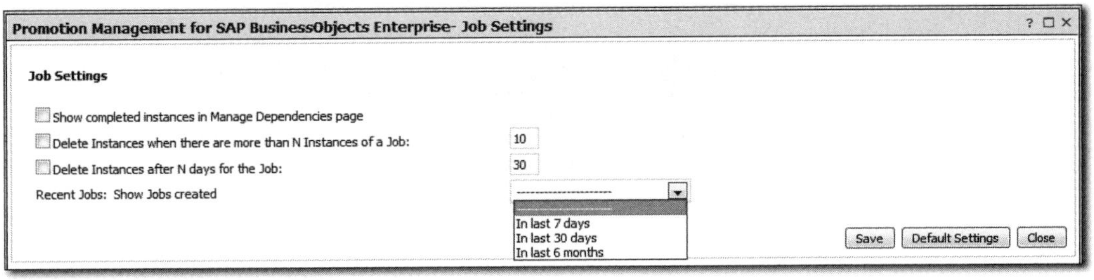

Figure 6.22 Scheduled Job Options

Much like normal CMS objects scheduled in other parts of the CMC, there are a few limits that can be placed on the scheduled jobs:

▶ SHOW COMPLETED INSTANCES IN MANAGE DEPENDENCIES PAGE
Well, you basically decide whether to show completed instances in the MANAGE DEPENDENCIES page.

▶ DELETE INSTANCES WHEN THERE ARE MORE THAN N INSTANCES OF A JOB
It's not always necessary to keep job history for a prolonged duration. Pick a number of job instances to maintain, and the CMS will automatically roll off the oldest instance when a new one is created.

▶ DELETE INSTANCES AFTER N DAYS FOR THE JOB
If an instance's age exceeds the number of days specified here, it will automatically be rolled off by the CMS.

▶ RECENT JOBS: SHOW JOBS CREATED
Merely a display parameter for the JOB HISTORY page, this setting limits the amount of history that is displayed by default.

Overrides

When you create objects in the development environment, such as connections or web services, these objects get bound to the system in which they were created. *Overrides* are a mechanism to automatically update those objects to use the correct host or a new connection as the move is made between environments. Overrides are tricky things. The context of overrides rests solely in the fact that as we create objects in the development environment, such as connections or web services, these objects get bound to the system in which they were created. Overrides are a mechanism to automatically update those objects to use the correct host or a new connection as the move is made between environments. Use the OVERRIDE SETTINGS menu to take control of them (see Figure 6.23).

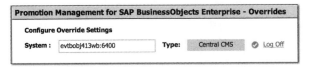

Figure 6.23 Default Override System

On the CONFIGURE OVERRIDES SETTINGS screen, overrides are managed based on the system to which you're currently logged on. In this example, we'll log off the environment and connect to it as an origin. Remember, the origin can be any CMS cluster you've defined in your systems list.

If successfully logged off, the icon changes, the system field goes blank, and you must log in to a source system (see Figure 6.24). Logically, the next step is to click LOGIN and select the system of choice for which to determine overrides.

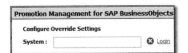

Figure 6.24 Valid Logoff

There you go. The system is intelligible because we named it in a friendly way, and Promotion Management let us know if the system we chose was the origin or not (see Figure 6.25). Given authentication credentials, we can start the overrides process.

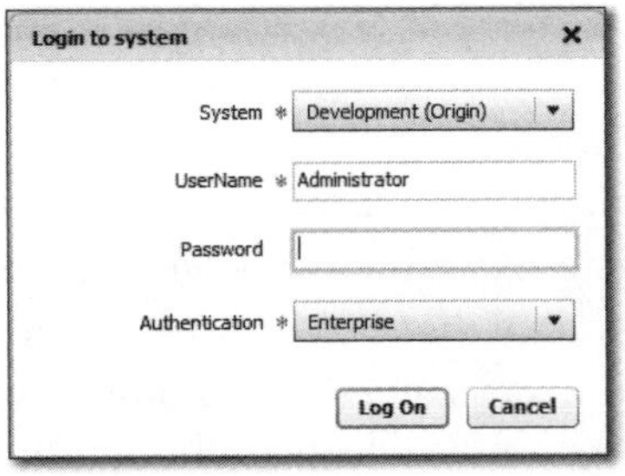

Figure 6.25 Establishing a New Connection

The difference is subtle, in this case, but it's there. We're authenticated back to the same system, but it's aware now that this is the origin system as well (see Figure 6.26).

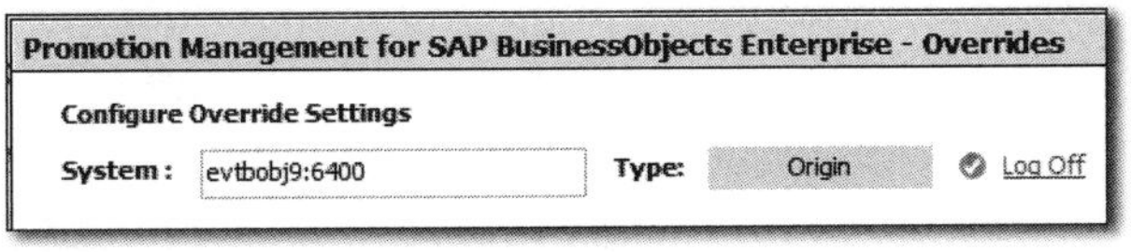

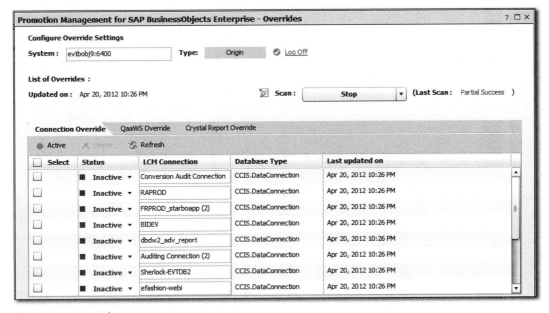

Figure 6.26 Successful Authentication

Now that we're squared away, let's look at the interface for a bit (see Figure 6.27).

Figure 6.27 Overrides

The list of overrides is broken into three distinct categories: CONNECTION OVERRIDE, QAAWS OVERRIDE, and CRYSTAL REPORT OVERRIDE. If your system hasn't been cataloged yet, now is as good a time as any. Simply choose the SCAN selector and the START option, and sit back and let the magic happen. The interface will populate the override page you're on with all of the available overrides you'll have to concern yourself with for moving content between environments.

As a best practice, this is an administrative function to be kept up with at all costs. You must have a communication mechanism in place with development teams to know when connection or service migrations are required and, when they are, if any overrides are appropriate. You won't be able to guess, and Promotion Management won't be able to make assumptions for you.

Yes. We said *best practice*. You should write that down as a to-do.

6.3   Migrating Content with Promotion Management

Planning and organizing content moves from one environment to another requires a Promotion Management ninja. OK, that may be a little on the overly dramatic side. However, knowing when and where to put jobs in folder structures requires some finesse and perhaps even some rework as you mature in your Promotion Management operations.

When it comes to planning migrations, the only best practice is the one that meets your organization's needs. Not every organization has a migration schedule on Tuesdays and Thursdays at 9:00 pm Central Time for universe X and reports Y and Z. Your organization may very well function on a loose implementation schedule where only reports and universes touched in a release are migrated and only when needed to fulfill the migration requirements.

As a general rule of thumb, though, you should think about structuring jobs in one of two ways: ad hoc migration requests for one-off needs and repeatable jobs in which content is moved with recurrence. These two types of structures certainly warrant two different types of promotion job folder structures. When organizing for either, let's be real and organize in a way similar to the public folder structure. This is the most visible and recognizable way to find report jobs for specific reports. From there, whether you have jobs that are repeatable for the singular purpose of mechanizing those regularly scheduled jobs or you create one-off jobs to move your content around, they'll be easily found.

6.3.1   Creating a Promotion Job

Let's start setting up some jobs in our new DEV TO TEST folder. The NEW JOB option says it all. If you remember, we created our folder to hold our jobs back on the CMC FOLDERS panel. From here, we'll kick things off by establishing a brand-new migration job. Click the NEW JOB button shown in Figure 6.28, which takes you to Figure 6.29.

Figure 6.28 Constructing a New Job

There are a few fields on this screen, so let's break it down:

▶ NAME
The first step is to name the job. If you think of the migration jobs as CMS objects, like reports or dashboards, this is just the object name.

▶ DESCRIPTION and KEYWORDS
Similar to other CMS objects, the description and key words strike the same chord as your other CMS objects, like Web Intelligence reports and so on.

▶ SAVE JOB IN
This is a required field and will only display folders created within the Promotion Management folder hierarchy that you've started to create.

▶ SOURCE
Your selection here will likely be the origin from which you're moving content. If it's more appropriate to migrate content from a nonorigin system, choose it.

▶ DESTINATION
Your selection here will be the target that will get the new objects upon migration.

The selection of the source SYSTEM in Figure 6.30 opens up the opportunity to migrate from any host. But, be sensible. Reverse migrations should only happen in the most rare of circumstances. The main path is up, not back down. It's not generally considered a best practice to permit changes to happen in higher environments and have them moved back down. In our illustration, we'll assume that this flow is taking a development to test migration path. You'll also note that when selecting the destination system, it narrows the available systems to only those not used as the source (see Figure 6.31).

Figure 6.29 New Job Properties

Figure 6.30 Setting the Source and Target System

Figure 6.31 Completed New Job Properties

And just like that, Promotion Management has validated our systems, taken our inputs, and we're ready to create a husk of a job with which to actually migrate our content. Click CREATE, and let's move along.

6.3.2 Adding Objects

With our job stubbed out, the only thing it's missing is the actual content to move. In the PROMOTION JOBS panel and with your job in EDIT mode, click the ADD OBJECTS button to move ahead.

Objects come in all shapes and sizes. Objects to move include reports, connections, users, groups, folders, services, rights—all of it. Figure 6.32 is a composite screenshot of all the available types within the ADD OBJECTS view of Promotion Management.

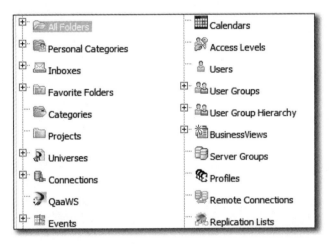

Figure 6.32 Objects Available for Migration

This does allow us to get really choosy about what we include in our migrations jobs, again, whether we're moving in an ad hoc migration or setting up a recurring migration job. In this case, let's single out a public folder titled EV TECHNOLOGIES from the selection list option ALL FOLDERS (see Figure 6.33).

Figure 6.33 Selecting Content to Migrate

After you've made your selection, clicking ADD AND CLOSE grabs all the CMS objects included within this public folder and includes them in your migration job. That's pretty easy. And, just like that, Promotion Management will drop you back to the job PROPERTIES screen to assess the full impact of all reports included in that migration (see Figure 6.34).

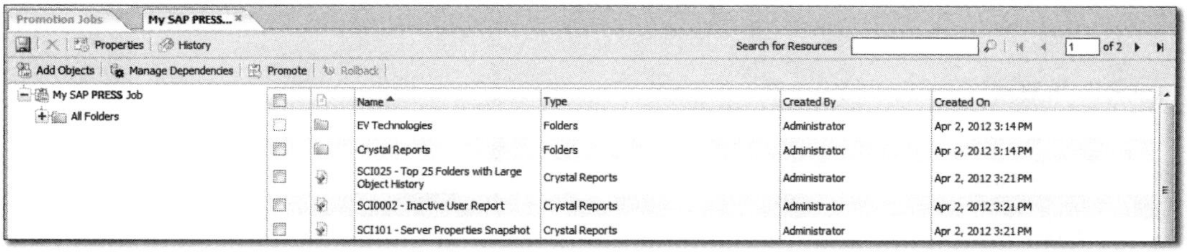

Figure 6.34 Selected Objects for Migration

6.3.3 Fulfilling Dependencies

It's important to let Promotion Management determine how to fulfill any dependencies when the migration is executed. A few examples might include connections for universes, universes for Web Intelligence reports, or lists of values for Crystal reports. The MANAGE DEPENDENCIES option in the JOB PROPERTIES will allow you to control how these dependencies are set.

Not all dependencies are required on each migration. As another illustration, after the initial migration of a connection to a target environment, it may no longer be necessary to remigrate this connection, and further, if using a different data source, may cause issues in the target environment. That said, use the screen shown in Figure 6.35 to control the migration of dependencies both on the initial move as well as subsequent migrations by selecting or unselecting the dependent options, such as connections, to determine whether they should be a part of the migration.

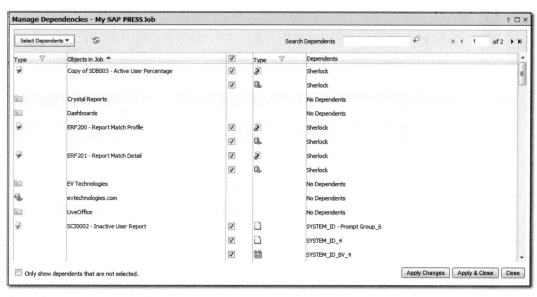

Figure 6.35 Viewing Dependencies

6.3.4 Viewing Properties

We've already established that a Promotion Management promotion job is just another CMS object. Viewing the properties of a Promotion Management promotion job reveals just that and a few extra nuggets (see Figure 6.36).

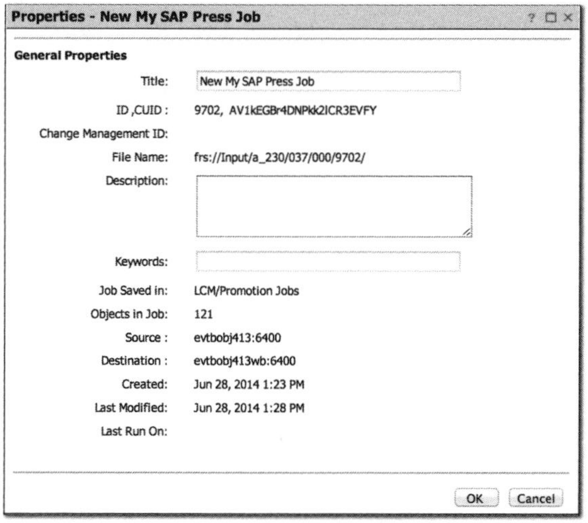

Figure 6.36 Promotion Job Properties

We've made it. The job is built. The content is defined. The source and target have been identified. The urge to leap in and click the PROMOTE button might be strong. But, we urge that you take the safe approach. Let's observe a few of the security settings before we leap in when promoting the job in Figure 6.37.

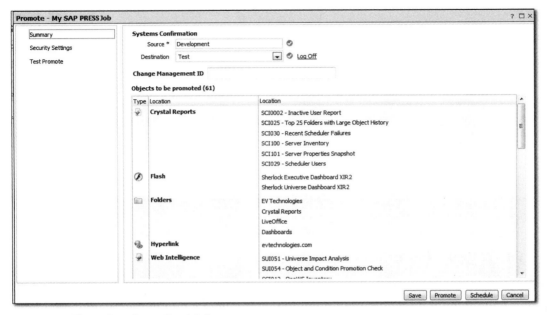

Figure 6.37 Promotion Job Summary

6.3.5 Choosing Security Settings

Oddly, you're presented with the option to modify security on the objects here versus when selecting all the objects. But alas, there are only two options for migrating content (see Figure 6.38):

▶ DO NOT PROMOTE SECURITY
This is really only appropriate *after* you've completed the initial migration of this content, when you need to adjust the security model as you move from development to test, or test to production, or lastly, if you want to define a new security model in the target environment (not likely).

▶ PROMOTE SECURITY
This is available in three flavors. The recommendation is to keep rights in sync between environments. Let Promotion Management do the heavy lifting of

setting up the rights between your environments now, in your development environment, based on a properly crafted security model (which you should definitely have after reading Chapter 5). The alternative is to reconfigure rights after each migration or rely on two distinct security models.

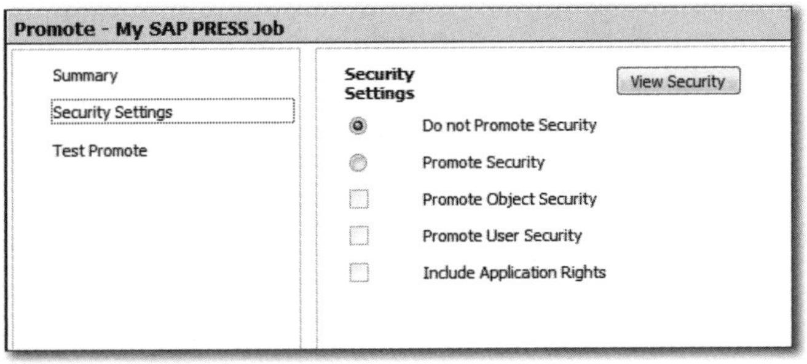

Figure 6.38 Migrating Security in a Promotion Job

We can take one more step before leaping into that full-on migration, and that is to test the migration.

6.3.6 Testing Migrations

One of the cool capabilities of Promotion Management is the ability to do a dry run without actually impacting your target environment (see Figure 6.39). The concept of a test migration provides a mechanism by which we can stage and simulate the migration and, hopefully, create the errors you might experience in an actual migration.

Figure 6.39 Test Promotions

When you're choosing to promote a Promotion Management job, this menu option will simulate the very migration you're about to get committed to. The TEST PROMOTE option lays out all the objects, once again, that will be moved ahead, with the exception that a new TEST PROMOTE button is present.

There really is no other trick to it than to click the button. The job will take all objects, complete the simulation, and return an item-by-item log of the state of the migration and the behaviors assumed during that move (see Figure 6.40).

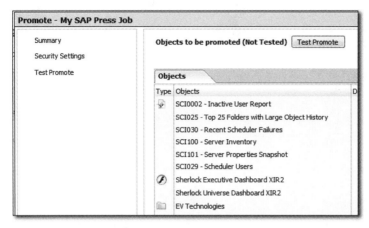

Figure 6.40 Review Before Promoting

If no errors came back with a nasty red warning, then you know the simulation was successful, and more than likely, your final move, barring surprises, will also be free from error (see Figure 6.41).

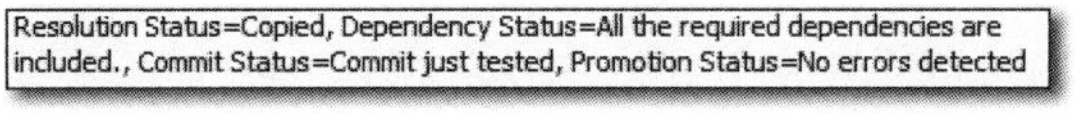

> Resolution Status=Copied, Dependency Status=All the required dependencies are included., Commit Status=Commit just tested, Promotion Status=No errors detected

Figure 6.41 Promotion Test Status

6.3.7 Executing Migrations

With that vote of confidence, pat yourself on the back. You can now click the *real* PROMOTE button. There is a fork in the road here, though. We can, in fact, click the PROMOTE button, on the one hand—or we can schedule it, on the other. Let's start with a real-time promotion. The move is going to happen on demand. The HISTORY button on the toolbar will review the pending job status and, with any luck, a successful execution in the end (shown both during and after in the composite screenshot in Figure 6.42).

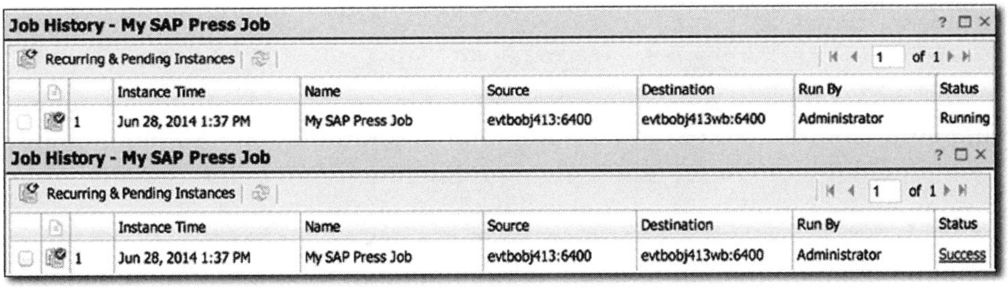

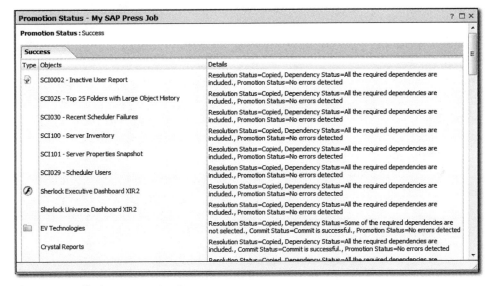

Figure 6.42 Migration Execution Status

A quick peek at the successful execution job log in Figure 6.43 should yield the exact same results as we saw in the test section of the job. If that is the case, you made it through the first of the two possible scenarios.

Figure 6.43 All Object Migration Status

In the job's alter ego as a report schedule, this may be a job we want to set to recur. The great news is that we get to leverage the same scheduling interface we know and **love** every day in scheduling our other content. Let's get through this. You're almost there (see Figure 6.44).

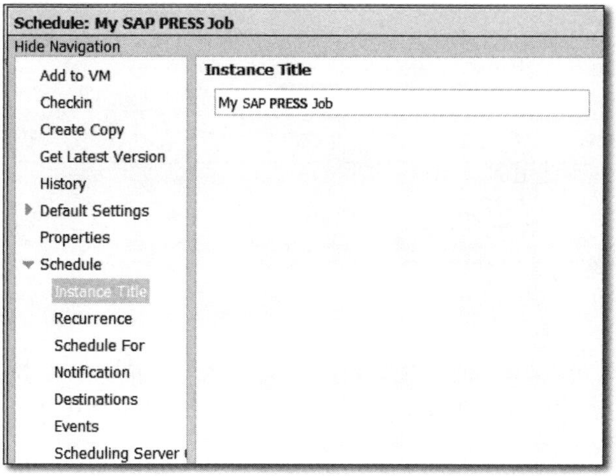

Figure 6.44 Setting a Promotion Job Schedule

Naming the job is no different, so move along, move along. A job is a job, and a Promotion Management job bears very little difference. The one factor we urge you to consider as you construct a recurring Promotion Management job is that the failure to move content is probably the one thing you really do want a heads up on. Fortunately, the CMC has the ability to use notifications to warn on failure or success of a scheduled job. The premise is easy: set your scheduled Promotion Management jobs to throw you or your change control administrator a warning email on any failed migrations (see Figure 6.45). Prevent surprises. Help prevent fires.

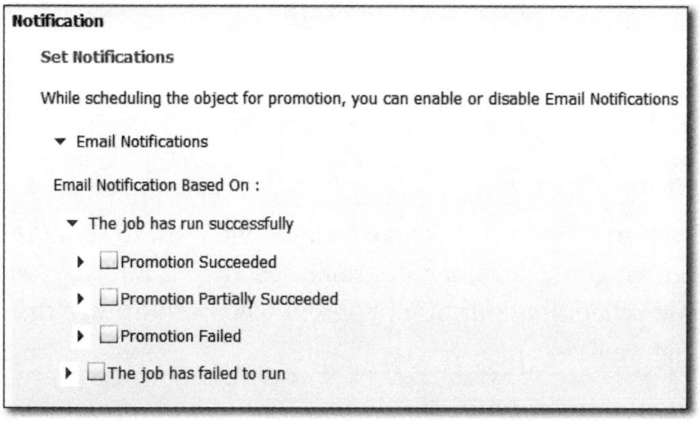

Figure 6.45 Scheduled Job Notification Options

6.3.8 Rolling Back Migrations

There really is a sweet feature here, and that is the ability to roll back. What? You weren't ready to move that content from test to production? What? You forgot to test that report before it went live, and your CEO just opened it up and wants to know who you are? Run. Hide. No, that's not right. Roll back.

The ROLLBACK button lives back on the promotion job PROPERTIES screen (see Figure 6.46).

Organize
Properties
History
Settings
Override Settings
New Job
Import
Edit
Promote
RollBack
VMS Actions

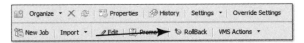

Figure 6.46 Rolling Back Migrations

While the jobs are racking up and tracking history, we do have some ability to revert changes from an environment. Promotion Management will review the jobs executed and give us valid rollback options. Simply put, choose a valid rollback scenario, full versus partial, to allow you to select individual items selected from the promotion job, and roll it back (see Figure 6.47).

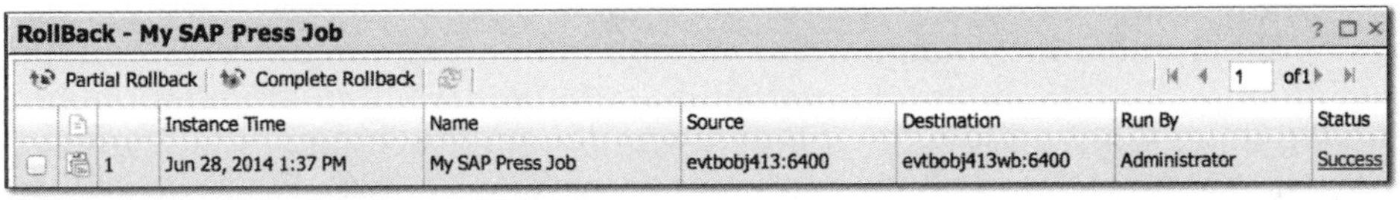

RollBack - My SAP Press Job
Partial Rollback
Complete Rollback
1
of1
Instance Time
Name
Source
Destination
Run By
Status
1
Jun 28, 2014 1:37 PM
My SAP Press Job
evtbobj413:6400
evtbobj413wb:6400
Administrator
Success

Figure 6.47 Rollback Status

Pop Quiz

1. Name the three possible overrides in a Promotion Management job.
2. True or False: The PROMOTION MANAGEMENT page of Promotion Management is now available within the CMC.
3. Which server in the SAP BusinessObjects BI 4.1 cluster handles scheduling within the environment?

6.4 Content Federation Using the Replication Service

Content federation exists in a completely separate domain from the UMT and Promotion Management. The idea behind content federation is that you have multiple production systems that have some common purpose but exist as two completely separate CMS clusters. Content federation creates an opportunity to help handle the overlap in utilization between one or more environments by using some CMS synchronization capabilities, as defined by you, the administrator, to keep them aligned. Do you have multiple production CMS clusters? If not, this section of the book may not be for you. However, if you're looking to understand the broader capabilities of replication, read on.

As you approach the CMC to manage this capability, there are three main tasks you have to know how to do: create replication lists, create remote connections, and create replication jobs.

6.4.1 Creating a New Replication List

Think of a replication list as a prebaked list of content on which you want to allow synchronization. It will be generated on the source system or the one originating the content for the relationship between the two CMS clusters. In reality, SAP BusinessObjects BI 4.1 sets up that list of content as a service that can be invoked to migrate content via the automation provided by federation. With that, the Replication Server calls this service when it wants to get the list of content to move about. We'll get to the federation part shortly, so let's focus on the replication list creation first.

Like other areas of the CMC, we're starting with a blank canvas. From the toolbar, click the button to create a new replication list (see Figure 6.48). This invokes a single screen to define the properties of the replication list, including the name and properties to include in the replication list (see Figure 6.49).

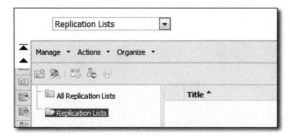

Figure 6.48 Replication Lists for Synchronization

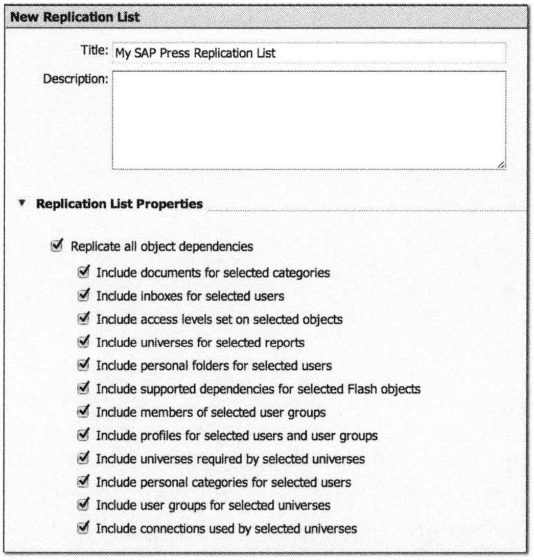

Figure 6.49 Objects to Replicate in a Replication List

Next up, based on those replication list properties, we're prompted to define what exactly we want to migrate. Not dissimilar to the UMT or Promotion Management, we can select from the various sets of CMS objects and tab those over to the SELECTED OBJECTS panel to include them in the replication list (see Figure 6.50).

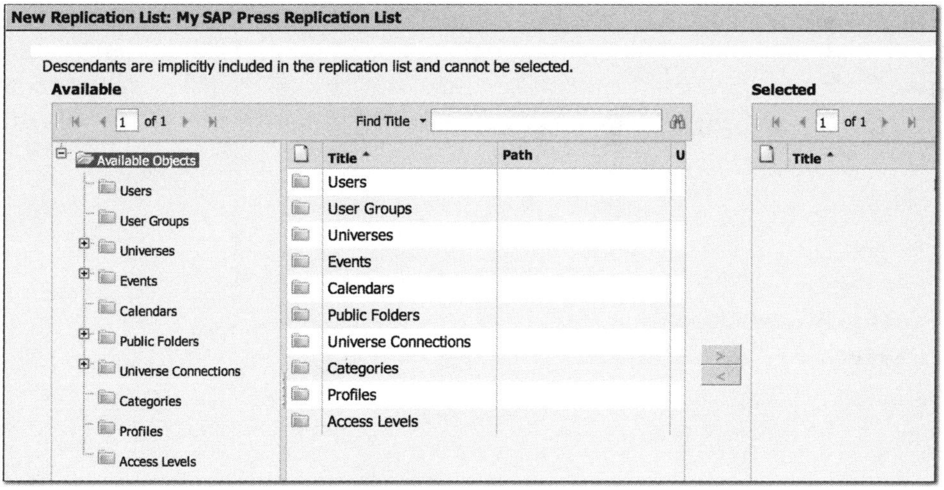

Figure 6.50 Selecting Content to Replicate

Save and close, and you're ready to go with this replication list (see Figure 6.51).

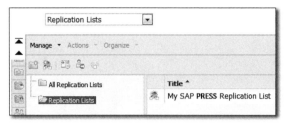

Figure 6.51 Reviewing the Finalized Replication List

6.4.2 Creating Remote Connections

We now have to flip to the destination environment. Again, the replication list was just the pointer to all of the reports we wanted to replicate. Using a second SAP BusinessObjects BI 4.1 CMS cluster, we now have to create the mapping back to the source system to be able to consume that replication list. Start out by accessing the FEDERATION panel in the CMC on the target system, and click the button to create a new remote connection (see Figure 6.52).

New Remote System Connection

Title:	My Other Production System
Description:	
Remote System Web Service URI:	http://evtbobj413.evtintranet.com:8080/dswsbobje
Remote System CMS:	evtbobj413
User Name:	administrator
Password:	•••••••••
Authentication:	Enterprise
Cleanup Frequency (in Hours):	24
☐ Limit the number of cleanup objects to:	150

Figure 6.52 A New Remote Connection

Create the remote system connection with a title that will make sense to identify it as a CMS object on the target cluster. Fill in the following fields as appropriate:

► REMOTE SYSTEM WEB SERVICE URI
This should follow a pattern of http (unless SSL is enabled), the appropriate server name (fully qualified domain name is recommended), the port, and finally, "/dswsbobje." This points the target host back to the right source system.

► REMOTE SYSTEM CMS
This is where you enter the simple CMS name for authentication purposes.

► USER NAME, PASSWORD, and AUTHENTICATION
Enter the appropriate information in the corresponding fields for the source CMS.

Saving that remote system connection allows the target server to federate the source system's objects, exposed through that replication list, to its own system.

6.4.3   Creating Replication Jobs

Still on the target CMS cluster, you now have to define the jobs that will actually perform the federation using the remote connection to the replication list. With the remote connection you've just created selected, click the CREATE NEW REPLICATION JOB button to invoke the process to create the job. First, simply name it.

Next, a list of available replication lists is presented from that remote connection (see Figure 6.53). In this case, we've only created one thus far, but support is provided for multiple, scaled-back replication lists.

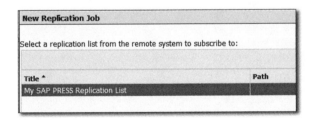

Figure 6.53 Selection of the Replication List

Next up, the replication job gets a little more complicated with options aimed at defining the synchronization between the source and target systems (see Figure 6.54). The options for the replication job provide the following capabilities during synchronization:

▶ CLEAN UP
This option synchronizes the source and target environment if delete actions were taken.

▶ AUTOMATIC CONFLICT RESOLUTION
This option determines which host wins should a newer copy be found on the target host. If the option NO AUTOMATIC CONFLICT RESOLUTION is chosen, the object isn't replicated.

▶ REPLICATION TYPE
This option determines if target system objects are replicated back to the source host. In ONE-WAY REPLICATION, they aren't; in TWO-WAY REPLICATION, they are.

▶ REPLICATION MODE
This option sets the direction of the replication, whether set to replicate in both directions or from a single direction only.

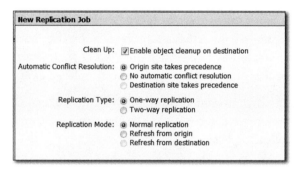

Figure 6.54 Replication Job Options

Well, that's it for options. The job template is now created and is yet another type of object that will coexist within the CMS (see Figure 6.55).

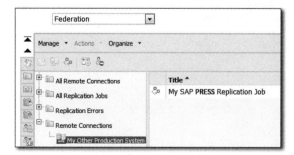

Figure 6.55 Completed Replication Job against Replication List

With the replication job in hand, it can now be executed as we might execute any other object capable of scheduling in the CMS. We can run it on demand or run it via the scheduler (see Figure 6.56).

Figure 6.56 Scheduling the Replication Job

Like other mission-critical content migrations, scheduling doesn't vary but does offer that one key capability for automated warnings: failed job notifications. Use them. We do. They'll give you advance warning of not being able to deliver content to your users.

Finally, whether you ran this as a one-time synchronization or scheduled a recurring sync-up between two environments, synchronized folders get a special designation that can be noted via the CMC FOLDERS view (see Figure 6.57). If you inherit a new system and are wondering what's up, it's federated content.

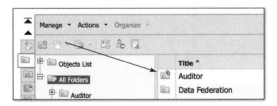

Figure 6.57 Viewing Replicated Content

Content federation is nifty. However, it's not suited for large-scale replication. Like its Promotion Management counterpart, we can't suggest you should consider replicating tens of thousands of reports or users. There are timing considerations, server performance considerations, and overall redundancy factors to take into account. Choose content federation ... wisely.

1. Contrast a replication job to a Promotion Management job.
2. The list of content to be replicated is contained within _____.
3. How are other CMS clusters referred to when mapping replication jobs from the source system to the target system?

6.5   Summary

If you're stepping into this book as an accomplished administrator on the SAP BusinessObjects XI 3.1 or older side of the fence, you might be asking yourself, "When is the Import Wizard coming back?" We're sorry to tell you, but we don't think you'll see it again. However, after reading this chapter, you should know that all is not lost. We've discussed the three tools currently at your disposal—Upgrade Management Tool, Promotion Management, and Replication Service/Data Federation Service—and you should now have a good understanding of when and how to use them.

With many more migrations under our belt since the first publication of this text, our points of view on the approach to migrations has varied. Customers of modest landscape size, say less than a few thousand objects, can consider "big bang" migration approaches by bulk moving content forward from SAP BusinessObjects XI 3.1 landscapes. Customers and users facing a mountain of report objects have to carefully weigh if those kinds of moves can happen in a time frame of an evening or a weekend to cause the least disruption possible. In these cases, a staged migration may be appropriate. Take stock and ensure you select the right content migration approach to cause the least disruption possible.

SAP BusinessObjects BI 4.1 includes some powerful technology for monitoring and alerting. This chapter focuses on how to set up monitoring and use it properly in root cause analysis situations.

7   Monitoring: Keeping an Eye on Things

Somewhere along the way, while we weren't looking, SAP BusinessObjects BI grew up on us. Having access to critical business information at all times is now the standard, and the backbone of that is a healthy and stable SAP BusinessObjects BI platform. Old-timer administrators like us used to have to get really creative when it came to implementing a monitoring plan for an SAP BusinessObjects BI environment—but not anymore. You lucky dogs get to start out with a pretty cool capability baked right into the SAP BusinessObjects BI Central Management Console, and that is the new monitoring engine. In this chapter, we'll help you get acquainted with the Monitoring application, which got a nice face-lift in SAP BusinessObjects 4.0 SP4 and has gotten better ever since. We'll discuss what metrics are, how to build them into watchlists, and the all-important alerting system that naturally follows. Sprinkle that with a little bit of savvy from Auditor and some best practices, and we'll call it a chapter. Let's dive right in, shall we?

7.1   Monitoring in the Central Management Console

There's a challenge you're going to face right off the bat with monitoring, so we might as well be completely up-front about it. The entire interface is written in Adobe Flash. Gasp! No mobile for you. So, that means you'll need to access the Central Management Console with a browser that has a Flash plugin installed. Why is this a challenge? Well, mainly because many administrators like to use the CMC that is actually on the server. It makes things a bit speedier in general. Have you ever tried to download a browser plugin from a server? It's not fun, especially not on Windows Server 2008 R2 with all of its Vista-esque "enhanced security." To make matters a bit worse, SAP didn't bundle a version of the Flash Player along with SAP BusinessObjects BI 4.1, so you have to get the Flash Player install-er from the Internet. Have fun with that. We didn't.

After you have Flash installed (or decided to use Google Chrome because it has Flash embedded in it already), log in to the CMC, and head on over to the MON-ITORING application (see Figure 7.1).

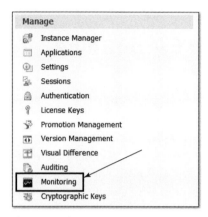

Figure 7.1 The Monitoring Application Location

Click on that bad boy, and after the Flash Player loads up the application, you'll land on the Monitoring Dashboard.

7.2 The Monitoring Dashboard

If you were lucky enough to get your hands on the first generally available release of SAP BusinessObjects BI 4.1, and you took the time to check out the Monitoring Dashboard in that version, you'll be pleasantly surprised at the work that went into this application in SP4. Take a gander at the entirely revamped Monitoring Dashboard (see Figure 7.2).

Looks pretty nice, doesn't it? Obviously a lot of thought went into this redesign. Let's explore each region of this new dashboard and explain what it does.

Starting from the top-left side, the first box you'll see is the overall health indica-tor. This is your hurry-up-and-tell-me-what-is-going-on-I'm-in-a-rush box. It's an aggregate summary of how your system is doing. It's a rather ubiquitous "traffic light" indicator that can be red, yellow, or green (see Figure 7.3).

Dashboard
Metrics
Watchlist
Probes
Alerts
Help
Overall Health :
OK
Recent Alerts (3) numbers in last 1 days.
View All
1 Consolidated Health Watch Danger Event May 10, 2012 6:13 AM Not Cleared
2 Service Categories Watch Danger Event May 10, 2012 6:13 AM Not Cleared
3 Crystal Reports Services Watch Danger Event May 10, 2012 6:13 AM Not Cleared
Graphical View of BI Landscape
Updated on:May 12, 2012 5:50:33 AM
Show Service Categories with State All Display only selected
Mini View
100% Zoom Levels
Crystal Re...
Core Servi...
Analysis S...
Lifecycle M...
Service Ca...
Connectivit...
Web Intelli...
Dashboard...
Data Feder...
KPI Status
May 12, 2012 5:51:32 AM
AdaptivePr ocessingSe rver Watch
CentralMan agementSer ver Watch
Recent Update
CrystalRep ortsCacheS erver Watch
Select KPI
Deployment Level Metrics
RunningJobs 0
Users 3
PendingJobs 0

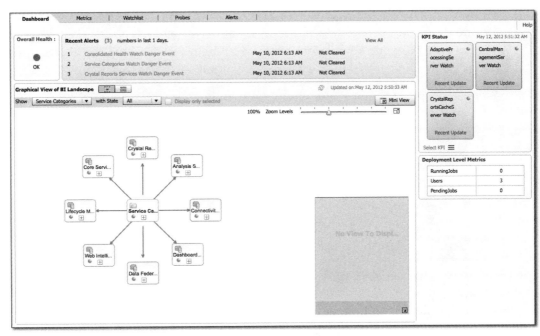

Figure 7.2 The SAP BusinessObjects BI Monitoring Dashboard

Overall Health :
OK

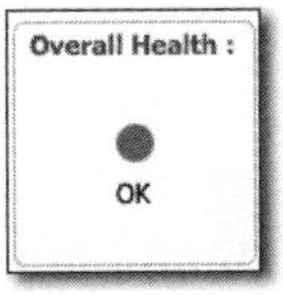

Figure 7.3 The Overall Health Indicator

Moving to the right, next is the Recent Alerts box (see Figure 7.4). This is a summary of any alerts that have been triggered and not yet cleared. (See Section 7.6 for specifics on alerts.)

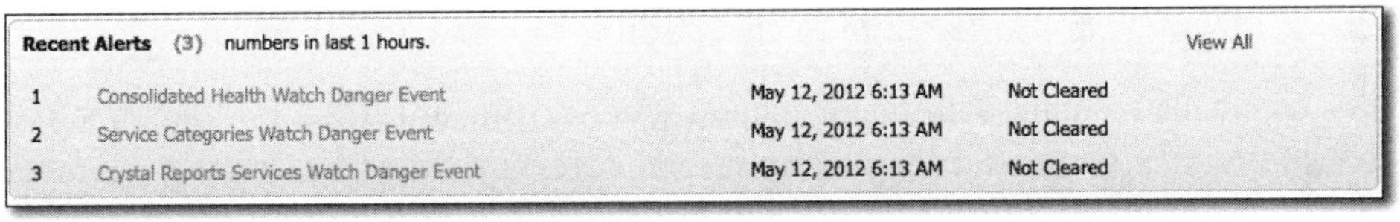

Recent Alerts (3) numbers in last 1 hours.
View All
1 Consolidated Health Watch Danger Event May 12, 2012 6:13 AM Not Cleared
2 Service Categories Watch Danger Event May 12, 2012 6:13 AM Not Cleared
3 Crystal Reports Services Watch Danger Event May 12, 2012 6:13 AM Not Cleared

Figure 7.4 The Recent Alerts Box

Moving across to the top right, we have the KPI STATUS box (see Figure 7.5). This one sports the current date and time on the server and has a list of watches you can define as your key performance indicators (KPIs). This will be different for each deployment, based on what your organization considers critical.

Figure 7.5 The KPI Status Box

Just below that is the DEPLOYMENT LEVEL METRICS box, which gives you a quick summary of more traditional metrics. You can see how many jobs are running right now, how many users are logged in, and how many jobs are pending (see Figure 7.6).

Deployment Level Metrics	
RunningJobs	0
Users	3
PendingJobs	0

Figure 7.6 The Deployment Level Metrics Box

That completes our trip around the outside of the Monitoring Dashboard. The largest pane on the dashboard is the GRAPHICAL VIEW OF BI LANDSCAPE box. This is where the pretty little star graphic is (see Figure 7.7). This pane is totally interactive (+1 for Flash), so feel free to click around and see what's what.

This is meant to start drilling in to your monitoring information. Metrics and watches have been preset for you by service category. Just like in the CMC Servers area, your watches can be broken down by their role (i.e., core services, Web Intelligence services, Data Federation Services, etc.). This is really handy when something is going wrong. You can get a quick visual on where the problem is.

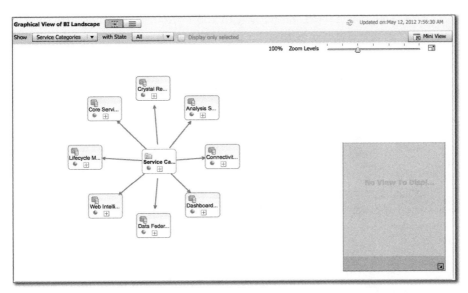

Figure 7.7 The Graphical View of BI Landscape Box

If you click into one of the categories, you'll see the view drill in even further. For example, click into the WEB INTELLIGENCE SERVICES box (see Figure 7.8).

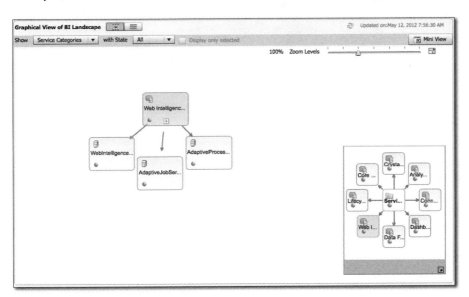

Figure 7.8 Graphical View of BI Landscape Box: Drilled in to Web Intelligence Services

Now the initial view has been put down in the bottom-left corner, so you can keep track of where you are in the stack. You'll see that the WEB INTELLIGENCE SERVICES box you clicked is now shaded. In the main window, you see the shaded WEB INTELLIGENCE SERVICES box again, plus it now shows you what three watches make up that parent service category. Pretty neat, huh?

If you drill in yet again, you'll go straight into the actual watch. All the way on the left, click into the WEB INTELLIGENCE PROCESSING SERVER watch (see Figure 7.9).

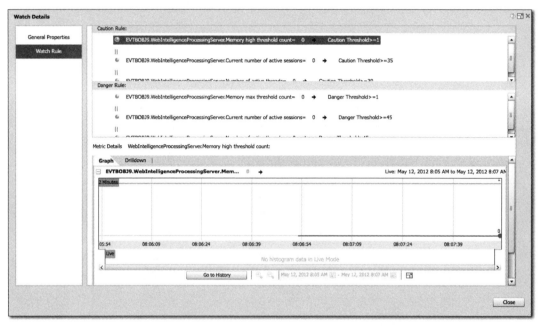

Figure 7.9 The Web Intelligence Processing Server Watch

We'll cover the specifics of watches and how they are made in Section 7.4. Let's stick with our dashboard tour for now. Close that WATCH DETAILS window, and return to the GRAPHICAL VIEW OF BI LANDSCAPE box. Along the top, you'll see a couple of dropdown boxes to change your views. The default view you started with was the SERVICE CATEGORIES view (see Figure 7.10). You can switch this to ENTERPRISE NODES for a different picture. This is especially helpful if you're working in a clustered environment and want to see how each node is behaving.

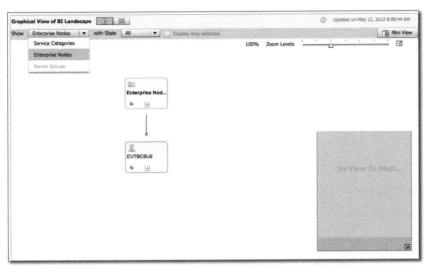

Figure 7.10 Graphical View of BI Landscape Box – Enterprise Nodes View

The demo server only has one node, so that's all you see here. If this was a three-node cluster, you'd see three boxes there by node name. Click on the node box (the bottom one), and you'll go to an expanded view of how each major service on the node is operating (see Figure 7.11). The other dropdown box on the top allows you to filter your view by state (see Figure 7.12).

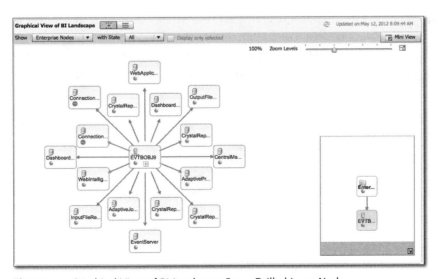

Figure 7.11 Graphical View of BI Landscape Box – Drilled in on Node

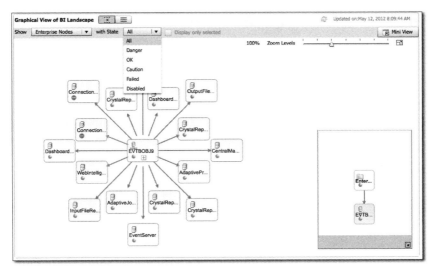

Figure 7.12 Graphical View of BI Landscape Box – State Filters

You can filter on ALL, DANGER, OK, CAUTION, FAILED, or DISABLED to help you hone in your triage quickly. It's important to note here that these states refer to the watches, and not particularly to the actual services. You can have a server that is running and enabled but a watch on it that is disabled. This watch would show up if you applied a DISABLED filter on this box.

Overall, that's pretty much all there is to the Monitoring Dashboard. It's meant to be your first stop and give you the lowdown on what is going on in your system all in one place. But what makes up all of that stuff we were just looking at? That is another great question. The basic building blocks of your Monitoring Engine are metrics, which we'll discuss next.

Pop Quiz

1. The browser component required to use the Monitoring Dashboard is _____.

2. True or False: The Monitoring Dashboard is used to monitor processes across all nodes of your CMS cluster.

7.3   Metrics

Metrics are really the foundation of the Monitoring Engine. A *metric* in its simplest definition is something to be measured. There are bunches and bunches of them predefined in the system for you: CPUs, CPU Utilization for the last 15 minutes, Total Memory, Number of Deadlocked Jobs, and so on. The list is very long. Use what has been prebuilt for you as a starting place, and build out if you need to. Let's take a look at the Metrics tab (see Figure 7.13).

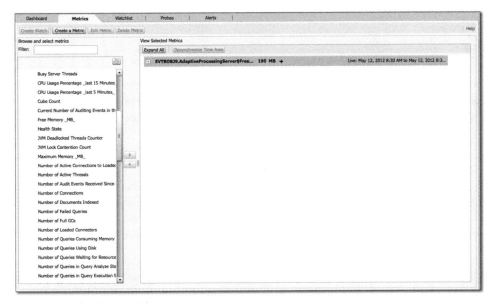

Figure 7.13 The Metrics Tab

On the right-hand side, you'll see your list of available metrics. It starts out collapsed, but you can plus it out and have a look around to find what you're looking for. For this example, we picked Servers • Adaptive Processing Server • Free Memory _MB_. The metric pops over into the main window, and you can see what it currently evaluates to. So right now, the APS is using 190MB of memory. If you plus out this metric, now you can see a trend over a larger window of time (see Figure 7.14).

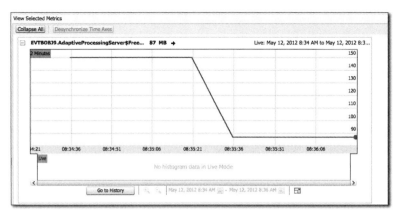

Figure 7.14 Expanded Metrics Window

This shows us the total memory being used by this server over the past few minutes. If you want to see more, click the Go to History button at the bottom.

If the predefined metrics don't give you enough information, or you want to have a new metric based on a few others, you can head over to the New Derived Metric screen (see Figure 7.15). This is where you can really get creative. Take a look at the formula syntax shown in Figure 7.16.

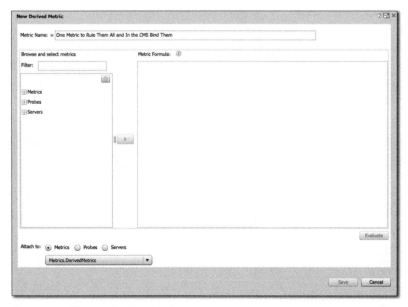

Figure 7.15 New Derived Metric Screen

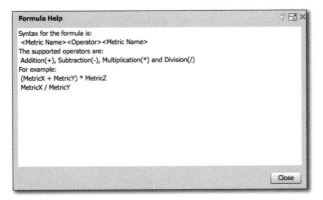

Figure 7.16 Metric Formula Syntax

As you can see, this will allow you to build some custom metrics that are based on an evaluation of another metric. Custom metrics can be useful when you want to see something in a way that isn't already there for you out-of-the-box; for example, if you want to see your free disk space for the Adaptive Job Server. There is only a disk size metric and a used disk space metric. You could easily create your own free disk space metric by creating a custom metric that subtracts the used disk space metric from the disk size metric. You're really only limited by your imagination here.

Metrics are to monitoring what dimensions are to a Web Intelligence query. They are the foundation of all that is done but need other things to be built on top of them to round out the service offering. A metric measures something, whether that is an amount of memory being used, number of CPUs in motion, number of reports running on a Processing Server, and so on. But, the measure itself doesn't do anything to tell you if that value is good or bad. To start doing some comparisons, you need to start building watchlists.

Pop Quiz

1. Describe the role of a metric in the Monitoring Dashboard.
2. Define the purpose that predefined metrics play in the Monitoring Dashboard.

7.4   Watchlists

Watchlists are what now allow us to use a metric to tell us if something is good or bad and to continue to watch (thus the name) for a specific condition to either be true or false. In this section, we'll show you some of the prebuilt watchlists offered by SAP BusinessObjects BI, and then we'll walk you through the steps of creating your own.

7.4.1   Prebuilt Watchlists

Head over to the WATCHLIST tab in the Monitoring application, and you'll see that SAP BusinessObjects BI 4.1 comes with some prebuilt watchlists already prepared for you.

In Figure 7.17 we clicked on the first watch, the ANALYSIS SERVICES WATCH, and in the lower pane, the watch popped up as a green bar. Just to the left of the watch in the list, you'll see the little stoplight status indicator, which is also green. This tells us at a glance that this watch is healthy, and there are no issues. You can expand the watch from the green bar in the lower pane, by clicking the plus sign in the left-most corner of the bar (see Figure 7.18).

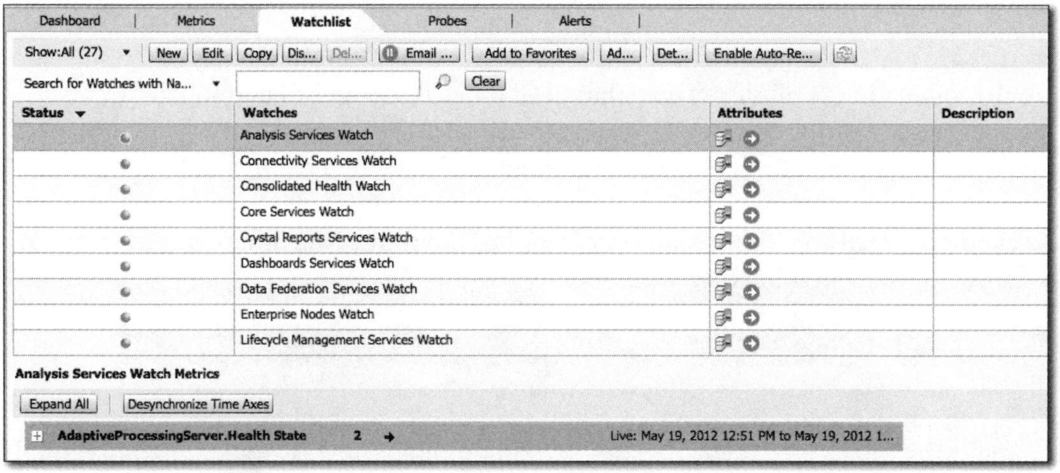

Figure 7.17 The Watchlist Tab

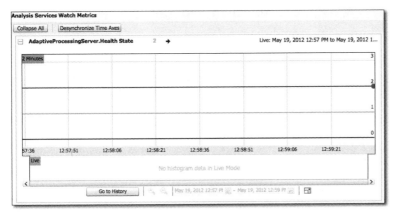

Figure 7.18 Analysis Services Watch: Expanded: Live Mode

In this expanded state, you can see that the value being measured is currently at 2, and that number is displayed in green to again tell you that this watch is healthy. The watch opens in LIVE mode, which means this is the value being measured for this watch right now, and shows you the value over the past two minutes. This is indicated by the purple line on the graph. The yellow line indicates where the caution rule is, and the red line shows where the danger rule is. We'll discuss the caution rule and danger rule in just a bit, so just tuck that bit of information away for a moment. You also have the option of viewing the history of this watch. Click the GO TO HISTORY button to switch it over. Once you do, you'll need to set the date range for the window you want to see displayed. In Figure 7.19, we set the watch to show us the past four weeks of data.

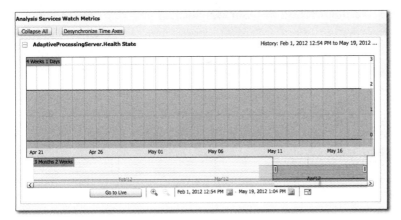

Figure 7.19 Analysis Services Watch: Expanded: History Mode

So, this watch has been steady at a value of 2 for the past four weeks. No problems here. If there had been any, you'd see it reflected in the data, where the purple line crossed either the yellow caution or red danger lines.

At the top of the WATCHLIST tab, there are a bunch of control buttons for you (see Figure 7.20).

Figure 7.20 Watchlist Tab Toolbar

Most of the types of controls you'd expect from a toolbar are here: NEW, EDIT, COPY, DISABLE, and DELETE. There's also a handy button to pause email notifications, which helps a bunch when you're in crisis mode or doing maintenance and want to stop the onslaught of your inbox. (We'll discuss how to set up the email alerts in Section 7.6.) To finish off the toolbar, you have ADD TO FAVORITES, ADD A KPI, DETAILS, and ENABLE AUTO-REFRESH.

7.4.2 Creating New Watchlists

To create a new watchlist, you'd start where you probably think you'd start, by clicking the NEW button on the WATCHLIST toolbar. This will land you in the NEW WATCH: GENERAL PROPERTIES window on the GENERAL PROPERTIES page (see Figure 7.21).

Here you'll need to enter a NAME for your watchlist. A best practice is to add as much specific information about the node, server name, and what you'll be watching in this name because if an alert fires, this will help you more quickly determine what is going on. For example, use *NodeName.ServerName_ThingIam-Watching* as a standard.

Also, do yourself a favor and enter a good DESCRIPTION here about what is being watched. After a few months, you'll forget what this watch was for, and a good description can help jog your memory.

Figure 7.21 New Watch: General Properties Screen

Next, you'll need to choose between a two-stage or three-stage watch. Two-stage is binary: either you're good or you're bad. No gray area here. Two-stage watches are great for things like server running state. Either your server is up or it's down, right? Three-stage watches are selected by default because most of the metrics you want to watch will be three-stagers. Three-stage has OK, caution, and danger states and are meant to help you know when things are starting to look bad, before things get catastrophic. Examples of good three-stage candidates are memory consumption, CPU utilization, number of active connections on your Web Intelligence Processing Server, and so on. These are things that you want some fair warning on that they are working hard. Working hard isn't always a bad thing, but getting a warning before things go south is pretty handy. Also, you should remember that the stages have a hierarchy. If both the caution and danger rules have evaluated to true, the watch will enter a danger state because danger is the more severe.

The final additional settings you'll want to consider are whether to write this watch to the trending database (highly recommended; data is *good*) and if you want to add this watch as a KPI so it will appear back on the main Monitoring Dashboard (refer to Figure 7.5). For this example, we've chosen a three-stage watchlist, and we're going to write data to the trending database and add this as a KPI (see Figure 7.22).

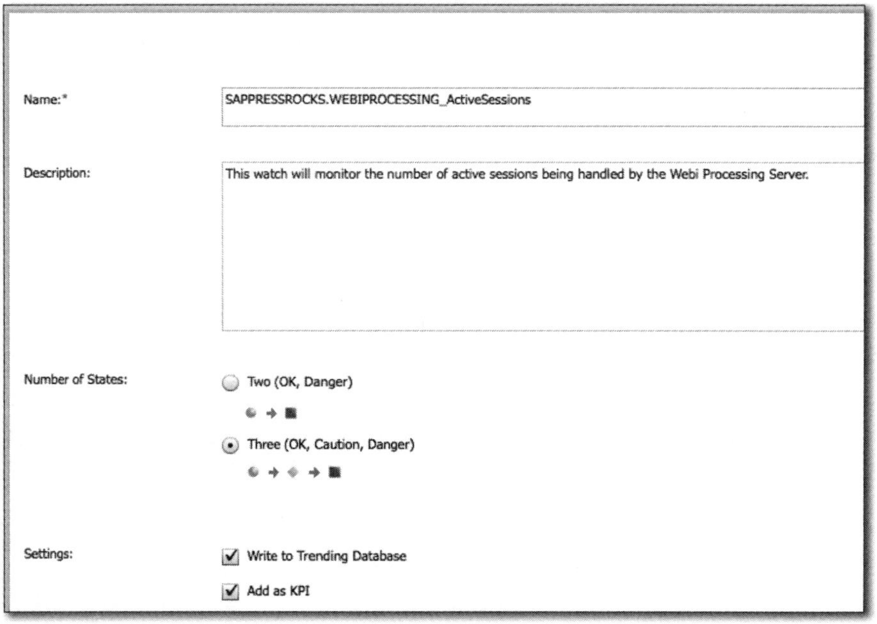

Name:*	SAPPRESSROCKS.WEBIPROCESSING_ActiveSessions
Description:	This watch will monitor the number of active sessions being handled by the Webi Processing Server.
Number of States:	○ Two (OK, Danger)
	● Three (OK, Caution, Danger)
Settings:	☑ Write to Trending Database
	☑ Add as KPI

Figure 7.22 The Watchlist General Properties Filled Out

Now that you have your watchlist named and described, stages chosen, and trending info decided, click NEXT.

Now, you'll want to define the caution rule. This is the phase where you want a warning that things are working hard but aren't necessarily in serious trouble yet. We like to consider the caution rule as the "heads up" rule.

In the left-hand pane, you'll see a list of available metrics, probes, servers, and topology available from which to choose to build your caution rule. We're going to use a metric for this example (see Figure 7.23).

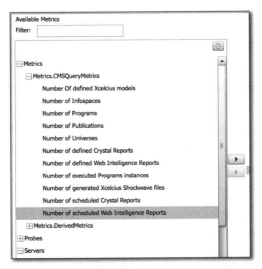

Figure 7.23 Choosing a Metric for Your Watchlist

We're going to make this watch keep watch on the number of scheduled Web Intelligence reports. So, select this metric, and then click the right arrow to push the metric over into the EXPRESSION pane. Here is where you'll build the watch logic that the Monitoring Engine will keep track of. This is where you'll need to do a little homework ahead of time, or be ready to hop back and forth between windows. To set up the logic here, you need to know what is good and what is bad, right? Let's jump quickly over to the SERVERS tab and open up the PROPERTIES of the Web Intelligence Cover Service (see Figure 7.24).

Web Intelligence Core Service	
☐ Use Configuration Template	
Timeout Before Recycling (seconds):	1200
Idle Document Timeout (seconds):	300
Server Polling Interval (seconds):	120
Maximum Documents per User:	5
Maximum Documents Before Recycling:	50
☑ Allow Document Map Maximum Size Errors	
Idle Connection Timeout (minutes):	20
Maximum Connections:	50
☑ Enable Memory Analysis	
Memory Lower Threshold (MB):	3500
Memory Upper Threshold (MB):	4500
Memory Maximum Threshold (MB):	6000
☑ Enable APS Service Monitoring	

Figure 7.24 Web Intelligence Core Service Properties

Here, you can see that the maximum connections are set to 50, so if 50 reports are running, you're out of capacity. In other words, 50 is the bad number that you really don't want to reach because that is where users will start seeing error messages. So for the caution rule, you'll want to set the number a bit lower than being in trouble, so you get your head up that something is working hard.

If 50 is terrible, a warning at 30 seems reasonable. It's a high enough number that things could continue and get worse, but early enough to do something about it. In the CAUTION rule, enter the number "30" (see Figure 7.25).

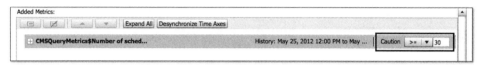

Figure 7.25 Building the Caution Rule Logic

If you want to see where this watchlist lies right now, at the bottom of your screen, click the CAUTION RULE CURRENTLY EVALUATES TO button, and you'll see where you stand at the moment (see Figure 7.26).

Figure 7.26 Caution Rule Currently Evaluates To

If you're satisfied, then go ahead and click NEXT and proceed to the danger rule. The danger rule is when you're in trouble, but hopefully not down yet. When this one fires, you want someone to act quickly to avoid an outage.

For this example watch, we said the threshold is 50, and we fired the caution rule at 30, so it makes sense to fire off the danger rule at 45. This puts it high enough to be concerned, but still low enough that there's some time to remedy the problem before an outage (see Figure 7.27).

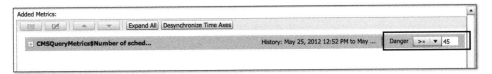

Figure 7.27 Setting the Danger Rule

You can check the danger rule as well and see how it currently evaluates by clicking the DANGER RULE CURRENTLY EVALUATES TO button at the bottom (see Figure 7.28).

Figure 7.28 Danger Rule Currently Evaluates To

When you're satisfied, click the NEXT button, and proceed to the NEW WATCH – THROTTLE AND NOTIFICATION screen (see Figure 7.29).

Figure 7.29 New Watch – Throttle and Notification Screen

The top portion of the window concerns throttling criteria, and the bottom the notification settings. Let's start with the top and discuss throttling.

The top two radio buttons allow you to decide what you want to do when your rules evaluate to true (see Figure 7.30).

○ Change watch state every time Caution or Danger Rule evaluates to true

○ Change watch state according to Throttling criteria below

Figure 7.30 Throttling Criteria Radio Buttons

The default selection is CHANGE WATCH STATE EVERY TIME CAUTION OR DANGER RULE EVALUATES TO TRUE. This means, quite simply, that the watch will change from OK to either a caution or danger state based on which rule was true, and it will do so every single time that condition exists. In most of your monitoring cases, this will be sufficient. But sometimes, you don't want to trigger the rule every time the condition exists. Sometimes, you need more information to determine if this is really something bad or just a busy server. That's where the customizable throttling criteria come in. If this is what you want, then change the radio button selection to CHANGE WATCH STATE ACCORDING TO THROTTLING CRITERIA BELOW, and proceed to set those criteria.

Let's set some throttling criteria for the caution rule. Following our example, we're setting up a watch to alert us when we're approaching the capacity for running scheduled Web Intelligence reports. We set the caution rule to 30 reports and the danger rule to 45 reports. Let's think about the caution rule a little more closely. As it stands, if you simply enacted this watch as-is, you would trigger the caution rule every single time the Web Intelligence Processing Server was running 30 simultaneous jobs. That watch might prove to be a little too "noisy," clutter up the alerts, and not be so meaningful. Maybe a better indicator that things are getting bad is if this condition were to persist for more than 15 minutes. To do that, set up the throttling criteria, as shown in Figure 7.31.

Now, the caution rule will only trigger if you have 30 simultaneous Web Intelligence reports on the server for more than 15 minutes. This is probably a better indicator that jobs aren't finishing up in a timely manner and the server is working pretty hard. You'll also notice that just below the time to wait options, you can also wait for a certain number of true evaluations over a set time period.

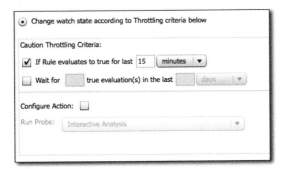

Figure 7.31 Caution Rule Throttling Criteria: Rule True Persistence

Rather than waiting for 15 minutes at that level, let's switch the throttling criteria to WAIT FOR 5 TRUE EVALUATION(S) IN THE LAST 30 MINUTES, as shown in Figure 7.32.

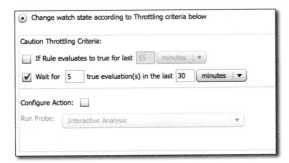

Figure 7.32 Caution Rule Throttling Criteria: Wait for True Evaluationsn

Now, the Web Intelligence Processing Server would have to hit 30 reports, then clear, and then hit 30 reports again five separate times within a 30-minute period to throw the watch into a caution state. Not too shabby.

The last throttling option is to take an action. To do this, select the CONFIGURE ACTION checkbox, and then choose your probe to run from the RUN PROBE dropdown list, as shown in Figure 7.33. For this example, we chose to run the START STOP SERVERS probe. (We'll discuss what the probes are in detail in Section 7.5.)

Figure 7.33 Caution Rule Throttling Criteria: Configure Action

All of the same options also exist for your danger rule. Again, the flexibility here is only limited by your imagination. Experiment with what works for you and your company. After you get this part set, you're pretty much done with throttling criteria. Now, it's time for everyone's favorite part: the notification settings.

Notification is the part that administrators dread: A message containing information about impending doom that typically comes in the middle of the night to roust you out of a comfy slumber. But, the servers need us sometimes. This is where you'll set up how your beloved server should contact you when the need arises, along with whom to contact.

Below the throttling criteria is where you'll find the NOTIFICATION SETTINGS pane (see Figure 7.34).

Figure 7.34 Notification Settings Pane

The ENABLE ALERT NOTIFICATIONS checkbox is selected by default. You can unselect it if you need to, and notifications won't go out for this watch.

The built-in ADMINISTRATOR account is the only one selected by default. To add other users, click the DIRECTORY button (see Figure 7.35).

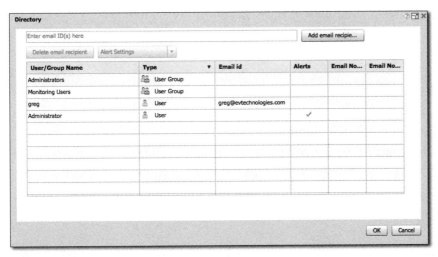

Figure 7.35 The Notifications Directory Window

When you enter in, you see that just the ADMINISTRATOR will get an alert. Alerts are discussed in detail in Section 7.6. You'll also notice that all of the groups and users are listed here as well. This test system has just a few, but let's add in some email notifications along with the alerts.

To do this, click on the user or group name you want, and then click the ALERT SETTINGS dropdown to select which ones you want to enable (see Figure 7.36).

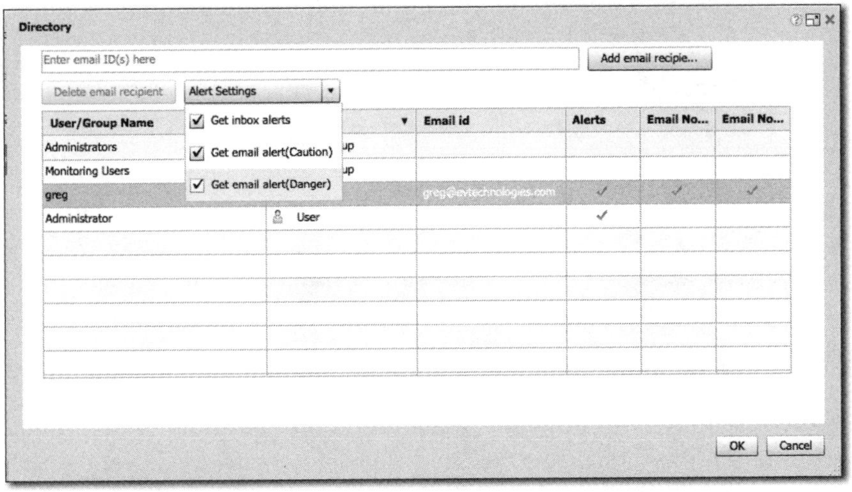

Figure 7.36 Adding Alert Settings

So, with this setup, you'll get the internal alerts for everything, plus an email to the email address specified when the caution rule and/or the danger rule evaluate to true. After you've picked all of the lucky candidates who should get these notifications, click OK , and you'll return to the NEW WATCH – THROTTLE AND NOTIFICATION window.

The last notification setting you can select is ADD METRIC TREND HISTORY AS ATTACHMENT (see Figure 7.37). This is handy because it will add a nice little graph of the metric trends for you to review if the caution or danger rules trigger. This is especially helpful when you're not logged into the server or if the rules fire after-hours.

Notification Settings:
Enable alert notifications
List of users to be notified
Administrator,greg
Directory
Add Metric Trend History As Attachment

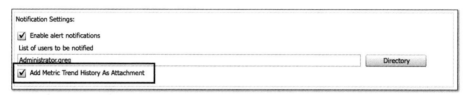

Figure 7.37 Add Metric Trend History as Attachment

Now you're all set. Click the SAVE button, and your new watchlist is live (see Figure 7.38)!

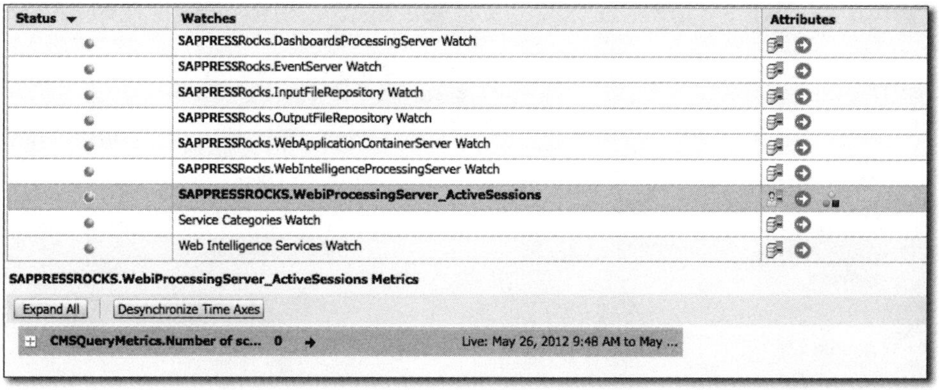

Status
Watches
Attributes
SAPPRESSRocks.DashboardsProcessingServer Watch
SAPPRESSRocks.EventServer Watch
SAPPRESSRocks.InputFileRepository Watch
SAPPRESSRocks.OutputFileRepository Watch
SAPPRESSRocks.WebApplicationContainerServer Watch
SAPPRESSRocks.WebIntelligenceProcessingServer Watch
SAPPRESSROCKS.WebiProcessingServer_ActiveSessions
Service Categories Watch
Web Intelligence Services Watch
SAPPRESSROCKS.WebiProcessingServer_ActiveSessions Metrics
Expand All
Desynchronize Time Axes
CMSQueryMetrics.Number of sc... 0
Live: May 26, 2012 9:48 AM to May ...

Figure 7.38 The Live Watchlist

Those are the basics for setting up your watchlists. Don't be afraid to experiment with these, and don't rely solely on the samples that are provided to you by SAP. The samples are a great start, but you should thoroughly review them based on your monitoring needs. Customize them as needed, or build your own from scratch now that you know how. Watchlists are only a piece of the monitoring puzzle, however, which brings us to the next major piece, the probes.

Pop Quiz

1. Describe the purpose of a watchlist.
2. True or False: Watchlists are predefined behaviours in SAP BusinessObjects BI 4.1 and can't be customized in an environment.
3. Describe a capability of a watchlist that ensures one-off events don't trigger the watchlist in a negative fashion.

7.5   Probes

So, just what are these funny things named probes? *Probes* are basically programs that you can schedule to run that will simulate different workflows or services provided by SAP BusinessObjects BI 4.1. The probes have actually been around for a long time, but this is the first version where they are officially a part of the product. The original probes were debuted by Business Objects Labs (pre-SAP acquisition) as a beta you could try out, and they have developed from there. Probes can be extremely useful for the administrator because they simulate things that your users will be doing and can help alert you to problems before your users do. Table 7.1 shows a list of probes you can use to help you monitor your system.

Probe Name	Probe Description
CMS Cache	This probe tests the availability and health of the CMS cache by executing the following query: `select SI_NAME from CI_SYSTEMOBJS where SI_ID=4` This query returns the system InfoObject that contains the CMS cluster name. After a warm-up period, it's expected that the CMS retrieves the system InfoObject from the cache rather than from the repository database. If the query fails, the cache might not be functioning properly or the cluster definition might be incorrect. No input parameters are required.

Table 7.1 Available Probes

Probe Name	Probe Description
CMS DB Connection	This probe tests the availability of the repository database by executing the following query: `select SI_NAME from CI_SYSTEMOBJS where SI_OBTYPE=13` This query returns the system InfoObject that contains the CMS cluster name. The CMS retrieves the system InfoObject from the repository database. If this query fails, there may be a connection problem between the CMS and repository database. No input parameters are required.
CMS Ping	This probe sends an empty query to the CMS. The test is considered successful if the CMS returns a parse failure error. Because query parsing is part of the CMS core functionality, the test is expected to complete quickly. No input parameters are required.
CMS Logon Logoff	This probe tests the availability of the CMS and the ability of users to log on to the system through client applications. The probe logs on a single user, tests session validity, and logs off the user. No input parameters are required.
Crystal Reports Service (Processing Server)	This probe will run a Crystal report (you specify the CUID in the input parameters) using page and Cache Servers and track how long it takes to refresh it. You can also optionally have the report export. Input parameters are required.
Crystal Reports Service (Report Application Server)	This probe will run a Crystal report (you specify the CUID in the input parameters) using the Report Application Server (RAS) and track how long it takes to refresh it. You can also optionally have the report export. Input parameters are required.
InfoView Probe	This probe will log in to the BI Launch Pad using an account and authentication type you specify. This will help you ensure the health of your web applications and your authentication systems. Input parameters are required.
Interactive Analysis	This probe will run a Web Intelligence report (you specify the CUID in the input parameters) and track how long it takes to refresh it. You can also optionally have the report exported to XLS or PDF formats. Note: The Web Intelligence report can't have any prompts. There is no way to pass in prompt values with a probe report. Input parameters are required.
Start Stop Servers	This one does just what it says, so use it carefully. It will stop and start all of your servers. Input parameters are required.

Table 7.1 Available Probes (Cont.)

If you click on the PROBES tab of the Monitoring Dashboard, you'll find the list of probes in all their glory (see Figure 7.39).

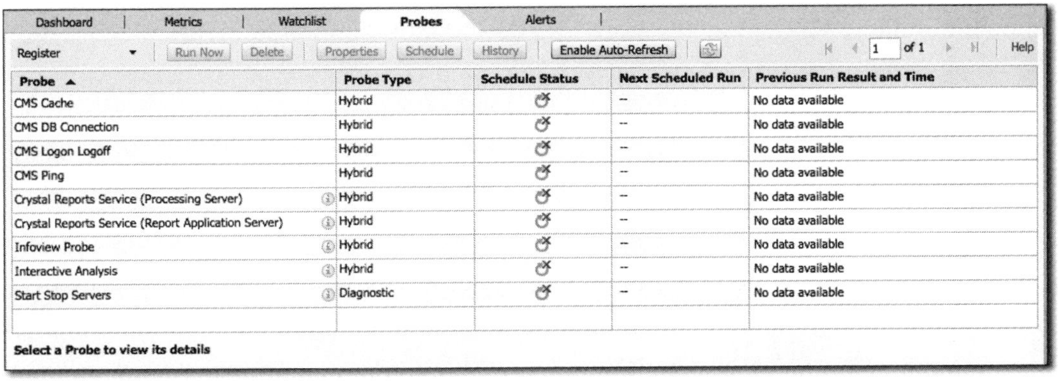

Probe ▲	Probe Type	Schedule Status	Next Scheduled Run	Previous Run Result and Time
CMS Cache	Hybrid	⏱	--	No data available
CMS DB Connection	Hybrid	⏱	--	No data available
CMS Logon Logoff	Hybrid	⏱	--	No data available
CMS Ping	Hybrid	⏱	--	No data available
Crystal Reports Service (Processing Server)	Hybrid	⏱	--	No data available
Crystal Reports Service (Report Application Server)	Hybrid	⏱	--	No data available
Infoview Probe	Hybrid	⏱	--	No data available
Interactive Analysis	Hybrid	⏱	--	No data available
Start Stop Servers	Diagnostic	⏱	--	No data available

Select a Probe to view its details

Figure 7.39 List of Probes in the Probes Tab

When you first arrive here after installing your SAP BusinessObjects BI 4.1 system, the probes will appear like they do in Figure 7.39 — no data available and not scheduled.

As we saw back in Section 7.4, probes can be run as throttling criteria if a caution or danger rule evaluates to true. It also appears that you can add additional probes in the future, whether these are probes you write yourself or probes that are provided to you by SAP at some point in the future. The REGISTER button in the top-left corner of the window lets you define a new probe. You can choose a JAVA-BASED PROBE or a SCRIPT PROBE (see Figure 7.40).

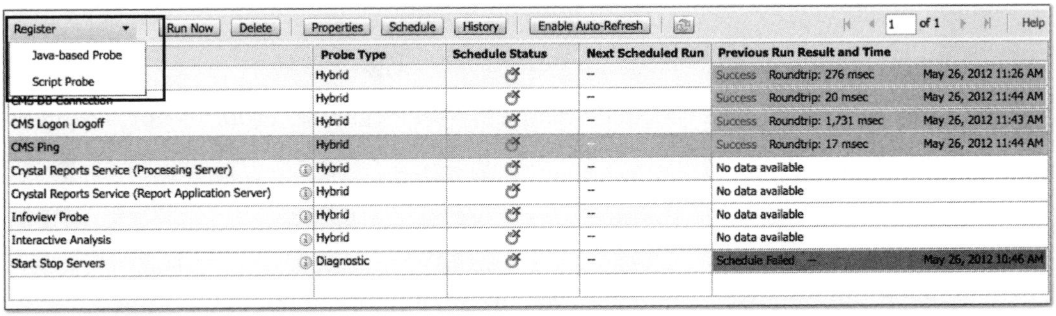

	Probe Type	Schedule Status	Next Scheduled Run	Previous Run Result and Time
	Hybrid	⏱	--	Success Roundtrip: 276 msec May 26, 2012 11:26 AM
CMS DB Connection	Hybrid	⏱	--	Success Roundtrip: 20 msec May 26, 2012 11:44 AM
CMS Logon Logoff	Hybrid	⏱	--	Success Roundtrip: 1,731 msec May 26, 2012 11:43 AM
CMS Ping	Hybrid	⏱	--	Success Roundtrip: 17 msec May 26, 2012 11:44 AM
Crystal Reports Service (Processing Server)	Hybrid	⏱	--	No data available
Crystal Reports Service (Report Application Server)	Hybrid	⏱	--	No data available
Infoview Probe	Hybrid	⏱	--	No data available
Interactive Analysis	Hybrid	⏱	--	No data available
Start Stop Servers	Diagnostic	⏱	--	Schedule Failed -- May 26, 2012 10:46 AM

Figure 7.40 Registering a New Probe

The first four probes in your list, CMS CACHE, CMS DB CONNECTION, CMS LOGON LOGOFF, and CMS PING (see Figure 7.41) don't require any input parameters to run. They already know where to find the information they need to run in the system. Schedule these to run as often as you need (or not).

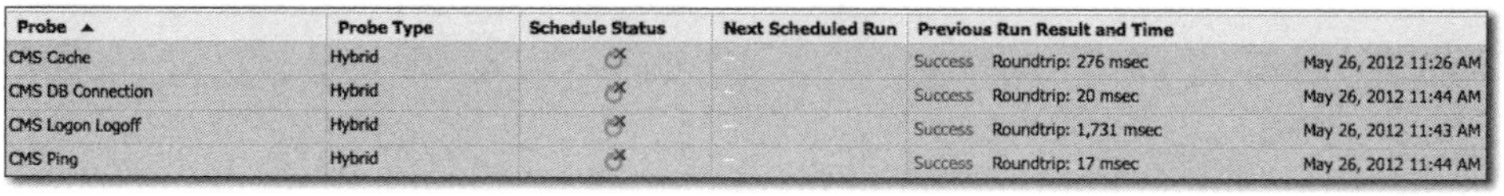

Probe ▲	Probe Type	Schedule Status	Next Scheduled Run	Previous Run Result and Time	
CMS Cache	Hybrid			Success Roundtrip: 276 msec	May 26, 2012 11:26 AM
CMS DB Connection	Hybrid			Success Roundtrip: 20 msec	May 26, 2012 11:44 AM
CMS Logon Logoff	Hybrid			Success Roundtrip: 1,731 msec	May 26, 2012 11:43 AM
CMS Ping	Hybrid			Success Roundtrip: 17 msec	May 26, 2012 11:44 AM

Figure 7.41 The CMS Probes

The rest of the five probes—CRYSTAL REPORTS SERVICE (PROCESSING SERVER), CRYSTAL REPORTS SERVICE (REPORT APPLICATION SERVER), INFOVIEW PROBE, INTERACTIVE ANALYSIS, and START STOP SERVERS—all have little information indicators in the name window, which indicates that these probes require input parameters before they will run successfully (see Figure 7.42).

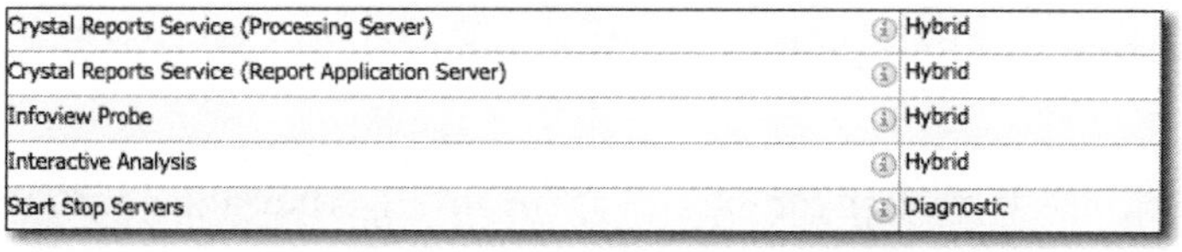

Crystal Reports Service (Processing Server)		Hybrid
Crystal Reports Service (Report Application Server)		Hybrid
Infoview Probe		Hybrid
Interactive Analysis		Hybrid
Start Stop Servers		Diagnostic

Figure 7.42 Probes That Require Input Parameters

Crystal Reports Service (Processing Server) Probe

To properly set this probe into action, you'll need to give it a little more information. Click this probe in the list to highlight it, and then click the PROPERTIES button in the toolbar above. This will launch the properties window, and you'll find where to enter in the input parameters (see Figure 7.43).

You'll have to find a candidate report that you want this probe to run and get the CUID from the report's properties page. Input that CUID here, and then tell the probe if you want to refresh the report and whether you want it to export or not using "true" or "false" to switch them on or off. It's important to note that the probe doesn't have a mechanism to pass in prompt values, so be sure to choose a report that doesn't require any interactive prompts.

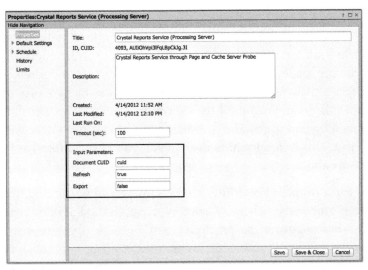

Figure 7.43 Crystal Reports Service (Processing Server) Probe Input Parameters

Crystal Reports Service (Report Application Server)

This probe is exactly the same as the previous one, except it will run your selected report via the RAS. As before, open up the properties, and input the CUID for the report you want this probe to run for you (see Figure 7.44).

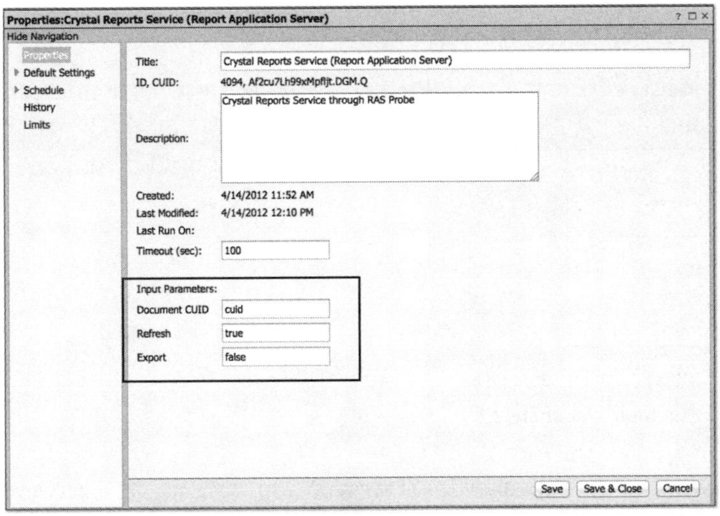

Figure 7.44 Crystal Reports Service (Report Application Server) Probe Input Parameters

InfoView Probe

The InfoView probe is meant to simulate the user experience of logging in to the BI Launch Pad. So, why isn't it named the BI Launch Pad probe? Great question! Sometimes SAP marketing makes product name changes faster than the product team can get those name changes into the code. This probe was likely a case in point for that. InfoView is the old name for the user portal though which analytics content is consumed by end users. The new name in SAP BusinessObjects BI 4.1 is the BI Launch Pad. This is important to note so you don't get confused as to what this probe is really about.

This probe is useful for a couple of reasons. First, assuming you're running this on a recurring basis, it's a constant check of your Web Application Server, even during times when users might not be on the system. Second, if you're using some sort of third-party authentication, this probe will be a constant check of your connectivity between the SAP BusinessObjects BI 4.1 server and your third-party Authentication Server.

To set up the InfoView probe, head on over to the PROPERTIES tab for the probe, and get ready to set up some input parameters (see Figure 7.45).

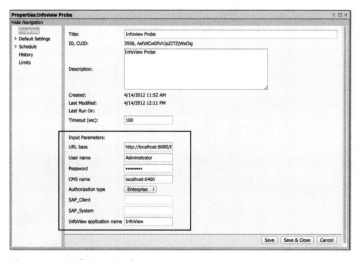

Figure 7.45 InfoView Probe Input Parameters

Here, you'll need to supply the URL BASE for your web applications, a USER NAME and PASSWORD to log in with, the CMS NAME and port, and what type of AUTHENTICATION type you want to use (ENTERPRISE, WINDOWS AD, LDAP, SAP, etc.).

Interactive Analysis Probe

This is another one that got caught in the onslaught of name changes that SAP marketing was trying to make with SAP BusinessObjects BI 4.1. At one point, Web Intelligence was supposed to be renamed to Interactive Analysis, but they changed their minds along the way. Again, not to be confused about what this probe does, this probe will run a Web Intelligence report against the Web Intelligence Processing Server. Open up the PROPERTIES page, and you'll find the input parameters required (see Figure 7.46).

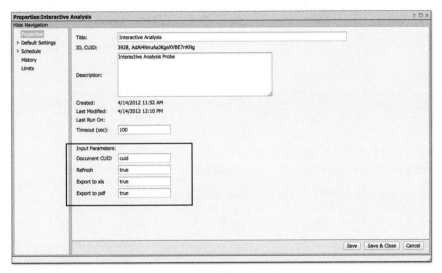

Figure 7.46 Interactive Analysis Probe Input Parameters

The probe needs a DOCUMENT CUID so it knows which report to run. You can also specify by entering "true" or "false" in the REFRESH box if you want the report to refresh, in the EXPORT TO XLS box to export to Excel format, or in the EXPORT TO PDF box to export to PDF format.

Start Stop Servers Probe

The Start Stop Servers probe can be useful, but it also can be a little disruptive. That's because this guy will do exactly what it says it does. It will stop and start your services. You can specify which services you want it to stop and start by heading over to the PROPERTIES tab and pulling out the text in the input parameters (see Figure 7.47).

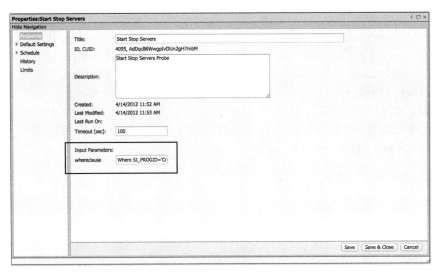

Figure 7.47 Start Stop Servers Probe Input Parameters

If you select all and copy that text out of the ridiculously small input window there, you'll see the following text in the WHERECLAUSE window:

```
Where SI_PROGID='CrystalEnterprise.Server' AND SI_SERVER_KIND NOT IN
    ('aps') AND SI_NAME NOT LIKE '%AdaptiveProcessingServer%' AND
    SI_NAME NOT LIKE '%AdaptiveJobServer%'
```

That's all well and good, but if you're not a Query Builder person, what does all that mean?

There's nothing like some antique Query Builder syntax to get the heart pumping. Even more exciting is that the good ol' Query Builder is still alive and well in SAP BusinessObjects BI 4.1. It lurks in your Web Application Server at *http://server-name:port/AdminTools* .

Login and land in the Query Builder. Enter the following query (based on the preceding input parameters), and you'll find out just which servers this thing is going to stop and start:

```
SELECT SI_NAME
FROM CI_SYSTEMOBJECTS
Where SI_PROGID='CrystalEnterprise.Server' AND SI_SERVER_KIND NOT
    IN ('aps') AND SI_NAME NOT LIKE '%AdaptiveProcessingServer%' AND
    SI_NAME NOT LIKE '%AdaptiveJobServer%'
```

That looks like Figure 7.48 in the actual Query Builder window.

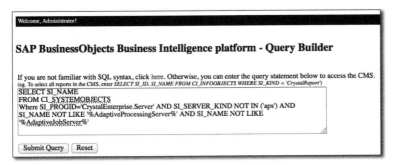

Figure 7.48 Using the Query Builder to Check the Probe

Submit the query, and you'll see that the result set is the list of servers that the Start Stop Servers probe will bounce (see Figure 7.49).

SAP BusinessObjects Business Intelligence platform - Query Builder

Number of InfoObject(s) returned: **12**

1/12

Properties	
SI_NAME	SAPPRESSRocks.CrystalReportsCacheServer

2/12

Properties	
SI_NAME	SAPPRESSRocks.CrystalReports2011ProcessingServer

3/12

Properties	
SI_NAME	SAPPRESSRocks.EventServer

4/12

Properties	
SI_NAME	SAPPRESSRocks.InputFileRepository

5/12

Properties	
SI_NAME	SAPPRESSRocks.WebIntelligenceProcessingServer

6/12

Properties	
SI_NAME	SAPPRESSRocks.DashboardsCacheServer

7/12

Properties	
SI_NAME	SAPPRESSRocks.ConnectionServer

8/12

Properties	
SI_NAME	SAPPRESSRocks.CrystalReports2011ReportApplicationServer

Figure 7.49 Query Builder Result Set

Now that you see what the query returns, the original probe `WHERE` clause might make a little more sense. First, it wants the list of all server names, but not any server names that are an Adaptive Processing Server. It also again filters out anything that has a name similar to Adaptive Processing Server or Adaptive Job Server.

There are 12 servers in all that it will bounce. If you want to customize this list, use the server names from your result set, and add them back into the original `WHERE` clause. Have someone help you if you aren't familiar with SQL syntax.

This probe can be helpful to see if your system is accepting shutdown and startup commands. It can also be rigged by altering the input parameters to restart your entire system, if desired. Conversely, you can also rig it to restart just one server.

Probes Summary

Use the probes to help you simulate user activities such as logging into the system or refreshing reports to alert you early to problems that could disrupt your users' experience. Trend the running of your probes, so you can see if certain operations are going faster or slower over time. Trending can help you spot problems before they occur.

> **Pop Quiz**
>
> 1. True or False: Probes support the implementation of CMS queries to extend the evaluation of a rule.
> 2. Distinguish a probe on Web Intelligence from that of other probes.

7.6 Alerting

Everything we've covered up to this point isn't worth a hill of beans unless you know what is going on. If something breaks, you have to be notified. That notification is an alert. An alert in SAP BusinessObjects BI comes in the form of a summary notice of which rule was triggered by which watch and under what conditions. An alert remains uncleared until an administrator goes in, reviews the alert, and manually clears it.

Aside from the email notifications you can set to receive in your watchlists, there are three main ways for you to review your alerts. First, in the Monitoring Dashboard, on the ALERTS tab, you'll find the entire list of uncleared alerts (see Figure 7.50).

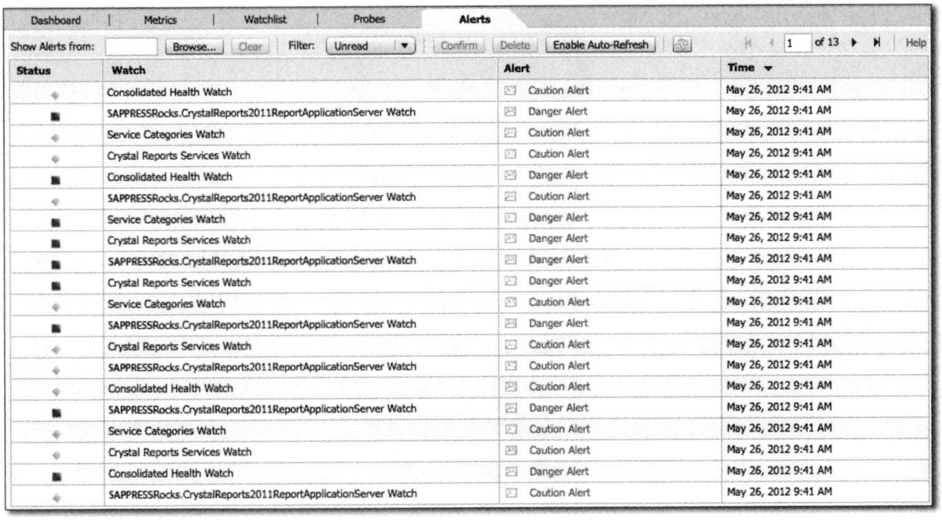

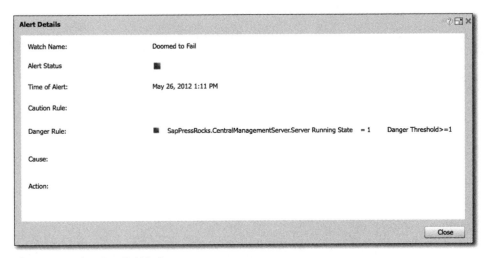

Figure 7.50 Monitoring Dashboard: Alerts Tab

To review an alert, click on the link that says CAUTION ALERT or DANGER ALERT, which will bring up the ALERT DETAILS window (see Figure 7.51).

Figure 7.51 Alert Details Window

This shows the name of the watch; the alert status, date, and time stamp when the rule evaluated true; what the rule criteria is; and, if available, the cause and any actions to take.

If you've reviewed the alert and remedied the situation, you can clear the alert out by clicking the CLOSE button on the ALERT DETAILS window. This will remove the alert from the alert list. If you have duplicate alerts and don't want to open and review each one, you can simply highlight the alert in the alert list and click the CLEAR button on the toolbar.

The second way to see your alerts is on the main Monitoring Dashboard (refer to Figure 7.4). This lists the last couple of alerts that were fired in the system and whether they have been cleared or not. You can click on the alert name right from this window to go to the ALERT DETAILS window.

The third way to see your alerts is in the BI Launch Pad. Every time you login, you'll find a summary list of alerts that need your attention (see Figure 7.52).

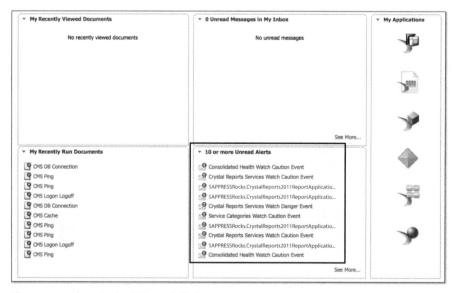

Figure 7.52 Alerts in the BI Launch Pad

This helps eliminate the need to constantly be inside the Central Management Console. You can't clear your alerts from the BI Launch Pad, but it certainly helps to have them listed here so you're aware of things that require your attention. An administrator's work is never done.

7.7 New Auditor Features

In reflecting upon the words of wisdom in Chapter 2, on auditing, we're not sure there is much more we can say about *why* you should be taking full advantage of Auditor. However, Chapter 2 was very centric to versions of Auditor predating SAP BusinessObjects BI 4.1. It's only natural as a part of this chapter that we dive deeper into what is new and exciting (you know it is) in Auditor for SAP BusinessObjects BI 4.1.

7.7.1 New Tables Galore

Auditor prior to SAP BusinessObjects BI 4.1 was a pretty straightforward model, as you saw deconstructed into the six most basic structures back in Chapter 2. Auditor in SAP BusinessObjects BI 4.1 takes on several new dimensions to be able to look into that rearview mirror of things happening in your environment (see Figure 7.53).

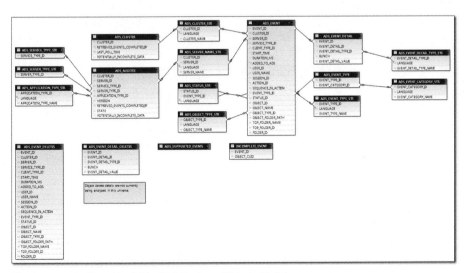

Figure 7.53 Auditor Model in SAP BusinessObjects BI 4.1

7.7.2   Third-Party Tools

Like the Activity – Reloaded universe we mentioned in Chapter 2, we'll be including a version of our take on the Auditor data model for SAP BusinessObjects BI 4.1 in the collateral included with this book. It's written specifically for Oracle, but you're free to craft it for your database *du jour*. Specifically note, however, this universe is based upon a multisource data source. If you want to redirect to a single-source universe, that is on you.

Now isn't the time to panic as you look at this model. There is a lot to consider, but we'll break it down into some bite-sized chunks to learn what has moved where:

- ▶ **ADS_EVENT**
  The table, formerly known as AUDIT_EVENT, should not be unfamiliar. It's still primarily responsible for capturing the core characteristics of the event that took place in the environment, such as a user logon, a report that was refreshed, or a schedule that failed. Table ADS_EVENT_TYPE provides the decode to each type of event that is being reported upon in the EVENT_TYPE_ID column.

- ▶ **ADS_EVENT_DETAIL**
  Like its predecessor, Table AUDIT_DETAIL, Table ADS_EVENT_DETAIL provides the granular details about each event. These details provide the administrator differing views of each event based upon the EVENT_DETAIL_ TYPE_ID contained within it, which is further extrapolated by reviewing Table ADS_ EVENT_DETAIL_TYPE_STR, as shown in Figure 7.54.

Figure 7.54 A Path from the Audit Event to the Type of Detail about It

- ▶ **ADS_STATUS_STR (new and notable)**
  Table ADS_STATUS_STR is one of the first examples we'll illustrate to demonstrate some of the new grains of reporting that are available in Auditor. This table, as an example, provides the reporting capability to roll up events into their higher level "success" or "failure" status types. It's based upon the STATUS_ID in ADS_EVENT, as shown in Figure 7.55.

Figure 7.55 Path from the Audit Event to Higher-Level Status Codes

▶ **ADS_OBJECT_TYPE_STR (new and notable)**

Prior to SAP BusinessObjects BI 4.0, object types were stored in a single column in Table AUDIT_EVENT. This has been denormalized in Table ADS_OBJECT_TYPE_STR, and it's apparent that many more types of objects are audited and listed here. The simple relationship between the two is demonstrated in Figure 7.56.

Figure 7.56 Path from the Audit Event to the Object Type

▶ **ADS_EVENT_CATEGORY_STR (new and notable)**

Event types have always been one-dimensional. In Auditor in SAP BusinessObjects BI 4.1, yet another new grain is a roll up of all events by their event category, as shown in Table ADS_EVENT_CATEGORY_STR. To make this walk, a cross-reference Table ADS_EVENT_TYPE is in place simply as a bridge between Table ADS_EVENT and Table ADS_EVENT_CATEGORY_STR, as shown in Figure 7.57.

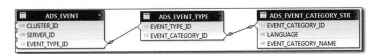

Figure 7.57 A Path from the Audit Event to the Event Category

▶ **ADS_EVENT_TYPE**

Replacing its predecessor, Table EVENT_TYPE, Table ADS_EVENT_TYPE gives the base-level decode for the EVENT_TYPE_ID, as shown in Table ADS_EVENT. SAP did a nice job of creating a more concise list of event types that are both rolled up to the category and detailed in Table ADS_EVENT_DETAIL, making reporting easier in this iteration of this database.

- **ADS_SERVER_NAME_STR (new and notable)**
We say new and notable only because Table SERVER_PROCESS from SAP BusinessObjects XI 3.1 and earlier days has been broken into smaller bits and replaced by Table ADS_SERVER_NAME_STR. Looking to identify which server serviced each event in Table ADS_EVENT? Read on.

- **ADS_AUDITEE (new and notable)**
Table ADS_AUDITEE serves as much as a cross-reference table to decode out the varying types for each server, but it's really just a series of server types, the state of the server, and the unique identifiers, as shown in Figure 7.58.

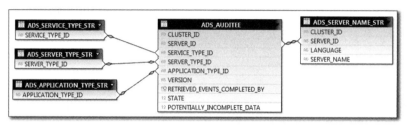

Figure 7.58 Server-Related Auditing

- **ADS_SERVICE_TYPE_STR (new and notable)**
Table ADS_AUDITEE gives way via the SERVICE_TYPE_ID. With it, Table ADS_SERVICE_TYPE_STR will roll the types of servers into nonaggregated service types such as Web Intelligence, SAP Crystal Reports, and—not that it's coming back anytime soon—Desktop Intelligence (see Figure 7.59).

Figure 7.59 Desktop Intelligence... Really? Nah.

- **ADS_SERVER_TYPE_STR (new and notable)**
Unlike Table ADS_SERVICE_TYPE_STR, Table ADS_SERVER_TYPE_STR actually does aggregate the servers into a higher-level organization such as Job Server, Dashboard Server, Connection Server, and so on. There can certainly be value in rolling up reporting for all types of servers to see what the most active in an environment is (it's all about understanding utilization).

_STR Suffixed Tables

The tables require an important distinction in all tables suffixed with _STR. These tables support all languages supported in the SAP BusinessObjects BI 4.1 platform. Therefore, the possibility exists to get errant results if the specification of the LANGUAGE attribute isn't selected properly. Either update the universe to limit to the desired language in all the joins, or remove the unneeded language codes from your lookup tables to avoid inflated numbers in your queries.

There are a few other tables in the model that we won't cover in detail here. Importantly, *always* consult the *BusinessObjects Platform Administrator Guide* accompanying any release of the product for the list of what is being audited in the release. Just like predecessors to auditing in SAP BusinessObjects BI 4.1, the combination of the event type and the detail type gives way to the combinations of reporting on events.

7.7.3   Getting the Data Out

Let's walk through a few practical examples of the new combinations of event types and detail types that allow us to report on events:

▶ **A scheduled job was run successfully.**
The EVENT_TYPE_ID is listed as 1011. The STATUS_ID is listed as 0.

```
ADS_EVENT.EVENT_TYPE_ID = 1011
AND ADS_EVENT.STATUS_ID = 0
```

▶ **A report was refreshed.**
The EVENT_TYPE_ID is listed as 1003. In other words:

```
ADS_EVENT.EVENT_TYPE_ID = 1003
```

▶ **A user failed to log on successfully.**
The EVENT_TYPE_ID is listed as 1014. In other words:

```
ADS_EVENT.EVENT_TYPE_ID = 1014
AND ADS_EVENT.STATUS_ID = 1
```

The universe mentioned previously, as included in the collateral, is a very high-level and not inclusive set of objects based on data available in Auditor for SAP BusinessObjects BI 4.1. If you look back to the approach we took in Chapter 2 to build aggregates to get data out of Auditor, the same types of approaches apply here. Let's build a simple example of extracting data from Auditor to calculate the total number of successful logons in our environment as shown here:

```
SELECT
  SUM(CASE WHEN
EVENT_TYPE_ID = 1014 AND STATUS_ID IN (0,2) THEN 1 ELSE 0)
  END AS NUMBER_OF_SUCCESSFUL_LOGONS
FROM
  ADS_EVENT
```

That was really it. We can build any number of KPIs into our universe in this way, slice and dice them by time dimensions and the various levels of hierarchy in our new Auditor database, and make better decisions about how we trend and analyze utilization within our environment.

7.7.4 Enabling Auditor

Huge strides have been made in managing Auditor in SAP BusinessObjects BI 4.1. The days of manually managing Auditor from a service level are gone. (This is where you cheer. Really.) Auditing is centrally managed via the CMC in the Au-DITING section. This unified interface alleviates the pain we as administrators once experienced in keeping auditing configured. Let's peel back this panel a bit to understand all of the things now happening in this console (see Figure 7.60).

Status Summary			
ADS Last Updated On	5/27/12 11:32:41 AM PDT	CMS Auditor	EVTBOBJ9.CentralManagementServer
Auditing Thread Utilization (%)	0	ADS Database Connection Name	BusinessObjects Audit Server 140
Last Polling Cycle Duration (seconds)	180	ADS Database User Name	boeuser

Figure 7.60 Auditor Health

The console's first look into Auditor, shown in Figure 7.60, is the state of auditing in the environment. In this case, Auditor is in good shape. However, if the connection to the Auditor database is lost, or extended delays are present, this console status updates to notify the administrator of issues in auditing.

Audit levels as shown in Figure 7.61, are predefined states that control the verbosity of the audit events being captured. Each level will toggle the list of event types in the SET EVENT DETAILS section of the AUDITING panel of the CMC (see Figure 7.62). These levels have a direct proportion to the number of events, and corresponding details that will be captured and written to the database. This is probably a good point to mention, again, that the auditing requirements come from you, your security organization, and your compliance organization.

Figure 7.61 Audit Levels

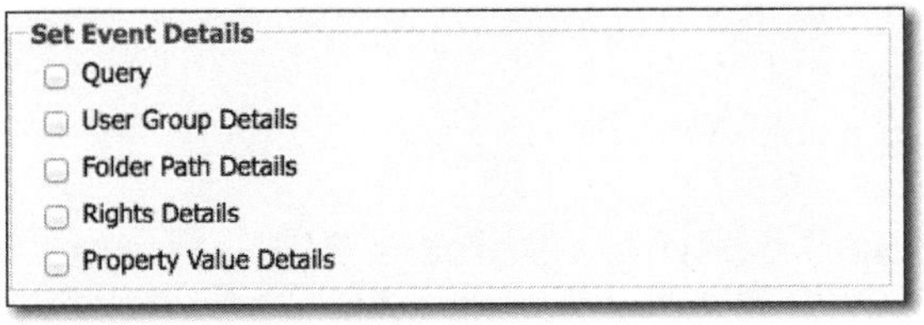

Set Event Details
- ☐ Query
- ☐ User Group Details
- ☐ Folder Path Details
- ☐ Rights Details
- ☐ Property Value Details

Figure 7.62 Audit Event Details

There are a handful of special detail types that control the grain of the details being returned to an even larger degree. It's probably worth noting that these are the pieces that make those character large objects (CLOBs) *huge* in the database. For example, saying "yes" to the query event detail means *every* query that runs in your environment is going to be written to that CLOB. In this case, it may be wise to consider only enabling when you're seeking to debug an active issue in the environment.

Lastly, the CONFIGURATION section of the CMC panel gives you a simple mechanism to modify the target database for your auditor data. Note, that in cases where ODBC references are required, they should already exist in the 64-bit ODBC console and be reflected in the CONNECTION NAME field, as shown in Figure 7.63.

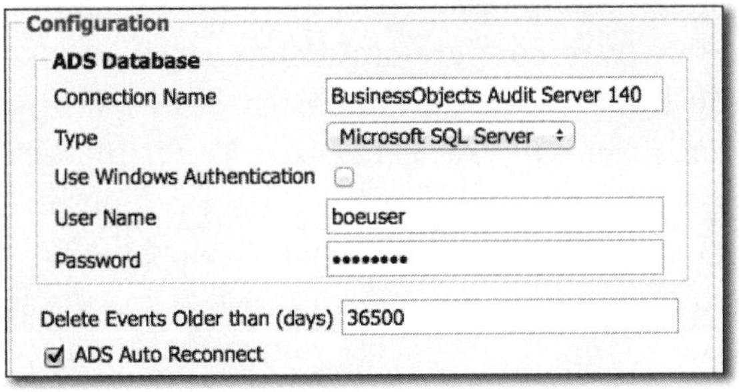

Configuration

ADS Database

Connection Name	BusinessObjects Audit Server 140
Type	Microsoft SQL Server ⬧
Use Windows Authentication	☐
User Name	boeuser
Password	••••••••

Delete Events Older than (days) 36500
☑ ADS Auto Reconnect

Figure 7.63 Audit Configuration

Pop Quiz

1. True or False: Existing Auditor universes will function in SAP BusinessObjects BI 4.1.

2. Describe the role of the LANGUAGE field in the lookup tables in the new Auditor schema.

3. Where are all the various auditing settings managed within the SAP BusinessObjects BI 4.1 environment?

7.8   Wily Introscope for SAP BusinessObjects BI Platform

No conversation about monitoring the SAP BusinessObjects BI Platform would be complete without mentioning Computer Associates' industry-leading, in-depth monitoring tool, Wily Introscope. SAP has had a long-standing relationship with Computer Associates for use of Wily in the Solution Manager tool suite. Solution Manager has been around for a long time on the "classic" SAP side (for SAP ERP, SAP CRM, etc.), but is likely foreign to "SAP BusinessObjects Agnostic" customers.

Wily Introscope is an in-depth monitoring system that allows data collection of system statistics (CPU, memory, disk, network traffic, etc.) down to an incredibly granular level on software that has been instrumented for Wily. SAP has fully instrumented SAP BusinessObjects BI 4.1 to communicate with Wily, so now you can use Wily to monitor internal traffic in the SAP BusinessObjects BI platform down to the individual Java methods being called. Yes, you read that correctly — down to the individual Java methods.

Installing, configuring, and using Wily Introscope are outside the realm of what we're trying to accomplish here on these humble printed pages. For specifics, start on SAP Community Network (SCN) and the SAP Help Portal. You'll find tons of excellent documentation on everything you need to get that task accomplished. In a nutshell, it consists of a "master system" or "managing host," called the Wily Introscope Enterprise Manager (WIEM). This is the master server that collects all of the data from your various servers. Then, on each server you want to monitor, or "managed host," you need to install a couple of diagnostic agents. These diagnostic agents are small pieces of software that allow for the collection of your system statistics and communication of those statistics to the WIEM server for storage and analysis.

Some important things to note here, though, are that Wily Instroscope is licensed to SAP for use by SAP customers under a Right-to-View license for no additional cost. Therefore, you can download and use Wily Introscope in Right-to-View mode for free (as long as you're current on your maintenance fees). Right-to-View means that Wily will monitor passively in the background, lacking any of the watchlist or alerting capabilities we discussed earlier in the SAP BusinessObjects BI 4 Monitoring Engine. You can purchase an Advanced Alerting license from SAP to unlock all of that if you so desire. Speak to your Account Representative for pricing. In many cases, Right-to-View is enough, coupled with using the SAP BusinessObjects BI 4 Monitoring Engine to alert you to system problems, and then using Wily to drill way down into the details of what is going on in your system (see Figure 7.64).

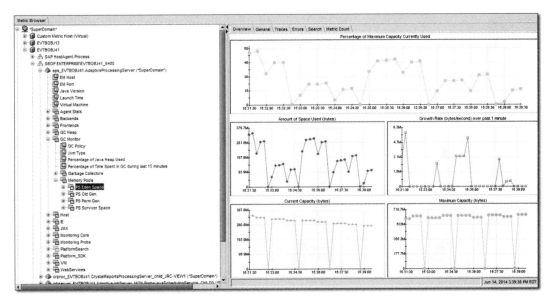

Figure 7.64 Wily Introscope Investigator Window

There are some serious benefits to putting Wily Introscope into your landscape:

▶ You have a treasure trove of detailed statistics about the behaviors of your system.

▶ SAP Support loves this stuff. This can help them help you better.

▶ Coupled with the SAP Passport browser plugin, you can replicate a user issue and trace the workflow through the entire SAP BusinessObjects BI stack to find out where the problem is, so there's no more guesswork.

▶ You can open the Live Error Viewer and watch system messages as they occur in real time.

▶ You get a suite of prebuilt monitoring dashboards that any administrator would love to have access to.

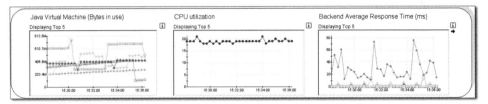

Figure 7.65 Small Section of the Wily Introscope Monitoring Dashboards

If this sounds like something you need in your SAP BusinessObjects BI landscape, head on over to SAP Community Network and start reading up on what it requires.

> **Mark of Excellence**
>
> If you're planning on building out a brand new SAP BusinessObjects BI 4.1 system and know you definitely want to include Wily Introscope, you'll need to build out your Wily Introscope Enterprise Manager (WIEM) server *first*. If you do that, then while you're installing SAP BusinessObjects BI 4.1, there are two screens that most people skip that you won't want to skip this time (see Chapter 3). These screens talk about the Solution Manager Diagnostics (SMD) configuration and Wily Introscope agents. If you configure these at installation to point to your existing WIEM server, then the diagnostic agents get installed right along with the software. It couldn't be any easier than that!

7.9 Monitoring Best Practices

Keeping your environment monitored and healthy over time is still critical as the users' behaviors change and developers build new and innovative visualizations on data that will continue to push and tax your environment. With that, keep in mind that your best practices will never be the same from year to year. Sure, many will carry forward, but if your best practices aren't evolving, you're doomed. Here are a few things to consider in monitoring your environment for better-assured success:

► Don't make your alerts too "noisy." All noisy alerts accomplish is to annoy people, who then end up ignoring them. Then when something really does go wrong, nobody knows about it because the alert was lost in the sea of noise. Make sure your alerts fire in a way that people know something serious is going on. Don't inundate your operators with a bazillion meaningless alerts. Basically, don't cry "wolf."

► Make sure that you can get critical alerts for critical servers from your mobile device. A critical alert that goes to your corporate email inbox late on Saturday night won't do you a lick of good if you can't see it until Monday morning once the business day has begun.

► Make sure your critical alerts are also going to a backup. Humans get sick or go away on vacation, and it just isn't feasible to think that only one person should be getting all of the server alerts.

► If your company has a 24x7 operations center or help desk, make sure your critical alerts get to them, too. And document as much as possible what these alerts mean and what those tier 1 operators should try first before calling and waking you up.

► Don't try to monitor the whole world at once. Start with your critical services and processes, and iron those out. Monitoring is a work in progress, sometimes for several months until you get the right mix that gets you the visibility you need.

► Conduct a review of your monitoring plan quarterly. Look at what is triggering and what isn't. If you have useless alerts or watchlists, get rid of them. Stick to what is meaningful, and don't be afraid to change the plan as your system changes and your company's needs evolve.

► Audit and report with frequency. Don't fire it up and forget it. Aside from third-party tools that report on content within the environment, it's the only SAP BusinessObjects BI 4.1 mechanism that allows you to analyze the behaviors of users within your environment.

While you finish this chapter and realize that SAP has added some very cool intra-application monitoring to SAP BusinessObjects BI 4.1, it's critical that you, as the caretaker of this platform, should not rely solely on an application monitoring platform that relies on itself to be up and running to function. What do we mean by that? Monitoring in SAP BusinessObjects BI 4.1 is dependent on the Server Intelligence Agent (SIA) and the CMS, processes that on their own are capable of failure prior to any other service running your cluster that you're hoping to monitor. What are you monitoring if, unbeknownst to you, your SIA crashes, and you didn't follow our advice on fault tolerance? Whoops. You must get engaged and rely on other enterprise monitoring solutions to maintain availability in your SAP BusinessObjects BI 4.1 platform.

Centralized Logging and Monitoring

Most organizations should have some type of enterprise monitoring solution in place. These types of platforms have the capability of monitoring many servers in your organization's data center. They are vendor agnostic. They can monitor systems running Windows, UNIX, Linux, and even Mac OS. So, how is this relevant? They don't depend on any SAP BusinessObjects BI service to be available to monitor your system. Let's slice and dice that:

▶ **Service level monitoring**
Since the invention of the SIA, monitoring individual servers for uptime has become more challenging. The SIA is in charge of spinning up individual servers and controls their uptime and downtime. Should the SIA itself be monitored? Absolutely. Can your enterprise monitoring tools watch for the presence of a CMS service where it's expected? You bet.

▶ **Performance monitoring**
Overall system utilization is a KPI that should not go unchecked. Whether you're using beefy physical servers or have virtualized parts of your cluster, these tools allow you to keep an eye on CPU utilization at an individual core level, but then also at an aggregate on the entire box. You can watch memory utilization over time to understand the peaks and valleys in the memory-hungry SAP BusinessObjects BI 4.1 platform throughout the online and offline day. Lastly, outliers such as disk I/O and network capacity can be watched to look for significant utilization.

Know, however, that definition of thresholds for when capacity is being reached may be out of your league. Each organization *should* already have standards in place to define what an acceptable and maximum utilization looks like. This is yet another reason to be buddies with your system administrator and capacity planning types, as they hold the keys to this information.

▶ **Application availability**

There is little you can do without custom code like the probes do to monitor whether SAP BusinessObjects BI is working. But, at a minimum, using technologies such as hardware load balancers gives you the ability to evaluate the availability of your web tier. If you believe that Tomcat or WebSphere is unfailing, you've got another thing coming. Load balancers redistribute HTTP traffic between servers. They then, by their nature, evaluate whether the server is alive so they can reallocate traffic in the event of a failure. This is a key warning if a box is going or has gone down.

As it pertains to SAP BusinessObjects BI 4.1, the probes are the only other mechanism that is going to give you any type of environmental health monitoring that you can rely on. But we can't impress enough the value of a cluster. Avoid putting all your eggs in one basket if at all possible.

Achieving a successful monitoring strategy takes work. Make nice with the system administrator and capacity planners in your organization to understand what enterprise monitoring tools have been acquired (assuming they are third-party vendors) and collaborate on that monitoring strategy to keep an eye on your environment as it gets used and grows up into a more mature/used platform.

7.10 Summary

The heart and soul of monitoring is that you want to be aware of problems in your system before your users are. Users who see error messages tend to panic, and panic is never a good thing.

SAP BusinessObjects BI 4.1 has a powerful, built-in Monitoring Engine to help you in your administrative cause. You can use metrics to build up a watchlist that will send you an alert when the criteria are met for your caution or danger rules. You can have your alert notifications sent to your email address, or you can simply consume them in the BI Launch Pad.

The probes are finally an official part of the product, and you can use them to simulate user activities such as logging in and refreshing reports. Schedule the probes to run on a regular basis, and you can keep tabs on critical customer touch points. You can also use probe runtimes as trend data to see if certain operations are speeding up or slowing down over time.

Fixing the hard problems is the task of every SAP BusinessObjects BI administrator. This chapter touches on some important areas that every administrator must know to fix critical issues and restore operations quickly and correctly.

8 Troubleshooting and Maintenance: What to Do When Stuff Breaks and How to Prevent It

This is the part of the job that every administrator dreads. You already put forth a monumental effort getting this system sized, installed, and configured properly; implemented a bulletproof security model; migrated your content; and set up your monitoring. In a perfect world, your job would be done, and you could kick back and surf Facebook for 8 hours a day while the system hummed along. Unfortunately, we don't live in a perfect world. Although it's light-years ahead of where it was a few years ago, SAP BusinessObjects BI 4.1 isn't a perfect piece of software. Users do unexpected things, and computer systems act strangely sometimes. The simple fact is that stuff breaks. And when it does, all eyes are on you to fix it.

There are two major activities that you, as the administrator, must have a firm grasp on in such troubling times. The first is troubleshooting. Troubleshooting is a process of elimination and requires an understanding of how things work in the SAP BusinessObjects BI architecture, so that you can start at the beginning of the workflow and step your way through to the end of the workflow with the hopes of figuring out where the issue you got woken up about exists. The second is maintenance. Just like your automobile, your SAP BusinessObjects BI 4.1 system needs periodic maintenance to keep it humming along and potentially avoid errors and outages that would induce the need for troubleshooting.

In this chapter, we'll walk you through the basics of the troubleshooting process. We'll go a little deeper and show you how to turn on trace or verbose logging and then how to read and analyze those logs. The discussion will then turn to server metrics and how those factor into your overall system health. Then to round out troubleshooting, we'll talk about some ways for you to get some more help. As we shift to discussing maintenance, we'll lay down the essential tasks you should be familiar with as an administrator and should be performing on a periodic basis. We'll also talk about managing patches and upgrades (even though you just did it, the time will come again). We'll wrap up maintenance with a heaping helping of backup and recovery and best practices.

8.1 Troubleshooting Basics

All wishful thinking aside, the day will come (probably sooner than you think) when your phone will ring, and a user will be calling you to report that something is broken, slow, wrong, or that you smell funny. It happens. Life as an administrator is seldom glamorous because much of what you do is deal with broken reports or crashing servers.

The good news is that with a little practice, troubleshooting will become as natural to you as breathing. The minute the phone rings, you'll know what questions to start asking, and you'll start breaking down the problem and zeroing in on the cause before you know it. The best place to start with troubleshooting is a solid understanding of SAP BusinessObjects BI 4.1 architecture.

8.1.1 Architecture Overview

If you're not an expert on the internal workings of SAP BusinessObjects BI, take another minute and go back to Chapter 1, Section 1.3, and review the high-level architecture overview there. We're about to get more detailed with it, so a review is definitely a good thing. Understanding architecture is important because it will help you hone in on where the problem is occurring. These systems can be complex, even in the simpler configurations. There are a lot of moving parts to creating and generating a report. Take a moment and review Figure 8.1 to see what we mean.

And, this is just a basic diagram of the different components. It gets even more complicated as you drill in deeper.

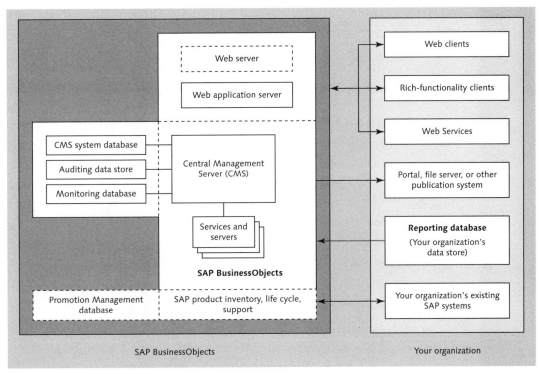

Figure 8.1 SAP BusinessObjects BI 4.1 Architecture

The best information to be had on the internal workflows is what you'll learn from becoming an SAP Certified Associate in SAP BusinessObjects BI. Certification is a great idea if you're planning on making a career out of SAP BusinessObjects BI.

Next, we'll discuss the three major portions of this system and how they come together in the two most common system workflows.

Architecture Tiers

SAP BusinessObjects BI 4.1 architecture can be broken down into three general tiers:

▸ **Web tier**

Regardless of what platform it's on, there is always a web component to SAP BusinessObjects BI. This consists of your web server and your Web Application

Server (which could be one and the same or separate) that house your SAP BusinessObjects BI web applications and make them available to end users via a web browser.

▶ **Application tier**
This is the section where all of your SAP BusinessObjects BI servers run, such as the Central Management Server, input and output File Repository Servers (iFRS/oFRS) (which is the same as the file repository tier mentioned in Chapter 1, lumped together here for simplicity), Web Intelligence and SAP Crystal Reports Processing Servers, and so on. Some will break the application tier down further, but for the purposes of troubleshooting, this isn't always necessary.

▶ **Data tier**
These are your corporate data sources: your data warehouse, operational data stores, data marts, unstructured data, and so on. This is the data from which your reporting and analytics content is being generated.

General System Workflows

Now that we have summarized the three major architecture tiers, it's important to discuss two major workflows that most commonly occur within these tiers. There are more, but we're being general here.

First, is an interactive report request by a user. This workflow starts and ends in the web tier:

1. A user logs in via his browser and requests a report that goes to the database to fetch data.

2. The report is then rendered and displayed back to the user in the web browser. The request makes a complete round trip.

This type of workflow is visualized in Figure 8.2.

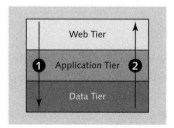

Figure 8.2 An Interactive Report Request General Workflow

The second major workflow is a scheduled report. This type of report typically starts and ends in the application tier, with no interaction in the web tier at all:

1. The Central Management Server determines it's time to run a scheduled report request and initiates the report. The report is handed off to the appropriate Processing Server, which connects to the data tier and fetches the data.

2. The report is rendered and exported, if specified, and stored in the defined destination for retrieval at a later time.

This type of workflow is visualized in Figure 8.3.

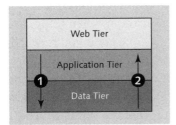

Figure 8.3 A Scheduled Report Request General Workflow

If you're scratching your head wondering why we're discussing architecture at this point instead of troubleshooting, let's take another minute to explain a few major points to take away here.

▶ Each architecture tier has distinctly different components. They all work together, but understanding which tier is having the issue will greatly speed up the troubleshooting process. Java errors from a web application are very different from database errors. It's imperative that you can distinguish the difference between them.

▶ Understanding what the user was doing when he received the error message is key. Different workflows touch different parts of the enterprise architecture.

8.1.2 Standardizing Your Error-Reporting Process

Many, but not all, organizations have an approved method for reporting problems with information technology. If you don't already have some sort of help desk or ticketing system, you have a little more work to do than those that do. Make sure that you get your new SAP BusinessObjects BI 4.1 system added into your ticketing system so users can log trouble tickets against it.

It's also a really great idea to require users to send in a screenshot of their error message. Often the error gets paraphrased when being transcribed by a nontechnical person, and with these types of things, it's best to get the information straight from the horse's mouth. Having the actual error message in its entirety is a good thing.

If you don't already have a service level agreement (SLA) with your customers on your BI systems, you should consider creating one. An SLA can help manage expectations when things get wonky. Without some sort of written expectations, often users think every issue is of the utmost priority and should be fixed immediately to the exclusion of all else. The SLA can help you define what is critical and what can wait, and what to expect from you as an administrator when things are truly bad. You'll understand the definition of *stress* pretty quickly if you're working a production outage without an SLA and have users and managers breathing down your neck not only for a resolution but also with demands to know the "root cause" before the issue is even resolved. Customers aren't at their best when things aren't working properly. At a minimum, the SLA should include what types of incidents classify as priority 1, how those problems will be supported, and how often you'll report the status until they are resolved. Throw in a dash of what you'll do with all of the other types of problems, and you have the framework for understood expectations.

8.1.3 Troubleshooting Basics Summary

At a very high level, you should now understand the basics of the SAP Business-Objects BI 4.1 architecture and the difference between an on-demand (i.e., interactive) report request and a scheduled report. While we haven't yet touched on exactly how to tell which tier an error code applies to, you should at least have a grasp of the concept that they will be different. We also discussed the basics of standardizing your error reporting, the ultimate goal of which is to get angry customers off of your back and let you do your work and bring them back to operational status faster. While you'll definitely be in the hot seat during an outage incident, you're certainly not alone in your quest. Before diving deeper into the specifics, it's important to take a moment and discuss where you can go to get more help when Murphy's Law is in full swing.

8.2 Where to Get More Help

Several community-type resources are available on the Internet for those willing to search around for them, but for the purposes of this discussion, we'll limit it to just what is officially under the SAP umbrella.

8.2.1 SAP Help Portal

Bookmark this site right now: *http://help.sap.com*. This is the official SAP site for all documentation (see Figure 8.4). If you find an "official" document somewhere else, chances are it's not really official or could be out of date.

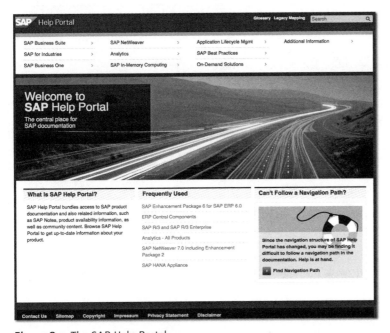

Figure 8.4 The SAP Help Portal

Finding all of the SAP BusinessObjects BI documentation just got a little trickier because they put it under the ANALYTICS section. Head in there, then go into the BUSINESS INTELLIGENCE section to find the SAP BusinessObjects BI 4.1 documentation (see Figure 8.5 and Figure 8.6). (Just a quick disclaimer: this is how this site looks today, and there is no guarantee that it will continue to look this way forever.)

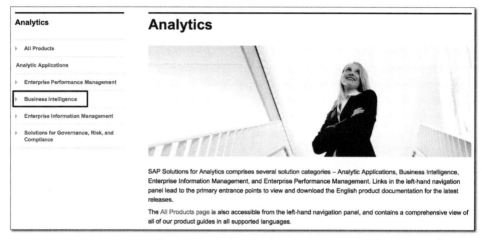

Figure 8.5 SAP Help Portal: Business Intelligence Documentation

Figure 8.6 SAP Help Portal: SAP BusinessObjects BI 4.1 Documentation

At a minimum, you should go and download the following documents so you have them on your computer where you'll be doing your SAP BusinessObjects BI administration work:

▸ *Sizing Companion for SAP BusinessObjects BI 4.1*

▸ *Installation Guide for [insert your platform here, e.g., UNIX, Windows, etc.]*

▸ *Web Application Deployment Guide for [insert your platform here]*

▸ *BusinessObjects Platform Administrator Guide*

▸ *Error Messages Explained*

There are more, and you can certainly download as many as you'd like. Keep in mind that you'll need to check periodically for updates on these, but you definitely want these documents on hand so you can reference them in times of trouble.

Another useful subsite of the SAP Help Portal is the online version of the Error Messages Explained document (see Figure 8.7). You can find this one at *http://help.sap.com/businessobject/product_guides/errors/12/0/en/html/default.htm*. This is invaluable when trying to chase down an error message you've never seen before.

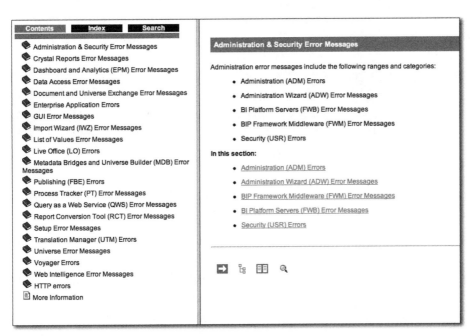

Figure 8.7 SAP Help Portal: Online Error Messages Explained Guide

Just looking at the index here helps reinforce what we discussed in Section 8.1 about understanding which part of the application (and which tier) an error message is coming from.

You should also take a spin through the pattern books that are available on *help.sap.com*. These are the de facto guides from SAP on SAP BusinessObjects BI architecture. You'll find a pattern book for each different platform (Windows, Linux, UNIX). At the end of each guide, there's a good troubleshooting section as well.

Spend some time and get familiar with the SAP Help Portal. It can provide you with hours and hours of reading material for times when you're finding it hard to sleep and will also help you answer any questions you might have that weren't already answered in this book.

8.2.2 SAP Support Portal

The SAP Support Portal is your central hub as an SAP BusinessObjects BI administrator. This is where you can maintain the information about your SAP BusinessObjects BI systems, request license keys, download installation and patch software, search the SAP Knowledge Base, and last but certainly not least, open up a support case. To access the SAP Support Portal, point your browser to *http://support.sap.com*. If you don't already have an account, known as an SAP user ID (i.e., S-ID) set up here, you'll need one because this site is password-protected. If you aren't the one that controls access to this site for your company, you'll need to determine who your company's "super-administrator" is so he can hook you up with a login. After you do login, you'll land on the home page (see Figure 8.8).

If you're a new SAP customer and haven't already done so, contact your account representative about a free tour of the SAP Support Portal. The tour led by your account representative is the best way for you to learn how to open a support request and use the other features of the SAP Support Portal.

After you get some more experience with your SAP BusinessObjects BI system, there are many common errors you'll come to recognize and understand how to fix quickly. Until that time, it's probably a good idea to open a ticket with SAP Support to help you figure out what the problem is. As a general rule, with non-production issues, you should spend an hour on your own trying to fix an issue and then open a support case. For production systems, you should open a support ticket immediately, then continue to work the problem on your own until the SAP Support engineer contacts you.

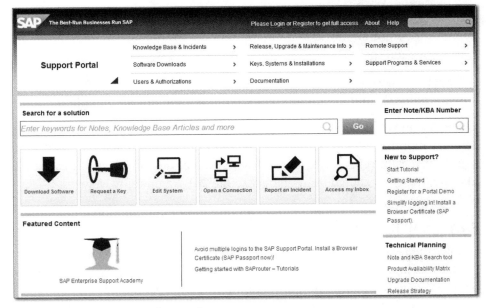

Figure 8.8 SAP Support Portal Home Page

To greatly speed up the processing of your support request, you must include some required information in your ticket. SAP Knowledge Base Article 1560818 has all of the details, but in summary, be sure to include the following information:

▶ One technical question, problem, or issue per incident

▶ Product version, service pack (SP), feature pack (FP), or any other applied patches

▶ Whether the problem is reproducible on the system as-is

▶ Description of the reproduction steps in detail with all necessary materials such as reports, universes, and so on

▶ Whether the problem is reproducible with the latest service pack or feature pack

▶ Whether the problem occurs on specific reports or universes

- ▶ Whether there is a workaround

- ▶ Captured dumps, event logs, trace logs, and other logs

- ▶ Any applied SAP Knowledge Base Articles and results

- ▶ Any attachments that could help SAP to investigate the problem (screenshots, etc.)

- ▶ Confirmation that the platform you're using is still supported

SAP Support loves trace logs. Hop on down to Section 8.3 to find out specifics on how to enable them. After you have, attach them to your support ticket.

While it's always best to utilize SAP Support whenever you have an issue (you're paying handsomely for it, after all), sometimes the do-it-yourselfer in us kicks in and we just can't resist trying to crack the problem nut ourselves. If this sounds like you, then you should head on over to the SAP Community Network (SCN).

8.2.3   SAP Router

Despite the fact that it sounds like a piece of hardware, SAP Router is actually a piece of software you can install that allows you to open up a secure connection between your company's systems and SAP Support. This doesn't open a back door to your systems that lets SAP connect whenever they want and go all willy-nilly. You, as the customer, initiate the connection when you want to grant access to SAP Support. And SAP Support only gets access to the specific portions of your system that you grant, such as the Central Management Console. This can be a really super-powerful tool in your toolbox to get SAP Support on your system quickly when you're having issues instead of the usual lead-time of phone tag it typically takes. Find out more about SAP Router in the SAP Support Portal.

8.2.4   SAP Community Network

With more than 2 million members and growing every day, you'd be hard-pressed to find another site of SAP experts as large and vibrant as the SAP Community Network (SCN). You'll find SCN at *http://scn.sap.com* (see Figure 8.9).

SCN recently underwent a major overhaul and is even easier to use than it ever was before. It's positively dripping with information. Of course, there are sections dedicated exclusively to SAP BusinessObjects BI where you can ask a question in the forums (which are routinely patrolled by senior engineers in the SAP

Support organization), blogs written by SAP employees and other customer and partner experts in the field, and tons of whitepapers and webcasts where you can learn more about the product you now support.

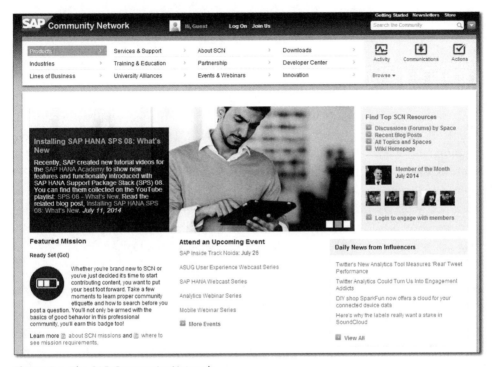

Figure 8.9 The SAP Community Network

As mentioned before, there are other online resources out there. Many regions of the world also have local user groups that meet a few times a year, where you can learn from others in your field. You get out of these communities what you put into them. If you have a story to share, go ahead and get involved, and help teach others as you were taught by them earlier.

The overarching message to take away from these resources is "You're not alone." There are lots and lots of other people out there who are in the same boat you are. Connect and learn. And, as long as you paid your bill, SAP will stand behind you when you have a product error, no matter what time of day it is. Now that you know where to go to find more information than you could ever read in a lifetime, let's get down to the specifics. First up, let's tackle trace logs.

Pop Quiz

1. Which of the SAP support resources is largely community driven?
2. Where does the SAP Knowledge Base reside?
3. What type of logon/site account is needed to access SAP support sites?

8.3 Enabling Trace Logs

One of the very first things that many SAP Support engineers will ask you to do to further diagnose an issue is to turn on trace logs. This is also known as verbose logging, and it's a staple of application troubleshooting. Trace logs, when set to their highest level, will record every single action taken by the server you enabled them on. As you can imagine, this causes extra work for the server and takes up extra space on your disk for the log files. Trace logging generates a bunch of files very quickly but is extremely valuable in finding the cause of a problem. In this section, we'll explain how to enable all the relevant trace logs.

8.3.1 Enterprise Service Trace Logs

This used to be much harder in past versions of SAP BusinessObjects BI, but with SAP BusinessObjects BI 4.1, you have it pretty easy. To turn on trace logging for any of your SAP BusinessObjects BI servers (anything in the application tier), start by logging in to the Central Management Console, head over to the SERVERS tab, and open up the properties for the server you want to enable trace on. Note, that you can also select multiple servers and enable tracing en masse if desired. Scroll down in the PROPERTIES window until you find the TRACELOG SERVICE box (see Figure 8.10).

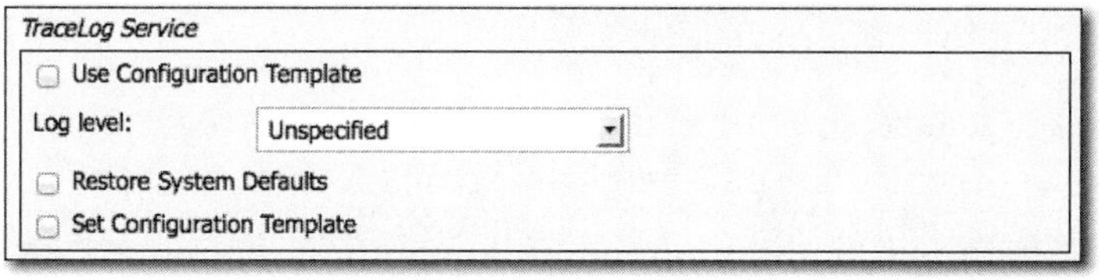

Figure 8.10 The TraceLog Service Box

Click the dropdown arrow in the LOG LEVEL box, and you'll see a few options you can choose from (see Figure 8.11).

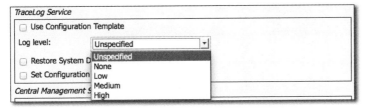

Figure 8.11 The TraceLog Service Box: Log Level Options

Table 8.1 shows what those different log levels mean to you as the administrator.

Level	Description
UNSPECIFIED	The trace log level is specified through another mechanism, usually an INI file.
NONE	The filter to optionally suppress traces below a specified importance level is deactivated. This doesn't mean that the tracing feature is totally turned off. Traces will still be logged for rare critical events such as failed assertions.
LOW	This level allows for logging error messages while ignoring warnings and most status messages. This level isn't recommended for debugging.
MEDIUM	This level includes error, warning, and most status messages in the log output. Status messages that are least important or highly verbose will be filtered out. This level isn't recommended for debugging.
HIGH	No messages are excluded. This level could affect system resources such as CPU usage and disk storage space in the file system.

Table 8.1 Trace Log Levels (Source: BusinessObjects Platform Administrator Guide)

While those other levels might be nice for some other purposes, if you're troubleshooting an error, you want to set this the level to HIGH. At the HIGH level, this service will log every single action it takes, with the hopes that it will also trap your error, and you can see what actions were happening leading up to the error occurrence. Choose HIGH from your dropdown list, and then click SAVE & CLOSE at the bottom of your screen. You'll return to the servers list and notice that the stale flag is present for the server you made the change on (see Figure 8.12). This indicates that you'll have to restart the service for the change to take effect.

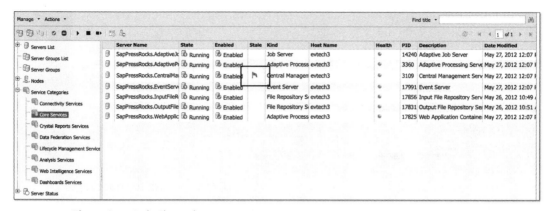

Figure 8.12 Stale Flag Indicator

After your restart is complete, your service will now be generating verbose logging. You'll find the logs on the server in your SAP BusinessObjects BI install root:

▶ On Windows: *<InstallRoot>SAP BusinessObjects Enterprise XI 4.0\logging*

▶ On UNIX/Linux: *<InstallRoot>/sap_bobj/logging*

Head on over to that directory, and you'll find your logs. Figure 8.13 shows an example on the Windows platform.

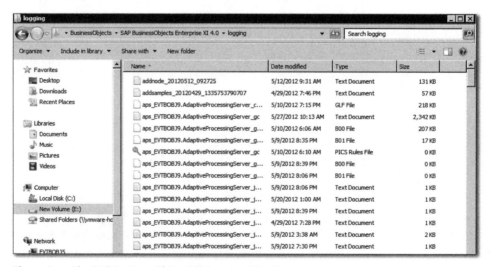

Figure 8.13 The SAP BusinessObjects BI Logging Directory

You'll notice that the trace files are named for the `SIA.Servername_trace.nnnnn`. Sorting the logs by their modified date is typically more useful than an alphabetical sort order.

As a general rule, you don't want to operate with high trace logging under normal circumstances. High trace logging should be tactical, turned on to diagnose an issue, and then turned back off. Turn the trace on, reproduce the error, then shut the trace back off. Copy the log files generated during this session off to a different folder. Here, you can review them later or zip them up and punt them to the SAP Support engineers working on your case. Typically you'll want to do this as a reflex action because 9 times out of 10, SAP Support is going to ask for trace logs anyway. Better to just get them done sooner so the diagnosis can begin. We'll discuss what to do with these logs in just a bit (see Section 8.4).

8.3.2 Web Application Trace Logs

SAP BusinessObjects BI 4.1 has taken another major leap forward with regards to web application trace logs. Instead of fumbling around with command-line switches, you can now set the trace log level for your SAP BusinessObjects BI 4.1 web applications right from the Central Management Console. You can set the following application trace logs from the CMC:

▶ CENTRAL MANAGEMENT CONSOLE

▶ BI LAUNCH PAD

▶ OPEN DOCUMENT

▶ WEB SERVICE

▶ PROMOTION MANAGEMENT

▶ VERSION MANAGEMENT

▶ VISUAL DIFFERENCE

If you need to trace any other web applications, you'll have to do that manually. (See Section 8.3.3 for details on manual trace logs.)

To enable trace logs in the CMC, head to the APPLICATIONS tab (see Figure 8.14).

Figure 8.14 The Applications Tab in the Central Management Console

Click the application you want to enable tracing on from the list. For this example, we'll be setting up tracing on the BI LAUNCH PAD (see Figure 8.15).

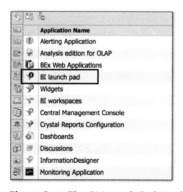

Figure 8.15 The BI Launch Pad Application in the Applications List

Double-click the application name, and select the TRACE LOG SETTINGS tab. Here, you'll find a familiar dropdown list, and you'll want to set your trace LOG LEVEL to HIGH for debugging purposes (see Figure 8.16).

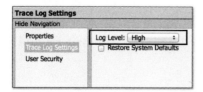

Figure 8.16 The BI Launch Pad Trace Log Level

The trace logs will be in effect immediately (without a reboot, which is nice) for every subsequent login to the web application. Existing sessions won't be traced until they log off and log back in. The log files generated will be located by default in the following directory: *$userHome/SBOPWebapp_$application_$IPaddress_ $port*.

You can also manually set up tracing on web applications using the same method as the servers discussed in Section 8.3.3, but it's strongly recommended to use the CMC method. Why fight easy?

8.3.3 Manually Enabling Trace Logs

The ability to enable and disable trace logging from the CMC has really eliminated most of the need to do tracing the manual way, but it's still worth understanding how to do it just in case. To enable trace logs manually, first head to your install root, to the *conf* folder:

▶ On Windows: *<InstallRoot>SAP BusinessObjects Enterprise XI 4.0\conf*

▶ On UNIX/Linux: *<InstallRoot>/sap_bobj/conf*

Here you'll find the *BO_trace.ini* file. Open the file in your favorite editor, and scroll down to the Trace Syntax and Setting section (see Figure 8.17). Here you'll find the settings you need to change.

```
//===================================================
//Trace Syntax and Setting
//
//uncomment the lines below to enable tracing via ini file.
//This will override the trace setting via command line
//
//===================================================

active = true;
importance = xl;
alert = true;
severity = 'E';
//keep = false;
//size = 100 * 1000;
```

Figure 8.17 BO_Trace.ini Trace Syntax and Setting Section

Uncomment and configure these settings according to your needs based on the possibilities shown in Table 8.2.

Parameter	Possible Values	Description
active	false, true.	If set to true, trace messages that meet the threshold set in the importance parameter will be traced. If set to false, trace messages won't be traced based on their importance level. Default value is false.
importance	'<<', '<=', '==', '>=', '>>', xs, s, m, l, xl importance = xs or importance = << are the most verbose options, while xl or '>>' are the least.	Specifies the threshold for tracing messages. All messages beyond the threshold will be traced. Default value is m (medium).
alert	false, true.	If set to true, trace messages that meet the threshold set in the severity parameter will be traced. If set to false, the trace messages won't be traced based on their severity level. Default value is true.
severity	'S', 'W', 'E', 'A', 'F' (success, warning, error, assert, fatal).	Specifies the threshold severity over which messages can be traced. 'S' consumes the most disk space. Default value is 'E'.
size	integers >= 1000.	Specifies the number of messages in a trace log file before a new one is created. Default value is 100,000.
keep_num	integers >= 1000.	Specifies the number of logs to keep.
administrator	Strings or integers.	Specifies an annotation to use in the output log file.
log_dir	Any directory on the file system.	Specifies the output log directory. Use this if you want to put the logs somewhere other than the default logging folder.
always_close	on, off.	Specifies whether the log file should be closed after a trace is written to the log file. Default value is off.

Table 8.2 BO_Trace.ini Parameters (Source: BusinessObjects Platform Administrator Guide)

Modify the file and save it. It should look something like Figure 8.18.

```
//============================================
//Trace Syntax and Setting
//
//uncomment the lines below to enable tracing via ini file.
//This will override the trace setting via command line
//
//============================================
active = true;
importance = xs;
alert = true;
severity = 'E';
keep_num = 600;
size = 100 * 1000;
```

Figure 8.18 BO_Trace.ini file Modified for Verbose Logging

Restart your SIA to put the trace in effect. This will put tracing on for all servers. If you want to enable tracing this way for just one server, you can add an IF statement to the beginning of your TRACE SYNTAX AND SETTING section (see Figure 8.19).

```
//============================================
//Trace Syntax and Setting
//
//uncomment the lines below to enable tracing via ini file.
//This will override the trace setting via command line
//
//============================================

if (process == "aps_MySIA.ProcessingServer")
{
active = true;
importance = xs;
alert = true;
severity = 'E';
keep_num = 600;
size = 100 * 1000;
}
```

Figure 8.19 BO_Trace.ini file with IF Statement for One Server

This option doesn't require a bounce of the server and will take effect within one minute. This will also override any trace settings you might have put in the CMC.

So, there you have it, manual tracing still lives, but cases where you'd really need to use it are limited. Don't fight easy. Wherever possible, take care of enabling and disabling tracing within the CMC.

8.3.4 Client Tool Trace Logs

Enabling trace logs on your SAP BusinessObjects BI client tools is still, unfortunately, manual. Luckily, the manual process we just described still holds true. You just have to do this on the individual client machines where the tools that you want to trace are installed.

Start by setting up three system environment variables (see Figure 8.20, Figure 8.21, and Figure 8.22).

Figure 8.20 BO_TRACE_CONFIGDIR Environment Variable

Figure 8.21 BO_TRACE_CONFIGFILE Environment Variable

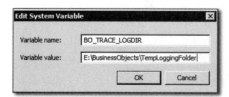

Figure 8.22 BO_TRACE_LOGDIR Environment Variable

You can, of course, make those paths in the variable value anything you want. This is just where we put ours for this example.

Now, you'll need to make a copy of your *BO_Trace.ini* file if you made one during the examples in Section 8.3.3. If not, go back there now, set one up, and then come back here with it copied to your clipboard.

Plunk that *BO_Trace.ini* file down in the folder you specified in your BO_TRACE_ CONFIGFILE environment variable. Now, when you start your client application, you'll see a trace log file appear in your logging folder. We launched Web Intelligence Rich Client (see Figure 8.23).

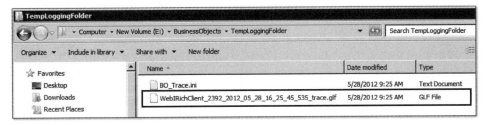

Figure 8.23 Web Intelligence Rich Client Trace Log

This method will work for the following client tools:

- Web Intelligence Rich Client
- Business View Manager
- Information Design Tool
- Report Conversion Tool
- Translation Management Tool
- Universe Design Tool

You can't trace the following client tools (at least not via this method) yet:

- Data Federation Administration Tool
- Query as a Web Service Designer

The Upgrade Management Tool (UMT), although technically a client tool, is really a server tool, and because it's brand new, it follows the server model of enabling trace.

Modify your *BO_Trace.ini* file in the *BOE root install\conf* folder as shown in Figure 8.24.

```
//==================================================
//Trace Syntax and Setting
//
//uncomment the lines below to enable tracing via ini file.
//This will override the trace setting via command line
//
//==================================================
if (process == "upgrademanagementtool")
{
active = true;
importance = xl;
alert = true;
severity = 'E';
keep = true;
size = 100 * 1000;
}
```

Figure 8.24 The BO_Trace.ini file Configured for the Upgrade Management Tool

Save and close the file, and the settings will go into effect within one minute.

Trace logs for client tools can be useful at times if you're having issues getting one of your users up and running, or if users are seeing a strange error. As with all trace logs, don't leave tracing on all the time. Those trace logs will grow like mold and fill up your entire hard disk before you know it. Turn them on, run your workflow to trap your error or process, and then turn them off.

8.3.5   Operating System Logs and Messages

It's common for new SAP BusinessObjects BI administrators to get completely fixated on the application logs and trace logs. But, it's super important (and often much quicker) to head over to your operating system (OS) logs and see what the OS says is going on. Often, you'll catch a succinct, pointed message in the OS log that will tip you off as to what is going on a lot faster than sifting through reams of trace logs.

In Windows, head on over to the EVENT VIEWER (see Figure 8.25).

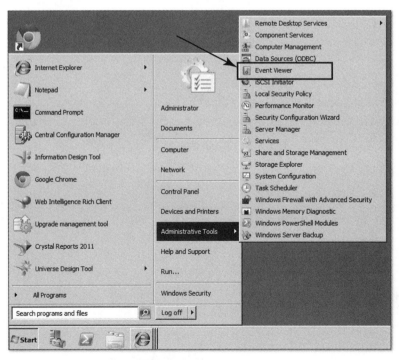

Figure 8.25 Windows Event Viewer

Expand out WINDOWS LOGS on the left, then select the APPLICATION log (*see* Figure 8.26).

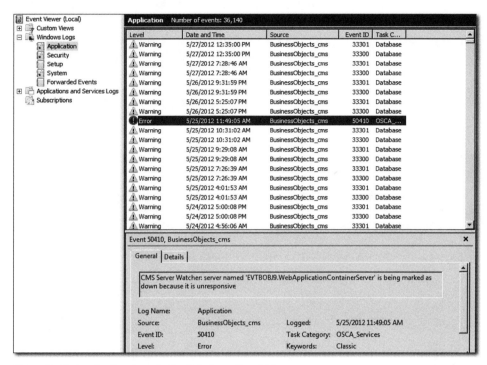

Figure 8.26 Application Logs in the Windows Event Viewer

For UNIX or Linux, ask your system administrators where the messages are being stored. Each flavor is a little different. This example is Red Hat Linux from the \var\log\messages file (see Figure 8.27).

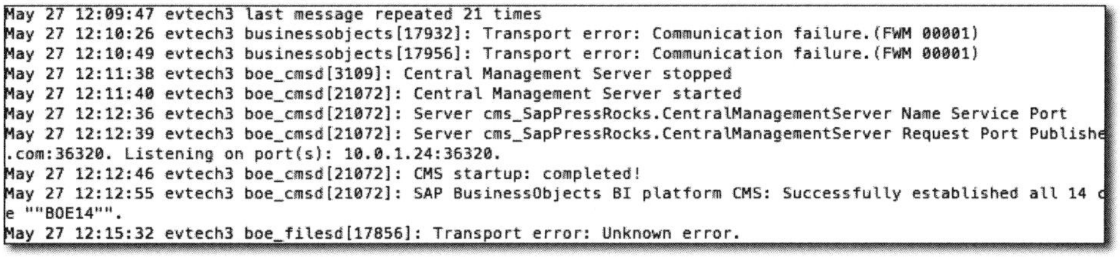

```
May 27 12:09:47 evtech3 last message repeated 21 times
May 27 12:10:26 evtech3 businessobjects[17932]: Transport error: Communication failure.(FWM 00001)
May 27 12:10:49 evtech3 businessobjects[17956]: Transport error: Communication failure.(FWM 00001)
May 27 12:11:38 evtech3 boe_cmsd[3109]: Central Management Server stopped
May 27 12:11:40 evtech3 boe_cmsd[21072]: Central Management Server started
May 27 12:12:36 evtech3 boe_cmsd[21072]: Server cms_SapPressRocks.CentralManagementServer Name Service Port
May 27 12:12:39 evtech3 boe_cmsd[21072]: Server cms_SapPressRocks.CentralManagementServer Request Port Publishe
.com:36320. Listening on port(s): 10.0.1.24:36320.
May 27 12:12:46 evtech3 boe_cmsd[21072]: CMS startup: completed!
May 27 12:12:55 evtech3 boe_cmsd[21072]: SAP BusinessObjects BI platform CMS: Successfully established all 14 c
e ""BOE14"".
May 27 12:15:32 evtech3 boe_filesd[17856]: Transport error: Unknown error.
```

Figure 8.27 Linux Messages File

Whether you're on Windows or not, here you'll find a plethora of errors and warnings SAP BusinessObjects BI throws as it operates from day to day. Do yourself a favor and check these logs early in your troubleshooting process, and make a habit of checking them at least weekly under normal operations. The OS logs can help clue you in on important things going on, and often you can spot trends of things that might be going bad before they actually do.

Now you know how to turn on trace logs on your SAP BusinessObjects BI servers, your web applications, and even your client tools. But, what do you do with all of those log files?

8.3.6 SAP Lumira—The Log Eater

One of the cool ideas we had when SAP Lumira went mainstream was to leverage it to analyze logs. There are a few, relatively painless things to do to effectively analyze trace logs, for example:

▶ Strip off any headers other than column names.

▶ Remove the funky delimiter at the end of each row. Note: Notepad++ is our favorite text editor for log munging.

▶ Rename your log files from .glf to .txt.

With that, your logs are easy to do analysis and cleansing on. You can easily sort by the trace type, severity, and more. This is just another handy tool to keep in the toolbox if nifty tools like Splunk aren't at your disposal.

Pop Quiz
1. Which trace level, accessible via the server's properties in the CMC, achieves the most granular level of tracing?
2. After tracing is enabled, where are logs located on the installation by default?
3. Other event notifications captured by the operating system are recorded in what system-based messaging logging application?

8.4 Reading and Analyzing Logs

All right, so now you have a ton of log files piling up on your application. They have all of these funny names and are busting at the seams with huge lines of text.

What are these things, anyway? You have a couple of options to explore for how to make any use out of these files. We'll introduce you to these options next.

8.4.1 The Laissez-Faire Approach to Trace Logs

By far the easiest, and probably the most efficient, approach to making use of your trace logs is to zip them up and send them off to SAP Support. Yup, that's right. Trace logs aren't for the faint of heart, so unless you're seriously ready for some hardcore troubleshooting, you're probably best off leaving this to the experts. It takes a lot of practice to get good at reading trace logs, let alone the really in-depth knowledge of how the platform operates, to make sense of the workflow being described in the logs.

No matter which method you end up using to analyze your trace logs, you should always do this step. Because you're always going to open a ticket in parallel with your own troubleshooting efforts, go ahead and package up the trace logs that have captured your problem, and attach them to your SAP Support ticket.

If you really want to read trace logs on your own, by all means, there is no intent to discourage on our part. Get in there and get your hands dirty. If you aren't daunted, then proceed.

8.4.2 The Go-For-It Approach to Trace Logs

If you're still here reading, you're either bold, brave, foolhardy, or all of the above. But congrats are in order because you're our kind of reader. Just because SAP discourages you from trying to read trace logs on your own doesn't mean you shouldn't try.

Before you start diving in, you'll need two things. First, you'll need trace logs. Seems a tad obvious, but hey, you do need them. Second, you'll need your favorite text editor. This can be Microsoft Notepad or WordPad, which come along with Windows. Our personal favorite is Notepad++. It's open source, and you can snag it at *http://notepad-plus-plus.org*. If you're not on Windows, you can, of course use `vi` or `emacs`. We're going to stick with Windows for this example. Head over to your logging directory, which is found at *<INSTALLDIR>\Program Files (x86)\SAP BusinessObjects\SAP BusinessObjects Enterprise XI 4.0\logging*. In here, you'll be in the candy store of trace logs. Don't get scared. If you're scared, go back to Section 8.4.1.

First, note that all of the trace log names follow a pattern. The very first part of the name tells you what service category the server is from. You'll see things like "aps," "cms," "dashboardEngine," "jobserver," and so on. Use your noodle and you'll detect the pattern pretty quickly. The second part of the name is the node name. So now, you have service category and node. Next then, you'll see the name of the server, and if it was a subservice of that main server, you'll see that too. There are some other things in there, but they aren't as important to you. Just look at the last part of the name before the .log extension, and that is the process ID (PID) from the process being logged. So if you're looking for a particular server, it's best to first go into the CMC SERVERS tab and find out what PID that server is running under. You can find the associated log files pretty fast by zeroing in on the PID.

Crack open one of the trace logs. We're using a Web Intelligence Processing Server log in this example (see Figure 8.28).

```
SEVERITY_MAP: |Information|W|Warning|E|Error|A|Assertion
HEADER_END
kc3xmlGenericParser.cpp:494:bool __cdecl Cube::xmlTools::ValueTypedConstant::validate(
|90633d55-39ac-3684-1912-11ca92a5eb2b|2012 05 31 05:47:06:635|-0500|>>|E| |webiserver_
kc3xmlGenericParser.cpp:463:bool __cdecl Cube::xmlTools::ValueTypedConstant::validate(
|89b7f0b0-a648-4d84-9aea-680cc5a0ac29|2012 05 31 05:47:06:650|-0500|>>|E| |webiserver_
kc3xmlGenericParser.cpp:494:bool __cdecl Cube::xmlTools::ValueTypedConstant::validate(
|7b17dd09-f683-2694-38b6-0ddf32111c12|2012 05 31 05:47:06:666|-0500|>>|E| |webiserver_
kc3xmlGenericParser.cpp:463:bool __cdecl Cube::xmlTools::ValueTypedConstant::validate(
|5fd3eaf0-7178-3c54-aa0c-47c2cf44820c|2012 05 31 05:47:06:666|-0500|>>|E| |webiserver_
kc3xmlGenericParser.cpp:494:bool __cdecl Cube::xmlTools::ValueTypedConstant::validate(
|09f59c75-ffc1-ecb4-abaf-fb7b998719aa|2012 05 31 05:47:06:682|-0500|>>|E| |webiserver_
kc3cdbtbdacs.cpp:1490:class ibo_ptr<struct ConnectionServer::JobResultSet> __cdecl tb(
|32d0d0ec-cc3c-8e34-ca0e-57ab6bee0832|2012 05 31 05:47:06:713|-0500|>>|E| |webiserver_
kc3cdbtbdacs.cpp:1494:class ibo_ptr<struct ConnectionServer::JobResultSet> __cdecl tb(
|32102957-5af5-f2d4-18c0-54871caff613|2012 05 31 05:47:06:713|-0500|>>|E| |webiserver_
kc3cdbtbdacs.cpp:1490:class ibo_ptr<struct ConnectionServer::JobResultSet> __cdecl tb(
|44c4c191-57d3-e2d4-3b9e-f3d1adc2e53b|2012 05 31 05:47:06:728|-0500|>>|E| |webiserver_
kc3cdbtbdacs.cpp:1486:class ibo_ptr<struct ConnectionServer::JobResultSet> __cdecl tb(
|0e070c46-1969-c414-0b49-350f3f75dbef|2012 05 31 05:47:06:744|-0500|>=|E|×|webiserver_
Error=GetDBConfigParam("DATABASE_DATE_FORMAT") failed.
kc3cdbtbdacs.cpp:1494:class ibo_ptr<struct ConnectionServer::JobResultSet> __cdecl tb(
|878f3333-eede-6074-e9ca-6767af0d8f09|2012 05 31 05:47:06:760|-0500|>>|E| |webiserver_
kc3cdbtbdacs.cpp:276:long __cdecl DoReportCSError(const class ConnectionServer::Error
|430de520-167c-f9a4-3aea-f2a8d7edf9fb|2012 05 31 05:47:06:775|-0500|>>|E| |webiserver_
kc3cdbgenda.cpp:198:long __cdecl cdbDARowsetCursor::doopen(bool): TraceLog message 407
|a2a69c7b-9cb6-7b54-095a-22eaffd15cf2|2012 05 31 05:47:06:791|-0500|>>|E| |webiserver_
kc3qtdataprovider.cpp:2770:long __cdecl cdbQTDataProvider::RefreshNoCommit(void): Trad
|73476f4c-6fce-cce4-ea91-93a54be32133|2012 05 31 05:47:06:791|-0500|>>|E| |webiserver_
kc3cdbdpmanager.cpp:1057:long __cdecl cdbDPManager::DoRefreshDP(class cdbDataProvider
|0e839ada-1691-e7f4-0941-c3c5e4ec0c20|2012 05 31 05:47:06:806|-0500|>>|E| |webiserver_
kc3CoreEngineImpl.cpp:3842:void __cdecl IECore::kc3CoreEngineImpl::ExecuteActionMDP(co
|38adeaaf-76cf-1a74-189e-6c74f79bfd55|2012 05 31 05:47:06:822|-0500|>>|E| |webiserver_
kc3CoreEngineImpl.cpp:3605:void __cdecl IECore::kc3CoreEngineImpl::ExecuteActionMDP(co
|447ad8b2-e8c9-49d4-ab04-85f4bd2d73d1|2012 05 31 05:47:06:838|-0500|>=|E|×|webiserver_
Error=ExecuteQuery/RefreshBatch failed : -2147191224 S(72)
```

Figure 8.28 Scary Web Intelligence Processing Server Trace Log

Now, before you fall down into the Pit of Despair, let's take a second and discuss what's going on here. First off, every single action this Web Intelligence Processing Server takes is being logged. The log is sequential, so the oldest actions are at the top, and the newest are at the bottom. There is a time stamp down to the millisecond in each entry. So, you can, in essence, follow the workflow of this server from action to action from the beginning of the log to the end. Now, before you start scratching your head and wondering what all of this has to do with any errors, scroll your window all the way over to the right. The end of each line is where the really interesting stuff gets written (see Figure 8.29).

```
325080:1||||||||||||GenericContainer_PluginActivityManagerImpl:notifyStopActivity: 0.25
:1||||||||||||**ERROR:C3_GenericParser:ValueTypedConstant::Validate - Client - Invalid value : false [kc3xmlGenericParser.cpp;463]
325080:1||||||||||||GenericContainer_EntityActivityNotifier:EntityActivityNotifier_DTor: 0.281
:1||||||||||||**ERROR:C3_GenericParser:ValueTypedConstant::Validate - Serial - Invalid value : false [kc3xmlGenericParser.cpp;494]
325080:1||||||||||||iboSynchronizedCUnknown::Release
325080:1||||||||||||iboSynchronizedCUnknown::Release: 0.016
t> *&): TraceLog message 40757
325080:1||||||||||||**ERROR:IESessionImpl:**EXCEPTION CAUGHT AT: [IESessionImpl.cpp;1155]
:1||||||||||||**ERROR:C3_GenericParser:ValueTypedConstant::Validate - Client - Invalid value : true [kc3xmlGenericParser.cpp;463]
325080:1||||||||||||**ERROR:RequestProc:Error stream : <ERRORS>
```

Figure 8.29 Scary Web Intelligence Processing Server Trace Log: Scrolled to the Right Showing Errors

Aha! Now there's something to chew on. Rather than trying to scroll through these logs manually, try a search instead. Some important key words you can search for to help you find a problem are listed here:

► Fail

► Cannot

► Assert

► Error

When you find one of these key words, read that entire line, and make a note of the time stamp when the event occurred. Then start stepping upward, line by line, to events that happened earlier. Many times, the error isn't the root cause but rather the end result of something that happened before it.

Manually sifting through trace logs is an art form. You'll need to practice and practice to get good at it. Reading trace logs is like reading Shakespeare. After you get used to the language and the rhythm, it starts making sense. You can do it successfully, given time. Remember, that nearly all of the really good, juicy error details are hiding in there, daring you to find them. You aren't going to take that from an error message, are you?

8.4.3 Cruise through Logs with the GLF Viewer

SAP has recently provided public access to a log parser, aptly named the GLF Viewer. Gain access by doing a quick search on SCN or the SAP Service Marketplace, where you can find this free download. It's a small Java program designed specifically to help you make some sense out of the log file gobbledygook. Pull in any of your enterprise log files that end with a .glf (generic log file), and the GLF Viewer stacks them up quite nicely for your viewing pleasure (see Figure 8.30).

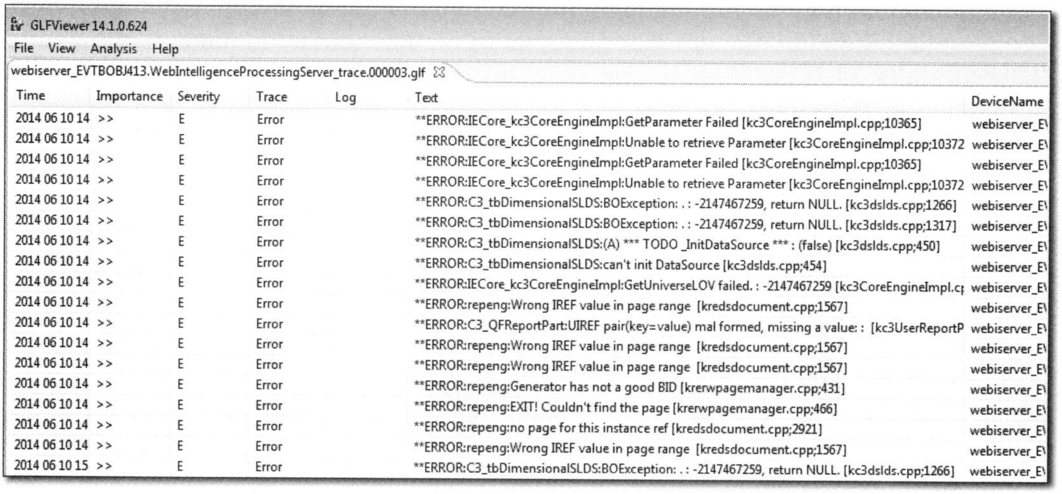

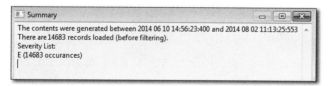

Figure 8.30 SAP GLF Viewer

There is even a handy Analysis view, which parses the entire file and does a summary of the error messages it finds (see Figure 8.31). Very handy, indeed.

Figure 8.31 GLF Viewer Summary

Take advantage of this free tool to help you speed through large amounts of SAP BusinessObjects BI logs, and save yourself some time.

8.4.4   The Cool Third-Party Tool Approach to Trace Logs

So, maybe the manual log parsing thing isn't your style. It's decidedly low tech. Or maybe the SAP GLF Viewer leaves you wanting more. We do live in the era of the "app." A quick Google search for "Visual Log Parser" will yield you a plethora of hits. While many of these are great for common types of logs (Windows system logs, web server logs, etc.), there isn't any third-party tool out there that will work out-of-the-box with SAP BusinessObjects BI logs. You can, with a little effort, practice, and good old tenacity, get some of these to yield pretty decent results for helping you to parse logs. One of our favorites is Splunk. You can download a free copy at *www.splunk.com.*

We'll leave the documentation on how to install and use Splunk to the experts on its website, but in summary, after you have Splunk running, you can load in your log files, and it will index them, making multiple individual log files into one big searchable one over a series of time. You can search for your key words and get very fast, very nice visualizations and time lines on where those key words appear (see Figure 8.32).

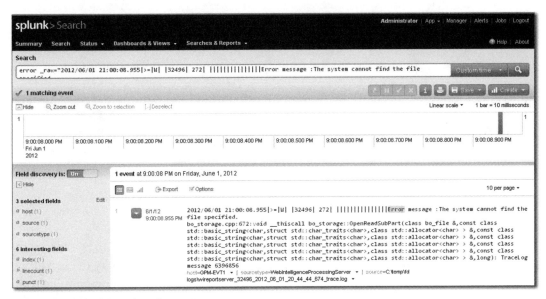

Figure 8.32 Splunk Search and Time Line

There are limits on what you can do with the free version, but, of course, paid versions are also available.

8.4.5 Reading and Understanding Log Summaries

There are ways to deal with your trace logs that range from avoidance to total geek nirvana. The method you take is really up to your appetite for such nitty-gritty things. At the very least, you should now know how to turn on trace logs, zip them up, and send them off to SAP Support. Trace logs are just a linear catalog of every action a particular server takes. As one log fills up, it will roll off and create a new file. You can track a specific server over multiple files by minding the process ID in the end of the file name and the time stamp to make sure you're following them in order.

Trace logs do come at a cost. While there are minor hits in performance for the most verbose of trace logs, the biggest cost comes at the space used by the ginormous logs being generated. Take a look for yourself. The size of the logs is directly proportional to the user activity and number of Web Intelligence Processing Servers. Do you have a busy box with a lot of users? Be ready for these logs to consume massive amounts of space quickly. You must not turn on trace logs and forget that they are running. This is an assured way to make your environment self-destruct.

Dive as deep as you dare. Remember to search for your key words and then step back in time to see if you can find the root cause. If you're serious about mining trace logs yourself, then practice, practice, and practice. Otherwise, it's completely acceptable to leave it to the experts at SAP Support.

Pop Quiz

1. True or False: Trace logs capture activity in reverse chronological order.

8.5 Periodic Maintenance

Not everything you do as an administrator is fixing broken things or breaking them yourself. What makes a good administrator great is his ability to keep things running smoothly so the users can continue to crunch their numbers. Periodic maintenance is a key element in having a smoothly operating SAP Business-Objects BI 4.1 environment. Think of this like taking your car in to have the oil changed every 3,000 miles or like mowing the lawn. This is stuff you have to do from time-to-time so things continue to run well and look nice. As far as your SAP BusinessObjects BI 4.1 platform is concerned, there are 4 lawns to mow, and those are instance management, managing log files, orphans (not the Annie kind), and controlling instances. Let's start with the Instance Manager.

8.5.1 Instance Management

Instances are pesky little things. They can grow really large, you can get lots and lots of them, and they can fail and cause you headaches. No tightly run SAP BusinessObjects BI 4.1 ship is complete without the use of the Instance Manager. Head on over to the Central Management Console, and under the MANAGE heading on the right, choose INSTANCE MANAGER (see Figure 8.33).

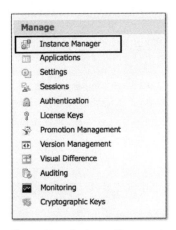

Figure 8.33 Instance Manager Location

Once inside, you'll find an entire console of instance management goodness (see Figure 8.34).

Starting at the top, you have some control dropdowns you're probably familiar with from other places inside the CMC, including MANAGE, ACTIONS, and ORGANIZE. Beneath those, there are buttons for (from left to right) INSTANCE DETAILS, PAUSE, RESUME, and RERUN AN INSTANCE (see Figure 8.35).

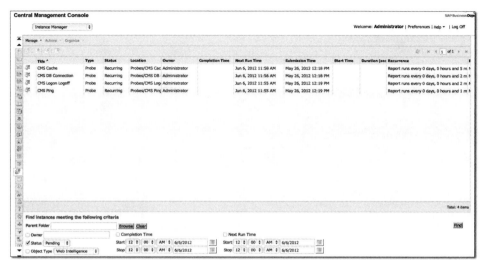

Figure 8.34 Instance Manager Console

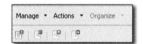

Figure 8.35 The Instance Manager Toolbar

In the middle, the list of instances appears (see Figure 8.36) with the following columns: TITLE, TYPE, STATUS, LOCATION, OWNER, COMPLETION TIME, NEXT RUN TIME, SUBMISSION TIME, START TIME, DURATION, RECURRENCE, EXPIRY, SERVER, and ERROR.

	Regional Sales Detail Rep Publication	Recurring	Sales/
	Regional Sales Detail Rep Publication	Recurring	Sales/
	Regional Sales Detail Rep Publication	Recurring	Sales/
	Regional Sales Detail Rep Publication	Recurring	Sales/
	Regional Sales Detail Rep Publication	Recurring	Sales/
	Regional Sales Detail Rep Publication	Recurring	Sales/
	Regional Sales Detail Rep Publication	Recurring	Sales/
	Regional Sales Detail Rep Publication	Recurring	Sales/
	Regional Sales Detail Rep Publication	Recurring	Sales/
	Regional Sales Detail Rep Publication	Recurring	Sales/
	Regional Sales Detail Rep Publication	Recurring	Sales/
	Regional Sales Detail Rep Publication	Recurring	Sales/
	Regional Sales Detail Rep Publication	Recurring	Sales/
	Regional Sales Detail Rep Publication	Recurring	Sales/

Figure 8.36 Instance Manager: Details Pane

And down below, you have your handy searching and filtering tool to help you sift through the entire population of instances you likely have (see Figure 8.37).

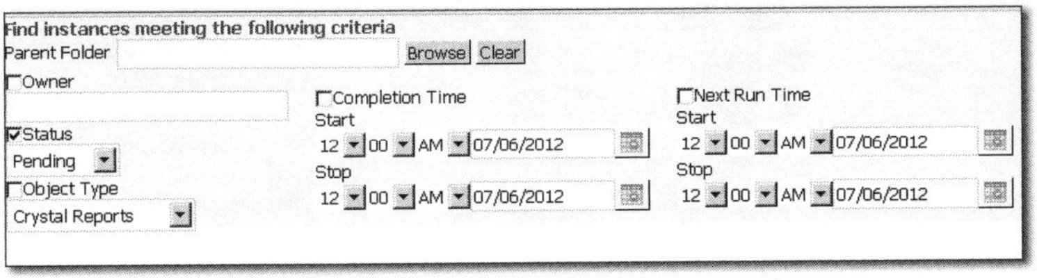

Figure 8.37 Instance Manager: Search and Filter Tool

You can search by PARENT FOLDER, OWNER, STATUS (SUCCESS, FAILED, RUNNING, PAUSED, PENDING, or RECURRING), or OBJECT TYPE (CRYSTAL REPORTS, OBJECT PACKAGE, PUBLICATION, WEB INTELLIGENCE, PROGRAM, or ADMINISTRATIVE TOOL). You can also filter by a starting and stopping COMPLETION TIME or a starting and stopping NEXT RUN TIME.

It becomes apparent pretty quickly that this is a really useful tool. It can help you keep the pulse of your Job Servers and scheduling activity all in one handy console. Watch for large numbers of pending jobs, as this can indicate issues. Also, keep an eye out for failures and errors. Use the searching and filtering to quickly narrow the list down to the useful information you want to see. And, don't forget to slide all the way over to the right and get at those juicy error messages.

8.5.2 Managing Log Files

Log files, if left unattended, as we said, will grow like mold. Make a point to check your log folder and clean it out from time to time. Put a reminder on your calendar to check it once a month. Your SAP BusinessObjects BI logs are in the *<INSTALLDIR>\SAP BusinessObjects Enterprise XI 4.0\logging* folder and on *<INSTALLDIR>/sap_bobj/logging* on UNIX and Linux.

If you're using Tomcat, that has logs, too. Those can be found in your Tomcat *<INSTALLDIR>\Tomcat6\logs* directory.

You should also consider, on Windows systems, doing a monthly archive and purge of your Windows event logs. Save them off, and then clear them out to keep things neat and clean. The example shown in Figure 8.38 is for a Windows 2008 R2 server. Launch the EVENT VIEWER, and then click CLEAR LOG on the right-hand side.

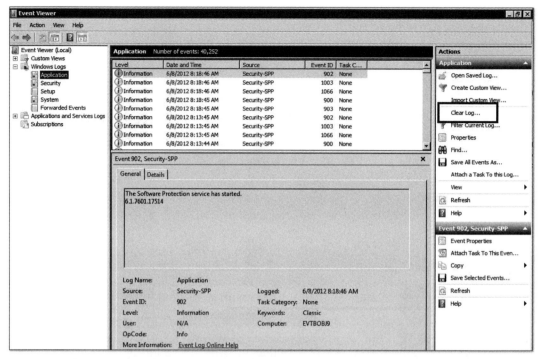

Figure 8.38 Windows Event Viewer: Clear Logs Option

Then choose SAVE AND CLEAR (see Figure 8.39).

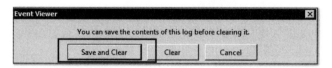

Figure 8.39 Windows Event Viewer: Save and Clear Option

Give the log a meaningful file name. It's a good practice to name it for what it is and put a date stamp into the file name so you'll easily be able to tell what this is in six months (see Figure 8.40).

After you click SAVE, then you have a nice clear log and are ready to start collecting more events. You can always load them back into the Event Viewer if you need to go back in time and renew. Just choose the OPEN SAVED LOG option from the main EVENT VIEWER screen (see Figure 8.41).

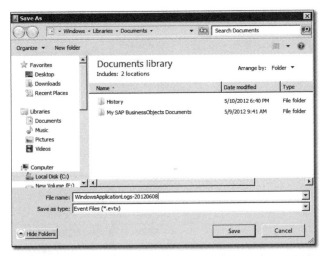

Figure 8.40 Saving Windows Event Logs with a Meaningful Name

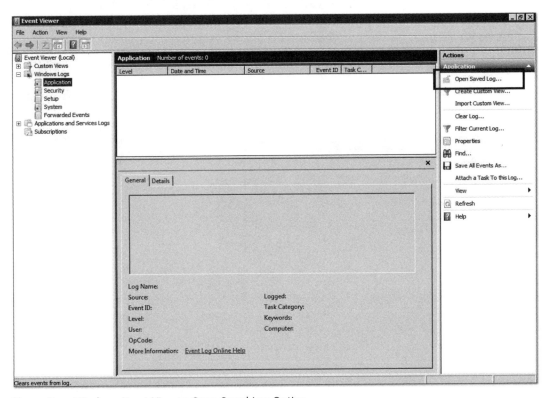

Figure 8.41 Windows Event Viewer: Open Saved Log Option

Choose your saved log file from the list, and then click OPEN (see Figure 8.42).

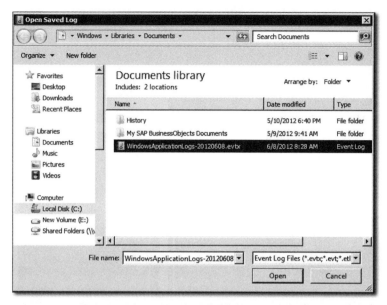

Figure 8.42 Windows Event Viewer: Restoring a Saved Log File

Choose a NAME, a DESCRIPTION, and a location for your restored logs (see Figure 8.43).

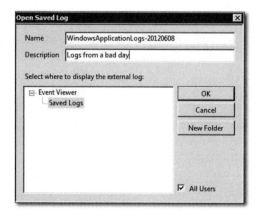

Figure 8.43 Windows Event Viewer: Choosing a Location for Your Saved Logs

After you click OK, you'll have your logs back where you can view them again (see Figure 8.44).

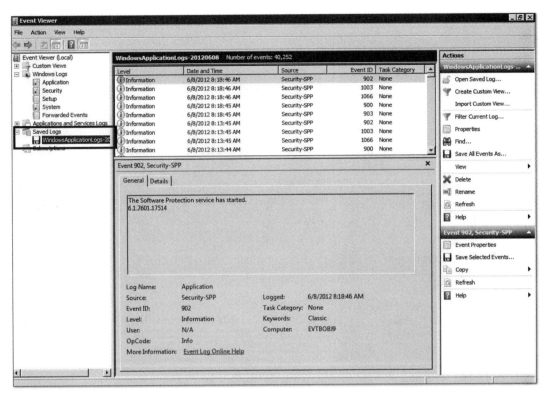

Figure 8.44 Windows Event Viewer: Saved Logs Restored

Logs can be a great source of information, but you don't need to keep them around forever. If you do want to retain them, zip them up with your favorite compression tool, and store them off your SAP BusinessObjects BI 4.1 system somewhere where they won't get in the way.

8.5.3 Orphans

Don't tell Angelina Jolie that there are orphans in your system, but there probably are. The longer you've been using your environment, the more likely you are to have some orphaned files in there. To remedy this, make running the Repository Diagnostic Tool (RDT) a monthly or quarterly exercise. See Section 8.7.3 for the skinny on running the RDT. You'll be surprised how much space you can save on your File Repository Server (FRS).

8.5.4 Controlling Instances

Users' inboxes, personal folders, and public folders are more places where you can seriously lose some storage space. People love to keep stuff in these spots forever and ever, never cleaning up instances or unread messages. There are several ways to manage this. Manually, of course, is least effective but is probably the least invasive. There are programmatic ways to do this as well, using the SDK. Your best bet is to set a limit on each user's personal folders based on established and documented guidelines that users can comprehend, and set retention rules for public folders, letting users know how long reports will live on. Pay attention to any retention rules dictated from above, especially if maintaining an environment that has anything to do with regulatory types of reporting. As an example, head into the CMC, and go to the PERSONAL FOLDERS section (see Figure 8.45).

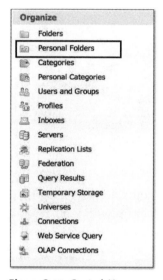

Figure 8.45 Central Management Console: Personal Folders Section

Then, choose the user folder you want to impose the limit on, and go to PROPERTIES • LIMITS (see Figure 8.46).

Here you can set a limit for how many instances a person can store in total. Add your restrictions as needed, and you'll be doing yourself a huge favor in the long run in preventing these personal folders from growing to massive sizes. Remember, if you don't set limits, they will.

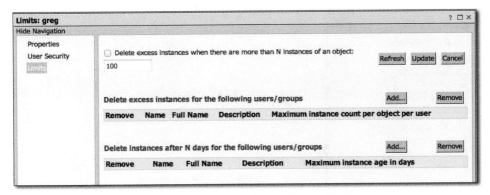

Figure 8.46 Limits Section of the Properties Window on Personal Folders

Users' inboxes will take more finesse. Without limits that can automatically delete these reports, you do need to leverage the SDK or third-party solutions to get rid of unread inbox documents.

8.5.5 Session Management

This feature has been so long in coming that many SAP BusinessObjects BI administrators might not even know that we ever used to have this feature. As of SAP BusinessObjects BI 4.1, we now have the ability to kill user sessions. Insert maniacal laugh here.

Until now, the only way to clear a session was to restart the SIA. Not a very elegant solution, but effective, and definitely disruptive. Now, there are two main ways to kill user sessions out of your system: discreetly and indiscriminately.

Discreet Session Killing (Sniper Mode)

You can kill sessions (baw-hahaha) straight from the CMC—either one at a time or a few at a time. This method, the discreet or sniper method (so coined by us, not SAP) is manual.

First, you have to log in to the CMC, and navigate to the SESSIONS screen (see Figure 8.47).

Figure 8.47 CMC Sessions Option

Once inside, you'll see a list of everyone that is connected to your BI system by user name, last logon time, first logon time, and even if they have any client tools open, and which ones those are. At the bottom of the screen, if you highlight the session or multiple sessions, there is now a little button with a big "X" next to it that says END SESSION (see Figure 8.48). That's your sniper rifle there. Click it, and the session is immediately terminated with extreme prejudice.

Figure 8.48 Killing a Discrete Session

Indiscriminant Session Killing (Battle Tank Mode)

Manually killing sessions is fine and dandy, but many times an SAP BusinessObjects BI administrator is too busy to worry about doing this on a regular basis. So, like any good admin, you want to automate this process to make your job as easy as possible. Thankfully our good friends over at SAP Support have just the thing. Log on to the SAP Service Marketplace, and search for SAP Knowledge Base Article #996692 – How to Automate the Cleanup of Stale BI 4 User Sessions. In a nutshell, this KBA will have you download a program object, which you then upload into SAP BusinessObjects BI 4, configure, and schedule to run on the recurrence schedule you desire (daily, weekly, monthly, etc.). It will then go through and clean out sessions based on the "staleness" criteria you define. Pretty cool, eh?

8.6   Managing Patches and Upgrades

There has been a lot of talk from SAP recently about non-disruptive upgrades. The goal is admirable, and one we'd certainly like to see come to fruition, but the simple fact remains that today, this is still just a dream. One of our past managers used to frequently say, "Whenever you open the patient, you risk infection," when we talked about patches and upgrades, and he was right. Patches can be devastating if you implement them improperly or don't test them thoroughly. Major version upgrades can turn your world upside down. Thankfully for you, if you're on SAP BusinessObjects BI 4.1, you're about as high as it goes as of the time this book was written. But time marches on, and it's only a matter of time before another major version comes along, and you'll be planning another upgrade. Because patches are coming out just about every two weeks, that is probably a good place to start.

8.6.1   Patches

Patches are an inevitable part of your administrative duties. At some point, one of your users is going to experience an issue that he just can't get over, and SAP Support is going to tell you that issue is fixed in a higher patch level. It happens. When that's the case, it's time to patch.

Download your patch installer files ahead of time from the SAP Support Portal. It's best if you can store them on a file server somewhere that is centrally located, especially if you have multiple SAP BusinessObjects BI servers to patch. It's also best if you make use of the SAP Download Manager tool because patch files tend to be quite large, and direct downloads can sometimes get wonky, especially on a server.

After you have the installation media, you're ready to start installing, right? Wrong! No system is too little or too unimportant to back up first. At a bare-bones minimum, you should make a backup of your FRS, your CMS and Auditor databases, and your web applications. That way, if you do get hit by Mr. Murphy's bus, you can restore those key pieces pretty quickly and restore your environment to working order. If you happen to be running on a virtual machine, it's pretty easy to just take a snapshot of the entire environment. If not, go for the traditional backup methods as described in Section 8.7.1. Long story short, make a backup!

Now that your backups are made and tucked away somewhere safe, and you've properly communicated your outage to your customers, you're ready to begin the patch.

One more thing before you start: you'll probably want to make sure that there are no users in the system. Having things changing or being used while the patch is running isn't a good idea. Do what you need to do to positively deny users access to log in, such as shutting down your web server so they can't get to the BI Launch Pad. This can be tricky if you don't have a distributed web and application tier in your environment. If that is the case, you could also revoke access to the BI Launch Pad from the CMC. In any case, get those pesky users out of the system before you start.

Okay, patch files downloaded, check; backups taken and stored, check; users booted out of the system, check—now is it finally time to get your patcher file running? Not quite yet. One final thing you'll need to nail down before you start is your patch deployment plan. Put simply, how are you going to deploy the patch on your server or servers, and in what order? Take the following into consideration when formulating your patch deployment plan:

▶ If your SAP BusinessObjects BI 4.1 server is a "black box" deployment, meaning everything is running on the same hardware, you must have the SIA up when the patch program runs. You can shut your web tier down to discourage pesky users from trying to log in during the patch, but the SIA must be up.

▶ If your SAP BusinessObjects BI 4.1 server is in a distributed landscape (separate servers for web and application tiers, not clustered), you can run the patch on the web tier and application tier in parallel to try to save some time, but the SIA must be up when you start the patch and must remain up during the entire process.

▶ If your SAP BusinessObjects BI deployment is complex (distributed landscape, clustered SIAs), this is where it can get tricky. In a clustered environment, every SIA must always be at the same patch level. No exceptions can be made, or bad things will happen. To manage this nuance while patching, shut down all of your SIAs except for one. Patch the running one first. Then, while remaining down, patch your remaining SIAs in the cluster, but use the first one that is still running as your authenticator for the patcher file. That way, the one patched SIA is the only one that stays up the whole time, and as the shutdown SIA completes its patch, the patch program will bounce it, and it will rejoin the cluster smoothly now that it's at the same patch level as the first SIA.

You also have the ability now to remove previous patches afterwards, so you can save disk space. For example, if you installed SAP BusinessObjects BI 4.1 at the FP3 level (base level GA release), then applied SP3, and then SP4, after you're done with SP4, you can go back into your Control Panel on Windows and uninstall the SP3 patch. The general rule is that you need to keep the base install (your first install level) plus the most current patch.

Now, you're finally ready to start patching. Go according to your patch deployment plan, and kick off the patch program. You'll be asked a few simple questions about your environment, CMS name, login, and so on, and then the patch will run.... and run... and run. On average, the patches for SAP BusinessObjects BI run for about three hours (depending on your system and whatnot). Each SIA will restart at the end of the patching process. Give it a few minutes to start everything back up, and then get in there and do some testing. Open up and refresh some reports. Kick the tires. If you have some users that can get in and test for you, all the better. Have them run through some of their daily tasks and make sure nothing is broken.

8.6.2 Upgrades

There could be a long, philosophical debate about what an *upgrade* is and what a *patch* is. But, for our purposes here, we're going to stick with some basics. SAP releases patches, service packs, and feature packs for SAP BusinessObjects BI now. The lowest level, and most frequent, is the patch. A patch typically contains bug fixes and improvements but usually not any new features or functionality. A patch is a patch. Everything else is an upgrade. Service packs are usually much larger than a patch, and less frequent in their releases, and often bring new functionality.

Feature packs are even bigger: they're loaded with new features and significantly change the system. So, if you're installing a service pack or feature pack, for all intents and purposes, you're doing an upgrade.

Upgrades need to be planned for in much the same way as a patch; it's just that the stakes are higher. More is changing, so there is more risk involved that something might go wrong. Be doubly sure you have good backups, ample disk space, and a solid test plan in place.

If you're adding new features with an upgrade, it really helps to get those changes out in front of your users ahead of time so they know what to expect. If you have a sandbox or demo environment, perform the upgrade there first. Then spend some time training your users on what the new version will look like and how it works. Get them interested in all the cool new toys they'll have to play with after you're done.

The importance of properly planning and testing the upgrade can't be stressed enough. If there are surprises in store for you with this upgrade, you don't want to find them on your production server. Test, test, test, and then test some more. Then go back and test it again—seriously. Every time you open the patient you risk infection. Make it into a contest. See who can find the most bugs with the upgrade and give out a prize for it (you'd be amazed what your coworkers will do for a $20 Starbucks gift card). Create your bug/issue list, and get your support tickets open with SAP if they are serious. Then fix your issues and keep a detailed list of what you had to do to resolve them. You're going to need that list when you get to your production box.

The actual upgrade files should be acquired and deployed just like we discussed in Section 8.6.1. The same rules apply as in patches. One SIA must always be up, and all of your SIAs in a cluster must be at the same patch level at all times.

Maintaining Your Patches and Upgrades

Theoretically, the patch frequency for SAP BusinessObjects BI 4.1 isn't the same as its predecessors. The frequency of patches and support packs has increased, and the inevitability that patching will be required throughout the year is a constant. As such, SAP has instituted a policy of maintaining two important documents to planning your SAP BusinessObjects BI 4.1 upgrades:

▶ **Forward-Fit Plan**

The Forward-Fit Plan is a document that is regularly updated by the SAP Support organization to inform you of the compatibility of patches with lower versions of the product and where they have been applied to higher-level support packs. This is vital! Are you considering an upgrade to a major support pack for a new feature but also to address a defect fixed in a fix pack? You must ensure that the fix pack has been applied to your target support pack level, or your issue may not be addressed! Search the SCN for the Forward-Fit Plan for SAP BusinessObjects, and bookmark it for future reference.

▶ **Maintenance Plan**

The Maintenance Plan falls into the same realm of knowledge transfer but fulfills a slightly different purpose. Also on the SCN, the Maintenance Plan provides a 60- to 90-day schedule, by product, indicating the week, month, and quarter for each fix pack and support pack release. The contents of those releases may be in the air. But, for the circumstances when a customer has a known issue solved by fix pack, SAP informs you on the targeted release, and the Maintenance Plan lets you know when you can expect the fix to roll.

8.6.3 Patches and Upgrades Summary

If there are only two words you remember out of this entire section, they should be *plan* and *test*. The Wild West cowboy method of patches and upgrades (also known as "winging it" or "just go for it" methods) just won't cut it. If we've said it once, we've said it a hundred times: Your SAP BusinessObjects BI 4.1 system is the lifeblood of your data-driven business. You can't risk breaking your system due to poor planning or poor testing of a patch or upgrade.

What is the appropriate way to test? There is no single magic bullet. You must base the decision about the degree of testing on how serious the upgrade is. Do you do a regression test on a representative sample of content, comparing a sandbox that is upgraded to a current production environment? Do you distribute responsibility for testing to application teams and wash your hands of any responsibility? Good luck. A structured test plan to ensure the stability, availability, and potential for error in the upgrade process will save your bacon.

Plan and test. Plan and test. Got it?

8.7   Backup and Recovery

Think of backups like you think about car insurance. Nobody likes them, nobody really wants to pay for them, and nobody likes dealing with them—until something breaks. Then, everybody wants them. Backups are your insurance policy against the evils of Murphy's Law. Something will go wrong, and it won't be a convenient time, so we best be prepared.

There are lots of types of backups that can be performed. Let's start with the higher level, general concepts and then get down into the weeds with it. There are three main types of backups:

▸ **System backup**
This is typically a backup of your entire server, OS, and all, bit for bit. Typically, a full backup is taken once a week, with an incremental backup taken daily. This certainly varies from organization to organization.

▸ **Database backup**
This is a backup taken of a specific database at a specific time. Typically, these are handled by your database administrators, but not always. This is a backup of the database structure and its contents. It doesn't necessarily include the OS files.

▸ **Directory backup**
These are files or folders or directories that are of special importance and are backed up on a periodic basis separate from any other backups. Often these are done more frequently, multiple times a day.

Now that we have those types of backups straight, let's speak generally about the important parts of your SAP BusinessObjects BI 4.1 system to back up. The truly valuable part is your content. Your reports, universes, dashboards, and so on are irreplaceable. If the server crashes, you can always reinstall SAP BusinessObjects BI, so that part really isn't as critical. But nothing will reinstall your content if it gets lost. There are two places where your content lives. The metadata about your content is all in the system or CMS database. The actual content files live on the

File Repository Server (FRS). So, the CMS database and the FRS file store are where you should focus your backup attention. We need to think about the timing and capability of both backups so that we maximize a recovery situation.

And, of course, what lengthy explanation would be complete without making the explanation just a bit more complicated? There are two ways you can back up your CMS database and FRS file store: hot backup and cold backup. We'll cover the difference between hot and cold backups, how to back up your server settings, and backing up your SAP BusinessObjects BI content. Next, we'll tell you what to do with those backups when you need to recover them and explain the difference between a "regular" restore and a disaster recovery.

8.7.1 Hot and Cold Backups

The difference between a hot and cold backup really is like night and day. A hot backup is a backup that is taken while the system is live, active, or hot. There are users in your system, and they are doing things. A cold backup, by contrast, is a system that is down or inactive. There are no users logged in, and no activity is taking place. Hot and cold backups are really a matter of preference and risk tolerance. Until very recently, the only recommended way to back up SAP BusinessObjects was a cold backup, and here's why. Because of how the system architecture works, your content has two parts that must match up, and those two parts are in two different places often on different servers. Those two places are the CMS database and the FRS file store. If you back up one and not the other, you can't recover. If you back up both, but at different times and in different states, you can have inconsistencies and errors after you recover. We'll cover the specifics about how to handle inconsistencies in Section 8.7.3. For now, let's stick with the backups.

Cold backups are still the single best way to ensure you're going to get a clean, complete backup of your CMS database and FRS file store. To execute a cold backup, shut down all of your SAP BusinessObjects BI 4.1 services and stop the SIA. After everything is down, you can safely back up your CMS database and FRS file store. After your backup jobs are complete, you can restart your SIA, and all will be well.

Hot backups, traditionally, were executed in the same way as a cold backup, except for the stopping-the-SIA part. You just took your chances and kicked off the backup job while everything was up. But now, with SAP BusinessObjects BI 4.1, you have a built-in way to help you get a cleaner hot backup. This feature will retain some change history for the period of time specified, so that when you run your CMS database and FRS file store backups, they will be in sync for the duration you specify.

To enable the hot backup feature in SAP BusinessObjects BI 4.1, follow these steps:

1. Log in to the Central Management Console.

2. Navigate to the SETTINGS page (see Figure 8.49).

Figure 8.49 CMC Settings Option

3. Click the ENABLE HOT BACKUP tab.

4. Enter the maximum number of minutes you expect the backup to take under HOT BACKUP MAXIMUM DURATION (MINUTES) (see Figure 8.50). Be sure to include the time required to back up both the CMS database and the file system of the SAP BusinessObjects BI host machine. If the actual duration of the backup exceeds the limit entered here, it may cause inconsistencies in the backed up data. It's better, and safer, to overestimate the time required.

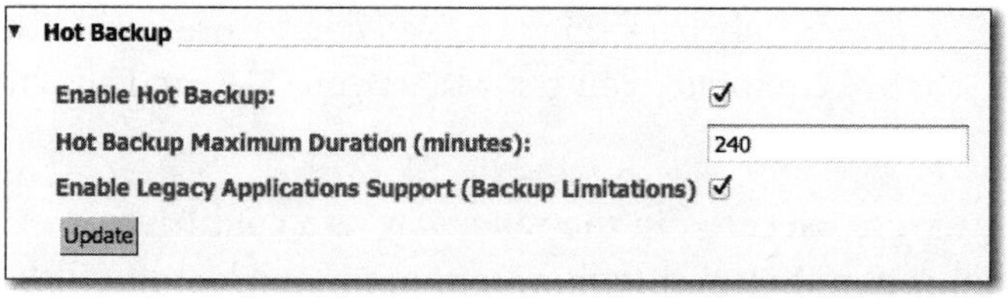

Figure 8.50 The Hot Backup Tab

5. To allow older (before SAP BusinessObjects BI 4.0 SP4) Web Intelligence Rich Client, SAP Crystal Reports Designer, or custom SDK thick client applications to modify documents on the system, select the ENABLE LEGACY APPLICATIONS SUPPORT (BACKUP LIMITATIONS) checkbox.

6. Click UPDATE, and hot backup will now be enabled.

If you aren't sure how long your backup will take, test it out a few times as a cold backup if you're able to. Monitor that length of time, and adjust the setting in the CMC if necessary. Definitely overestimate here.

Besides the CMS database backup and the FRS file store backup, there are two other types of backups you as the SAP BusinessObjects BI administrator should be aware of because they are backups that you control and should be conducting on a regular basis. Those two types of administrator-controlled backups are server settings backups, and SAP BusinessObjects BI content backups.

Backing Up Server Settings

To speed along your recovery process, you now have the ability to backup all of your server settings as well. This is something you should do on a regular basis, especially before and after any patches or upgrades are applied. Having available backups of your servers allows you to restore settings without having to restore your CMS system database, FRS file store, or SAP BusinessObjects BI content. You should also backup your server settings whenever you make any changes to your system's deployment. This includes creating, renaming, and deleting nodes and creating or deleting servers.

You can backup server settings on the Windows platform using the Central Configuration Manager (CCM). Open the CENTRAL CONFIGURATION MANAGERscreen, and on the top toolbar, click the BACK UP SERVER CONFIGURATION button (see Figure 8.51).

This will launch the SERVER CONFIGURATION BACKUP WIZARD. On this welcome screen, click NEXT (see Figure 8.52).

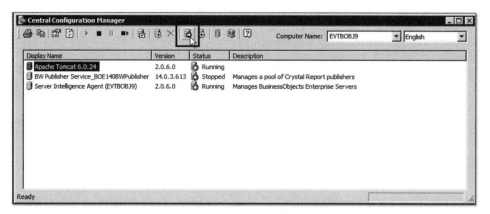

Figure 8.51 The Backup Server Configuration Button on the CCM

Figure 8.52 Welcome to the Server Configuration Backup Wizard Screen

Enter your SYSTEM name, USER NAME, PASSWORD, and AUTHENTICATION method to log in to your SIA (see Figure 8.53).

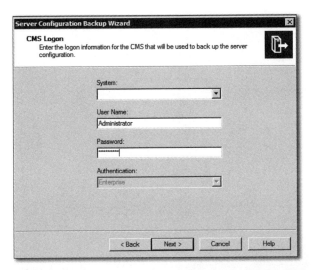

Figure 8.53 Server Configuration Backup Wizard: CMS Logon Screen

Specify a name and location for where you want to put the BI Archive Resource (BIAR) file. Don't forget to add the .biar extension to your file name yourself (see Figure 8.54). This ancient limitation still exists.

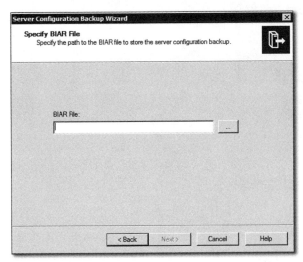

Figure 8.54 Server Configuration Backup Wizard: Specify BIAR File Screen

Next, you'll land on the CONFIRMATION screen. Click FINISH, and your configuration backup will commence (see Figure 8.55).

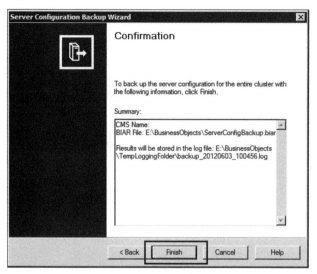

Figure 8.55 Server Configuration Backup Wizard: Confirmation Screen

You'll watch the progress bar with glee as it shows you how long it has left to complete (see Figure 8.56).

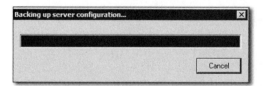

Figure 8.56 Server Configuration Backup Wizard: Backup Progress Bar

Once complete, you'll get a happy little confirmation message that all went swimmingly (see Figure 8.57).

Figure 8.57 Server Configuration Backup Wizard: Backup Complete

To backup server settings on UNIX or Linux, use the `serverconfig.sh` script. Launch the script, choose option 5 – BACK UP SERVER CONFIGURATION, and press Enter (see Figure 8.58).

```
---------------------------------------------------
            SAP BusinessObjects

What do you want to do?

1 - Add node
2 - Delete node
3 - Modify node
4 - Move node
5 - Back up server configuration
6 - Restore server configuration
7 - Modify web tier configuration
8 - List all nodes


[quit(0)]
---------------------------------------------------

[8]
```

Figure 8.58 serverconfig.sh Script Main Screen

Specify whether to use an existing CMS to back up server settings or to create a temporary CMS. To backup server settings from a system that is running, select EXISTING, and press Enter. To either back up server settings from a system that isn't running or to restore server settings, select TEMPORARY, and press Enter (see Figure 8.59).

```
-----------------------------------------------------------------
            SAP BusinessObjects

* Select a CMS *

Select a CMS that will be used to back up a cluster.

existing
    (Select when at least one CMS is running.)
temporary
    (Select when cluster has no running CMSs. A temporary CMS will be automatically started. Upon completion, it will be stopped.)

[existing(3)/temporary(2)/back(1)/quit(0)]
-----------------------------------------------------------------

[existing]
```

Figure 8.59 serverconfig.sh Script: Backup Server Settings – Select CMS Type Screen

Enter your CMS name, and then press Enter (see Figure 8.60).

```
--------------------------------------------------------
            SAP BusinessObjects

* CMS Logon *
Enter the name of the CMS that will be used to back up the server configuration.



[back(1)/quit(0)]
--------------------------------------------------------
```

Figure 8.60 serverconfig.sh script: Backup Server Settings – Specify CMS Name Screen

Enter the port that your CMS is running on, and press [Enter] (see Figure 8.61).

```
--------------------------------------------------------
            SAP BusinessObjects

* CMS Logon *
Enter the port number of the CMS that will be used to back up the server configuration.
Or press ENTER to use the default.


[back(1)/quit(0)]
--------------------------------------------------------
[default (6400)][]
```

Figure 8.61 serverconfig.sh script: Backup Server Settings – Specify CMS Port Screen

Now, enter the user name you want to use to authenticate, and press [Enter] (see Figure 8.62).

```
--------------------------------------------------------
            SAP BusinessObjects

* CMS Logon *
Enter the user name to connect to this CMS.
Note that only Enterprise authentication is supported.


[back(1)/quit(0)]
--------------------------------------------------------
[Administrator][]
```

Figure 8.62 serverconfig.sh script: Backup Server Settings – Specify User Name Screen

Then, enter in the password for the user you chose, and press [Enter] (see Figure 8.63).

```
--------------------------------------------------
            SAP BusinessObjects

* CMS Logon *
Enter the password to connect to this CMS.




[back(1)/quit(0)]
--------------------------------------------------
[]
```

Figure 8.63 serverconfig.sh script: Backup Server Settings – Enter Password Screen

The script will ask you to wait one moment, but it lies. Give it a couple of minutes, and you'll be able to proceed (see Figure 8.64).

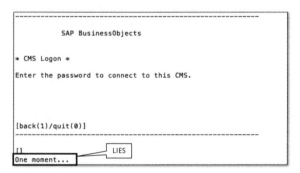

Figure 8.64 serverconfig.sh script: Backup Server Settings – One Moment... Lies

When it finally does fess up the next screen, you'll be asked to put in the full path for where you want the BIAR file to be written (see Figure 8.65).

```
--------------------------------------------------
            SAP BusinessObjects

* Specify BIAR File *
Enter the full path of the BIAR file to store the server configuration backup.



[back(1)/quit(0)]
--------------------------------------------------
[]/app/serverbackup.biar
```

Figure 8.65 serverconfig.sh Script: Backup Server Settings – BIAR Path Screen

And, finally, you'll come to the confirmation that this script will now backup your entire cluster settings for you where you asked it to. Bravely enter YES, and press ⌷Enter⌷ (see Figure 8.66).

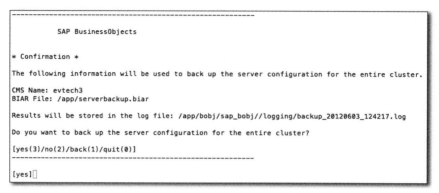

```
            SAP BusinessObjects

* Confirmation *

The following information will be used to back up the server configuration for the entire cluster.

CMS Name: evtech3
BIAR File: /app/serverbackup.biar

Results will be stored in the log file: /app/bobj/sap_bobj//logging/backup_20120603_124217.log

Do you want to back up the server configuration for the entire cluster?

[yes(3)/no(2)/back(1)/quit(0)]

[yes]⌷
```

Figure 8.66 serverconfig.sh Script: Backup Server Settings – Confirmation Screen

Whether it's Windows or Linux, if you really want to keep these server configuration backup BIAR files safe, it would be best to store them off of the SAP BusinessObjects BI 4.1 server. If it's your SAP BusinessObjects BI system that crashes, what good is a backup file that's on the crashed system? Put them out on a file server or SAN somewhere that gets backed up regularly to tape. Keep them secret; keep them safe.

Backing Up Your Business Intelligence Content

Several of these other backup methods will get your SAP BusinessObjects BI content as well, but sometimes you just want your reports and universes and such and not all of the extras. If this is the case for you, kindly refer to Chapter 6 and take a hard look at the Promotion Management tool. This guy is your pal for backing up and restoring your reporting and analytics content.

So, now you have your backups. But, how do you use them when you need them?

8.7.2 Restoring and Recovering

After years of experience in recovering failed SAP BusinessObjects BI environments on various platforms, one lesson that is indelibly etched on our brains is that you don't want a moment of crisis to be the time when you test your backups. Backups aren't foolproof. They aren't perfect. Just because you think you have a clean backup doesn't mean you can use it to recover. When you have a system down and customers screaming at you to get it back up and running, it's not the time you want to discover that your backup was incomplete or corrupt. Trust us on this one. It's definitely an experience you can live without. That being the case, there's no better way to preface a section on restoring from backup and disaster recovery than stressing the fact that you must test your backups from time to time. Take a day out of your schedule once a month, pull a random backup, and restore it somewhere in a lab or sandbox environment and see what it does. You'll thank us later, when something really breaks, and you know you have good backups.

Let's take a moment and discuss briefly the difference between a restore recovery and a disaster recovery. A restore from backup typically happens on the same server system from which the backup was taken. For example, we take a backup of SAP BusinessObjects BI 4.1 server PROD111 on Monday, January 1, and on Tuesday, January 2, something bad happens, and we have to restore. We pull the backups from January 1 and apply them back to the same hardware and OS from which it was taken. That's a restore.

Disaster recovery, however, is more serious. You're still restoring from the same backup but typically to a totally different piece of hardware, which could even be in a totally different location. This is when something really bad happens. Your server overheated and melted down. Your data center got hit by a meteor and is now a steaming crater. The Zombie Apocalypse hit the Northeast, and they ate the power lines feeding your company's buildings. That's a disaster recovery.

Restoring from Backup

The best way to restore from a backup is to do a cold restore. Just like in the cold backup, you'll want to stop the SIA, and then restore your CMS database and FRS file store. After the restore is complete, bring the SIA back up, and run some tests yourself before you release the environment to users. It's always best to open up the BI Launch Pad, log in, and run some reports. Make sure you spot check a few reports before letting the system go. But, be ready to respond if there are errors or inconsistencies.

Disaster Recovery

At a minimum, you should try to restore your backups on a totally different piece of hardware. If your company has a server lab or if you're lucky enough to have a sandbox server you can use, those are perfect. There are multiple ways to conduct a disaster recovery, but, in general, as far as SAP BusinessObjects BI goes, there are really only two:

▶ **Method 1: Full restore**
Use this method if you have the entire operating system, file system, and application backed up on one master backup. Use the server backup, and restore that first onto the new server (get some help from a system administrator if you're unfamiliar with how this is done to avoid things such as IP address conflicts). After the operating system up and running, and you've tested it, then shut down your SIA and perform your SAP BusinessObjects BI 4.1 restore, just like you did in a regular restore. Put the CMS database and the FRS file store back on, and then restart the SIA. Log in to the BI Launch Pad and run some reports.

▶ **Method 2: Rebuild and partial restore**
Use this method if you only have a CMS database and FRS file store backup. This means you'll have to do a reinstall of SAP BusinessObjects BI 4.1 and patch it up so it's at exactly the same build level as the system you're recovering. After the install is completed, run your restore operation just as before. Stop the SIA, run the restore, restart the SIA, log in to the BI Launch Pad, and run some reports.

Disaster recovery can get tricky because of server names and IP addresses. You're basically building an exact copy of a failed server. If that failed server is down never to see the light of day again, you're less likely to have problems. But, if the old and new servers are up, you can sometimes run into problems because of this. In any case, if you're in a disaster situation, get help. System and database administrators are your pals.

If you're really lucky (or unlucky), your company already conducts annual or bi-annual disaster recovery exercises where you get to travel somewhere off-site and work all weekend doing a recovery in a remote location. These are extremely taxing but extremely valuable learning experiences. After you've done a few, you won't break a sweat in an actual crisis situation. You'll know just what to do.

In any case, no matter what your company policy is, you need to practice your restores from time to time. As soon as something breaks, and you don't know how to or can't recover, your management will realize the value in allowing you a little practice time.

Restoring Server Settings

To put your server settings back, you'll use nearly the same method we described to back them up, just in reverse. Make sure you have those server configuration BIAR files saved somewhere safe off of your SAP BusinessObjects BI server. On Windows, follow these steps:

1. Stop all SIAs and nodes in your cluster and in the CCM, and, this time, click the RESTORE SERVER CONFIGURATION button (see Figure 8.67).

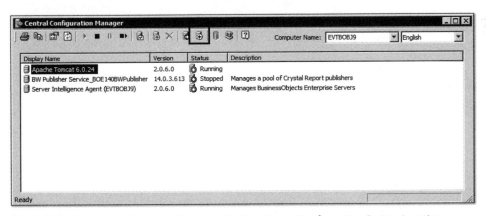

Figure 8.67 Central Configuration Manager: Restore Server Configuration Button Location

2. You'll need to use a temporary CMS this time to do the restore because your target CMS is down. Provide a port number for the temporary CMS to use and the information to connect to the CMS system database. Then click NEXT.

3. Enter the cluster key, and then click NEXT.

4. When prompted, log on to the CMS by entering the CMS name, user name, and password of an account with administrative privileges, and click NEXT.

5. Specify the location and name of the backup BIAR file that has the configuration settings you want to restore.

6. Click NEXT to continue.

7. Review the summary page, click FINISH to continue, and click YES on the warning message to start the restore.

To restore your server setting on Linux/UNIX, follow these steps:

1. Launch the `serverconfig.sh` script, choose option 6 – RESTORE SERVER CONFIGURATION, and press Enter.

2. Enter a port number for the temporary CMS to use, and press Enter.

3. On the next screens, specify the connection information to the CMS system database.

4. When prompted, log on to the CMS by specifying the system, user name, and password of an account with administrative privileges, and then press Enter.

5. When prompted, specify the location and name of the BIAR file that you want to restore the server configuration settings from, and press Enter.

6. Verify that the information displayed on the screen is correct, and press Enter to continue. The `serverconfig.sh` script restores the server configuration settings for the entire cluster from the BIAR file that you specify.

Now you have everything back—your CMS database, your FRS file store, your server settings, and your SAP BusinessObjects BI content. Everything is going to magically work just fine now, right? Maybe if you're really lucky. If so, go play the lottery that day as well. If things aren't quite right, or you have users reporting strange errors when they try to run a report, it's time to turn to our good friend, the Repository Diagnostic Tool.

8.7.3   Repository Diagnostic Tool

Back in the beginning of Section 8.7 we touched on the fact that your CMS database and FRS file store must be backed up in the same state. We discussed the various strategies to accomplish that. Let's recap briefly why that is important. Remember, that the CMS database holds all the metadata the SAP BusinessObjects BI 4.1 Central Management Server needs to do its job. It tells the CMS where every report is, who owns it, where it lives on the FRS, how big it is, when it's scheduled to run, and on and on and on. The FRS file store physically houses all of your SAP BusinessObjects BI 4.1 platform content—every Web Intelligence report, every Crystal report, every universe. If the metadata is out of sync with the physical files, you'll get errors. If the physical files are out of sync with the metadata, you'll get errors. So, what do you do when you have inconsistencies like this? Enter the Repository Diagnostic Tool.

Getting to Know the RDT

The Repository Diagnostic Tool (RDT) is a command-line tool that scans, diagnoses, and repairs inconsistencies that may occur between your CMS database and FRS file store, or inconsistencies that can occur in the metadata of InfoObjects stored in the CMS database.

During normal operations of your SAP BusinessObjects BI 4.1 platform, it is not common for the CMS system database to develop inconsistencies. It *is* common, however, for inconsistencies to occur during disaster recovery, backup restoration, or network outages. During such events, the CMS system database might be interrupted while performing a task, and thus an inconsistency occurs.

The RDT will scan the CMS system database and identify inconsistencies in reports, users, user groups, folders, servers, universes, universe connections, and other objects. The RDT scans for two major types of inconsistencies:

► **Object to file inconsistencies**
These are inconsistencies that can occur between InfoObjects in the CMS database and the corresponding files in the FRS file store. For example, a file that exists in the FRS is missing a corresponding metadata object in the CMS system database.

► **InfoObject metadata inconsistencies**
These are inconsistencies that may exist in an InfoObject's metadata in the CMS database. For example, an InfoObject may reference another InfoObject that doesn't exist in the CMS database.

The RDT performs two functions, depending on the parameters you provide when you run the tool:

► RDT scans the CMS system database and the FRS file store, reports inconsistencies, and outputs a log file in XML format with suggested actions to repair the inconsistencies.

► RDT scans and repairs the inconsistencies identified in the CMS system database and FRS file store and then outputs the actions taken to a log file in XML format.

Running the RDT

First, before you go and try to run the RDT, read this section through all the way. Then go back and read it again. There is a bunch of information you need to collect before you can run the RDT because the RDT requires it to be passed in the command line. This tool isn't user-friendly. Do some homework first and save yourself the gray hairs.

To execute the RDT on Windows, open a command prompt window, and run the following command:

```
<INSTALLDIR>\SAP BusinessObjects Enterprise XI 4.0\win64_x64\
reposcan.exe <arguments>
```

In this command, `<arguments>` is the list of parameters you want to specify.

To execute the RDT on UNIX, run the following command:

```
.<INSTALLDIR>/sap_bobj/enterprise_xi40/<platform>/boe_
reposcan.sh <arguments>
```

In this command, `<platform>` is either `linux_x64`, `solaris_sparcv9`, `hpux_ia64`, or `aix_rs6000_64`, and `<arguments>` is the list of parameters you want to specify.

The arguments you can (or must) specify are shown in Table 8.3.

Parameter	Optional or Mandatory	Description
dbdriver	Mandatory	Type of driver used to connect to the CMS database. Following are the accepted values: ▶ db2databasesubsystem ▶ maxdbdatabasesubsystem ▶ mysqldatabasesubsystem ▶ oracledatabasesubsystem ▶ sqlserverdatabasesubsystem ▶ sybasedatabasesubsystem
connect	Mandatory	The connection details that are used to connect to the CMS database. For example: -connect "UID=root;PWD=<pass- word>;DSN=<dsn>; HOSTNAME=<host- name>;PORT=<portnumber>"

Table 8.3 Arguments in the RDT (Source: Repository Diagnostic Tool User Guide 4.0)

Parameter	Optional or Mandatory	Description
dbkey	Mandatory	Enter the cluster key for your SAP Business-Objects platform deployment.
inputfrsdir	Mandatory	The file path of the input File Repository Server (iFRS). Be sure that the user account you're logged in as has full control of the file location.
outputfrsdir	Mandatory	The file path of the output File Repository Server (oFRS). Be sure that the user account you're logged in as has full control of the file location.
outputdir	Optional	The file path where the RDT will write its log files.
count	Optional	The number of approximate errors to scan. This can help performance. The default value is 0, which means the entire repository.
repair	Optional	Tells the RDT to repair all inconsistencies it may find. The default behavior is to only report inconsistencies and not to perform any repairs. If the -repair parameter exists in the command line, the RDT reports and repairs all inconsistencies. This process will delete any orphaned objects or files in the repository database.
scanfrs	Optional	Specifies whether the RDT scans the CMS and FRS for inconsistencies. Acceptable values are True and False. Default value is True.
scancms	Optional	Specifies whether the RDT scans the CMS for inconsistencies between InfoObjects. Acceptable values are True and False. Default value is True.

Table 8.3 Arguments in the RDT (Source: Repository Diagnostic Tool User Guide 4.0) (Cont.)

Parameter	Optional or Mandatory	Description
submitterid	Optional	Specifies the user ID to replace missing or invalid IDs for scheduled objects. If no value is provided, the RDT doesn't replace invalid IDs. If the provided user ID doesn't exist in the CMS, the RDT prompts for a valid ID. This parameter is only used when the RDT operates in REPAIR mode.
started	Optional	Specifies the object in the CMS database to start the scan for. For example, if you've already scanned the first 500 objects in your repository, you can set the -startid=501 to start a new scan on the 501st object. The default value is 1.
optionsfile	Optional	Specifies the file path to the parameter file. The parameter file is a text file that lists each command-line option and its values. The file should have one parameter per line. With this option, you can set all the parameters in a text file as described previously. Use this option to point to a parameter file without entering the parameters on the command line.
syscopy	Optional	This parameter is used when you copy the repository database. You must run the tool on the newly created copy, which will update the copy to prevent it from clustering with the source system servers. If the copy won't be able to communicate with the source system, this isn't necessary. It should only be used with the mandatory parameters and not be combined with other optional parameters in this list. Be careful not to run the RDT with the syscopy parameter on your source system.

Table 8.3 Arguments in the RDT (Source: Repository Diagnostic Tool User Guide 4.0) (Cont.)

Parameter	Optional or Mandatory	Description
`requestport`	Optional	The port number that the RDT uses to communicate with the CMS. Accepts whole, positive numbers. By default, the tool uses the value from the OS of the machine the RDT is running on.
`numericip`	Optional	Whether the RDT users the numeric IP address instead of the host name for communication between the CMS and the machine the RDT is running on. Acceptable values are `True` and `False`. Default is `True`.
`ipv6`	Optional	The `ipv6` name of the machine the RDT is running on. Accepts a string. Default value is the host name of the machine the RDT is running on.
`port`	Optional	The `ipv4` name of the machine the RDT is running on. Accepts a string. Default value is the host name of the machine the RDT is running on.
`threads`	Optional	The number of threads to use. Accepts whole, positive values. Default value is `12`.
`protocol`	Optional	Specifies whether the tool should run in SSL mode. The only accepted value is `ssl`.
`ssl_certdir`	Optional	The directory that contains the SSL certificates.
`ssl_trusted-certificate`	Optional	The file name of the certificate.
`ssl_mycerti-ficate`	Optional	The file name of the signed certificate.
`ssl_mykey`	Optional	The file name of the file that contains the private SSL key.
`ssl_mykey_passphrase`	Optional	The file name that contains the SSL passphrase.

Table 8.3 Arguments in the RDT (Source: Repository Diagnostic Tool User Guide 4.0) (Cont.)

There exists a very detailed, living document on the SAP Community Network that goes through the Repository Diagnostic Tool in great detail. You can find this wiki page at *http://wiki.scn.sap.com/wiki/pages/viewpage.action?pageId=143065487*.

The RDT is a helpful tool that will scan your CMS database and FRS file store and find and/or repair any inconsistencies that may exist between the two. The RDT is run from the command line and requires several mandatory arguments to work properly. Use the RDT as a standard every time you have to do a restore or disaster recovery. It can help you save time by finding those pesky inconsistencies before your users do.

Pop Quiz

1. True or False: The timing of backups for the file stores and the CMS database is irrelevant.
2. Describe the characteristics of a cold backup.
3. True or False: Incremental recoveries from a tape backup are advisable.
4. The Repository Diagnostic Tool scans for _____ .

8.8   Troubleshooting and Maintenance Best Practices

Take a few minutes and read through this list of best practices, or just overall good ideas. These are things we've learned from years on the job as SAP BusinessObjects BI administrators. These things can help you in your time of need. Go ahead and poach these ideas; they're yours for the taking:

▶ Make a diagram of your major application tiers that includes actual server names. Keep this handy so that when things break, you have an at-a-glance guide to help you zero in on the error. If all of those servers aren't under your control, add names and contact numbers to your diagram as well—"If web server 01 breaks, call John Smith at x4242," for example. This is also great when you head off for your well-deserved vacation to hand to your backup, who might not be as familiar with the systems as you are.

▶ Nearly everyone knows how to take a screenshot these days. Make it a standard in your organization that whenever possible, users provide you with a screenshot of the error messages they get. A user paraphrasing an error message is decidedly less helpful.

▶ When you're facing an incident that is stopping your users from working, whether it's a development or testing environment, or especially if it's a production environment, open a support ticket with SAP Support as your first action. You can always start working the problem yourself while you wait for SAP Support to call, but often you'll want to know the cavalry is coming to help you out when you're knee-deep in the soup.

▶ Establish service level agreements (SLAs) with your customers wherever possible. SLAs can help calm frayed nerves in a crisis. Nothing is worse than trying to work a critical outage and having the customers constantly wanting status updates. Let them know what to expect in your SLA. For example, "When a production system goes down, we'll provide 24-hour support until the issue is resolved. A high-priority support ticket will be opened with SAP immediately, and status updates will be sent by the incident manager hourly."

▶ Designate a substitute for your inbox in the SAP Support Portal when you're going on vacation. Even administrators need a break from time to time. Let your backup work your open tickets for you while you take a breather.

▶ Bookmark the SAP Support Portal and SAP Help Portal in your favorite web browsers. You'll be spending a lot of time there, so keep them somewhere handy so you don't have to go searching for them.

▶ Set up single sign-on for your login to the SAP Support Portal. If you don't want to, go ahead and try to use it without for a few times. Trust us on this one.

▶ Start every support ticket in the SAP Support Portal with the following standard information: your environment details (version, platform, patch level, application server, system database platform and version, etc.), your contact details (name, phone number, email address, time zone), and the best time you can be reached. Then, go into describing your issue. It may seem redundant, but trust us on this one, too.

▶ Whenever you have an error or outage on a production server, the first thing you should do is open a support ticket with SAP Support. Do that first, then start working the problem. It will take some time, even for the highest-priority tickets, to get assigned to an engineer. You might as well spend your wait time working the problem, so when the engineer does call you, you have some more information to give him. It also helps to get an SAP engineer on your team quickly, so if things progress for an extended period of time, you have expert help.

▶ Turn on high-level trace logs when you can repeat your error. Get the error captured in your trace logs, and then turn the high-level trace back off. Backup the log files that were generated during the trace session to a different directory.

You can then zip them up with your favorite compression tool and attach them to your SAP Support case. SAP Support engineers love trace logs (LOL). Seriously.

▶ If you choose to be brave and analyze trace logs on your own, remember that they have a specific naming convention, and they are a linear record of all actions taken by that particular server. Search for a key word that indicates something went wrong, and then step up line by line until you find something that caused the issue.

▶ Check your operating system logs at least weekly during normal operations. Check them immediately if you are having troubles. These logs contain things from the operating system's perspective and often have blinding insight into what is going on.

▶ Despite what any marketing material might tell you, patches and upgrades are disruptive to your SAP BusinessObjects BI 4.1 system. Test them out on a development or sandbox server first if you're lucky enough to have one. Make sure you have a test plan to implement and thoroughly check the system out after the patch has been applied.

▶ Applying patches to your SAP BusinessObjects BI 4.1 system is more about planning than it is about patching. Plan your outage window, plan your backup and recovery strategy, plan your post-patch testing, and plan your patch deployment strategy. Plan, plan, plan! And be ready to back out if things get ugly.

▶ Practice restoring from backup from time to time. This will help you assess the quality of your backups and give you practice in all of the quirks and nuances involved in the process. Know the difference between a restore and a disaster recovery, and know how to do both. When you're in the middle of a crisis that requires recovery, it's not the time to practice.

▶ Use the Central Configuration Manager to backup server configuration settings to a BIAR file before and after every system change you make. That includes adding nodes or services, and especially applying patches or upgrades.

▶ Learn how to use the RDT and make it a regular part of your operations when you do a content restore.

▶ Zip up and backup your log files on a periodic basis. Log files can needlessly consume precious disk space.

▶ Set limits on your users' personal folders and public folders alike so they can't grow to ridiculous and often unused sizes.

▸ Remember, always, you don't just troubleshoot and tune an SAP BusinessObjects BI system once. It's an ongoing and critical responsibility for the SAP BusinessObjects BI administrator.

8.9   Summary

This is a doozy of a chapter. But troubleshooting and maintenance are the core of what you'll be doing as an SAP BusinessObjects BI administrator. Remember, first and foremost, you're not alone. Use those other resources available to you to get help when you need it, especially leveraging SAP Support (because you're likely paying for it). Open up a support ticket in parallel with any of your own troubleshooting efforts until you get to the point where you're more comfortable handling issues on your own. Even after you learn more, only spend an hour or so trying to figure out a problem on your own; then, go open up a support ticket.

If you have a pesky problem, and the error message isn't helpful, enable your trace logs and capture the problem in action. Those trace logs should be sent to SAP Support, but don't be afraid to dig through the trace logs yourself. We showed you how.

Conduct your periodic maintenance to keep your system humming along as clean and as smooth as possible. This involves watching your instances and inboxes, along with keeping up your system log files. And, don't forget the lessons from Chapter 2 about sizing. Periodically rerun your sizing exercise, and make sure you aren't running out of capacity as well.

And, to round things out, you'll invariably have to apply a patch, service pack, or upgrade to your SAP BusinessObjects BI 4.1 system. Patching is more about planning than executing. Make sure you have your backups, and practice restoring those backups once in a while. You should also practice running the RDT from time to time, so you know how to use it when you really need it. Remember, the midst of a crisis isn't the time to practice doing a system recovery.

All in all, maintaining an SAP BusinessObjects BI 4.1 environment will be the bulk of your tasks as an administrator. The more you practice and learn, the better at it you'll become.

Apparently, mobility is the new big thing. In this chapter, we'll introduce you to the SAP BusinessObjects Mobile solution.

9 SAP BusinessObjects Mobile: Taking It on the Road

Mobility in the business intelligence space is far from a constant today. As we write this chapter, SAP's "mobile first" message is very pervasive and beginning to emerge as fact versus fiction. By the time this chapter gets through final edits and out to publishing, you may very well find that it has gone through even more metamorphosis. As a matter of fact, between the time it took for this book to get from concept for the first edition of this book, to table of contents, to written text, it changed again. The same is true based on when we agreed to write a second edition until now. Buckle up. Here we go. Stay close to us.

This chapter will use a broad brush to illustrate the new and improved deployment mechanism for mobile for your SAP BusinessObjects BI environment, the way we configure it now (hint: it's a vast improvement), and finally, how we actually get SAP BusinessObjects Mobile BI in our users' hands. As if that weren't enough, we'll try to connect some dots on common troubleshooting approaches to keep mobile users in motion. You'll find that the SAP BusinessObjects Mobile app has become the "one app to rule them all," taking on the needs of SAP BusinessObjects Web Intelligence, SAP Crystal Reports, SAP BusinessObjects Explorer, SAP Dashboards, and SAP Lumira all in one app.

9.1 Supported Mobile Platforms

If you've kept up with the mobile technology supported by Business Objects, pre-SAP, you know that the actual mobile solutions available within the past five years have changed the way we interact with our phones. The arrival of the iPhone, arguably the turning point in the usage of mobile technologies, has fostered much-needed innovation in the support of mobile business intelligence applications that support not only the iOS platform (thanks, Steve), but also Android-based devices as well.

Heading back over to our trusty pal, the Product Availability Matrix (PAM), we need to seriously consider the supported platforms for SAP BusinessObjects BI 4.1. It's worth noting that in atypical deployments, it may very well be required to stand up additional servers in this environment to support the mobile components, whether it's due to sizing considerations already assumed for the base product, OS, or web tier requirements to support SAP BusinessObjects Mobile. Before we move on, we should note that as of the writing of this chapter, the SAP BusinessObjects BI 4.1 PAM is available and referenced here. Let's dig in, shall we?

First and foremost, as your organization is selecting a device standard for mobility, there is a broad field to choose from that comes with a varying user experience. BlackBerry devices, the granddad of the mobile platforms, have been around for many years, and penetration within enterprise customers is high. However, user experience suffers based on the dreaded click wheel, historically. As of the publication of this book, we've not been able to interact with SAP BusinessObjects BI Mobile on any of the more modern BlackBerry devices. On the other hand, handheld devices with interactive screens offer a richer way to interface with reports, which, in addition, creates a more elegant user experience.

Enterprise standards will dictate device selection, more often than not. But, there are strong arguments made in each camp. This is a discussion to be had by you, your SAP BusinessObjects BI architect (if not you), your enterprise/strategic architect, your network architect, your chief security expert, and the mobility guru in your organization. Why all of those people?

▶ The enterprise/strategic architect is responsible for overall technology decisions, and a mobile device strategy is a big one.

▶ The network architect knows the ins and outs of mobile device traffic both internally via Wi-Fi and externally via the Internet.

▶ The security expert understands what organizational policies exist for mobile device security, remote network access, and more.

> ▸ Your mobility guru must be current on mobile technologies and how they interface with all the various layers of enterprise architecture, and must also know how to support them.

Above all, remember that *you* are a driver for change here and a champion for your end users' requirements. If your organization doesn't already have a mobile device strategy, this is a good reason to start. (That's for another book; for example, pick up *Mobilizing Your Enterprise with SAP* [SAP PRESS, 2012].)

With all of that, let's consider mobile device support in this first look at the PAM. However, before we do, we have to make another important note, and that is a mention of the change in direction that SAP has taken with the mobile platform. The components for mobility are now covered within the SAP BusinessObjects BI 4.1 PAM.

The big driver for this, as we'll talk about in a bit, is that we no longer have to deal with managing stand-alone mobile servers. Thanks to the Sybase Unwired Platform, the deployment has become loads easier. For now, let's go over the PAM in Figure 9.1.

SAP BusinessObjects Mobile Clients
Supported Platforms (SAP BusinessObjects BI)

Mobile Client	Mobile Client Version	Mobile Client Platform	Mobile Client Platform Version(s)	Sybase Mobile Platform Version(s)	Mobile BI Server Version(s)
SAP BusinessObjects Mobile	5.0(*1)	Blackberry	4.7-6.0	N/A(*2)	BI 4.1 and Edge BI 4.1
SAP BusinessObjects Mobile SAP BusinessObjects Mobile iOS SDK	6.0.3	iOS	iOS 6-iOS 7	SUP 2.1 and above	XI 3.1 and Edge XI 3.1: SP03 FP6 and above / BI 4.0 and Edge BI 4.0: SP02 and above / BI 4.1 and Edge BI 4.1 / Crystal Reports Server XI 3.1: SP03 FP6 and above / Crystal Server 2011: SP02 and above / Crystal Server 2013
SAP BusinessObjects Mobile SAP BusinessObjects Mobile Android SDK	6.0.0	Android	4.0.3-4.4	SUP 2.1 and above	BI 4.0 and Edge BI 4.0: SP02 Patch 13 and above / BI 4.1 and Edge BI 4.1
SAP BusinessObjects Explorer	4.1.10	iOS	iOS 6-iOS 7	N/A(*2)	XI 3.2 and Edge XI 3.2: SP4 and above / BI 4.0 and Edge BI 4.0: SP2 and above / BI 4.1 and Edge BI 4.1

Based on the backend server version, the features supported will be different. Please read the admin guide for the features that will be supported with different versions of backend servers

(*1) SAP BusinessObjects Mobile Client for Blackberry is shipped along with the respective BI Platform for versions below BI 4.1

(*2) The connection based on Sybase Mobile Platform is not supported

Figure 9.1 The PAM for Mobile Technologies in All Its Glory

The great news is that historical support for RIM, iOS, and Android devices is still there, tried, and true. Interestingly absent are the Windows Mobile and Sybian devices. Perhaps, this is a sign of the reality of the mobile market today. SAP BusinessObjects Mobile does continue to dominate from a feature and version perspective on iOS (the way Steve would have wanted it).

The operating system support for SAP BusinessObjects Mobile, shown in Figure 9.2, does require you to pay close attention in decentralized web tier architectures or within environments not running Windows at all. Any flavor of Linux or UNIX will be off limits prior to SAP BusinessObjects BI 4.1. SAP BusinessObjects BI 4.1 caught up on support for other operating systems for mobile. Is that all bad? This should not be considered a showstopper. If your environment has standardized on these distributions in any way, this is another great example of where virtualization can be your friend.

SAP BusinessObjects BI Platform 4.1
Server Components by Operating System

	Windows (*1)				Linux			AIX		Solaris	
	Server 2008 x64	Server 2008 R2 x64	Server 2012	Server 2012 R2	Suse SLES 11 x86_64	Red Hat EL 5 x86_64	Red Hat EL 6 x86_64	AIX 6.1 Power	AIX 7.1 Power	Solaris 10 SPARC	Solaris 11 SPARC
64-bit BusinessObjects BI Server Products	SP2	SP1			(*2)	Update 3 (*2)	Update 2 (*2)	TL6	TL1 SP1		
SAP BusinessObjects BI platform	✓	✓	✓	SP02+ (*6)	✓	✓	✓	✓	✓	✓	✓
SAP BusinessObjects Analysis, edition for OLAP	✓	✓	✓	SP02+ (*6)	✓	✓	✓	✓	✓	✓	✓
SAP BusinessObjects Explorer	✓	✓	✓	SP02+ (*6)	✓	✓	✓	✓	✓	✓	✓
SAP BusinessObjects Web Intelligence	✓	✓	✓	SP02+ (*6)	✓	✓	✓	✓	✓	✓	✓
SAP Crystal Reports for Enterprise	✓	✓	✓	SP02+ (*6)	✓	✓	✓	✓	✓	✓	✓
SAP Crystal Reports 2013	✓	✓	✓	SP02+ (*6)	✓	✓	SP01+	✓	✓	✓	✓
SAP BusinessObjects Dashboards	✓	✓	✓	SP02+ (*6)	✓	✓	✓	✓	✓	✓	✓
Mobile Server (*4)	✓	✓	✓	SP02+ (*6)	✓	✓	✓	✓	✓	✓	(*5)

- SAP BusinessObjects BI server components only support 64-bit operating systems. This is not a complete list of platform/connectivity services
- (*1) Data Center Edition, Enterprise Edition, Standard Edition, Web Edition.
- (*2) Minor versions of RHEL 5/6 and SPs of SLES 11 above the minimum supported versions listed on this slide are supported by reference. Refer to Page 25 of this document for more information about minimum OS patch requirements for Linux.
- (*4) Operating systems support applies to both Mobile server (<MobileBIservice.war>) and Mobile OTA (<MobileOTA.war>) required for over-the-air download of the Mobile client onto the mobile devices.
- (*5) Mobile Server support for Solaris 11 is planned for a later SP.
- (*6) Windows Server 2012 R2 is supported for server components as of BI 4.1 SP02; please note that IE11 is supported only as of BI 4.1 SP03.

Figure 9.2 OS Support for Mobile Devices

Consider it a best practice that your mobile servers *should* stand on a distinct environment in a perfect world. Let that mobile HTTP traffic funnel from independent mobile servers from the rest of your presentation layer traffic. Your visitors can still reference SAP BusinessObjects Mobile from a separate load-balanced DNS address to access independently of the BI Launch Pad traffic. Remember, this isn't a bad thing.

Another relevant area to focus on is the Java Application Server support (see Figure 9.3). While there is broad support, there are minor nuances in support required for SAP BusinessObjects Mobile. Again, this isn't to be considered a catastrophe if you've already standardized in another path. Consider virtualization or stand-alone mobile nodes in your cluster to support this deployment.

SAP BusinessObjects BI Platform 4.1
Java Application Server Support by Operating System [1/2]

The platforms on this slide are supported as application servers. For more information, please refer to the Web Application Deployment Guide.

See next slide for footnotes 2-3 and explanations on how to read the table.

Application Server (*2)	Version	Java Version	Windows Server Oracle/Sun JDK	Linux Oracle/Sun JDK	AIX IBM Java	Solaris Oracle/Sun JDK
JBoss Application Server (*1)	7.1.1 (*1)	Java 6, Java 7	✓	✓	✓	✓
SAP NetWeaver Java Application Server	7.3, 7.31 SP4+	SAP JVM 6.1 (*3)	✓	✓	✓	✓
	7.40 SP2+	SAP JVM 6.1 (*3)	SP01+	SP01+	SP01+	SP01+
Apache Tomcat	6.0.20	Java 6, Java 7	✓	✓	✓	✓
	7.0	Java 6, Java 7 (*6)	✓	✓	✓	✓
Oracle WebLogic Server	10.3.5	Java 6	✓	✓	✓	✓
		JRockit 6.0	✓	✓	-	✓
	10.3.6	Java 6, Java 7	✓	✓	✓	✓
		JRockit 6.0	✓	✓	-	✓
IBM WebSphere Application Server	7.0.0.11	Java 6 (*2)	✓	✓	✓	✓
	8.5 (*4) (*5)	Java 6, Java 7 (*2)	✓	✓	✓	✓
	8.5.5 (*4) (*5)	Java 6, Java 7 (*2)	SP02+	SP02+	SP02+	SP02+

(*1) JBoss Application Server 7.1.1 is supported for pre-deploy only and is not visible as an option in the Wdeploy GUI.
(*2 - *3) See next page.
(*4) Support for the WebSphere On Demand Router is described in SAP Note 1869511.
(*5) The WAS Liberty Profile is not supported.
(*6) Apache Tomcat 7 is also supported with SAP JVM 6.1 on all supported operating systems.

Note: Any HTTP server supported by the application server vendor can be used with the supported application server

Figure 9.3 Java Application Support

Pop Quiz

1. True or False: You should deploy SAP BusinessObjects Mobile on Solaris because it's the most stable platform available to date for this technology.

2. Name the two mobile technologies that support the iOS platform.

3. What online guide provides instruction on the supported technologies for SAP BusinessObjects Mobile?

9.2   Installation and Deployment of SAP BusinessObjects Mobile

We hinted in Section 9.1 that SAP did something awesome with mobile in SAP BusinessObjects BI with the implementation of the Sybase Unwired Platform. If you ever deployed mobile prior to SAP BusinessObjects BI 4.0, particularly for anything other than iOS-based devices, you ran into the brick wall that was configuring the VAS and VMS servers. This deployment required a great deal of complex configuration file editing, trial, and error.

SAP got it right with SAP BusinessObjects BI 4.0 by making the Sybase Unwired Platform and a simple Web Archive (WAR) file deployment the new bar for ease of installation for its mobile products (see Figure 9.4).

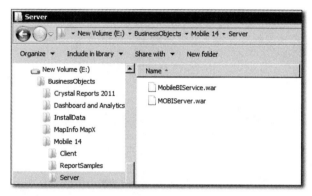

Figure 9.4 WAR File Deployment

This directory structure should seem familiar to you. This path is where you'd commonly find the VAS and VMS configuration servers. Not anymore. Today, we're presented with the two WAR files we are to deploy in our application server. Yep. Seriously. That's it. In SAP BusinessObjects BI 4.1, this path is empty. Instead, back during our installation, we had the choice to automatically deploy the WAR files during the installer. If you were paying attention, this will save you steps and start you out with a mobile-ready SAP BusinessObjects BI 4.1 landscape!

In the case of SAP BusinessObjects BI 4.1, our local build is still in the same path as SAP BusinessObjects BI 4.0 in *e:\BusinessObjects\Tomcat6*. The only step required for an out-of-the-box deployment is to copy these two WAR files into the *webapps* folder. Tomcat here is smart enough to deploy those WAR files on the fly and leave you with a working mobile deployment.

Now that each server is deployed, some configurations can be made to both the MobileBIService and MOBIServer specifically. When we first encountered the new SAP BusinessObjects Mobile in SAP BusinessObjects BI 4.0, we were handed a stack of configuration files and asked to go manage them. SAP did good things in SAP BusinessObjects BI 4.1, and those settings are now in the CMC. For the purposes of helping out those still stuck on SAP BusinessObjects BI 4.0, those configurations remain intact here. The new CMC specifications will follow.

MobileBIService

The first file encountered for fine-tuning is the *clientsettings.properties* file. Simply put, this file is used to define the mobile client-side parameters that are set to enforce security on the mobile device. The security requirements imposed by your security guru and network architect will help in defining the configuration in this file (see Listing 9.1).

```
# This file should be modified carefully with the settings defined in
# SAP BusinessObjects Mobile Administration guide.
#
savePassword=false
offlineStorage=false
offlineStorage.ttl=365
offlineStorage.appPwd=true
```

Listing 9.1 clientsettings.properties File

The *mobi.properties* file, conversely, contains application-specific configurations for the mobile server itself (see Listing 9.2). While many of the default properties will suffice, the best property of all in this file is the ability to fine-tune the categories used to display mobile content. No more sticking everything in a "Mobile" category.

```
# This is a configuration file for Mobi. This file should
# be carefully edited.


#
# Definition of 'Mobile-ready' documents for different request sources
#
# <requestSrc>.corporateCategory=cat1,cat2
# <requestSrc>.personalCategory=personalCat1,personalCat2
#
```

```
# Only documents that belong to the specified categories will be
# returned for a particular requestSrc.
# If the entries for a particular requestSrc is missing, then the
# values mentioned for "default" requestSrc will be used.
#
#
# Define the report format in which you need to get it from the server.
# Provide different options for page mode and
# output type for the data.
#
#
# Valid values for requestSrc are:
#        default, iphone, ipad, bbphone, bbtablet, androidphone,
#        androidtablet
#
#


#default
default.corporateCategory=Mobile
default.personalCategory=Mobile
default.category.mobileDesigned=MobileDesigned
default.category.secure=Confidential
default.docTypes=Webi,CrystalReport
default.imageSize=100000
default.lov.size.limit=50
default.search.resultsPerPage=10
default.search.maxDocuments=500
default.search.maxInstanceOfDocument=5
default.map.rootnode.prefix=$a_root_
default.map.node.prefix=$a_
default.save.maxPages=20
default.discover.maxrows=100




#ipad
ipad.corporateCategory=Mobile
ipad.personalCategory=Mobile
ipad.category.mobileDesigned=MobileDesigned
ipad.category.secure=Confidential
ipad.pagemode=true
ipad.outputDataType=convertChartToTable
ipad.docTypes=Webi,CrystalReport


#iphone
iphone.corporateCategory=Mobile
iphone.personalCategory=Mobile
```

```
iphone.pagemode=true
iphone.outputDataType=convertChartToTable
iphone.docTypes=Webi,CrystalReport


#blackberry mobile
bbphone.pagemode=false
bbphone.outputDataType=XML


#blackberry Tablet
bbtablet.pagemode=false
bbtablet.outputDataType=XML
```
Listing 9.2 mobi.properties File

The *sso.properties* file doesn't get much easier (see Listing 9.3). With support for one or more CMS clusters with trusted authentication enabled, the mobile server can be configured to allow for Single Sign-On (SSO).

```
# This is a configuration file for setting up trusted authentication
# between Mobi Server and BOE Server
#
# Administrator first needs to enable trusted authentication on
# BOE server, then download the shared secret and maintain it as
# follows
#
# cms1.aliases = <IP Address 1>, <Qualified Name 1>, <Alias 1>
# cms1.secret  = <Shared Secret Key 1>
#
# cms2.aliases = <IP Address 2>, <Qualified Name 2>, <Alias 2>
# cms2.secret  = <Shared Secret Key 2>
```
Listing 9.3 sso.properties File

Finally, the *sup.properties* file provides integration to the existing Sybase Unwired Platform for integrated authentication (see Listing 9.4).

```
#This file must have the following lines for each supported
#SUP Security Configuration:
# <SecurityConfigName_as_defined_in_SUP>.cms=xxxx
# <SecurityConfigName_as_defined_in_SUP>.auth=[secEnterprise|secWinAD|
    secLDAP|secSAPR3]
#
# example:
#
# MobiSec.cms=11.22.33.44
# MobiSec.auth=secEnterprise
#
```

```
# MobiSecAnother.cms=myserver.company.com
# MobiSecAnother.auth=secLDAP
#
```
Listing 9.4 sup.properties File

MOBIServer

The MOBIServer contains one properties file for configuration to provide default connections for the mobile device that can be imported to the iPad application (see Listing 9.5).

```
#
 This file is used to configure connections for import from the client.
# Please refer to the product documentation on syntax for the same.


# Sample:
#
# mobi.connections=sampleconnection
# sampleconnection.displayname=sample
# sampleconnection.serverURL=http://experience.sap.com/explorer/
#
#
#mobi.connections=connection1,connection2
#
#connection1.DisplayName=Sample
#connection1.BOBJ_MOBILE_USER_NAME=Sample
#connection1.BOBJ_MOBILE_URL=http://11.22.33.44:8080
#connection1.BOBJ_MOBILE_CMS=55.66.77.88
#connection1.BOBJ_MOBILE_AUTH_METHOD=secEnterprise
#
#connection2.DisplayName=Sample
#connection2.BOBJ_MOBILE_USER_NAME=Sample
#connection2.BOBJ_MOBILE_URL=http://11.22.33.44:8080
#connection2.BOBJ_MOBILE_CMS=55.66.77.88
#connection2.BOBJ_MOBILE_AUTH_METHOD=secEnterprise
```
Listing 9.5 MOBIServer Properties File

Application Settings for SAP BusinessObjects Mobile in SAP BusinessObjects BI 4.1

Still unworthy of a coveted spot on the Central Management Console home page, SAP BusinessObjects Mobile is relegated to the Applications section of the CMC. That's OK SAP BusinessObjects Mobile, we still love you. We especially love that

SAP cared enough to axe a significant number of the settings covered in the properties files of the SAP BusinessObjects BI 4.0 days and wrap them into configuration screens. While almost there, these screens simply encapsulate the settings for the *clientsettings.properties* file (see Figure 9.5) and the *mobi.properties* file (see Figure 9.6).

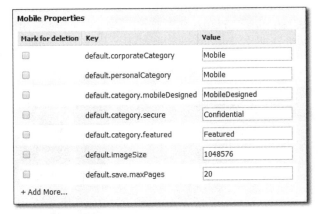

Figure 9.5 mobi.properties File with a Frontend

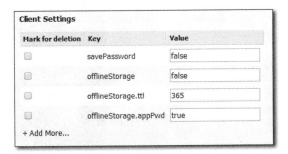

Figure 9.6 clientsettings.properties File with a Frontend

Pop Quiz

1. What is the new technology used to support mobility in the SAP BusinessObjects BI 4.0 platform forward?

2. True or False: The VMS and VAS services require hours of configuration to support SAP BusinessObjects Mobile.

9.3   Configuring Mobile Devices

The simplicity of defining a server deployment for a mobile server is complemented nicely, for example, in the configuration of an iPad with the mobile server.

The device connection itself provides common logon attributes to the BI Launch Pad (when enabled) or the CMC, shown in Figure 9.7. If not already shared with the device owner, the only fields of any complexity to guide the users through are SERVER URL and CMS NAME.

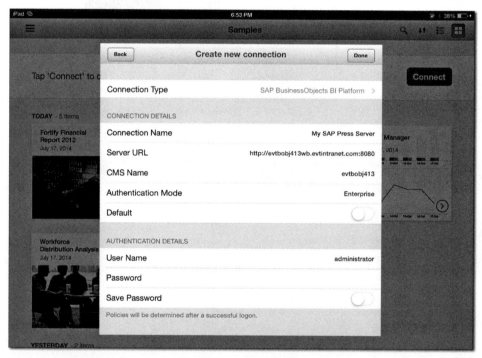

Figure 9.7 Create New Connection Screen for SAP BusinessObjects Mobile

The SERVER URL should reflect the absolute URL of your server, including the relevant port (if not using standard port 80 or 443). The CMS NAME should reflect the CMS host name for your CMS cluster.

With that, in conjunction with the user's user name and password (and appropriate authentication type), the user may now create a connection to the SAP BusinessObjects BI 4.1 environment and any reports accessible in the assigned categories.

Figure 9.8 shows an example of user functionality to set up disconnected/local reports, where the content can be browsed and selected on device without being connected to the SAP BusinessObjects BI landscape.

Figure 9.8 Downloading Reports from the SAP BusinessObjects BI Landscape

The compelling part about using SAP BusinessObjects Mobile in this way is that a Web Intelligence report can drive a display on the device that provides a richer experience by leveraging the multitouch features of the device (see Figure 9.9).

Chart/table components of the dashboard may respond to touch and, in addition, provide deeper drill levels that expand the chart view into a larger focus or even enable interactivity similar to input controls in Web Intelligence (see Figure 9.10).

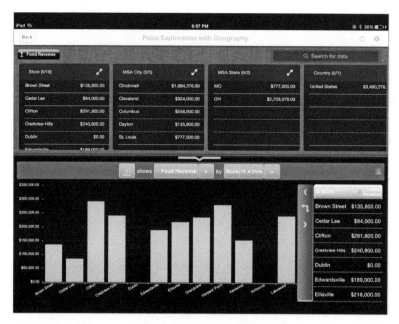

Figure 9.9 An Interactive Mobile Information Space

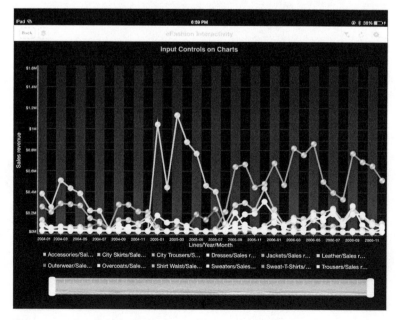

Figure 9.10 A Mobile Web Intelligence Report Drill-Down

One of the striking things about the configuration files for the new mobile server, the documentation, and the applications being released for mobile is that iOS support is the most robust (and arguably attractive) deployment option, from both an ease-of-use perspective and a capability perspective.

For more on device-specific configuration for RIM or Android-based devices, we recommend that you refer to the specific deployment guide for that device. Similar to the iPad, these guides will contain specific device and report-configuration instructions to optimize the experience on each type of device.

> **Note**
>
> A fuller discussion is beyond the scope of this book, but a full capability list for customizing Web Intelligence reports for the iPad is available in the *Administrator and Report Designer's Guide for SAP BusinessObjects Mobile* for iPad 4.1.0, or greater.

9.4   Troubleshooting SAP BusinessObjects Mobile

The marketing firm 11Mark surveyed 1,000 Americans and found that 75% of them admitted to using smartphones while using the restroom. The first piece of advice before you troubleshoot SAP BusinessObjects Mobile is, for the love of all things, wear rubber gloves when you touch someone else's phone. Second, if troubleshooting connectivity because someone dropped his device in the commode, *don't touch it.*

Kidding aside, there are some logical steps to debugging mobility issues inside the SAP BusinessObjects BI platform:

▸ Get back to the most basic of security and access configurations before any others are tested. In other words, does the wireless device work on the internal network (versus extranet/external connections), and will it work with SAP BusinessObjects BI authentication? If you can't confirm that those two scenarios are functional, you should probably get back to the basics and ensure it's working there first.

▸ Is it an authentication error with Active Directory, LDAP, or SAP authentication? Validate that those authentication types work for the BI Launch Pad or the CMC for starters, and debug if necessary.

▶ Does the mobile device have trouble communicating with the SAP BusinessObjects Mobile server via the intranet? Have you validated that other devices can, in fact, utilize the mobile servers?

▶ For externally accessing devices, can the device reach other internal servers (such as—in a most basic test—the BI Launch Pad) in a web browser?

We should mention at this point that this is (obviously) not an exhaustive list. However, the goal here is to get your creative juices flowing as to where you should begin to debug. That is a totally valid cop-out because every customer's architecture is different. If you haven't already referenced your architecture diagram and started looking for faults, this is your first chance. We'll also suggest that the SAP Community Network wiki has an evolving set of troubleshooting pages centered on SAP BusinessObjects Mobile applications.

This chapter hasn't delved into the depths of the various network architecture options that exist for deploying mobile products. Going back to our cast of players from Chapter 1, the network administrator will play a critical role in helping you understand the resources and capabilities of your network, as well as the standards for letting traffic through the various firewalls and DMZs in your infrastructure. Now, would be a good time to buy him that coffee he is due.

9.5   Summary

You should be excited that your organization has made the leap into mobility. While it may seem like just another platform to manage, mobility is highly likely to be the future of business intelligence. Our friend Donald MacCormick made a very astute observation about the future of SAP BusinessObjects BI applications:

> *Your operational business people (who are in the majority in all organizations) are just the same [Donald is referring to an example of doctors consuming data from an application], they need easy-to-use, no-training-required interfaces to the data they need to do their jobs. These are what I call BI apps, and I am certain that they are the next evolution of dashboards.*

Wow. Did you catch that? The idea is that the majority of users (we can argue this has been said for years) only want to consume content. We've tried for years to get users to do this through simply viewing a Web Intelligence report in a web browser. But, with the number of people in the world with a smartphone growing every day, and your own device policies becoming pervasive in many work-forces, it's hard to ignore the fact that we can give our users access to real data in an easily consumable fashion on mobile devices now. The message here is *embrace mobile now*. It's coming whether you expect it to or not.

Congratulations—you're among the first in the world to be deploying SAP BusinessObjects on the Sybase Unwired Platform. And for the rest of the world, you're blazing new trails.

You've got your system sized, installed, configured, and secured, and you're totally on top of the monitoring and troubleshooting thing. Now how do you make it pretty?

10 Customization and Enhancement: SAP BusinessObjects BI Colors Are Boring

First things first—we don't want you to put this chapter down and think: "By golly I'm not a report developer. I don't need this stuff." This is especially true because *everybody* says that in our line of work. To be a great administrator, it's truly important to grasp that you may be asked to support customizations to Web Intelligence reports, to Crystal reports, to dashboards, and to the BI Launch Pad.

In this chapter, we'll introduce you to the basics of doing this. You'll learn that reports come with a host of properties and layout options that allow you to include style sheet references. You'll also learn that you can modify the style sheet and images in your BI Launch Pad. Finally, we'll conclude with some general recommendations about when to use software development kits (SDKs).

Further References

This chapter is only an introduction to the basic concepts behind SAP BusinessObjects BI customization for an administrator. SAP has gone to significant, new lengths to make the deployment and customization of SAP BusinessObjects BI a tailored fit for customers. For more information on this topic, we recommend two SAP guides:

▶ **SAP BusinessObjects Original Equipment Manufacturer (OEM) Customization Guide for SAP BusinessObjects BI 4.0 customers or the SAP BusinessObjects BI Customization Guide for SAP BusinessObjects BI 4.1 customers**
The OEM guide was originally for SAP partners that have a solution which bundles SAP BusinessObjects BI but has information about the programmer's approach to updating the look and feel of the platform. There's a lot of material in here that is specific to creating a customized delivery of both the software and the branding SAP BusinessObjects BI.

> ▶ **BusinessObjects Platform Administrator Guide**
> This guide has a chapter called "Managing Applications" that is dedicated to the configuration and customization of the applications contained within the SAP BusinessObjects BI platform. It defines object-by-object reference for what can be modified stylewise.

10.1   Customizing Client Tools

SAP BusinessObjects BI is in the business to visualize your data, in case you missed that memo. As a facet of that, there's a need for a creative touch to make all that data look pretty when you do finally present it. Is that necessarily your job, as the administrator? Not really. However, you're the great facilitator. You empower the application developers that will utilize your environment for dashboards, reports, and BI applications to create dead sexy content.

A marketer or graphics designer-type will tell you that a branding strategy is important to any successful project. What is a branding strategy, you might ask? Well, according to Wikipedia (wait, we can cite Wikipedia at this point, right? It's Chapter 10 and all), a brand itself is a "name, term, design, symbol, or any other feature that identifies one seller's good or service as distinct from those of other sellers."

That said, a branding strategy is the process by which we define how to effectively define and communicate that brand. Your company is highly likely to be already doing this with its own brand. That same brand is just as important to your BI project and how it identifies itself, so you're going to want to put it on reports.

Design techniques in the SAP BusinessObjects BI family of products vary wildly from product to product. If we look at product history:

▶ Web Intelligence was developed in house at Business Objects prior to the SAP acquisition.

▶ SAP Crystal Reports has a history going back several decades and several acquisitions. The developer experience is largely unchanged over quite some time.

▶ SAP Crystal Reports Enterprise is brand new and rethinks the way Crystal reports are developed.

► Dashboards was acquired as Xcelsius and maintains much of its developer interface.

The thing that resonates here is that each of these products, with their genesis in other companies acquired by SAP, presents the content developer with varied ways of creating highly formatted content. Will you or your development teams be masters of each? That will ultimately be up to the tool standards set by your organization.

Because this is simply an overview for administrators, this chapter doesn't seek to be an all-inclusive discussion of any particular customization capability within a report or dashboard. But, to give you the big picture, we'll dive into a general overview of report design techniques for the three biggest SAP BusinessObjects BI tools: SAP Crystal Reports, SAP BusinessObjects Web Intelligence, and SAP BusinessObjects Dashboards.

10.1.1 SAP Crystal Reports

We already know at this point that we have to consider branding in two ways, both from an SAP Crystal Reports 2013 point of view and from an SAP Crystal Reports Enterprise interface. In this chapter, we're only going to focus on SAP Crystal Reports 2013 and the characteristics of the tool that apply to formatting a report.

SAP Crystal Reports 2013 has long been known as the tool used to create "pixel-perfect" reports. The fine-grained control we've already discussed is pretty awesome (that coming from a long-time Desktop Intelligence guy right here). As you can see in Figure 10.1, a simple report with no formatting gives you a very plain look and feel. But, we can make it less vanilla with the capabilities of SAP Crystal Reports 2013.

Every object on the body of the report has a common set of properties, as shown in Figure 10.2. While there may be subtle variations based on the data type, this is a very consistent properties window for the object on the body of the report. In addition to usability properties, the most general of formatting capabilities, such as alignment control and referenced style sheet names, make this the first stop for customizing the display of a field in a Crystal report.

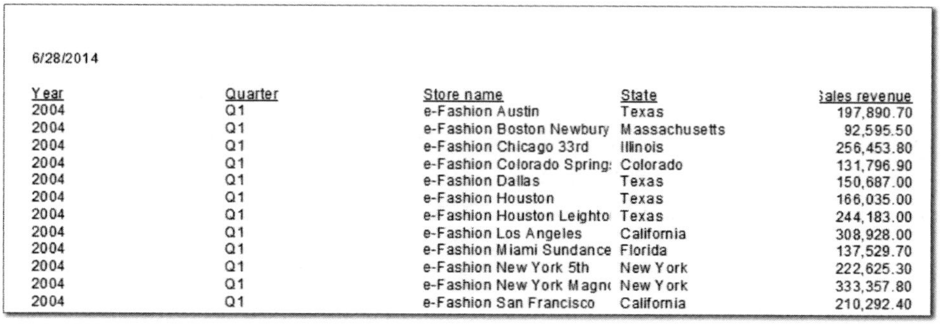

6/28/2014				
Year	Quarter	Store name	State	Sales revenue
2004	Q1	e-Fashion Austin	Texas	197,890.70
2004	Q1	e-Fashion Boston Newbury	Massachusetts	92,595.50
2004	Q1	e-Fashion Chicago 33rd	Illinois	256,453.80
2004	Q1	e-Fashion Colorado Spring:	Colorado	131,796.90
2004	Q1	e-Fashion Dallas	Texas	150,687.00
2004	Q1	e-Fashion Houston	Texas	166,035.00
2004	Q1	e-Fashion Houston Leighto	Texas	244,183.00
2004	Q1	e-Fashion Los Angeles	California	308,928.00
2004	Q1	e-Fashion Miami Sundance	Florida	137,529.70
2004	Q1	e-Fashion New York 5th	New York	222,625.30
2004	Q1	e-Fashion New York Magn(	New York	333,357.80
2004	Q1	e-Fashion San Francisco	California	210,292.40

Figure 10.1 A Vanilla SAP Crystal Reports 2013 Output

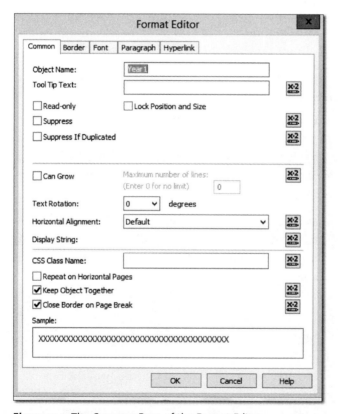

Figure 10.2 The Common Pane of the Format Editor

Like any good publishing tool, a Crystal report can make use of lines—basic, colored, weighted, and so on, and even based upon a formula—as shown in Figure 10.3.

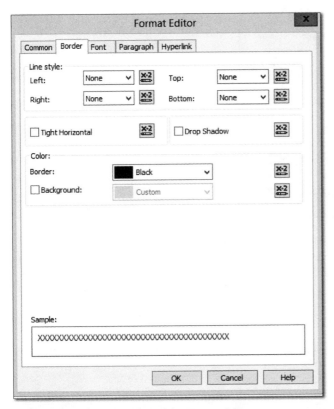

Figure 10.3 The Border Pane of the Format Editor

As opposed to other HTML-based reporting tools, which must rely on web standard fonts, the ability of SAP Crystal Reports to utilize a viewer allows SAP Crystal Server and SAP BusinessObjects BI to leverage a more robust font library, as shown in Figure 10.4.

In the example in Figure 10.5, we're working with a text field. SAP Crystal Reports presents the report designer with a view based on the data type of the object, whether date, alphanumeric, or numeric.

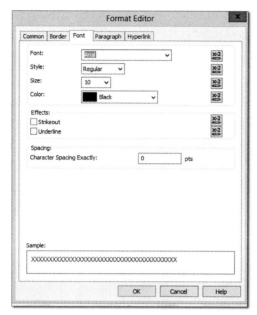

Figure 10.4 The Font Pane of the Format Editor

Figure 10.5 The Paragraph Pane of the Format Editor

Most of the capabilities of SAP Crystal Reports allow for rule-based formatting based on a formula. Whether formatting a section or one of the properties in the FORMAT EDITOR, formulas are a very rich way to create the format of your report in an extremely flexible manner. Figure 10.6 demonstrates a simple example of alternate row shading based on a formula.

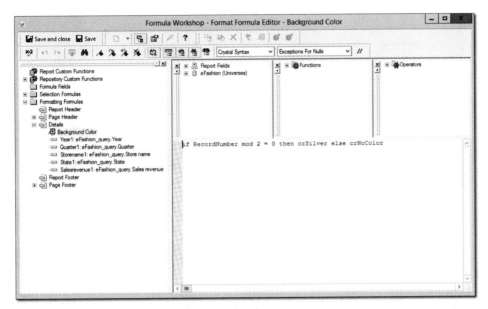

Figure 10.6 Custom Formatting via the Formula Editor

Well, there. That's better. With a company logo, some header information, a little more readable formatting with the alternate line shading, and some grouping with subtotals, that boring report just got a wee bit fancier. We're not graphic designers, but we can tell you that what you see in Figure 10.7 took about 15 minutes and creates a common report-style guide that users can follow and become accustomed to.

The new Customization Guide goes into extensive detail for customers and even further for OEMs. In this guide, you can learn how to customize the installer for either SAP Crystal Reports 2011+ or SAP Crystal Reports Enterprise. This information guides you through customizations such as installation-specific components, menu customization, splash screen changes, and more.

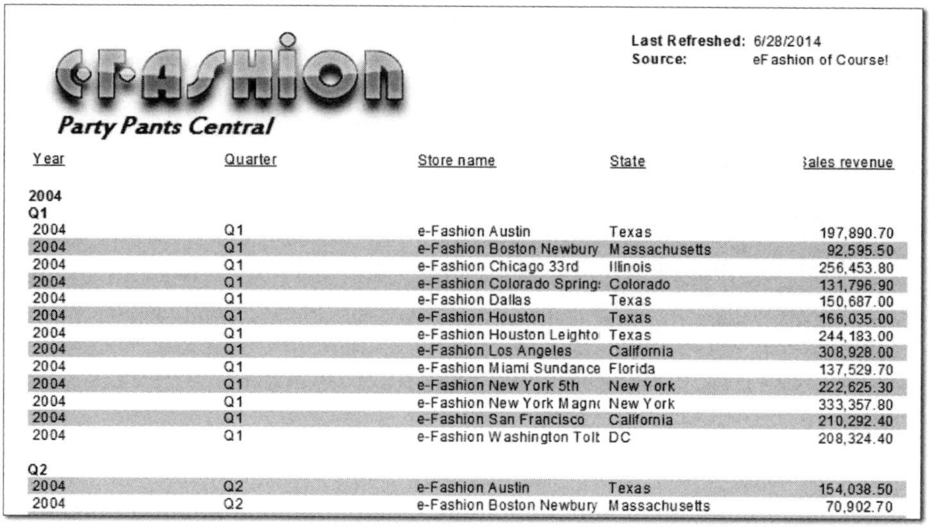

Party Pants Central

Last Refreshed: 6/28/2014
Source: eFashion of Course!

Year	Quarter	Store name	State	Sales revenue
2004				
Q1				
2004	Q1	e-Fashion Austin	Texas	197,890.70
2004	Q1	e-Fashion Boston Newbury	Massachusetts	92,595.50
2004	Q1	e-Fashion Chicago 33rd	Illinois	256,453.80
2004	Q1	e-Fashion Colorado Spring:	Colorado	131,796.90
2004	Q1	e-Fashion Dallas	Texas	150,687.00
2004	Q1	e-Fashion Houston	Texas	166,035.00
2004	Q1	e-Fashion Houston Leighto	Texas	244,183.00
2004	Q1	e-Fashion Los Angeles	California	308,928.00
2004	Q1	e-Fashion Miami Sundance	Florida	137,529.70
2004	Q1	e-Fashion New York 5th	New York	222,625.30
2004	Q1	e-Fashion New York Magn(	New York	333,357.80
2004	Q1	e-Fashion San Francisco	California	210,292.40
2004	Q1	e-Fashion Washington Tolt	DC	208,324.40
Q2				
2004	Q2	e-Fashion Austin	Texas	154,038.50
2004	Q2	e-Fashion Boston Newbury	Massachusetts	70,902.70

Figure 10.7 The Same Report with Some Chocolate on Top

10.1.2 SAP BusinessObjects Web Intelligence

Web Intelligence takes a different approach to design. Instead of freestanding cells, content is organized into tables known as blocks and styled in many of the same ways, but from a slightly different approach.

One could argue that a Web Intelligence report in SAP BusinessObjects BI 4.1 has a little more pizazz. Reports get a nice gradient header and a clean body, all in a nice block, as shown in Figure 10.8. But really, the similarities start to peel apart from there.

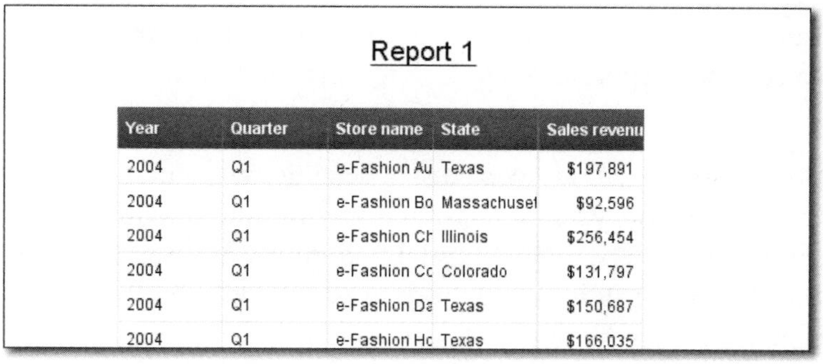

Report 1

Year	Quarter	Store name	State	Sales revenu
2004	Q1	e-Fashion Au	Texas	$197,891
2004	Q1	e-Fashion Bo	Massachuset	$92,596
2004	Q1	e-Fashion Ch	Illinois	$256,454
2004	Q1	e-Fashion Cc	Colorado	$131,797
2004	Q1	e-Fashion Da	Texas	$150,687
2004	Q1	e-Fashion Hc	Texas	$166,035

Figure 10.8 A Vanilla Web Intelligence Report

The properties of anything in a Web Intelligence report are context sensitive. So if you're modifying a freestanding cell, a table, a chart, a header cell, whatever, the format options will vary much like they do in a Crystal report. The general properties of the Web Intelligence report shown in Figure 10.9 are the simplest possible. While there are shortcuts on the ribbons on the report designer, a concise view of all settings is achieved here.

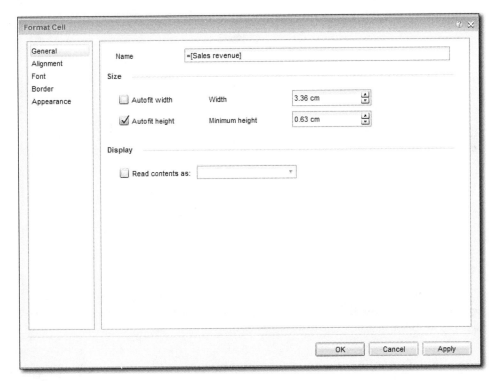

Figure 10.9 The General Pane for Format Properties

The ALIGNMENT pane in Figure 10.10 gives the simple behaviors for how text acts within a cell, whether it's in a freestanding cell or in a column or row in a block of data.

Fonts and borders (not shown) have nothing magical here, but like any good Microsoft Office document, or a Crystal report, you can refine the style of a report to conform as closely as you can to your corporate style guide. Contrary to the capabilities of SAP Crystal Reports, you can't apply formulas to format the style in this case *unless* you use the capabilities included in Alerters (not shown). This is another fine reason to snag a fine SAP PRESS publication on Web Intelligence. (We specifically recommend *SAP BusinessObjects Web Intelligence*, third edition by Jim Brogden et al. [SAP PRESS, 2014]).

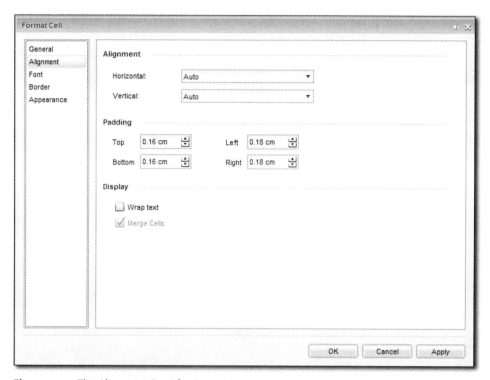

Figure 10.10 The Alignment Pane for Format Properties

With a little formatting, we achieve a very similar result between the two report types. That is some nifty stuff right there, and it improves the user experience through a consistent look and feel.

There is a tiny catch in the screenshot you see in Figure 10.11, though. SAP Crystal Reports allows you to embed a graphic quite easily. However, in Web Intelligence, to effectively set a server-side graphic on your application tier, you must first make this graphic available to your users.

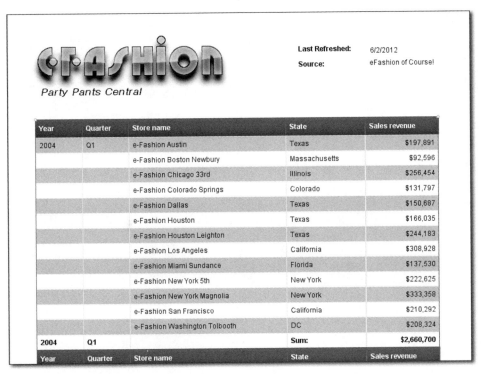

Figure 10.11 The Same Report with Some Chocolate on Top

The path in Figure 10.12 displays the location on the application tier where your images must reside to be used by Web Intelligence. When multiple servers exist in the cluster, the identical image must be placed on each server in this path. This will allow your users to reference an image path when embedding their images in a manner such as the following:

boimg ://some_image_file_name.jpg

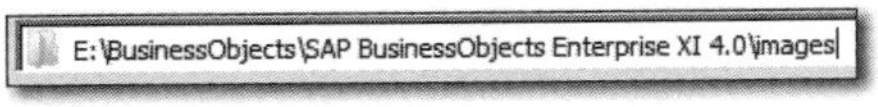

E:\BusinessObjects\SAP BusinessObjects Enterprise XI 4.0\images|

Figure 10.12 The Path to Images on the Server for Web Intelligence

In addition to being able to customize the style of a Web Intelligence report through toolbars and property panels, Web Intelligence supports style sheet references. No, you won't be running out and designing an entire HTML5 website, but you can create a style sheet that is capable of being imported directly into an existing report to override the default style.

The PROPERTIES ribbon has a DOCUMENT option that allows for access to the document summary (see Figure 10.13).

Figure 10.13 Accessing the Document Properties

Tucked away at the bottom of the document summary in Figure 10.14 is the ability to change the default style for the report. Click the CHANGE DEFAULT STYLEbutton to get access to this report's style sheet.

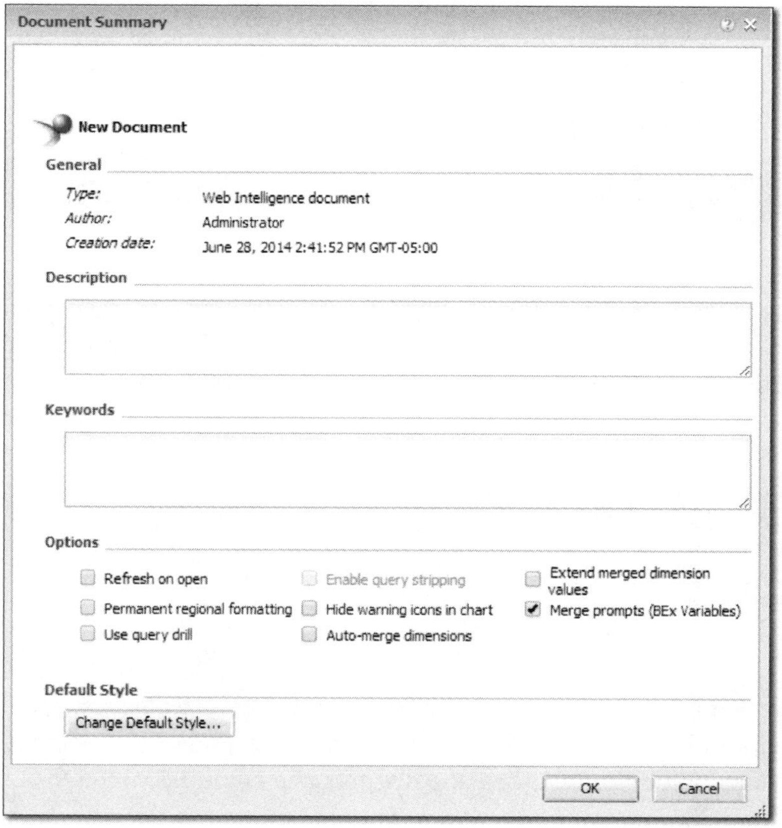

Figure 10.14 Web Intelligence Document Summary

The options in Figure 10.15 are quite simple. The IMPORT STYLE button takes a compliant style sheet and replaces the current style. Do you seem to be missing the starting point of the style sheet? Start by clicking the EXPORT STYLE button to get the Web Intelligence default CSS.

Figure 10.15 Web Intelligence Default Style

The style sheet in Figure 10.16, compared to the BI Launch Pad default style (more on that in Section 10.2), is tidy and well formatted. These CSS properties allow you to modify block, border, font, and other miscellaneous properties to be loaded into your reports.

These style sheets are local and specific to the Web Intelligence document being modified here. At the time of the development of this chapter, a global version of this option wasn't available.

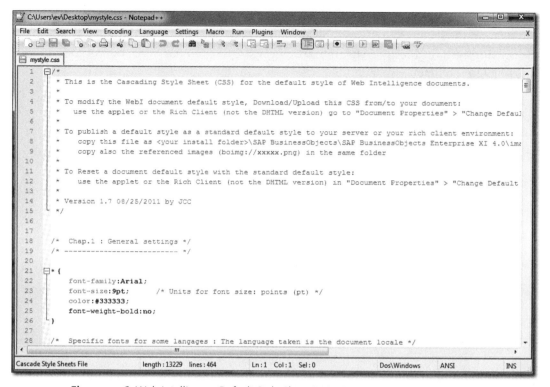

Figure 10.16 Web Intelligence Default Style Sheet in Action

10.1.3 SAP BusinessObjects Dashboards

You won't see us creating a cool tabular report in an SAP dashboard. It's just not the same thing. However, just like its reporting-tool counterparts, Dashboards gives you many ways to make data look awesome, as well as a simple way to brand dashboards in a manner consistent with reports in your deployment (see Figure 10.17). Hopefully you're getting the message here: next to data and usability, style is everything.

Underscoring the fact, once again, that we aren't graphic designers, an SAP dashboard should at least fall into the same realm as the style guide created for your reports and the BI Launch Pad. Now, we'll argue that you *should* have a graphic designer help contribute to your overall branding strategy for SAP BusinessObjects BI, but that's a longer chapter.

Dashboard components, like those of reports in Web Intelligence or SAP Crystal Reports, get their own fine-grained controls for styling. Figure 10.18, while different in options, has a few of the same controls provided in the reporting tools, enabling users to modify borders and text flow, to name a few. While not shown, the TEXT tab provides extensive format styles for the individual components on the canvas.

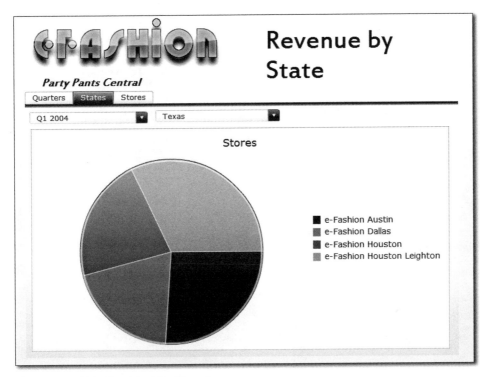

Figure 10.17 Style-Consistent Dashboard

Just like Web Intelligence and SAP Crystal Reports, objects on the canvas in Dashboards have panels to style the appearance of the objects. And also just like Web Intelligence and SAP Crystal Reports, the APPEARANCE panel in Dashboards is context sensitive, changing based on the type of object being modified. When contrasting the Web Intelligence examples in Figure 10.15 and Figure 10.16, it's easy to see the rather extensive differences in styling capabilities based on the type of object on the canvas, as demonstrated in Figure 10.18, Figure 10.19, and Figure 10.20.

Figure 10.18 The Layout Tab of the Appearance Panel

Figure 10.19 The Color Tab in the Appearance Panel for a Text Box

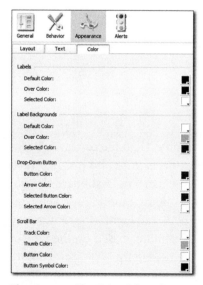

Figure 10.20 The Color Tab in the Appearance Panel for a Combo Selector

10.2 Customizing the BI Launch Pad

Before we even talk about how to give the BI Launch Pad a facelift, there is something really simple you need to run out and do before you do anything else. You have a server or servers in your SAP BusinessObjects BI web tier, and they have really painful names assigned by your system administrators. Maybe one of those server names is something like:

stlbobjsrvp01web.thisismycompany.com/BOE/BI

Is that really something you want to make your users remember? Domain name systems (DNS) will make your users' experiences much easier. You can easily ask your network administrator to create new domain aliases for your server. Think of it as an "also known as" for your server. Maybe something like *bo.thisismycompany.com* (nobody really uses "bo" thanks to the negative connotation) or *bobj.thisismycompany.com* or *awesomebusinessintelligence.thisismycompany.com*. The sky is the limit as long as nobody in your organization is already squatting that domain name. While you're at it, if at all possible, request the non–Fully Qualified Domain Name (FQDN). So, instead of *bobj.thisismycompany.com*, just get *bobj* in DNS. As long as your network administrators have DNS set up properly on all the user workstations, it'll work. Taking this one step further, consider a simple JavaScript redirect at the root of your Tomcat application (*/webapps/ROOT*). Using a JavaScript redirect in a new *index.jsp* file, your users simply have to hit that root domain such as *bobj.thisismycompany.com* and automatically be redirected to the BI Launch Pad at *bobj.thisismycompany.com/BOE/BI*. A simple JavaScript redirect might look like the following:

```
<script type="text/javascript">
  window.location = "http://bobj.thisismycompany.com/BOE/BI/"
</script>
```

With that little tasty bit out of the way, we can move on to actually making the BI Launch Pad and friends look pretty.

In this section, we'll dig primarily into the BI Launch Pad, but give honorable mentions to other customization opportunities. With that, on the server side, there are a few components of the architecture that can be rebranded to be consistent with your company or BI branding strategy. At the highest of possible levels, they are the following:

▶ BI Launch Pad

▶ OpenDocument

▶ SAP Crystal Reports JavaScript viewer

Note

Keep in mind that SAP isn't going to provide support if you stray beyond the included custom style references for the BI Launch Pad. It's a narrow scope, but it does give quite a bit of customization in creating that branding for your portal.

Prior to SAP BusinessObjects BI 4.0, it can be said that it was actually a wee bit easier to brand InfoView. Anyone with some basic HTML and CSS skills would be able to update the style sheets, a little code, and the images that made up InfoView. You and your web developer have your work cut out for you to dig in and update the BI Launch Pad in a semi-crude approach.

SAP is very explicit in the new SAP BusinessObjects BI 4.1 Customization Guide regarding what can be customized, as in, implied support, which are cited here from Chapter 4 of that guide:

▶ Favicon

▶ Logos

▶ Certain background patterns and colors

▶ Certain animated gifs

▶ Certain CSS styles

▶ JavaScript files for the Crystal Reports JavaScript Viewer

We're going to begin by looking at customizations via CSS modification. Yes, you do have to traverse 10 folders to get to the CSS. The BI Launch Pad CSS folder in Figure 10.21, as well as the images folder, is located deep within the *Tomcat6* folder in the location in which you installed SAP BusinessObjects BI. Please note, that this also applies only to the server in which you've installed your web tier, not your application tier.

E:\BusinessObjects\Tomcat6\webapps\BOE\WEB-INF\eclipse\plugins\webpath.InfoView\web\css

Figure 10.21 The BI Launch Pad Path

As with all configuration changes you may make inside your SAP BusinessObjects BI cluster, it's always a good idea to backup your style sheet, as shown in Figure 10.22. Eventually, you (or someone else, of course) will mess up a config file and will need to get that back.

default - Copy.css
default.css

Figure 10.22 Back It Up

The OEM actually has a bit of an easier task with the ability to customize at install time. While you can certainly follow this process, you may not want to have to deal with deploying and redeploying WAR files each time you need to tweak the style of your site the way that the OEM customization guide leads you to do. Either way you go, an effective way to identify where a style reference is coming from is to take advantage of modern browser capabilities.

If you're a cool hipster like us, you're using a Mac. Further, if you're trendy, to boot, you're using Google Chrome or Mozilla Firefox. In each, the right-click context in your browser window provides an option to INSPECT ELEMENT, as shown in Figure 10.23. In the old days, only add-ons such as Firebug provided this capability. INSPECT ELEMENT is really quite awesome.

Figure 10.23 Browser Style Inspection

The INSPECT ELEMENTcapability is contextual to where you have your mouse cursor on the page. When this occurs, it highlights the selected HTML object and even provides you with the style reference in a popup box above it, shading out all other content on the page (see Figure 10.24).

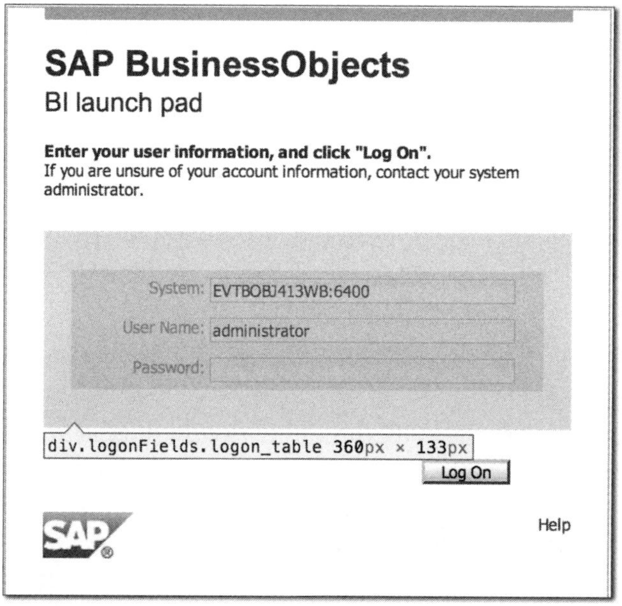

SAP BusinessObjects
BI launch pad

Enter your user information, and click "Log On".
If you are unsure of your account information, contact your system administrator.

System: EVTBOBJ413WB:6400

User Name: administrator

Password:

div.logonFields.logon_table 360px × 133px

Log On

Help

Figure 10.24 The Inspected Element

Toward the bottom of the inspected page, the browser gives you a little more help, as shown in Figure 10.25. It actually demonstrates hierarchically where the containers in the HTML nest, allowing you to drill up or down interactively in that code—but in a visual way, to see where style references are taking place.

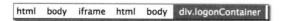

html   body   iframe   html   body   div.logonContainer

Figure 10.25 Inspected Page Object Hierarchy

To put a bow on visualizing style elements, the browser sets up a few different views inline on the page to allow you to view the HTML being generated by all of those JSPs in the BI Launch Pad, as well as the inheritance of the style sheets across the board (see Figure 10.26). We love that. With our nifty style inspection tools pinned down, we can actually go back a few steps to that *default.css* file we found and get ready to hack it apart.

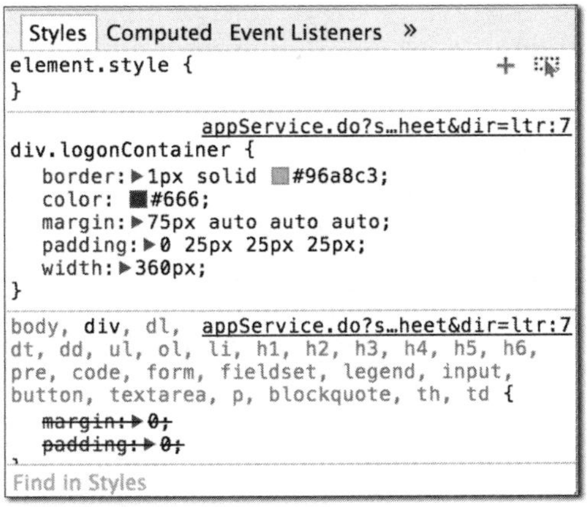

Figure 10.26 Inspected Page Views

Let's start with the real step 1. Don't panic. The first time you open *default.css*, it's kind of a mess (see Figure 10.27). This file appears to have no formatting in terms of line breaks or other characteristics that a good web developer might consider ... well, good. On the flip side, the lack of additional formatting, extra spaces, line returns, and so on makes for a smaller and more optimized file that will get loaded over and over again. Frankly, reformatting this file is probably not a good investment of your time. So, start in small swipes, and work from the preceding example in our initial inspection with a simple "find" in your favorite text editor. If you don't have one already, Notepad++ is a gem.

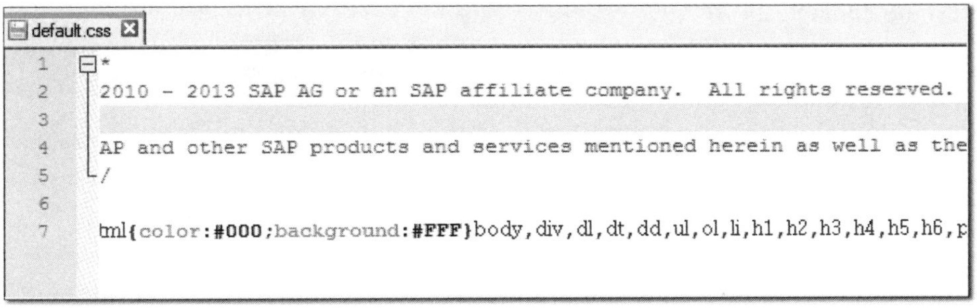

Figure 10.27 The Default Style Sheet

The inspection gave the name of `logonfields` for the piece of code that contains the logon box for the BI Launch Pad. That's easy enough. Search for it, as shown in Figure 10.28.

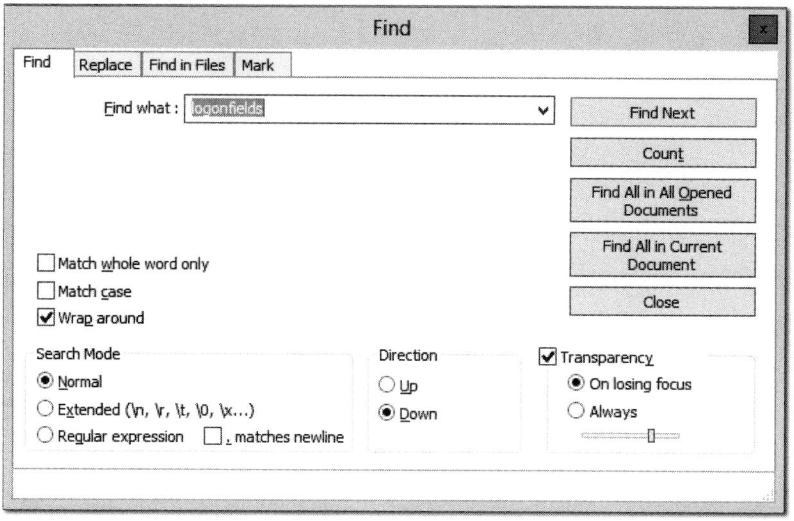

Figure 10.28 The Style Search

For SAP BusinessObjects BI 4.1, in the search for `logonFields`, the following code snippet, all shoved into that one continuous line of styles, is displayed in Figure 10.29. Your results will vary in prior versions, as this code was changed along the way of the SAP BusinessObjects BI 4.0 code line. To demonstrate, the highlighted text was tweaked to give this `div` a background color of red. This should really make your BI Launch Pad pop. Either that or it will incite rage in your users—whatever works for you. Let's go ahead and put some well-formed CSS changes into the code:

```
/* This was added by Super Admin on 6/29/2014*/
.logonFields{
    padding:25px;
    border:1px solid #CACAD9;
    background-color:red;
    text-align:right;
}
```

That wasn't so scary now was it?

```
.logonFields{background-color:red;border:1px solid #cacad9;padding:25px 18px}
```

Figure 10.29 The Search Result

The next tough part here is that Tomcat is a fickle beast. Even a knowledge base reference on SAP's own support portal indicates you may need to both clear the

Tomcat cache and restart Tomcat. The rule of thumb here is simple: do both and save yourself time. With that restart out of the way, clear your browser cache to make triple sure you don't have a cached style sheet, and let's see what magical user experience we've just created together.

Figure 10.30 is tough to look at. But with a little work, you can make it look a lot better.

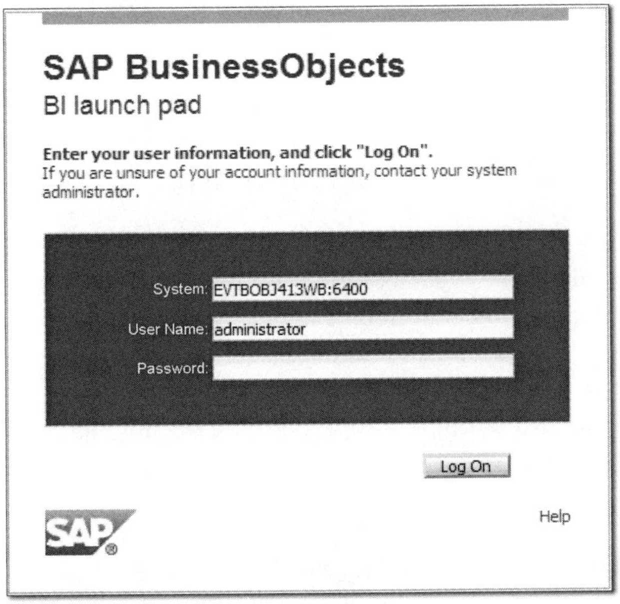

Figure 10.30 The New, Awesome BI Launch Pad: Before Customization

That all being said, we don't recommend that you run off with the browser tricks mentioned previously and start redesigning the BI Launch Pad. Partner up with your graphic designer and come up with a look and feel for your BI Launch Pad that is consistent with your corporate branding or SAP BusinessObjects BI branding, and comply with the styles that SAP has provided in its style sheet references.

Lastly, follow just as rigid a systems development lifecycle as you should be following with your SAP BusinessObjects BI content. Make changes to your BI Launch Pad in your development environment, evaluate performance and usability, and promote these code changes in a structured way to your test and production environments as you go. In addition, if you don't commit the changes you're making to the *BOE.war* files, they are susceptible to being overwritten if the war file is redeployed. Further, any changes to the pages based on service packs or patches may require you to reintegrate your changes into these styles.

Pop Quiz

1. Which guide contains detailed references to aspects of the BI Launch Pad that can be customized?
2. What web template file is used to style the BI Launch Pad visually?
3. True or False: Modifying JSPs within the BI Launch Pad to customize functionality is supported.

10.3   When to Use the Software Development Kit

The SAP BusinessObjects BI Software Development Kit (SDK) is the type of library that SAP uses to implement things such as the BI Launch Pad, but it's abstracted and made public so that customers can extend SAP BusinessObjects BI. On the remote chance that your organization doesn't use SAP NetWeaver, Microsoft SharePoint, or some other supported portal technology that integrates with SAP BusinessObjects BI, the SDK is your only mechanism to integrate SAP BusinessObjects BI content into your portal.

This is the part where we tell you we don't envy you.

Seriously though, you can certainly build some basic "grab a report and display it in a web page" code via the SDK and integrate it into any site. But try to imagine the vast amount of time SAP has already put into the BI Launch Pad. Do you want to be led down a path to rebuild that? The answer is no. Can it be done? Yes. Should you? The answer is still a no.

So, with that, why might you want to use the SDK to integrate SAP BusinessObjects BI into your existing web page or portal? Let's think through a few possibilities:

▶ **An application needs to view a simple report or dashboard from within its own template.**
It could be argued this is a better fit for OpenDocument. No coding is required. Simply supply the needed parameters, such as the report's CUID, and open the link up.

▶ **Display a list of reports to which a user has access in SAP BusinessObjects BI.**
A little more complex, but really relatively easily accomplished. This requires use of authentication APIs, the listing of folders the user has access to, and also returning the list of reports available in each folder. Again, this is a great use case for OpenDocument, preventing you from the need to code more extensively with the viewers.

▶ **Schedule and distribute a report.**
A known report and a list of recipients for the report can be used to schedule and blast the report out to a broader audience without the need to log on and schedule the report via the BI Launch Pad or CMC.

▶ **I don't want my users to have to log into the BI Launch Pad.**
This certainly isn't an invalid request. Could single sign-on accomplish this? Certainly, single sign-on has been a well-documented and integrated component of SAP BusinessObjects BI forever. In addition, capabilities such as trusted authentication can be used to accept logon tokens from a separate web application and pass them to SAP BusinessObjects BI, bypassing the logon page in the BI Launch Pad.

You can bet there are scores of scenarios in which you might build a simple web application that integrates with SAP BusinessObjects BI. But, as mentioned before, don't put yourself in the role of re-creating the BI Launch Pad. There may be no greater effort in futility. Don't forget to acknowledge the fact that with each release of SAP BusinessObjects BI, you must also do rigid regression testing for your code for any new release of the platform, as the underlying SDKs may change on each release. Consult the release notes on each new release for any clues as to what may be changed in a service pack or patch.

10.4   Summary

SAP BusinessObjects BI gives us the means to get gobs of data and visualize it. It's the job of the developer to help your end users make sense of all that data. However, as a collective, the developer on your team, the graphic designer defining the branding strategy for your organization, and you, the administrator, must make a concerted effort to get it together for your BI implementation. This means an end-to-end approach to branding, reports, and portal alike.

The visualization tools will give your development teams plenty of opportunity to stay busy in applying that style guide. Despite the complexities of modifying style sheets and graphics, you can give the BI Launch Pad a look and feel that is familiar to your users. Give it a try.

Here's the general rule of thumb to follow, whether customizing the frontend, a report, or a dashboard: If SAP has documented it in the official release documentation, then there's a high to almost-certain likelihood that the change is supported. That's a pretty easy rule to follow. When in doubt, log an SAP incident and get clarification before you begin. You just might end up saving yourself from a miserable experience later in developing an unsupported user experience in SAP BusinessObjects BI.

With that, folks, we conclude our SAP BusinessObjects BI administration journey. You should now know every single thing you possibly could ever need to know about SAP BusinessObjects BI administration! Okay, maybe not *every* single thing. But you should feel confident in your ability to administer an SAP BusinessObjects BI system, and know that, if you encounter questions during the process, you can refer back to this book for answers.

Go forth and administer!

A   Answer Key

A.1   Chapter 1

Section 1.1

1. The UNV is a single-source universe with a history in classic SAP BusinessObjects BI reporting, while the UNX supports multiple sources and was introduced in SAP BusinessObjects BI 4.0.

2. The sole purpose of the universe should be to obscure the complexities of the data from the business user, creating a mechanism for self-service reporting and analysis.

Section 1.2

1. The Information Design Tool.

2. SAP BusinessObjects Analysis, edition for Microsoft Office.

3. SAP BusinessObjects Explorer.

Section 1.3

1. Crystal Decisions Crystal Enterprise.

2. The web tier.

3. The Product Availability Matrix.

4. The application tier houses the components of the SAP BusinessObjects BI architecture that are responsible for creating and storing reports for consumption.

Section 1.4

1. Art, science, and trial and error.

2. The development environment is as important to development teams as production is to end users. Without it, projects can't continue and organizations may certainly experience monetary loss.

A.2 Chapter 2

Section 2.1

1. SAPS is an accepted, industry standard measurement, adhered to by major server manufacturers to provide hardware that scales to the SAPS number prescribed to support a given SAP environment.

2. An active-concurrent user is logged on to the system and is actively interacting with the UI and reporting capability.

Section 2.2

1. The SAP BI 4 Sizing Estimator takes estimated utilization for SAP BusinessObjects BI content and creates a measure in SAPS and Memory for purchase of hardware.

2. SAP BusinessObjects Analysis, edition for OLAP; SAP Crystal Reports 2011; SAP Crystal Reports Enterprise; Dashboards; and Web Intelligence.

3. Information consumers, business users, and expert users.

4. Expert users.

5. SAP Community Network.

Section 2.3

1. After SAPS rates are determined and hardware vendor selection has begun, the Product Availability Matrix (PAM) is the key resource to ensuring that the selection criteria fall within the supported platforms list for SAP BusinessObjects BI.

Section 2.4

1. Table AUDIT_DETAIL captures granular details about each event that takes place in the environment, whether a user refreshes a report or simply logs on.

2. Unless space and time are no concern, no. Audit just what is needed to effectively measure utilization and satisfy compliance audit concerns.

3. Not only is Auditor data a historical accounting of what has taken place in an environment, but it also serves as a model to forecast growth month over month to help predict future growth as well.

Section 2.6

1. The processing tier fulfills reporting requests such as view and refresh events for authenticated users.

2. All of them.

3. One now that it can span child processes.

4. The Adaptive Job Server.

A.3   Chapter 3

Introduction

1. Flash cut.

2. The SAP BusinessObjects BI 4 Sizing Estimator.

Section 3.2

1. 64-bit.

2. Custom/expanded.

3. Subversion.

4. The Product Availability Matrix (PAM).

Section 3.3

1. The CMC, or Central Management Console, is the web-based application for addressing application administration tasks within SAP BusinessObjects BI 4.1. The CCM, or Central Configuration Manager, is responsible for creating the base services such as the Server Intelligence Agent on a server.

2. A configuration template creates a blueprint by which other servers of like type can inherit the properties and subsequent changes to the parent server.

3. False. You must use the Central Configuration Manager (CCM).

Section 3.4

1. Never. Always ask questions and ensure everyone understands the capacity demands.

A.4   Chapter 4

Section 4.2

1. Each server consists of several smaller components that can be split into their own processes, consuming their own Java heaps and memory allocations.

2. True.

Section 4.3

1. The Data Federation Administration Tool.

2. An explain plan.

3. Statistics.

4. Content federation is the process of synchronizing data across disparate systems with logically separate CMS clusters.

5. Data federation is the process of combining disparate data without physically co-locating it via ETL or other materialization techniques at a database level.

Section 4.4

1. Servers you aren't using will consume precious CPU and memory resources. Choose wisely. Only run servers needed to support the reporting tools to be deployed in your environment.

A.5   Chapter 5

Section 5.1

1. A principal is a user or group as defined either via enterprise or third-party authentication systems.

2. Denied.

3. Application rights are specific to individual facets of the SAP BusinessObjects BI 4.1 platform, such as Web Intelligence or SAP Crystal Reports, which control the access and behaviors of each technology for a principal.

4. VIEW ON DEMAND.

5. Often advanced rights may be required that aren't satisfied by VIEW, SCHEDULE, VIEW ON DEMAND, or other predefined access levels. Avoid advanced rights with custom access levels.

Section 5.2

1. True.

Section 5.3

1. The CRYPTOGRAPHIC KEYS MANAGEMENT area in the CMC.

2. The cluster key is used to encrypt all of the cryptographic keys in the CMS repository.

3. Next chapter, please....

Section 5.4

1. Whichever port will be accessed via a user's web browser; typically port 80 for IIS, Apache, HIS, or port 8080 for other Java application containers.

2. 6400, unless overridden.

3. If port availability on a server is limited to a specific range by information/network security, or the server co-locates more than one SAP BusinessObjects SIA and CMS cluster.

4. Hang out enough with Jamie Oswald and the Diversified Semantic Layer podcast crew, and you'll get there. You can find us at *http://dslayer.net/dslayer*.

A.6   Chapter 6

Section 6.1

1. The Upgrade Management Tool provides a migration path from supported versions of SAP BusinessObjects prior to release 4.0.

2. A full migration moves all content in the source CMS cluster, while an incremental migration provides the chance to selectively upgrade content.

3. False.

4. Rename object to avoid name conflict and Do not import object.

5. Promotion Management is responsible for moving content between like versions of SAP BusinessObjects BI 4.1.

6. Decentralized Promotion Management environments call for the movement of content between just two environments for the Promotion Management Server.

7. True.

Section 6.3

1. Connection overrides, QaaWS overrides, and SAP Crystal Reports overrides.

2. True.

3. The Adaptive Job Server.

Section 6.4

1. Replication jobs replicate, possibly in one-way, or two-way directions, the content between two CMS clusters for the purpose of synchronizing content, while Promotion Management is a one-way move used for code promotion.

2. A replication list.

3. Remote connection.

A.7   Chapter 7

Section 7.2

1. Adobe Flash (ack).
2. True.

Section 7.3

1. A metric provides some measure of performance for a specific server in the CMS cluster.
2. Predefined metrics in the Monitoring Dashboard serve to give the administrator a starting point for monitoring the system without the need to create metrics from scratch.

Section 7.4

1. A watchlist is a mechanism in which metrics are evaluated as to whether they provide a positive or negative state for a monitored metric.
2. False. Custom watchlists can be created on any server or metric set.
3. By using throttling criteria, watchlists can ensure that a single occurrence of a trigger must happen more than n times before indicating that a threshold has been crossed, and says "Houston, we have a problem."

Section 7.5

1. True.
2. Probes on Web Intelligence will actually interact with the report and ensure that it opens and can be refreshed. This tests the entire report refresh workflow, from logging on (security permissions), to refreshing the report (data access and database connectivity), to rendering the report and creating the formatted output (Web Intelligence Processing Service).

Section 7.6

1. An alert takes into account the activity in a watchlist and notifies the administrator of the condition level.

2. True, of course. You're indispensible and irreplaceable. This system will keep you gainfully employed. You can count on it.

Section 7.7

1. This is really a trick question. While true, it will only allow you to report on historical usage information from your old SAP BusinessObjects XI R2 or XI 3.1 database.

2. Multilingual support is ready to go within the Auditor database and must be filtered based on the appropriate language set.

3. In a single AUDITING panel in the Central Management Console.

A.8   Chapter 8

Section 8.1

1. On-demand and scheduling workflows.

2. Another type of workflow might include a simple report view, a user logon, or sending a report to a destination.

Section 8.2

1. The SAP Community Network (SCN).

2. The SAP Support Portal.

3. An S-ID.

Section 8.3

1. High.

2. Trace logs are placed in the SAP BusinessObjects BI install directory in the logging folder.

3. The Event Viewer.

Section 8.4

1. False. Trace logs capture data sequentially.

Section 8.5

1. The Instance Manager.

2. False. The Instance Manager allows you to reschedule a failed instance.

3. Limits ensure that the scheduler isn't accumulating too many copies of the same report that are resultant from the recurring jobs in the environment.

Section 8.6

1. Did you really have to flip back to the answer on this one? False, of course.

Section 8.7

1. False. Common backup times are crucial.

2. A cold backup implies that SAP BusinessObjects BI has been stopped so that any locked files can be backed up as well.

3. False. A partial recovery is like a needle in a haystack. If a partial recovery is required, it's necessary to recover to a separate system and then migrate using the Promotion Management BIAR.

4. Inconsistencies between the file store and the CMS database.

A.9 Chapter 9

Section 9.1

1. False. Solaris isn't supported until a later SP release.

2. SAP BusinessObjects Mobile and SAP BusinessObjects Experience.

3. The Product Availability Matrix (still).

Section 9.2

1. Sybase Unwired Platform.

2. False. The Sybase Unwired Platform requires the deployment of just two WAR files for all mobile platforms.

A.10   Chapter 10

Section 10.1

1. A Cascading Style Sheet (CSS).

2. *Install Directory/SAP BusinessObjects XI 4.0/images*.

3. False. Go back and read Section 10.1. We get a great number of opportunities to build a consistent style in reports and dashboards.

Section 10.2

1. The OEM Customization Guide in the help document portal.

2. CSS.

3. False.

B   The Authors

Greg Myers has worked in the analytics industry for the past 16 years, specializing in Business Objects tools for 12 years. He is primarily focused on the operational side of analytics, working with SAP BusinessObjects BI architecture, performance, and administration. He is an SAP Certified Associate in SAP BusinessObjects, as well as an SAP Mentor and active volunteer with America's SAP User Group (ASUG). He has a Bachelor of Science degree in Business and Information Systems, and a Master of Business Administration. Greg lives in the suburban Philadelphia area of Pennsylvania, and when he's not working or speaking at a conference, he can be found outside running, training for his next marathon.

Eric Vallo has been a part of the greater Business Objects community since 1999, and involved in business intelligence as a whole since early 1998. He has had the opportunity to cover all facets of reporting and analytics, ranging from report and universe development through to business intelligence platform architecture and strategy. Eric is one of the co-founders of EV Technologies in the United States and Australia, and the managing partner at EV Technologies in the United States, an SAP Certified Associate in SAP BusinessObjects, an SAP Mentor, and, along with Greg, a co-host of the Diversified Semantic Layer podcast network. Eric currently lives in St. Louis, MO.

Index

S

T